Rethinking Mahler

Rethinking Mahler

EDITED BY
Jeremy Barham

OXFORD
UNIVERSITY PRESS

OXFORD
UNIVERSITY PRESS

Oxford University Press is a department of the University of Oxford. It furthers
the University's objective of excellence in research, scholarship, and education
by publishing worldwide. Oxford is a registered trade mark of Oxford University
Press in the UK and certain other countries.

Published in the United States of America by Oxford University Press
198 Madison Avenue, New York, NY 10016, United States of America.

Library of Congress Cataloging-in-Publication Data
Names: Barham, Jeremy, 1963– editor.
Title: Rethinking Mahler/[edited] by Jeremy Barham.
Description: New York, NY: Oxford University Press, [2017] | Includes
bibliographical references and index.
Identifiers: LCCN 2016047149| ISBN 9780199316106 (pbk.: alk. paper) |
ISBN 9780199316090 (hardcover: alk. paper)
Subjects: LCSH: Mahler, Gustav, 1860–1911—Criticism and interpretation. |
Music—19th century—History and criticism.
Classification: LCC ML410.M23 R47 2017 | DDC 780.92—dc23 LC record available
at https://lccn.loc.gov/2016047149

9 8 7 6 5 4 3 2 1

Printed by Sheridan Books, Inc., United States of America

In memoriam

George Sidney Barham (1929–2013)

Zoltan Roman (1936–2015)

Henry-Louis de La Grange (1924–2017)

Contents

List of Figures and Tables   *ix*

List of Music Examples   *xiii*

Acknowledgements   *xvii*

List of Contributors   *xix*

Introduction: Mahler's Times   *xxv*
JEREMY BARHAM

I Repertoires and Structures of the Past

1   Fantasy, Denial, and Virtual Reality in Mahler's Fourth Symphony   3
    BENJAMIN K. DAVIES

2   Mining the Past for New Expressions: Song Form as Narrative
    Device in Mahler's Ballads from *Des Knaben Wunderhorn*   25
    MOLLY M. BRECKLING

3   The Earliness of Mahler's Late Romanticism: The Poetics
    of the 'Deceptive Perfect Cadence' in the Ninth Symphony
    and *Das Lied von der Erde*   51
    MARK SUMMERFIELD

4   'Pedester ist der Musikstoff, sublim der Vortrag': Mahler's Scherzos
    as Impulses for the Evolution of Musical Language   73
    MATHIEU SCHNEIDER

5   Forming Form through Force: Bruckner, Mahler, and the
    Structural Function of Highpoints   85
    ALESSANDRO CECCHI

6   *Die Meistersinger* in Mahler's Seventh Symphony   105
    ANNA STOLL KNECHT

7   Idyllic Masks of Death: References to *Orphée aux Enfers* in
    'Das himmlische Leben'   127
    LÓRÁNT PÉTERI

II Stage, Screen, and Popular Cultures

8 Mahler and the Myth of the Total Symphony   141
   JAMES BUHLER

9 On the British Reception of Ken Russell's *Mahler*   163
   EFTYCHIA PAPANIKOLAOU

10 Popular Music and the Colloquial Tone in the Posthorn
   Solos of Mahler's Third Symphony   183
   TIMOTHY FREEZE

11 Gustav Mahler's Eighth Symphony and Max Reinhardt's
   Concept of *Massenregie*   203
   PETER REVERS

III Varieties of Historical and Aesthetic Experience

12 The Particularity of the Moment   219
   JULIAN JOHNSON

13 Gustav Mahler and the Aesthetics of De-Identification   237
   FEDERICO CELESTINI

14 Decadent Transitions: Mahler, Modernism, and the Viennese
   Fin de Siècle   253
   ZOLTAN ROMAN

15 Justine Mahler's *Faust* Notebook: An Introduction   271
   STEPHEN E. HEFLING

16 Abridging Mahler's Symphonies: A Historical Perspective   299
   MATTHEW MUGMON

17 Mahler and the Game of History   315
   JEREMY BARHAM

Bibliography   353
Index   381

Figures and Tables

Figures

1.1	Tonal centres in Mahler's Fourth Symphony, first movement: exposition and development (1)	15
1.2	Tonal centres in Mahler's Fourth Symphony, first movement: development (2), recapitulation and coda	16
2.1	'Der Schildwache Nachtlied', Poem and Song text	31
2.2	'Des Antonius von Padua Fischpredigt' Poem and Song Text	36–37
2.3	'Nicht Wiedersehen', Poem and Song Text	39
2.4	'Wo die schönen Trompeten blasen', Poem and Song Text	42
5.1	Diagram of formal tensions in Bruckner's Ninth Symphony, first movement	95
5.2	Diagram of formal tensions in Mahler's First Symphony, first movement	100
6.1	Initial part of the *Meistersinger* Overture (bb. 1–58) and Mahler's ritornello (bb. 1–23)	106
8.1	Classic shot/reverse-shot cinematic editing pattern with concluding 2-shot in *Now, Voyager* (1942)	148
8.2	Cinematic reflections, *mise en abyme* and fractured subjectivity: a: *The Apartment* (1960); b: *Lady from Shanghai* (1947); c: *Citizen Kane* (1941)	156
9.1a	Robert Powell as Gustav Mahler. *Mahler*	164
9.1b	Georgina Hale as Alma Mahler. *Mahler*	164
9.2	Advertisement for *Mahler* in *The Guardian*, 5 April 1974, 11	170
9.3	Mahler alive in the coffin. *Mahler*	171
9.4	Allusion to Visconti's *Death in Venice. Mahler*	172
9.5	Alma dances on Gustav's coffin. *Mahler*	174
9.6	Intertitle for the beginning of the conversion fantasy sequence. *Mahler*	175
9.7	Cosima Wagner as Nazi dominatrix. *Mahler*	176
9.8	Mahler as Siegfried. *Mahler*	176

 9.9 Robert Powell as Gustav Mahler and Antonia Ellis as Cosima
      Wagner at the end of the conversion fantasy sequence. *Mahler*   177

11.1 Alfred Roller's poster advertising the première of the Eighth
      Symphony   204

11.2 Mahler rehearsing the Eighth Symphony   206

11.3 Max Reinhardt: Sophocles, *King Oedipus* (London, 1912)   208

14.1 Ernst Stöhr's 'Vampire'   260

15.1 Justine Mahler Rosé's *Faust* Notebook, p. 1   272

15.2 Letter of 28 April [1894] to Mahler from his sister Justine, who
      was then visiting Rome   273

15.3 Justine Mahler Rosé's *Faust* Notebook, p. 77   274

15.4 Siegfried Lipiner, Adam, manuscript copy in the hand
      of Justine Mahler [1899]   275

15.5 Siegfried Lipiner   276

15.6 Letter of [22 (?) June 1909] from Mahler to his wife Alma, p. [4]   280

15.7 Letter of [22 (?) June 1909] from Mahler to his wife Alma,
      bifolio 2 (=p. [5])   281

15.8 Letter of [22 (?) June 1909] from Mahler to his wife Alma, p. [6]   282

15.9 Letter of [22 (?) June 1909] from Mahler to his wife Alma, p. [7]   283

16.1 Deletion marked in Koussevitzky's piano score of Mahler's Ninth
      Symphony   305

16.2 Deletion marked in Koussevitzky's full score of Mahler's Ninth
      Symphony   306

17.1 Paul Klee, 'Angelus Novus' (1920)   322

17.2 Still from Syberberg, *Hitler, a Film from Germany*, Part 2,
      'A German Dream . . . Until the End of the World' (1977)   324

17.3 Still from Farocki, *Zwischen zwei Kriegen* (*Between Two Wars*), 1978   328

17.4 Paul Klee, 'The Twittering Machine' (1922)   334

17.5 Lyrics of 'I'll Be Seeing You' and first verse of 'White Christmas'   339

Tables

 2.1 Gustav Mahler's Ballads based on texts from *Des Knaben
      Wunderhorn*   26

 4.1 Structural Outline of the Movement (final version)   81

 4.2 Structural Outline of the Movement (draft and score)   82

7.1   The Number of Performances of Offenbach's Theatrical Works
      Conducted by Mahler   132

15.1 From Justine Mahler's Faust Notebook, pp. 116–22, transl.
      Stephen Hefling and Friedrich Thiel.   284

15.2 Comparison of Schlußszene passages in Justine's Notebook to
      Mahler's 1909 Faust Letter   290

16.1 Deletions in Serge Koussevitzky's Score of Mahler's
      Ninth Symphony   309

Music Examples

1.1 Mahler's Fourth Symphony, first movement, bars 233–38   10

1.2 Mahler's Fourth Symphony, first movement, appoggiatura
functions   12

1.3 Mahler's Fourth Symphony, first movement, melodic recycling   13

1.4 (a) Mahler's Fourth Symphony, first movement, 'dream ocarina',
bars 126–31; (b) and (c) related figures in Mahler's
First Symphony, first movement, bars 135–39, 220–24; d) related
figure in Dvorak's Eighth Symphony, first movement, bars 18–22.   18

1.5 Mahler's Fourth Symphony, first movement, sequence and 'clone',
bars 187–99, 199–212   20

1.6 Collapsing gestures in Mahler's Fourth Symphony and Sixth
Symphony, first movements   21

2.1 'Der Schildwache Nachtlied', bars 1–4, the guard's soundworld   32

2.2 'Der Schildwache Nachtlied', bars 17–21, the maiden's soundworld 32

2.3 'Der Schildwache Nachtlied', bars 9–12, a musical yawn   33

2.4 'Der Schildwache Nachtlied', bars 66–8, frustration boils over 34

2.5 'Des Antonius von Padua Fischpredigt', bars 16–24, flowing river 37

2.6 'Des Antonius von Padua Fischpredigt', bars 52–57, klezmer melody 38

2.7 'Nicht Wiedersehen!', bars 1–4, tragedy beckons   40

2.8 'Nicht Wiedersehen!', bars 55–9, a hopeful reunion   41

2.9 'Wo die schönen Trompeten blasen', bars 15–20, a knock at the door 45

2.10 'Wo die schönen Trompeten blasen', bars 36–43, *Ländler* motive 46

2.11 'Wo die schönen Trompeten blasen', bars 169–73, the soldier's
military theme   47

2.12 'Wo die schönen Trompeten blasen', bars 5–8, premonition from
a nightingale   48

3.1 Agawu's 'conflated' cadence: Ninth Symphony, first movement,
bars 53–54   53

3.2   Modulating Deceptive Cadence: *Das Lied von der Erde*, 'Der
       Trunkene im Frühling,', bars 6–8   53

3.3   Modulating Deceptive Cadence: Fifth Symphony, 'Adagietto,'
       bars 45–47   54

3.4   Hybrid Cadence: *Das Lied von der Erde*, 'Das Trinklied Jammer
       der Erde,' bars 225–30   55

3.5   *Das Lied von der Erde*, 'Von der Jugend,' bars 22–25   56

3.6   *Das Lied von der Erde*, 'Von der Jugend,' bars 107–11   57

3.7   Ninth Symphony, second movement, bars 429–32   57

3.8   *Das Lied von der Erde*, 'Das Trinklied Jammer der Erde,'
       bars 147–53   58

3.9   Ninth Symphony, second movement, bars 564–71   59

3.10a *Das Lied von der Erde*, 'Der Einsame im Herbst,' bars 98–103   60

3.10b *Das Lied von der Erde*, 'Der Einsame im Herbst,' bars 98–103
       (voice leading graph)   61

3.11a *Das Lied von der Erde*, 'Der Abschied,' bars 213–21   61

3.11b *Das Lied von der Erde*, 'Der Abschied', bars 213–221 (voice
       leading graph)   62

3.12a Ninth Symphony, second movement, bars 295–99   63

3.12b Ninth Symphony, second movement, bars 295–99
       (voice leading graph)   64

3.13   *Das Lied von der Erde*, 'Das Trinklied Jammer der Erde,' bars
       311–26   68

4.1   The octave leaps in the scherzo of Mahler's First Symphony   75

4.2   The Ländler-theme in the scherzo of the Ninth Symphony
       (bars 9–16, reduced to strings, horn 1 and clarinet 1)   77

4.3   Harmonic reduction of the first Ländler's entire section in the
       Scherzo of the Ninth Symphony   78

4.4   Harmonic reduction of the waltz theme at its first appearance
       (bars 90–102)   80

4.5   First bars of the second Ländler (bars 218–21, reduced to strings) 81

6.1   Mahler's ritornello theme (MA1 + MA2) framing Wagner's
       theme (A)   107

6.2   Wagner's theme B and the introductions to the Seventh's first
       and last movements   108

6.3   Cadences in the *Meistersinger* Overture and in Mahler's Finale   108

6.4   Deceptive cadences in Mahler's ritornello and *Meistersinger* III, 5 110

6.5   The first movement of the Seventh, end of the introduction
       (bars 45–50)   113

6.6   *Meistersinger* II, 7 'Auf, schreit zu Hilfe: Mord und Zeter, herbei!'   115

6.7   Mahler's sketchbook (6v) and Beckmesser's serenade   116

6.8   Mahler's sketchbook (5v), Beckmesser's serenade, the Sixth and
       Seventh symphonies   117

6.9   *Meistersinger* III, 1 'Wahn, Wahn, überall Wahn!'   118

6.10   *Götterdämmerung* III, 2 and *Meistersinger* III, 5   119

7.1   Jacques Offenbach, *Orphée aux enfers*, Act I (1858 version),
       'chanson pastorale' of Aristaeus, excerpt from the refrain   128

7.2   Gustav Mahler, 'Das himmlische Leben' (1892 version), entry of
       the singer   129

7.3   Gustav Mahler, 'Das himmlische Leben' (1892 version), ending   130

8.1a   Mahler, Sixth Symphony, I, bars 77–80   154

8.1b   Mahler, Sixth Symphony, I, bars 91–94   154

8.2   Mahler, Sixth Symphony, I, bars 99–102: dissolve from B to A   157

10.1a Adolf Müller, Sr., "Der Postillion", mixture of signals and
       lyrical phrases   185

10.1b Adolf Müller, Sr., "Der Postillion", tune at the cemetery   185

10.2   Viktor Nessler, *Trompeter von Säkkingen*, "Behüt Dich Gott"
       (excerpt)   186

10.3   Mahler, *Blumine*, trumpet theme   187

10.4   Heinrich Schäffer, 'Die Post im Walde'   188

10.5   Viktor Nessler, *Trompeter von Säkkingen*, no. 13 (excerpt)   189

10.6   Mahler, Symphony no. 3, third movement, first posthorn
       episode (excerpt)   190

10.7   Posthorn signals of the Deutsche Reichspost with closing
       gesture paralleling *Abblasen*   192
       (a) No. 1, Für Estaffeten
       (b) No. 2, Für Kuriere
       (c) No. 3, Für Extraposten
       (d) No. 5, Für Güterposten

12.1   Mahler, First Symphony, Finale, bar 519   219

12.2   Mahler, First Symphony, Finale, bars 519–21 and 524–35   220

12.3   Mahler, Fourth Symphony, first movement, bars 237–41   224

12.4   Mahler, Fourth Symphony, first movement, bars 330–37   225

12.5   Mahler, Ninth Symphony, final movement, bars 180–85   233

12.6   Mahler, 'Der Abschied' from *Das Lied von der Erde*, reduction
        of bars 27–32; First Symphony, Finale, reduction of bars 511–20   233

12.7   Mahler, 'Der Abschied' from *Das Lied von der Erde*, bars 166–71   234

13.1   Mahler, *Lieder eines fahrenden Gesellen*, no. 4, 'Die zwei blauen
        Augen'   248

13.2   (a) Mahler, *Lieder eines fahrenden Gesellen*, no. 4 'Auf der
        Straße steht ein Lindenbaum'; (b) J. Strauß, 'Eine Nacht
        in Venedig', 3rd. Act, Caramello: 'Ach, wie so herrlich
        anzuschaun'; (c) Wagner, *Das Rheingold*, 1st. Act, 2nd Scene,
        Loges: 'Die goldnen Aepfel'; (d) Folk song, 'Es wird scho glei
        dumpa'   249

14.1   Attack (a) and Accent/duration (b) patterns, in Mahler's Ninth
        Symphony, first movement: a. bars 1–6; b: bars 1–7   264

14.2   Mahler's Ninth Symphony, third movement, bars 1–7   265

17.1   (a) opening bars of McCartney's 'Yesterday'; and (b) bars 101–2,
        24–27, and 119–21 of Mahler's Third Symphony, fourth
        movement   336

17.2   (a) opening bars of the refrain from 'I'll Be Seeing You'; and
        (b) the four statements of the secondary motive in Mahler's
        Third Symphony, last movement: (i) bars 8–11; (ii) bars 99–102;
        (iii) bars 206–8; and (iv) bars 275–78   338

17.3   (a) 'Slip Away': opening bars; chromatic dominant substitutions;
        (b) Mahler 'Adagietto', chromatic dominant substitutions, bars
        15, 28–30, 46, 59–60, 62–64, 71–72, 94–95   341–42

17.4   (a) reduction of *Interstellar* score at 19:18; (b) Mahler,
        Symphony no. 9, fourth movement bars 165–67   343

17.5   Reduction of *Interstellar* score at 38:42 (first and second
        systems) and 39:59 (third system); Mahler, Symphony no. 10,
        fifth movement, bars 29–31, 66–68, 322–24 and 352–54.   344

Acknowledgements

I would like first to thank all the contributors for the diligence and rigour with which they prepared their work, and for their patience and understanding in awaiting the book's completion. The origins of the volume lie in an international conference convened by the editor at the University of Surrey, July 2011: 'Gustav Mahler Centenary Conference. Mahler: Contemporary of the Past?' I gratefully acknowledge the following for their generous support of this event: the Institute of Advanced Studies (University of Surrey), the British Academy, the Royal Musical Association, the *Music & Letters* Trust, the Institute of Musical Research, the Austrian Cultural Forum (London), the Department of Music and Sound Recording (University of Surrey), Stephen Downes, Julian Johnson, Uri Caine, the Endymion Ensemble, Stephen Goss and the Tetra Guitar Quartet, Emilie Capulet, Maureen Galea, Michelle Castelletti, Caroline Tate, Matthew Sansom, Keith Clarke, Mirela Dumic, Hera Yoon, Laurence Willis, Julian Fagan-King, Peter Bryant, Julie Barham and Georgina Barham.

For the production of the present book, I would like to express my profound thanks to Suzanne Ryan, Adam Cohen, Daniel Gibney, Andrew Maillet, Jessen O'Brien, and Eden Piacitelli at Oxford University Press for their unstinting support and encouragement; to Jake Willson and Harry Barham for producing the music examples; and to the following institutions for permission to reproduce materials: the Mahler-Rosé Collection (Gustav Mahler-Alfred Rosé Room, Music Library, University of Western Ontario), the Pierpont Morgan Library, New York, the Trustees of the Boston Public Library, and the Serge Koussevitzky Music Foundation, Inc.. I am grateful to my colleagues past and present in the Department of Music at the University of Surrey for their collegiality and intellectual curiosity. Finally I thank my family Julie, Georgina, Samuel, and Harry for their love and support throughout all the years.

Contributors

Jeremy Barham is Reader in Music at the University of Surrey. His Mahler-related publications include most recently a chapter on politics and philosophy in the de La Grange Festschrift *Naturlauf: Scholarly Journeys Toward Gustav Mahler*, as well as 'Mahler: Centenary Commentaries on Musical Meaning' (guest-edited issue of *Nineteenth-Century Music Review*), *The Cambridge Companion to Mahler, Gustav Mahler: New Insights into His Life, Times and Work*, and *Perspectives on Gustav Mahler*. He also researches in the fields of screen music and jazz. He is series editor of the *Oxford Studies in Recorded Jazz* and co-editor of *The Music and Sound of Experimental Film* (Oxford University Press). He is currently working on the monographs *Post-Centenary Mahler: Revaluing Musical Meaning* (Indiana), and *Music, Time and the Moving Image* (Cambridge University Press); and the edited volume *Global Screen Music in the Early Sound Era*.

Molly M. Breckling serves as an instructor of musicology at the University of West Georgia in Carrollton (Georgia). She has previously taught courses in music history, popular music, and voice at several institutions in North Carolina and Tennessee. She holds a PhD from the University of North Carolina and master's degrees from Austin Peay, the University of Wisconsin, and North Carolina. Her background is in vocal performance, and her research interests include issues of narrative and epistemology in the songs of Gustav Mahler, on which she has published several articles in journals such as *MLA Notes, Ars Lyrica*, and *Music Research Forum,*. She is completing her first monograph, which examines Mahler's musical and textual narratives in his Lieder from *Des Knaben Wunderhorn* as platforms for cultural and political commentary.

James Buhler is a Professor in the Sarah and Ernest Butler School of Music at the University of Texas at Austin, where he teaches courses in music theory and film music. He is the co-author of *Hearing the Movies* (Oxford University Press), now in its second edition, and is currently completing a manuscript, *Theories of the Soundtrack*, for Oxford University Press.

Alessandro Cecchi is a Lecturer in Musicology at the University of Pisa. His main research topics are music theory and aesthetics, the symphonies of Bruckner and Mahler, the theory and history of film music, and musical performance. His articles appear in musicological journals including *Il Saggiatore musicale, Studi musicali, Musica/Tecnologia, Rivista di Analisi e Teoria Musicale*, and *Music, Sound, and the Moving Image*. He has contributed chapters to several books published by Carocci, Kaplan, Libreria Musicale Italiana, and Pavia University Press. He is the editor of a special issue of the *Rivista di Analisi e Teoria Musicale* entitled 'Schenker's *Formenlehre*.' He participates in the editorial board of the online journal *Analitica*, and in the scientific committee of the Gruppo di Analisi e Teoria Musicale. He collaborates with the Institute of Music of the Giorgio Cini Foundation, Venice, where he serves as editorial board member of the online journal *Archival Notes*.

Federico Celestini is Professor of Music at the Institute of Musicology at the University of Innsbruck. He received his doctorate in 1998 and the Habilitation in 2004, both in musicology, at the University of Graz. At the same time, he worked as a member of the University's research project 'Modern—Vienna and Central Europe around 1900'. From 2008 to 2011, Celestini was a lecturer at the Institute of Music Aesthetics at the University of Music and Performing Arts, Graz. From 2010 to 2012 he ran the project 'Scelsi and Austria,' with the support of the Austrian Science Fund. Since 2011 he has been co-editor of the journal *Acta Musicologica*. He has held fellowships and visiting professorships at the University of Oxford, the Riemenschneider Bach Institute, the Free University of Berlin, and the University of Chicago. His areas of interest include music of the seventeenth to the twenty-first centuries, approaches to music from cultural studies, music aesthetics, and medieval polyphony.

Benjamin K. Davies is a composer, theorist, and improvising pianist. He graduated in philosophy and social and political sciences at Cambridge University in 1983, and obtained a PhD in composition from Southampton University in 2009, supervised by Michael Finnissy. In between, he worked extensively in theatre—both experimental and commercial—and contemporary dance, as composer and musical director. Resident in Barcelona since 1988, he joined the Conservatori del Liceu in 2009 and currently holds the posts of academic director and head of the composition and theory departments. His research areas include post-tonal harmony, the ontology of jazz, music and truth, Beethoven and Habermas's theory of communicative action, and studies of works, generally viewed as problematic with respect to analytic strategies, by composers such as Webern, Birtwistle, and Janacek.

Timothy Freeze is visiting Assistant Professor at the College of Wooster. He has published research on Gustav Mahler, Viennese operetta, and Aaron Copland in several journals and collected volumes. He is currently working on a critical edition of Gershwin's Concerto in F for the George and Ira Gershwin Critical Edition. Before coming to Wooster, he taught at Indiana University and IES Abroad in Vienna. He earned a PhD in historical musicology from the University of Michigan and has held research fellowships from the Berlin Program for Advanced German European Studies, the German Academic Exchange Service, and the Fulbright Program.

Stephen E. Hefling is Professor Emeritus of Music at Case Western Reserve University, and has also taught at Stanford and Yale universities as well as the Oberlin College Conservatory. Hefling received the AB in music from Harvard and the PhD from Yale, with a dissertation on Mahler's 'Todtenfeier.' He is vice president of the Internationale Gustav Mahler Gesellschaft as well as co-director of the Neue Kritische Gesamtausgabe of Mahler's works, for which he edited the autograph piano version of *Das Lied von der Erde*. Author of *Gustav Mahler: Das Lied von der Erde* (Cambridge University Press, 2000) and editor of *Mahler Studies* (Cambridge University Press, 1997), he has published over two dozen articles and book chapters on Mahler and his music. Currently he is working on a two-volume study entitled *The Symphonic Worlds of Gustav Mahler* (Yale University Press) and completing *The Reilly Catalogue of Mahler's Musical Manuscripts*. Other areas of interest include chamber music (editor, *Nineteenth-Century Chamber Music* [Routledge 2003] and historical performance practice (*Rhythmic Alteration in 17th- and 18th-Century Music* [Schirmer, 1993]).

Julian Johnson is Regius Professor of Music at Royal Holloway, University of London, having formerly been Reader in Music at the University of Oxford (2001–7), and Lecturer at the University of Sussex (1992–2001). In the early part of his career he combined research into musical aesthetics with working as a professional composer, an experience that continues to shape his thinking in musicology. He has published widely on music from Beethoven to contemporary music, but with a particular focus on Mahler, Viennese modernism, musical aesthetics, and the wider idea of musical modernity. His monographs include *Webern and the Transformation of Nature* (Cambridge University Press, 1999), *Mahler's Voices: Expression and Irony in the Songs and Symphonies* (Oxford University Press, 2009), and *Out of Time: Music and the Making of Modernity* (Oxford University Press, 2015). He is the co-editor of *Transformations of Musical Modernism* (Cambridge University Press, 2015) and of the Cambridge University Press journal *Twentieth-Century Music*.

Matthew Mugmon is Assistant Professor of Musicology at the University of Arizona. His research focuses on the relationship between Gustav Mahler's music and four influential figures in American modernism—Nadia Boulanger, Aaron Copland, Serge Koussevitzky, and Leonard Bernstein. Publications include articles in *Music & Letters* and the *Journal of Musicological Research*, as well as the volume *Ambrosiana at Harvard: New Sources of Milanese Chant*, which he co-edited with Thomas Forrest Kelly. Mugmon received his PhD in historical musicology from Harvard University in 2013, and he has served as the New York Philharmonic Orchestra's Leonard Bernstein Scholar-in-Residence.

Eftychia Papanikolaou is Associate Professor of Music History at Bowling Green State University (Ohio), where she also serves as musicology coordinator.

She holds a BA in English philology and literature from the University of Athens, Greece; music theory degrees from the National Conservatory of Athens; and master's and PhD degrees in historical musicology from Boston University. Her publications (ranging from Haydn, Schumann, and Brahms to Liszt and Mahler's fin-de-siècle Vienna) focus on the interconnections of music, religion, and politics in the long nineteenth century, with emphasis on the sacred as a musical topos. Other research interests include music and film (*The Last Temptation of Christ, Battlestar Galactica, Mahler*), and interdisciplinary and dance studies. Forthcoming publications include essays on Mahler's Eighth Symphony and the choreographic work of Uwe Scholz. She is currently completing a monograph on the Romantic symphonic mass.

Lóránt Péteri is Professor, and head of the musicology department of the Liszt Academy of Music (State University), Budapest. As a postgraduate research student, he received supervision from the University of Oxford in 2004–5 and received his PhD from the University of Bristol, UK, in 2008 with the dissertation entitled 'The Scherzo of Mahler's Second Symphony: A Study of Genre'. He has given papers about the musical life of state socialist Hungary and about the music of Gustav Mahler in international conferences (in Bristol, Brno, Budapest, Canterbury, Cardiff, Guildford, New York, Pittsburgh, and Radziejowice). His latest contribution is the study 'The "Question of Nationalism" in Hungarian Musicology during the State Socialist Period,' in Słavomira Żerańska-Kominek (ed.), *Nationality vs. Universality: Music Historiographies in Central and Eastern Europe* (Cambridge Scholars Publishing, 2016).

Peter Revers is Professor of Music History at the University of Music and Performing Arts in Graz and has been president of the Austrian Musicological Society (2001–9). He studied musicology and composition at the Universities of Salzburg and Vienna as well as at the University 'Mozarteum' in Salzburg. From 1980–96 he taught at the University of Music and Dramatic Arts in Vienna and completed his Habilitation in 1993 (University of Hamburg). In 1988–89 he was fellow of the Alexander von Humboldt-Foundation, Germany. In 1996 he became full professor in Graz. His publications list runs to eight books and more than 120 articles, and includes volumes on Mahler, *Mahlers Lieder* (Munich, 2000), and *Gustav Mahler—Interpretationen seiner Werke* (Laaber, 2011); and the European reception of Far-Eastern music: *Das Fremde und das Vertraute—Studien zur musiktheoretischen und musikdramatischen Ostasienrezeption* (Stuttgart, 1997).

Zoltan Roman's scholarly work was devoted chiefly to the biographical, analytical, editorial, and bibliographic study of the lives and music of Mahler and Webern, as well as, latterly, interdisciplinary studies relating to the turn of the twentieth century. He held elected positions on the councils of the American Musicological Society and the International Musicological Society, on the board of the International Webern Society, and for the Internationale

Gustav Mahler Gesellschaft (Board of Directors, Executive Committee, and Academic Advisory Board). He edited several fascicles of Mahler's songs for the Complete Critical Edition and was author or co-author of four books on Mahler and Webern, including *Gustav Mahler's American Years, 1907– 1911: A Documentary History* (1989) and *Gustav Mahler and Hungary* (1991). His numerous studies have been published in the *Music Review*, the *Musical Quarterly*, the *International Review of the Aesthetics and Sociology of Music*, *Muzyka*, *Acta Musicologica*, and *Studia Musicologica*.

Mathieu Schneider is Associate Professor and Pro Vice-Chancellor at the University of Strasbourg. A specialist of German post-romanticism, he is the author of a book-length monograph on the relationship between music and literature in the symphonic works of Gustav Mahler and Richard Strauss and has published essays in various scholarly journals both in France and internationally. He has served as chief editor of *Cahiers Franz Schubert* and was the curator of an international exhibition on Richard Wagner's reception in France, which was displayed in Bayreuth and Berlin. An additional field of interest is the study of representations of Switzerland in nineteenth-century music, on which he recently published the book *L'Utopie suisse dans la musique romantique* (Paris, 2016).

British Academy postdoctoral fellow at the University of Oxford (Jesus College), **Anna Stoll Knecht** conducts research on Mahler's interpretation of Wagner, both as a conductor and as a composer. She took her MA in musicology and ancient Greek at the University of Geneva (with a Diploma in music theory at the Conservatory of Music), and her PhD at New York University (2014). Her publications include a forthcoming monograph on Mahler's Seventh Symphony (*Studies in Musical Genesis, Structure and Interpretation*, Oxford University Press), several essays (*Naturlauf: Scholarly Journeys Toward Gustav Mahler*, Peter Lang, 2016; *Texts and Beyond: The Process of Music Composition from the 19th to the 20th century*, Ad Parnassum Studies, 2016) and a study of Henri Dutilleux's *Métaboles* (*Annales Suisses de Musicologie*, 2006). She has been the recipient of several fellowships (Fulbright, the Swiss National Science Foundation, and non-stipendiary Junior Research Fellowship at Jesus College).

Mark Summerfield studied music at Royal Holloway and Bedford New College, University of London and completed a PhD with the Open University entitled 'The Construction of Closure and Cadence in Gustav Mahler's Ninth Symphony and *Das Lied von der Erde*.' He is interested in closure, the sublime and shock from a music theoretical perspective, particularly in the music of Mahler. He has taught as an associate tutor and summer school tutor on a number of courses for the Open University and is currently preparing further articles on cadences and closure in Mahler and on the psychoanalytical implications of the ways that expectation is invoked in music theory.

Introduction

Mahler's Times

Jeremy Barham

Mahler was far from overlooked in the concert hall up to the late 1930s,[1] but if he truly was 'reborn' in the 1960s, then he is very close in age to myself. The similarities may end there, but though I can lay no claim to artistic greatness it is interesting to consider how in times chronologically distant from his own he re-emerged and re-developed within the same postwar, Western-dominated but increasingly globalised, cultural environment: an age of extremes and fracture as Eric Hobsbawm would have it. My generation grew up alongside the re-awakening Mahler. Caring adults nurtured his fragile second infancy, including, towards the end of her own days, the sometimes over-protective 'mother' figure of his afterlife, Alma Maria. Godparents were an initially select but later expanding, second-generation group—from Schoenberg, Berg, and Webern to Berio, Schnittke, and Rochberg; from Walter and Mengelberg to Bernstein and Haitink; and from Stefan, Bekker, and Specht to Cooke, Mitchell, and de La Grange. He was frequently scolded, but his potential was understood all too well by generous spirits, among them beloved eccentric uncle, Ken Russell. He has since become a global godchild, though attempted baptisms have been inconclusive. Teenage years were full of awestruck, first-time musical discoveries of world sorrow, mortality, and yet radiant life-intensity—all equally essential parts of an inwardly heroic youthful mindscape from which to forge meaningful identities, to locate formidable truths amid uncertainty and chaos. As they sometimes do, maturity and acceptance came at a price. While Beethoven was strong enough to cope with Alex DeLarge's violent, anarchic championing in Kubrick's filmic realisation of Burgess's future social dystopia *A Clockwork Orange*, in the same year (1971) Mahler's fledgling status allowed him, through Visconti's re-working of Thomas Mann's past artistic dystopia *Death in Venice*, readily, thoroughly, and enduringly to colonise the public consciousness in frameworks of overripe artistic decay and a transgressive pathos and pathology of personal longing. Whether this early stereotyping and synechdochical interpretative confinement have been, will be, or should be displaced is open to question.

There is considerably more to Mahler, of course, than that which narrow streams of media appropriation (whether populist or 'art-house'), however powerful, would have us believe. But, should we wish to, it remains difficult to extricate Mahler from the over-determined, inflexible world of 'applied' or 'functional' music, partly because it has proved so tempting and gratifying to read this or that meaning in his music (a process in which Mahler himself was complicit) and so easy to remain attached to it, and partly because so many composers for mass screen media have called upon his music's surface-level mechanics. The foster children we once never knew he had include not just the likes of Shostakovich, Britten, and Weill, but also Korngold, Steiner, Herrmann, and many of their more recent descendants.

It could be argued that the way in which Mahler has been approached and understood in scholarly contexts (and certainly in the concert programme note) has also tended to be methodologically and ideologically circumscribed, if less stringently so. Aside from titanic biographical accounts, there remains in the first place something of a bifurcation between music-analytical and cultural-hermeneutic impulses, and in the second place prevailing, historically synoptical, scholarly assumptions and preferences that commonly (and not without justification) configure Mahler as proto-modernist. In the years since I previously referred to the first of these tendencies in the introduction to *Perspectives on Gustav Mahler* (2005), during which the composer's intervening anniversaries (2010–11) might have provided opportunities for reassessment, that situation does not seem to have significantly changed. The continuing divide, which in part has been intellectually bound up with North American disciplinary distinctions between music history and music theory, is demonstrated by two recent monographs. Seth Monahan's *Mahler's Symphonic Sonatas* concerns itself analytically with the works as 'intramusical narratives' and as 'abstract dramatic scenarios: expressive but not illustrative, volitional without depicting extrinsic agents'.[2] Thomas Peattie's interdisciplinary *Gustav Mahler's Symphonic Landscapes* by contrast invokes external tropes of 'Alpine journeys', 'cowbells and solitude', the paintings of Turner and others, 'Wanderers', and 'Mahler's walks' as means of approaching the composer's 'symphonic dramaturgy' which he describes, after critic Richard Heuberger and notably in terms not dissimilar to Monahan's, as 'abstract theatre'.[3] This is perhaps an example of Schopenhauer's provocative image of 'two miners digging a shaft from opposite ends and then meeting underground', used by Mahler in a letter of 1897 to Arthur Seidl to differentiate his and Strauss's brands of programmaticism, and originally by Schopenhauer in 1836 to demonstrate his metaphysical philosophy's relation to empirical science.[4] Both volumes offer sophisticated re-castings of older questions of where and how to locate meaning in Mahler's music, and more precisely the extent to which this meaning and the methods employed to derive it are internally and/or externally oriented.

While my future work will address this question more fully,[5] the present volume contributes to re-emphasising a sense of change in the second tendency identified above. Exploring an intermittent thread in Mahler scholarship that can be traced erratically back to the 1970s,[6] a time when modernism in music arguably began to experience serious threats to its hegemony, this collection emerges from the centenary conference held at the University of Surrey in 2011, themed 'Mahler: Contemporary of the Past?', an intentional play on the title of Kurt Blaukopf's 1969 study of the composer, *Gustav Mahler oder der Zeitgenosse der Zukunft [Gustav Mahler or the Contemporary of the Future]*. Its principal rationale, therefore, is to re-evaluate the 'modern-izing' of Mahler that has come as an inevitable consequence of reflection constructed through the lenses of historical linearity and teleology combined with continuing desires to get to grips with modernism's highly potent, more than century-old claim on Western thought, which is now straining at the limits of living, social memory. One of the most devoted exponents of that modernism and a prolific performer of Mahler's music, Pierre Boulez, within the same text seems to hold in tension contradictory diagnoses of his predecessor's historical status:

> There is no sense in looking for the clear markers we find in classical music ... There is [in Mahler] ... a determination to disregard the categories of the past.

> There is too much nostalgia, too much attachment to the past in Mahler's music for him to be declared, without any qualifications, the revolutionary who initiated an irreversible process of radical renewal in music.[7]

If this seems confusing, it also suggests a need not only to rethink Mahler's debt to, and re-fashioning of, the legacies he inherited from his own past as a musician working at the end of one and the beginning of another century, deeply involved in the re-creation of earlier repertoires in the opera house and concert hall, but also to re-conceptualise a modernity that, in the face of political catastrophes, was as much about preservation and restoration as it was about destruction, forgetting, superseding and advancement.

Under the title *Bahnbrüche: Gustav Mahler*, incorporating an intriguing neologism stemming from *Bahnbrecher/bahnbrechend* (pioneer, ground-breaking, or paving the way for) that could translate as 'acts of breaking (or preparing) new ground', a third recent volume on the composer at least starts by seeming to recognise these subtleties of modernist culture, and the conceivably irreconcilable plurality of Mahler's creative output: 'In many respects Gustav Mahler's works constitute an initial surge in the unfolding of a multi-faceted modernism. In his music, tradition and the avant-garde, awareness of established forms and experimental structural daring, early romanticism and modern consciousness of the self and reality, enter into thoroughly "impossible syntheses"'.[8]

In facing the challenge to (re-)address 'impossible', paradoxical questions of past, present, and future in Mahler's creative practice and interpretation, the (initially Freudian) concept of 'Nachträglichkeit', 'après-coup', or 'afterwardsness' may be of help, alongside the historical acceptance that Mahler 'came after' just as much as he 'came before'. 'Nachträglichkeit' does not mean simply the process whereby, with the benefit of hindsight, the historian creates meaningful order out of piecemeal, intractable, and sometimes contradictory, evidence of past events. Rather, it involves 'revision of a memory ... into a form that it could take only later',[9] an understanding of history as a 'living experience of the past whose meanings change with new or different interpretive contexts', and an acknowledgement that historians themselves are 'historically in process' and 'cannot simply confront events that happened in the past as if these events were unmediated by subsequent experiences that shift their valencies and change their meaning'.[10] This complex of temporalities and perspectives entails not just past and present being grasped reciprocally through each other, nor merely the commonplace idea of poststructural relativism, but also notions of belatedness, especially in the sense of assimilating much later the effects of initially unassimilable traumatic events. Such events may stretch from, on one level, the deaths of loved ones and artistic idols, devastating romantic rejection, perceived artistic failure, or regime-sponsored personal and cultural prohibition, to, on another level, wider processes and movements of geopolitical history: the destabilising revolutions of 1848 built on contrasting yet highly prophetic centripetal and centrifugal forces in Germany and the Austrian Empire, respectively; the Franco-Prussian war of 1871 and the string of Austrian defeats that preceded it; the melancholy collapse of older, more benignly idealist forms of nineteenth-century political Liberalism coupled with the rise of competing nationalisms and institutionalised anti-Semitism; or the rapidly shifting sociocultural landscapes of early and postwar twentieth-century modernism experienced in various forms of secessionist and insurrectionist art, politics, and philosophy.

This mode of thought also entails recognising that if Mahler's widespread reception was deferred to a significant historical period in the second half of the twentieth century which was supposedly witnessing the twilight of that modernism and the coming of its heterogeneous aftermath which some label postmodernism, then in a temporal reversal the roots of the former may enigmatically lie in the latter, as Lyotard once suggested.[11] (Mahler's technical recourse to more traditional (early nineteenth-century and older), 're-booted' forms of strongly tonal voice leading and periodic phrasing were, after all, one of several developments that only in retrospect might seem surprising in a sensuously and sinuously chromaticised, post-Wagnerian modernist environment, heady with the perfume of fin-de-siècle Vienna—Mahler's contemporary critics were largely silent on these facets of his language.) Furthermore, it involves the realisation that, like contemporary commentators and critics, Mahler himself only had his own past (and evanescent present) as reference points for his current artistic creativity, and that his (and critics') crucial understanding of that past and fleeting present was partial, fragmented, and contingent. It means accepting that certain important periods of *his* future reception and of fashions in his interpretative history—whether positive or negative, long-lasting or short-lived—lay in *our* past; that different works have had different histories in this regard; and finally that large parts of those reception histories have been, and continue to be, mediated and mediatised by all manner of cultural custodians, themselves with equally varied personal and sociopolitical contexts, agendas, and histories at work that create, as much as clarify, modes of appreciation and consumption. How far Mahler can be taken to have been, for example, a 'model of the postmodern' from the 1970s onwards, such that he is now 'entirely emblematic of the emancipation from modernism',[12] when he himself contributed to destabilising the very meaning and constitution of these assumed historical categories, is a question worth interrogating.

It is in this spirit that the following collection of chapters pursues ideas of nostalgia, historicism, and 'pastness' in relation to an emergent pluralist sense of modernity (retrospectively seen as progressive), in its wide-ranging explorations of Mahler's relationship with music, media, and ideas, past, present, and 'future anterior' (what will have been). It does so in three broadly themed and interconnected sections, between them addressing, from a variety of discrete and blended historical-cultural, empirical-analytical, and critical-interpretative methodological standpoints, issues in musical structure and allusion across song and symphony, inherited forms, narrative process, harmonic formulae, and intensifying sonata procedures (Part I); correlations of spatial and social organisation, mythologising, and musical portraiture and tone, in stage, screen, and popular cultures (Part II); and networks of aesthetic and historical-temporal experience brought to bear on notions of radical particularity, fragmentation of identities and of the musical work in performance, intermediate cultural states of decadence, Goethean literary allegory, and the very possibilities and limits of Mahler historiography (Part III).

Notes

1. See Werner, "The Popularity of Mahler's Music."
2. Monahan, *Mahler's Symphonic Sonatas*, 5.
3. Peattie, *Gustav Mahler's Symphonic Landscapes*, preliminary text n.p., 81, 104, 119–28, 152, and 163–69.
4. See Martner, *Selected Letters*, 213; and Schopenhauer, *On the Will in Nature*, 22: 'Therefore the two bodies of investigators [philosophers and scientists] must really feel like miners in the bowels of the earth who drive two galleries toward each other from two widely separated points, and who, having long worked from both directions in subterranean darkness and relied only on compass and spirit-level, at last experience the longed-for joy of hearing each other's hammer blows.'

5. Jeremy Barham, *Post-Centenary Mahler: Revaluing Musical Meaning* (Indiana University Press, forthcoming).

6. See Mitchell, "Influences and Anticipations"; Floros, *Gustav Mahler II*; Spinnler, "Zur Angemessenheit traditioneller Formbegriffe"; Kapp, "Schumann-Reminiszenzen bei Mahler"; de La Grange, "Music about Music in Mahler"; Sponheuer and Steinbeck, *Gustav Mahler und die Symphonik des 19. Jahrhunderts*; Kubik, "Spuren in die Vergangenheit"; and Partsch, "Alte Tonartensymbolik in Mahlers Liedschaffen?"

7. Boulez, "Mahler: Our Contemporary?", 299, 303.

8. 'Gustav Mahlers Schaffen steht in vieler Hinsicht für einen Aufbruch in eine sich facettenreich auffächernde Moderne. In seinem Werk gehen Tradition und Avantgarde, überkommenes Formbewusstsein und experimentelle Strukturwagnisse, Frühromantik und modernes Ich- wie Wirklichkeitsbewusstsein geradezu "unmögliche Synthesen" ein.' Berger and Schnitzler, "Vorwort", in *Bahnbrüche: Gustav Mahler*, 7 (my translation).

9. Figlio, "Historical Imagination", 201.

10. Rauch, "Post-Traumatic Hermeneutics," 112–13.

11. Lyotard, "Answering the Question: What Is Postmodernism?", 79.

12. Botstein, "Whose Gustav Mahler?", 4.

Rethinking Mahler

I

REPERTOIRES AND STRUCTURES OF THE PAST

1

Fantasy, Denial, and Virtual Reality in Mahler's Fourth Symphony

Benjamin K. Davies

An incursion into the secondary literature on Mahler's Fourth Symphony swiftly encounters highly contrasted—when not directly contradictory—statements. Thus, for Floros, 'the Fourth is the exact opposite of . . . absolute music',[1] while for Bruno Walter (letter to Schiedermair), 'it is absolute music from beginning to end . . . organic in every movement.'[2] In this particular case, Adorno's suggestion that the symphony 'has swallowed its programme'[3] offers an honourable compromise, but other stand-offs are perhaps not so elegantly to be mediated. While for de La Grange, 'The initial movement of the Fourth . . . can hardly be thought of as anything but a homage to Haydn and Viennese classicism',[4] Zychowicz asserts that 'Mahler was not attempting to write an overtly neoclassical work'.[5] Nor is there consensus over the general emotional tone of the first movement: Bruno Walter hears 'exultant happiness', 'a great cheerfulness, an unearthly joy'[6] while Adorno perceives it 'deeply impregnated with sorrow'.[7] Specific elements are heard in contrasting ways: Deryck Cooke characterises the flute theme at bar 126 of the first movement as 'untroubled, like a boy whistling',[8] while for Knapp it is 'mocking';[9] and if for Robert Samuels the pause in bar 37 before the start of the second group is 'a mark of a genuine aporia',[10] Seth Monahan regards it as 'an utterly conventional . . . gesture'.[11] Similarly, a passage at the end of the development that for Samuels is 'the most enigmatic and magical episode of the movement',[12] Knapp regards as 'a nightmare experience too extreme to be tolerated'.[13] Perhaps, in this latter case, the music must itself take some blame for the confusion: Floros believes that 'the strange as well as unexpected happenings at the end of the development defy strict musical explanation',[14] while Bonds, comparing development with exposition, finds that 'the elaboration seems incommensurate with the opening proposition'.[15] Samuels duly identifies the problem:

> several codes of listening are required at this point. Codes of thematic continuity, motivic development and formal scheme conflict in a way which leaves as the only way of "making sense . . . the resort to a code of "musical narration," referring exclusively intertextually within the institution of symphonic composition.[16]

Expressed thus, the technical demands made on listeners may seem fearsome; but this has not deterred audiences from flocking to the Fourth, one of the most played and recorded of Mahler's symphonies, even if they have done so handicapped by ignorance, as Donald Mitchell suggests: 'It says something about the symphony that it could speak so directly, eloquently, and expressively in virtually the total absence in those far-off days of anything like the contextual information we have ready to hand.'[17] Yet, on occasion, such contextual information is itself contradictory. For instance, it is difficult to reconcile the two similes Mahler himself is purported to have offered for the prevailing ethos of the Fourth, 'the undifferentiated blue of the sky',[18] and 'a primitive picture, painted on a gold background'.[19] Other statements are directly problematic: is it self-evidently the case, for instance, that the theme in bars 3–6—with its ornamental turn, accented chromatic passing note and wealth of rhythmic figuration—is 'childishly simple and quite unselfconscious'?[20]

While the first movement of the Fourth has almost invariably been perceived as innocent, naïve, and optimistic, an evocation of past elegance, and a vision of future happiness—for Diepenbrock, the whole possesses a 'childlike, happy mood',[21] and Adorno calls it a 'fairy-tale', complete with 'once upon a time' preamble[22]—the musical surface is in fact far from placid and untroubled. Repeats at all levels fail to be literal; there are peremptory overlaps and strange elisions; rhythmic patterns are shifted by beats or fractions of them; and bar- and phrase-structure struggle to maintain regularity. Overall, the movement is rife with discontinuities in texture, orchestration, and thematic development. More particularly, as it unfolds, the apparently effortless and flawless weave of the opening is increasingly subject to various degrees of warping, as if—perhaps as in all fairy tales—darker energies conspire to disrupt the idyll. Eventually—inevitably?—rupture occurs. However, the sonata movement, far from assimilating and resolving these impulses, simply ignores them: the recapitulation seems more a wilful refusal to engage with events in the development than a resolution of them. In effect, it comprises an escapist fantasy. Might not the seeming classical restraint and decorum be, in fact, strategies of denial and tokens of artificiality?

What to do, then, with the 'context' Mitchell deems necessary to a full understanding of the work? It can be summarised briefly: the symphony's final movement is a setting, sung by an adult female soprano, of a spurious mediaeval text in which a child describes the supposed joys of heaven; Mahler composed it some years prior to the rest of the symphony, and at one point had intended including it in the Third; he reportedly stated that the song 'explains what [the symphony as a whole] means', and that it forms the 'apex of the edifice';[23] finally, in composing the other movements, he employed elements from the song. The conclusion drawn is that the song both culminates, and provides an explanatory dénouement for, everything that has preceded it. In one celebrated, if problematic, formulation, it is said to provoke '*retrospective*

enlightenment',[24] the suggestion being that we revise our understanding of the
first three movements upon hearing the last. However, Mahler may not in fact
have made any remark about apexes (to take just one example); and even if we
were sure he had, we still could not know precisely what he meant by the analogy; and even if we knew that he had made the remark, and understood what he
meant by it—if we knew his exact structural intentions, as it were—and could
also be certain that he himself felt that he had achieved his aims, we would
still need to understand the statement in terms of the music. Meaning—even
structural meaning, which is to say, function—cannot be imbued by an act of
will (it is, in fact, a specific kind of madness to believe that it can be). Meaning
accrues by complex diachronic social processes that cannot be telescoped into
a single act, no matter how intense, by one person.

Even assuming that the apex simile can correctly be attributed to the composer, the clearest implications are in fact contrary to the standard interpretation. The top stone or apex of, for example, a pyramid is essentially bound by
the structure which it tautologically completes: it is an inevitable and technically redundant detail. Mahler's compositional problem was how to integrate his
song into a symphonic argument. Tovey discusses how Brahms, in his Fourth
Symphony, faced the problem of what sort of finale would be appropriate after
the first three highly dramatic movements.[25] Mahler's conundrum is similar, but
inverted: he needed a sequence of three movements to which the essentially static
song could form an epilogue. If 'heaven' was to be the theme, it is one that has
little place in a symphonic argument, since—axiomatically—it is a realm of per-
petuity and stasis. The song could not fulfil a role in a continuing dramatic cycle,
since it contains no argument of its own. In consequence, any integration with
the other movements must be in terms of common musical elements: hence the
fragments from the song woven throughout the symphony. But compositional
timeline is one matter, aesthetic listening is another: we experience elements in
the last movement as reprises, variants, concatenations, or developments of ideas
already heard. The opposite suggestion—that we somehow (retrospectively) hear
the last movement as 'generating' the first three—is perhaps attractive as a poetic
conceit (although would the suggestion have arisen without contextual information?) but problematic in terms of how music—any music—is actually heard.

These are issues that touch on the phenomenology of listening, and
cannot be addressed here. However, other problems that concern talk of
heaven require comment. The most obvious, and fundamental, is ontologi-
cal: heaven does not exist. Another is epistemological: if it does exist, we can
know nothing of it. Then, there are ethical issues: for an atheist, the promise of heaven seems at best a kind of wishful thinking, at worst an ideological justification for social injustice and, somewhere in the middle, an evasion
of the categorical imperative to face fundamental existential uncertainties.
While for many decades, at least in Western Europe, these issues have been
dormant, limited to the sphere of lifestyle choices, the recent growth in

Christian and Muslim fundamentalism has returned them to both the political and social agendas. Recent times have witnessed children—presumably having been promised heavenly life, perhaps even with a song about it on their lips—sent into public places in Afghanistan and Iraq, strapped into explosive waistcoats.

If the promise of heaven has perhaps, on balance, not added to the sum of human happiness, why should the Fourth Symphony interest us? As already noted, evasion and denial go deep in the work: particularly in the first movement, the music seems explicitly to turn away from the implications of its own trajectory. Commentators have variously identified the dreamlike, fictional, 'past-tense' or 'quotation-mark' qualities inherent to the movement. Such non-reality can readily be associated with stylistic evocations, of which Roger Scruton has written in another context, which project 'The lingering backward glance toward that which can never be recovered (and which is falsified by the yearning for it) . . . it involves a "turning away" from the present reality, a desire to lock emotions into a narrow and predetermined world of fantasy, a world which *you yourself* control.'[26] But such control is ultimately unsustainable. The 'narrow and predetermined world of fantasy' propagated by the Fourth becomes destabilised by the contradictions inherent to any denial: the fantasy consumes itself and the illusion crumbles. In the case of the Fourth, this involves the opening of windows onto the darker and more humanly tragic worlds of the Fifth and Sixth symphonies. But what exactly is being denied? If we maintain 'heaven' as our theme, the answer is that we are in denial over the fact that life is frequently unjust, painful and unpleasant—that bad things happen to good people. But other candidates may be conscripted from the convulsive intellectual and social life of the late nineteenth century. We might, for instance, recall Mahler's early interest in Nietzsche and read into the Fourth a drama wherein the Dionysian urge, initially thwarted and denied by an Apollonian superstructure that has forgotten its radical interdependence, breaks through and wreaks havoc. Or we might look to Mahler's Vienna, and recall the overlap between his circle and Freud's, whose *Interpretation of Dreams* was published in 1899. Freud's ideas posit a radical limit to our transparency to ourselves. Certain impulses need to be denied for the good of society and culture; yet their repression can lead to outbreaks of irrationality. Adorno suggests that 'no father figures' are admitted to the Fourth.[27] But such an evocation of a pre-Freudian paradise is as unattainable as it is undesirable: arrested Oedipal development has severe clinical and social consequences.[28] Another possible formulation of denial might be to see late Habsburg society as stifling a series of necessary social and ethical evolutions, with a consequent explosion of murderous irrationality in the years after 1914. Thus, while in appearance civilised, cultured, and elegant, the society was in fact premised on social myopia and injustice, a hollow pretence expending its last energies in ignoring the impending catastrophe.

Doubtless many more possibilities exist. Perhaps none will be self-evidently incorrect, provided we endorse the analogising of conceptual content from musical syntax and morphology. Equally, no interpretation would be even minimally binding upon a listener. One further option is to take the work as a parable of musical evolution, a demonstration—proto-Brechtian in its embodiment of its negative paradigm—that the role of tonality in the definition of form and time-scale had been seriously compromised by expressive innovations (particularly in the harmonic field) over the preceding fifty or sixty years. On this reading the Fourth embodies the thesis that tonality's days as a vital and rigorous organising principle were numbered. While I will not pursue this reading explicitly, it may be taken, if not to underpin the remainder of the chapter, then at least as offering little narrative lubrication to its dryer analytical aspects.

Notwithstanding Rosen's appraisal that Mahler 'employed sonata-forms with the same mock respect that he gave to his shop-worn scraps of dance-tunes',[29] the first movement of the Fourth represents one of the most radical of Mahler's sonata proposals, the enactment of an issue that has dogged sonata thinking almost since its inception: the status of the 'double return'. This apotheosis of teleological fulfilment had become generalised practice in around 1770 (Mozart and Schubert retained older strategies on occasion). Its historical ascendancy derives from the synthesis it effects of binary and ternary forms (which until that point had comprised opposing conceptions of contrast and coherence), which made of it a highly efficient 'engine' for transforming the latent energy of tonality into aesthetic work. Yet, before long, the double return—the moment at which the dominant's aspirations to tonicity are definitively repudiated—became subject to creative subversion. As metaphysical thinking turned from Kantian to Hegelian premises (with digressions through Fichte and Schelling), and subsequently to the systems or anti-systems of Schopenhauer and Nietzsche, it was perhaps inevitable that sonata thinking should undergo its own, parallel, evolutions. Thus, the sense or truth obtaining from simplistic and mechanical restorations of the order overthrown in the exposition became less than self-evident. If we regard sonata form as a forum for speculation on the nature and meaning of rupture, restoration, progress, and fulfilment (rather than as a series of pre-established formal segments), as these basic categories of human experience are reformulated and questioned throughout the nineteenth century, composers use the form to reappraise and conjugate anew these concepts in musical terms. Beethoven, in his two op. 14 sonatas, already lays out the two broad alternative strategies—of transfigured first group (op. 14/1) and 'false recapitulation' (op. 14/2)—which were to be greatly elaborated and enhanced by symphonists in the second half of the nineteenth century. Other manoeuvres include the elision of the development and recapitulation sections (an element of Mahler's strategy in the Fourth, but for which precedents can be found in many earlier works, such as the first movements of Haydn's string quartet op. 50/1 and Beethoven's Eighth Symphony), and directing the development towards the 'wrong' key (Haydn's piano sonata H. 38 ends the development on a perfect cadence on vi; Beethoven's sonatas op. 7 and 28 end the discursive part of the development on V/vii and V/VI, respectively). By the final quarter of the nineteenth century, composers had found myriad ways of parsing the scansion between development and recapitulation: an unambiguously affirmative double return is by no means the most frequently chosen alternative. This is the case with Mahler's symphonies prior to the Fourth. The First reaches an exuberant tonic, albeit not from a dominant, but only connects with the 'Ging heut' Morgen' theme seventeen bars later, and then almost casually, in mid-phrase. The Second generates extraordinary tension on a massive dominant but places the hiatus after the resolution to the tonic, causing the passage to sound more like an ending than a new beginning. In the Third, the music dwindles to almost nothing—a side drum, *pppp*—having reached the flimsiest imaginable dominant, a D♭ that is only potentially the enharmonic equivalent of the leading note of D minor. Thus, the 'strange happenings' in the Fourth at the interface between development and recapitulation are not entirely incommensurate with practices in other composers', and in Mahler's own, works.

However, in the Fourth, the denial of a teleological double return has a quality not so much of a cognisance of metaphysical complexities as of a negligent refusal to engage with the music's recent past. It thus represents what might be termed a 'structural evasion', one of two I identify in the movement. Discussion of the other—perhaps more an 'attempted evasion'—requires addressing how the movement is to be parsed in terms of exposition, development, recapitulation, and coda. Most commentators place the beginning of the development at bar 102, following what is regarded as an incomplete repeat of the exposition with an 'epilogue' in the home tonic. On my reading, bars 72–101 would constitute a 'fake exposition repeat.'[30] The strategy—generally traced to Beethoven's op. 59/1, although it is found in Haydn's Sonata H.51—had been taken to elaborate lengths in two recent symphonies written shortly before Mahler's Fourth: Brahms's Fourth and Dvorak's Eighth.[31] This division correlatively suggests placing the coda from bar 298 (rather than 340, a mere ten bars from the end). Taken together, the juncture between exposition and development becomes thematically and tonally congruent with that between recapitulation and coda: in bars 69–71 the music cadences in D major, moving to the sleighbell theme in B minor at bar 72; while in bars 295–97 the cadence in G major gives way to the sleighbells in E minor. There are further advantages to my scheme: bars 72–101 cease to be an anomaly (an 'episode' or a rondo refrain); and the proportions between the various structural units seem more harmonious (exposition—71 bars; development—165 bars; recapitulation (from hiatus)—60 bars; coda—52 bars). The point at which the 'fake' repeat diverges from its model is no more delayed in Mahler's Fourth than in the Dvorak and Brahms symphonies mentioned earlier. The principal difference—and this will probably be the main objection to my suggestion— is that Mahler's music slows to a standstill on the tonic rather than picking up pace and initiating tonal expansion, as do the Brahms and Dvorak works. I view this, however, as an instance of attempted denial, the first 'structural evasion': how better to safeguard the hermetic fantasy of the exposition than by avoiding the development and its attendant dangers of motivic and tonal confrontation? The music expands a little counterpoint that has appeared in the tenor immediately before the two perfect authentic cadences in G major (bb. 21 and 80) heard so far, suggesting that here the cadential moment is being prolonged indefinitely (the melody never reaches the first degree) in a dilation of time entirely in keeping with a pathology of prevarication. To Adorno, this passage suggests the vision of a 'village . . . that might be what [the listener] seeks';[32] but, as the theoretician of *Negative Dialectics* was aware, all such idylls are ultimately illusory.

However much structural innovations may resonate with the intellectual *zeitgeist*, formal events need to be motivated by musical material. A work will convince only if its unfolding dramatic succession does not feel forced or imposed in an arbitrary manner. Beethoven's use, in the *Waldstein* Sonata, of the major mediant in the second group is justified because the tonicised V in bar 3 has rendered the dominant key unviable. In the op. 90 sonata, the 'discovery' of the recapitulation—an effect Tovey admires[33]—is only possible because the sequential harmony of the main theme (i—VII7—III—II7—v), with its ephemeral tonic, makes dominant preparation inappropriate. In Beethoven's Eighth Symphony, the elision of development and recapitulation occurs because the first theme in the treble would be incapable of bearing the weight of an affirmative double return: the solution is for it to sound in the basses as part of a cadential 6/4 at the development's climax. Mahler's opening string theme in the Fourth is equally unsuited to the task of teleological culmination. But rather than seeking a solution (as does Beethoven), Mahler seems effectively to ignore the problem. That this failure to engage with one of the central premises of sonata thought be heard as the creative and vivid dramatisation of a disjunction, rather than as mere incompetence, will depend on the musical material, and on how it instigates the formal processes.

Mahler reportedly stated that the Fourth completes a 'perfectly self-contained tetralogy' with the first three symphonies.[34] The comment serves to remind us that the two harmonies that open the Prelude to *Götterdämmerung* are in the same relation as those which open Mahler's work: E♭ minor and C♭ major in Wagner, B minor and G major in the Fourth. In both cases, there exists a radical uncertainty as to the chords' functions: whether they are, respectively, minor tonic and major submediant, or minor mediant and major tonic. This ambiguity (perhaps analogous to Escher's investigations of the phenomenology of background/foreground perception) runs throughout

the first movement of the Fourth. The iii–I progression is heard memorably
in Beethoven's *Diabelli Variations*, op. 120, where the C major of the closing
Tempo di Minuetto is reached from an E minor triad. The passage marks a
point of inflection in the erosion of the dominant function, a process itself in-
timately linked to the evolution of the development-recapitulation nexus. As
musical language evolved during the nineteenth century, the range and force
of the tensions that a work might generate became so great that the dominant
was no longer capable of its main structural task: that of concentrating all tensions metonymically within itself and subsequently discharging them in a resolution to the tonic. It is notable how few syntactically crucial, form-defining
dominants there are in the Fourth: for all its deployment of classicising tropes,
the dominant is not the definitive dissonance in this work and has lost almost
entirely its capacity for structural leverage. The device by which Mahler regains
the tonic at the end of the development is thus of great significance. Following
an 'outburst' in C major (bb. 209–20) the music moves to a crisis chord and
collapses, the attenuation playing out over the slow grinding of tonal gears.
The recapitulation emerges tenuously and elongated (b. 233), and concurrently
the tonic is reached—almost casually—via a chain of descending thirds, each
successive harmony giving way to its own diatonic submediant (an extension
of the harmonic relation found at the opening of the movement). As Ex. 1.1
shows, F♯minor drops to D major, and thence to B minor, G major, E minor
and C major (overshooting the tonic, such is the lack of importance given it).
This same structure of thirds, in the form of alternating of major and minor
keys, underpins the tonal organisation of the Fourth (this is shown in Figs. 1.1
and 1.2, and is discussed below). Thus, this 'enigmatic and magical' moment
is also one of the most prosaic in structural terms, the point where (in the
best Viennese tradition) the constructive principle is exposed on the musical
surface.

Ex. 1.1 Mahler's Fourth Symphony, first movement, bars 233–38

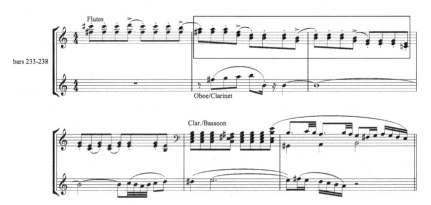

Earlier I described aspects of the Fourth as an 'escapist fantasy'. The denial of the dominant function is one aspect of this. The nature of the material itself—themes, motives, rhythmic devices—is also significant, specifically in its tendency to a certain artificiality. Perhaps our closest present-day experience of non-pathological fantasy worlds is granted by computer-generated graphics. Certain aspects of the Fourth might be seen—anachronistically and fictionally—as 'representations' of musical elements, resulting from what I will term 'algorithmic', as opposed to organic, processes. One example is the movement's almost obsessive dependence on 6–5 appoggiaturas, from its opening sonority onwards.[35] Ex. 1.2a shows the some of the instances (bracketed). Further, when themes are intensified or expanded, it is almost invariably this element that is exploited. The result is a self-absorbed quality, of dislocation from the flow of time, as if a moment were expanded from within. This is in part a consequence of privileging voice-leading resolutions over harmonic ones. The extreme instance is when, in the course of repetitions of a particular figure, the appoggiatura actually takes over the harmony, undermining any directionality (this is shown in Ex.1.2b).

The prevalence of appoggiaturas has structural, as well as expressive, importance: in the absence of dominant leverage, Mahler employs appoggiaturas to toggle the music up and down the mediants. The open fifth that begins the movement and that signals a new cycle at various crucial junctures has two upper neighbour notes. In the minor mode these are the minor sixth degree and the major second degree, and it is by inflecting these that Mahler moves between keys: for instance, the flattened second degree of the implied B minor, C♮ (a Phrygian inflection) eases the music into G major in bar 4; and the sharpened sixth-degree (Dorian inflection) of F♯ minor, D♯, nudges the music into C♯ minor in bar 147.

Another characteristic of the movement is its marked tendency to a proliferation of material that is not developmental in a dynamic sense. Melodic canons emerge fleetingly like mirages and just as quickly peter out, pleonastic melodic inversions masquerade as consequents, and random counterpoints germinate, almost parasitically, in any available fissure. There is a generalised stacking or burgeoning of material that tends to saturate available space without creating meaningful contrapuntal tensions. A further avoidance of dynamism can be seen in the fact that the two principal melodies from first and second groups share a basic outline. To an extent this merely demonstrates the kind of motivic unity we trace with pleasure in the Viennese classicists;[36] but there is a sense here of modular recombination rather than organic flexibility. As Ex. 1.3 suggests, each element of the melody from bars 3–7 is recycled in bars 263–71 (from the recapitulation, for ease of comparison), only minimally varied and in permutated order. The common elements are labelled A to D in Ex.1.3.

Ryan Kangas draws attention to how the first theme closes on a perfect authentic cadence after just four bars, which makes finding a suitable consequent

Ex. 1.2 Mahler's Fourth Symphony, first movement, occurrences of appoggiaturas: a) bars 1, 2, 4–5, 10–11, 12–17, 20, 39, 44–45, 50–52, 56–57, 69, 93–96, 109–110, 128–29, 148–49, 196–97, 338–40; b) bars 13, 15, 29, 88

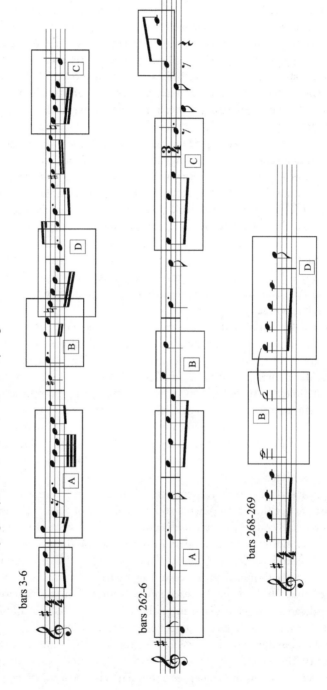

Ex. 1.3 Mahler's Fourth Symphony, first movement, melodic recycling

decidedly problematic. His observation that 'the music is somehow simultaneously classical and impossible for the classical era'[37] captures the ambivalence of much of the material: its superficial appearance is just that—there is no deep grammar driving its behaviour. The anomalous rhythmic behaviour of the second group is a further instance. Here, it is as if the operations of elision and expansion have been applied without cognisance of the mediating role of bar structure. Thus, bar 40 is a truncated version of 38–39, omitting the first and last two beats respectively; bar 41 gets confused between two and four beats, and ends up being three, a limping phrase in this ostensibly most lyrical of passages. In bars 56–57 the melody initiates a syncopation (a dotted rhythm straddling the strong beats) but promptly forgets where the downbeat is, requiring a scrambled bar change to square the expected cadence. A similar sensation is given by the quirky and idiosyncratic closing group (built, not incidentally, almost exclusively from the three-note scalar lead-in to the main theme), which follows on from this point. Here, elementary figures are recycled by means of relatively unsophisticated combinational protocols. There is also a strange sensation, prompted by the melody's wayward chromatic inflections, that tonality is somehow external, rather than intrinsic, to the music: it operates within the prescribed limits of tonic, and enhanced dominant and subdominant, but does so only because when it collides with tonality's constraints, it rebounds.

  None of this bodes well for the remainder of the sonata, but as has been suggested, the fantasy aspect of the piece has a vested interest in never reaching a development section. Perhaps here we can flesh out Mitchell's observation that the development is 'virtually self-contained':[38] at its start, the exposition material almost manages to slow time to a standstill, prompting the sleigh-bells—with a markedly more aggressive stance than previously—to initiate a third beginning; and come the recapitulation the materials' only feasible strategy—given the tonal and motivic distance travelled—is to pull the plug on the sonata process, and start over as if re-booting. We will now chart this latter process more closely.

  Figs. 1.1 and 1.2 present respectively the tonal centres in the exposition and the first part of the development, and second part of the development, recapitulation, and coda. (The division occurs in bar 167, upon reaching F minor: the corresponding column appears in both charts.) The left- and right-most columns reproduce the array of mediant-related keys, alternating major and minor, with the former in upper case. The top row gives the bar in which each key is reached; the bars spent in each key are indicated in the individual cells; a cross indicates a key centre that might have been expected (the number in the same column indicates the key in fact employed).

  The first bars present the music's basic tonal strategy, and its fundamental ambiguity. The second group is in $\underline{D}$,[39] reached by a bifocal cadence. From here, the key centres follow the sequence in the chart's leftmost column: $\underline{D}$, $\underline{b}$, $\underline{G}$, $\underline{e}$, $\underline{C}$.

	EXPOSITION						DEVELOPMENT-1											
Bar	1	4	38	72	77	102	109	115	119	125	145	148	151	155	158	160	163	167
E													x					
c#												3						
A										20								
f#											3						4	
D			34															
b	3			5		7												
G		34			25													
e							6		6									
C								4	(6)				4					
a										x								
F																		
d																		
Bb																		
g																		
Eb																		
c																		
Ab																		
f																		18
Db																		
bb																		
Gb																	x	
eb														3		3		
Cb																		
ab															2			
Fb																		
db																		

Fig. 1.1 Tonal centres in Mahler's Fourth Symphony, first movement: exposition and development (1)

	DEVELOPMENT-2														RECAPITULATION				CODA		
	167	185	188	190	192	196	204	209	221	227	229	230	234	235	239	287	289	298	302	308	311
E																					
c#																					
A																					
f#												5									
D																					
b													2			2					
G						(9)									49		9				39
e														3				4			
C								12													
a								x											6		
F																					
d							5														
Bb																				3	
g						9															x
Eb					4																
c																					
Ab																					
f	18			2					6												
Db			2							x											
bb		3									1										
Gb												x									
eb																					
Cb																					
ab																					
Fb																					
db										2											

Fig. 1.2 Tonal centres in Mahler's Fourth Symphony, first movement: development (2), recapitulation and coda

Within this progression, Mahler backtracks twice, revisiting b̲ between G̲ and e̲, and insinuating e̲ after C̲, this latter move creating a sort of dead-lock (bb. 115–20) which results in the movement's first crisis and collapse (bb. 121–24). Following this, we find the principal strategy used to vary the se-quence of keys: the music moves to the tonal centre next on the chart, but in the parallel mode. Thus, from C̲ the music passes to A̲, rather than to a̲. Coinciding with this first change in tonal protocol, we hear the celebrated 'dream ocarina' in bar 126 (see Ex. 1.4a).[40]

This theme is frequently cited as an important instance of the insertion of material from the song that 'explains' what the symphony 'means'. On certain readings, it is conceived as encroaching upon, or even requisitioning, the sonata plot followed up until now. Yet there is perhaps little that will prompt us—if not predisposed by contextual knowledge—to such a perception. The gesture is generic: in tessitura, scoring, and construction (a major triad, an appoggiatura, and a passing note) it is similar to figures in Mahler's First Symphony (closing group: Ex. 1.4b), and in Dvorak's Eighth (first theme after introduction: Ex. 1.4d). In addition, while in certain respects a 'new' theme—by no means un-usual in development sections: interestingly, in his First, Mahler employs the flute motive in counterpoint to the new theme in the cellos (Ex. 1.4c)—it can be derived from preceding music. Thus, the initial high E retakes the pitch reached at the point of collapse in bar 121, while the rhythm and figuration can be assembled from snippets of previous themes: the repeated notes at the start of the of the second group theme; the dotted rhythm from the 'village' theme (heard in counterpoint to the flutes and immediately prior to their entry); the insistence on the 6–5 appoggiatura; and so on. An unprejudiced hearing will find nothing that obliges it to realign the terms of the movement's sonata argu-ment (even assuming that such cognitive appraisal can be said to form part of the phenomenology of aesthetic attention).

The change of mode that results in A̲ prompts the music (following a brief shading of f♯ in b. 145) to retrace its steps from this new point in the chart: c♯ is reached at some point between bars 146 and 148, and the sequence continues upwards, but with another change of mode, to e̲ (rather than E̲), a key already investigated at some length, and which gave rise to the first crisis and collapse. Perhaps to avoid the same fate, the music here effects a more radical move, not immediately to be assimilated within the sequence of mediant-related keys. Using standard second-practice harmony (a diminished-seventh chord with common-tone resolution), the music modulates down a semitone, written as e♭ (the key signature is given) although technically it is d♯. The sequence of four minor keys between leaving A̲ (b. 145) and reaching e♭ (b. 191)—f♯, c♯, e̲, e♭—is reproduced (a further algorithmic procedure) one tone higher (a♭, e♭, f♯, and f♯ are reached in bars 158, 160, 163, and 167, respectively) in a passage which offers a highly telescoped summary of events in bars 103–54. The final key reached, f̲ (key-signature given), is the antipode of the b̲ that opens the

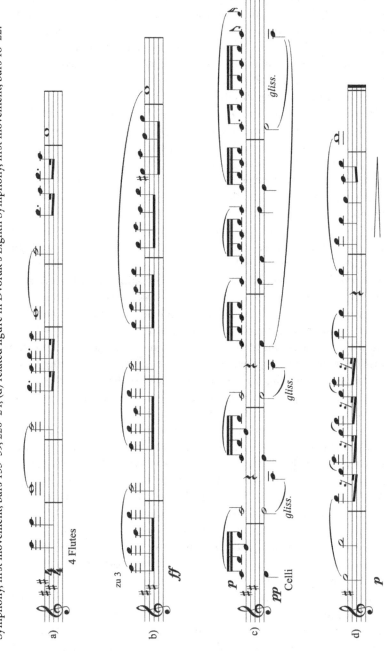

Ex. 1.4 (a) Mahler's Fourth Symphony, first movement, 'dream ocarina', bars 126–31; (b) and (c) related figures in Mahler's First Symphony, first movement, bars 135–39, 220–24; (d) related figure in Dvorak's Eighth Symphony, first movement, bars 18–22.

work, and represents an important structural division in the development (hence the 'story so far' summation that immediately precedes it). The sleigh-bell theme appears in a variant including the lower chromatic neighbour note to the upper fifth, which gives rise to augmented-sixth harmony, an innocent enough device, but one which will eventually provoke the development's terminal collapse. Barring some Phrygian inflections that nudge it towards b̲♭, the tonality is relatively stable until a series of references to the first group begins in bar 187. This is developed for a further eight bars, whereupon a dissonant climax is reached (b. 196), which lasts four bars. The last of these, bar 199, sees the start of a 'cloned' version of the music from bars 187–95. In this latter case, the climax is the consonant (if raucous) outburst in C̲ (with key signature) that Adorno terms a 'noisily cheerful field'.[41] The sequence and its 'clone' are shown in Ex. 1.5, aligned on two staves each (the last bar in the top two staves is the first in the lower two). The movement's most dissonant passage follows this 'noisily cheerful field', leading to crisis and complete collapse. Here sounds the fanfare that will open the Fifth Symphony: but blithely ignoring this portent, the recapitulation enters stealthily, feigning ignorance of previous events. What motivates this failure of sonata protocol? How does it convince?

The immediate origin of the crisis is to be found in the two climatic moments, one dissonant (b. 196), the other consonant (b. 209). Clearly, neither represents a double return: both, however, exhibit traits associated with the device and may be understood as (failed) attempts at teleological fulfilment. Each is preceded by a passage developing first-group material in rising sequence, a common retransitional strategy. The climax in bar 196 is the first time since bar 101 that the tonic key has been heard. An important token of this is that the timpani plays on G, *forte*: the first time this instrument has played the tonic, only its third intervention in the piece so far, and first at this dynamic. The harmony evinces major/minor ambiguity, however, and while the material is first-group-derived, and certain rhythmic elements are correctly aligned (the rhythm in violins in b. 197, and basses in b. 198, corresponds to that of the main theme in bb. 4 and 5), it is beset with variants that have not been sufficiently untangled. If the music from bar 4 onwards, with its characteristic falling sixth, turn, and chromatic passing note were spliced, perhaps suitably re-orchestrated, on to bar 195, the result would not be absurd: while unconvincing in terms of resolution (why this is so is the crux of the movement, and of this chapter), it would be syntactically correct. If bar 196 can be viewed as a botched recapitulation, the cloned passage that ensues would represent the music—in a desperate measure—taking a second run at it, but with even worse fortune. In bar 209 the appropriate affirmative energy is achieved, and the bass is correct, but this second would-be recapitulation is doubly false: while it apes the gestural quality of a double return—the tone is irremediably forced, even parodic—it is the wrong material (derived from the 'dream ocarina' and the transition theme from the exposition) in the wrong key (C major). The second-inversion orientation of the harmony suggests a cadential

Ex. 1.5 Mahler's Fourth Symphony, first movement, sequence and 'clone', bars 187–99, 199–212

Ex. 1.6 Collapsing gestures in Mahler's Fourth Symphony and Sixth Symphony, first movements

6/4 (shades of Beethoven's Eighth?), but the customary resolution would define the home tonic, G̲, as a dominant. The only alternative, a resolution upwards over the same pedal, produces a combination of French and German augmented sixths which can be interpreted functionally as a pre-dominant in f̲. While this tonality is not the supposed goal, it is the key that started the second half of the development (b. 167) and thus represents the most recent moment of tonal stability prior to the 'noisily cheerful field'. It cannot represent a long-term solution, however, and far from resolving and stabilising, the music collapses.

The onset of this collapse evidently made an impression on Mahler himself, for he paraphrased it in his Sixth Symphony.[42] The principal elements from the two passages are clearly related, as Ex. 1.6 shows: the upbeat gestures in strings share rhythm and contour; the underlying harmony is identical; the melodic figures, entrusted to the trumpets in both cases, patently issue from a common gene pool; and the figuration in the woodwind is well-nigh identical.

Taking the 'crisis chord' to imply f̲, the subsequent keys follow the cycle of mediant-related keys, with changes of mode in the second and fourth steps: f̲, d♭, b♭, g♭. This latter is written enharmonically as f♯: from here the flutes take the music stepwise down to G and beyond as discussed in connection with Ex. 1.1. The stealthy recapitulation that starts in bar 234 is rhythmically elongated (six beats are added before the turn, and two after the chromatic passing note, and two beats of rest before the hiatus). The lead-in figure offers a b (Aeolian), rather than G, orientation, although it seems to correct itself by falling an octave rather than a sixth (thereby landing on the same B as the melody in b. 4). But bars 234–35 in fact reproduce bars 120–21 (the site of the first disintegration of the texture) a fourth lower, at the same time as insinuating that b minor is the home tonic after all. The opening of the main theme is, in fact, never heard again verbatim: although allusions are rife, even the closest (in bb. 341–42) has subdominant orientation. The double return is thus utterly negated: neither is the tonic affirmed (the flutes 'overshoot') nor is the main theme heard in its original form, and far from issuing in teleological manner from the development, the recapitulation treats it as irrelevant.

From this point, the recapitulation is relatively straightforward, although there are a couple of moments where the unfinished business of the development seems about to break through: the 'noisily cheerful field' makes a sly bid for first-group status in bar 240, insinuating itself as a counterpoint (in canon) to the music previously heard in bars 20–23; then it appears in full, but in G major, in the transition. Another intrusion is in the closing group which, aside from suffering incursions from derivations of the first group, includes a strange episode in B♭ major, a key not heard up to this point. In all, the rampant burgeoning of material now traverses sectional boundaries. The coda (b. 298 onwards in my reading) exhibits traits of a second development (more than usually appropriate here given the first development's failure to resolve anything), but finds its way back into the 'fake exposition repeat' and a peroration on the music that ebbs away on 6–5 appoggiaturas, here with even less cadential finality. The last ten bars gather together motives and figures from the cheerier parts of the movement, but perhaps its true conclusion lies in the Fifth and Sixth symphonies, works more prepared to contemplate the reality of the human condition, while the escapist element—courtesy of Irving Berlin—finds a home on Broadway.

Notes

1. Floros, *Gustav Mahler: The Symphonies*, 113.
2. Cited in Floros, *Gustav Mahler: The Symphonies*, 115.
3. Adorno, *Mahler* [English edition], 58.
4. La Grange, "Music about Music," 136.
5. Zychowicz, *Mahler's Fourth Symphony*, 16.
6. Walter, *Gustav Mahler*, 83 and 84 (author's translation).

7. Adorno, "Mahler (Centenary Address, Vienna 1960)," 90.

8. Cooke, *Gustav Mahler*, 67.

9. Knapp, "Suffering Children," 248.

10. Samuels,"Music as Text", 155.

11. Monahan, *Mahler's Symphonic Sonatas*, 154.

12. Samuels, "Music as Text," 156.

13. Knapp, "Suffering Children", 249.

14. Floros, *Gustav Mahler: The Symphonies*, 121.

15. Bonds, *After Beethoven*, 190.

16. Samuels, "Music as Text," 156.

17. Mitchell, "'Swallowing the Programme'", 207.

18. Bauer-Lechner, *Recollections of Gustav Mahler*, 152.

19. Bauer-Lechner, *Mahleriana*, unpublished MS, cited in de La Grange, *Vienna: The Years of Challenge*, 757.

20. Bauer-Lechner, *Recollections of Gustav Mahler*, 162.

21. Cited in Floros, *Gustav Mahler: The Symphonies*, 115.

22. Adorno, *Mahler* [English edition], 57 and 96.

23. Bauer-Lechner, *Recollections of Gustav Mahler*, 151 (author's translation) and 178.

24. Mitchell, "'Swallowing the Programme'", 194 (emphasis in original).

25. Tovey, *Essays in Musical Analysis. Volume I: Symphonies*, p. 115.

26. Paddison, *Adorno's Aesthetics of Music*, 492.

27. Adorno, *Mahler* [English edition], 53.

28. Adorno's comment is pertinent in another context, too: the years between the completion of the Third and the composition of the Fourth saw the demise—symbolic or actual—of a large number of father figure candidates. Bruckner died in 1896 and Brahms in 1897, the same year that Hugo Wolf succumbed to final madness (after declaring himself director of the Vienna Opera, a post Mahler actually held); Hans Richter was ousted from the Vienna Philharmonic in 1898, and Johann Strauss died in 1899, while Dvorak never really recovered his hold on public life after returning from America in 1895. Adorno suggests that Mahler reduced the scale and innovation of the Fourth because he had gone out on a limb in the Third, in which sonata form is 'no more than a husk' (Adorno, *Mahler* [English edition], 77). But perhaps the circumstance of finding himself with neither living role models nor effective competition freed him from the compulsion constantly to go one better.

29. Rosen, *The Classical Style*, 522.

30. This possibility is discussed but rejected in favour of a reading in terms of rondo form by Julian Johnson in *Mahler's Voices*, 111.

31. Historically, the motivation behind the 'fake exposition repeat' is not primarily that of fooling an audience. It is rather that, in the absence of a full repetition of the exposition, it offers a double return after the second-group modulation in a manner that can be perceived as inadequate, thus making patent the requirement for a development capable of engineering a truly satisfactory tonal and thematic restoration.

32. Adorno, *Mahler* [English edition], 44.

33. Tovey, *A Companion to Beethoven's Pianoforte Sonatas*, 200.

34. Bauer-Lechner, *Recollections of Gustav Mahler*, 154.

35. It is probably entirely coincidental, but for that reason the more intriguing, that Irving Berlin's *Cheek to Cheek*, from the 1935 musical *Top Hat*, sets the opening lyric 'Heaven' with a 6–5. Even more remarkably, bars 7–10 of the song exactly reproduce the melody in bars 54–55 of Mahler's Fourth.

36. See Rosen, *The Classical Style*, 121, for one of countless examples.

37. Kangas, "Classical Style, Childhood and Nostalgia", 226.

38. Mitchell, " 'Swallowing the Programme' ", 213.

39. In the following discussion, major keys are indicated by higher case letters, and minor keys by lower, in both instances underlined.

40. The key signature changes here (it has already changed from G to D and back, coinciding with the second group and the start of the development, respectively). There are three further key signature changes—far fewer than the number of key centres actually transitioned—before the recapitulation, each one coinciding with a 'non-standard' (i.e., non-consecutive in the chart) modulation.

41. Adorno, *Mahler* [English edition], 54.

42. The connection seems to have escaped comment in the literature. The passage in the Sixth comes just at the end of the first group, immediately before the first timpani strokes and the horns' major-minor gesture. There is an implied intensification of the form: in the Fourth it is at the end of the development, traditionally a moment of high tension, whereas in the Sixth it occurs at a point of transition.

2

Mining the Past for New Expressions

Song Form as Narrative Device in Mahler's Ballads from
Des Knaben Wunderhorn

Molly M. Breckling

In his ballads based on texts from Achim von Arnim and Clemens Brentano's 1805–8 folksong anthology *Des Knaben Wunderhorn: Alte Deutsche Lieder*, Gustav Mahler used familiar tools such as folk-like melodies, memorable accompaniment figures, simple diatonic harmonies, and mimetic gestures to create something quite extraordinary. With these elements he could convince his listeners that they were hearing something innocent and naïve. But once his audience stripped away the comforting veneer supplied by these seemingly commonplace techniques, they would find that Mahler had manipulated the tropes in complex ways, and in doing so, he presented his listeners with a dilemma: one could either take the songs at face value or look a little more deeply at a level of sophistication that challenged established norms, assumptions, and values. A fascinating friction lies between the old and conventional and the new and innovative in these works. This liminal space refers to a glorified folkloric past that is not as enchanting as it is made to seem and points to an environment that depends on musical trompe l'oeil.

Much of this deceptive complexity stems from Mahler's unusual approach to narrative within the *Wunderhorn* ballads (Table 2.1). Stated simply, ballads relate tales. But they are not merely diegetic, as Goethe observes in his classic definition, describing the ballad as a poetic form in which information can be relayed to the listener using 'all three basic poetic modes': the epic, dramatic, and lyric. Goethe also points out that the poetic flexibility offered by ballads allows poets or singers to 'rush to the end or draw it out', based on the amount of detail they choose to reveal.[1]

Most ballads combine these lyric, epic, and dramatic elements, pairing dialogue (dramatic action) with narrative distance (epic neutrality) or with lyrical forms of verse. Some, however, function purely dramatically, with a text entirely of dialogue, while other poems dwell purely in the epic, featuring only narration.

A song composer can most directly impart his intended narrative sources and trajectories by allowing the musical narrative to mirror that of the spoken text; for example, providing contrasting stanzas with differing music or

Table 2.1 Gustav Mahler's Ballads based on texts from *Des Knaben Wunderhorn*

Song	Plot	Song form	Poem form
'Um schlimme Kinder artig zu machen' c. 1887	Stranger visits a castle offering gifts to a mother if her children are well behaved. She says they are not, and he leaves.	Modified strophic (AA¹)	Four 4-line stanzas
'Ich ging mit Lust' c. 1887	A young man walks through the woods to reach the home of his love. On the way he may have strayed.	Extended ternary form (AABA¹)	Five 5-line stanzas
'Aus! Aus!' c. 1887	A young soldier bids farewell to his sweetheart before riding into battle.	Rondo (ABACA)	Three 5-line stanzas, one 6-line stanza, and one 10-line stanza
'Starke Einbildungskraft' c. 1887	A maiden wonders why her sweetheart has not asked for her hand in marriage; he cleverly dodges the question.	Modified strophic (A A¹)	Two 7-line stanzas
'Zu Straßburg auf der Schanz' c. 1890	A young, homesick soldier is punished for trying to return to his homeland.	Modified bar form (AAAB)	Six 5-line stanzas
'Scheiden und Meiden' c. 1890	Two lovers are saying farewell.	Extended ternary form (ABBA¹)	Three 5-line stanzas

Title	Summary	Form	Structure
'Nicht wiedersehen' c. 1890	A young man leaves for the summer. When he returns, his sweetheart has died of a broken heart.	Bar form (AAB)	Four 4-line stanzas and one 5-line stanza
'Der Schildwache Nachtlied" 1892	A guard imagines a conversation with his sweetheart during night duty.	Strophic (paired verses)	Six 4-line stanzas
'Verlor'ne Müh' 1892	A maiden tries unsuccessfully to woo her laddie.	Modified strophic	Five sets of 4-line stanzas with 2-line responses
'Trost im Unglück' 1892	While parting, a couple downplay their feelings for each other.	Extended ternary form (AABA')	Five 4-line stanzas with 4-line refrain
'Das irdische Leben' 1893	A starving child is ignored by her mother, busily baking bread.	Modified strophic	Five stanzas: first omits two lines, which appear at end
'Des Antonius von Padua Fischpredigt' 1893	St. Anthony takes his sermon to the river. While the fish are entertained by his performance, his words do not change their behavior.	Extended ternary form (AAABAA)	Nine 6-line stanzas
'Rheinlegendchen' 1893	A peasant dreams of being reunited with her sweetheart who works for the king.	Ternary form	Eight 4-line stanzas

(continued)

Table 2.1 Continued

Song	Plot	Song form	Poem form
'Lob des hohen Verstands' 1896	A cuckoo challenges a nightingale to a singing contest to be judged by a donkey.	Extended ternary form (ABA¹)	Five 6-line stanzas
'Lied des Verfolgten im Turm' 1898	A prisoner refuses to submit his thoughts to his captivity.	Modified strophic (paired verses)	Four 8-line stanzas with three 5-line responses
'Wo die schönen Trompeten blasen' 1898	A maiden is visited by the ghost of her beloved soldier.	Free-form scena	Both poems have 4-line stanzas, 9 & 4
'Revelge' 1899	Soldiers' sense of duty stays with them after death.	Free-form scena	Eight 5-line stanzas
'Der Tamboursg'sell' 1901	A young drummer is punished for military wrongdoing.	Modified bar form (AAAB)	Five 6-line stanzas

creating unique sonic spaces for individual characters in a dialogue. While sometimes we hear these types of techniques in Mahler's ballads, he does not always opt for this simplistic approach. Instead, he frequently allows his music to play an independent role, one that weaves in and out of the story regardless of the narrative voices present in the text. Sometimes the music serves as an epic narrator, sometimes as a dramatic character, and sometimes it merely supports the poetry in an essentially lyrical fashion. This fluidity brings to the musical work a unique narrative interaction that neither text nor music can provide alone. The listener learns things about the characters in the stories that the protagonists do not know about themselves, allowing the audience to become increasingly engaged with events as they unfold.

This chapter explores the various formal techniques that Mahler used to contribute to the process of storytelling in his ballads from *Des Knaben Wunderhorn*. Mahler used song form as a type of narrative device, setting stories that progressed at similar rates or with plots analogous to the same kinds of formal structures. Numerous studies have examined the various formal structures at play in Mahler's Lieder.[2] None, however, have attributed those forms with the ability to convey narrative.

Most earlier German Lieder featured musical forms that followed the mechanical elements of the chosen poetry, such as poetic rhythm, rhyme scheme, stanzaic structure, and the like. Mahler's innovative method allows formal concerns to follow not the sound of the words but what the text actually means, allowing the narrative flow to hold primacy over all other matters. Mahler seems to have viewed these poems as remnants of a mutable oral tradition, as indicated in his often-quoted statement noted by Alma Mahler, 'It always seems barbaric to me when musicians undertake the setting to music of completely beautiful poetry. These [the *Wunderhorn* texts] are not completed texts, but blocks of stone that anyone might make his own.'[3] As such, he made numerous changes to his poetic sources, leaving none of his chosen *Wunderhorn* poems unaltered to some degree, and allowing his song texts to be re-imagined in the form best suited to the musico-poetic stories he wished to tell. In Mahler's *Wunderhornlieder* the text and music fuse together, creating a semiotic unit far greater than the sum of its parts. Mahler's musical storytelling demands this close level of scrutiny due to its purposeful combination of old, universal tales with modern, experimental composition. This juxtaposition of the old with the new accords with Mahler's burgeoning modernist aesthetic and the universality of folk stories.

Modified Strophic Forms

In traditional ballads, strophic settings occur almost exclusively, and modified strophic forms commonly appear in musical settings of *Kunstballaden*—poems, rather than balladic song texts, written in a folk style by nineteenth-century

poets such as Goethe and Heine during a period when the perceived simplicity offered by 'all-things-folk' became the vogue. Decades later in the 1880s,
Mahler himself would (by then, somewhat unfashionably) participate in this
trend, as seen in his texts for *Lieder eines fahrenden Gesellen* and in a more
extended fashion in *Das Klagende Lied*. The regularly recurring musical pattern heard in a ballad's traditional strophic form maintains consistency and
provides a sense of the gradual passage of time as the music takes a backseat to
the text, which allows the action to progress with each successive verse.

While he never applied strophic form in the strictest sense, Mahler utilised
a variation of this structure for six of his eighteen balladic *Wunderhorn* lieder.[4]
This includes paired verse forms—groups of two contrasting verses appearing
repeatedly in tandem—which are used in two of his ballads. The more complex examples of Mahler's modified strophic forms use the similarities contained within each verse to ground the passage of time in the story. Meanwhile,
the musical elaborations that take place within each successive verse build the
drama as the story unfolds, allowing the listener to recall previous events, recognise that the circumstances portrayed by the music have changed, and see the
situation in a different light.[5]

Anyone who has ever been forced to work overnight while seemingly everyone else sleeps will understand the circumstances that Mahler has illustrated
musically in 'Der Schildwache Nachtlied' (Fig. 2.1). While the chosen poem
features six stanzas of identical poetic rhythm and rhyme scheme, Mahler
adapted his text to create a ballad featuring a modified strophic setting of paired
verses, which alternate between two characters, one the very real protagonist
and the other appearing only in his dreams. The night watchman, at first filled
with dutiful enthusiasm, finds it difficult to stay awake, and he drifts into sweet
dreams of his beloved back home, only to be instantly snapped awake by his
responsibilities, to begin the cycle anew. Mahler narrates the story by creating
two distinctive musical environments: the sentry's actual surroundings in the
guard tower, created with steady 4/4 time, declamatory vocal lines, diatonic
and triadic harmonies, fanfares, and drum cadences (Ex. 2.1); and the dream
world of his imagined sweetheart with its soft woodwinds and harp, legato
melodies backed by lushly chromatic dissonances, flexible metre, and slow
tempo. And as it happens in real life, the waking world gradually gives way
to the world of dreams, through a three-measure transition where the martial
sound world dissipates into the dream soundscape. (Ex. 2.2).

The vocal melody in this short passage with its long pitch followed by an
octave descent could be interpreted as the musicalisation of a yawn (Ex. 2.3).

But in each successive verse, the watchman falls asleep only to find himself
jolted awake by two abrupt notes on the timpani and low strings, as the reality
of military life returns instantly.

As the story progresses through successive pairs of verses, subtle changes
in the music illustrate the growing frustration experienced by the young man.

'Der Schildwache Nachtlied' (Boxberger)	'Der Schildwache Nachtlied' (as set by Mahler)
"Ich kann und mag nicht fröhlich sein.	Ich kann und mag nicht fröhlich sein!
Wenn alle Leute schlafen,	Wenn alle Leute schlafen!
So muβ ich wachen,	so muβ ich wachen! Ja, wachen!
Muβ traurig sein."-	Muβ traurig sein!
"Ach, Knabe, Du sollst nicht traurig	Lieb' (Ach) Knabe, du muβt nicht traurig
sein!	sein!
Will Deiner warten	Will deiner warten
Im Rosengarten,	im Rosengarten!
Im grünen Klee."-	Im grünen Klee!
	im grünen Klee!
"Zum grünen Klee da komm ich nicht;	Zum grünen Klee da komm ich nicht!
Zum Waffengarten	Zum Waffengarten!
Voll Helleparten	Voll Helleparten!
Bin ich gestellt."-	Bin ich gestellt!
	Bin ich gestellt!
"Stehst Du im Feld, so helf Dir Gott!	Stehst du im Feld, so helf' dir Gott!
An Gottes Segen	An Gottes Segen
Ist Alles gelegen,	ist Alles gelegen!
Wer's glauben thut."-	Wer's glauben tut!
	wer's glauben tut!
"Wer's glauben thut, ist weit davon;	Wer's glauben tut, ist weit davon!
Er ist ein König,	Er ist ein König!
Er ist ein Kaiser,	Er ist ein Kaiser! Ein Kaiser!
Er führt den Krieg."	Er führt den Krieg!
Halt! Wer da? – Rund! Wer sang zur	Halt! Wer da!! Rund'!?
Stund? -	Bleib' mir vom Leib!
Verlorne Feldwacht	Wer sang es hier? Wer sang zur Stund'?
Sang es um Mitternacht. -	Verlorne Feldwacht
Bleib mir vom Leib!	sang es um Mitternacht!
	Mitternacht! Mitternacht!
	Feldwacht!

Fig. 2.1 'Der Schildwache Nachtlied', Poem and Song text

A new element appears the third time the watchman emerges from his dreams at bar 63 (Ex. 2.4).

The reality of the waking world abruptly returns with the same crashing timpani and low strings heard twice before, but after only three bars: suddenly the key changes from B♭ Major to G Major, and a steady military cadence arises from the snare drum, along with a thinning of the texture and a new fanfare figure in the horns and trumpet. These new musical clues signal a shift

Ex. 2.1 'Der Schildwache Nachtlied', bars 1–4, the guard's soundworld

Ex. 2.2 'Der Schildwache Nachtlied', bars 17–21, the maiden's soundworld

Ex. 2.3 'Der Schildwache Nachtlied', bars 9–12, a musical yawn

in the watchman's attitude toward his position. His frustration boils over into this overly militaristic, almost ceremonial passage as the watchman sarcastically blames God for his unfortunate predicament. With each verse, his resentment has grown, until this moment, when his grumbling causes a commotion that attracts the attention of another guard, bringing in the coda.

Ex. 2.4 'Der Schildwache Nachtlied', bars 66–68, frustration boils over

The listener who observes this gradual change over time is forced to wonder whether the sentry will give into temptation, abandoning his post in order to join his distant sweetheart. But, alas, we are left only to wonder what became of him, and the story is left unresolved. The music of the coda with its similarly militaristic motives, however, points to the maintaining of the status quo. If our protagonist himself will not remain at his post, there are plenty of other eager young men willing to take his place, and his post will not go unfilled for long.

Ternary Forms

The use of ternary form in the musical setting of a ballad brings with it certain challenges to the process of storytelling. The most prominent of these difficulties lies in the inherent qualities of narrative and arched forms. The very nature of a balladic story implies that the characters' actions and experiences should alter their environment so that their circumstances change in the process; by the end the world is somehow different. The structure of ternary form, on the other hand, requires that the music of the beginning and its recapitulation after a contrasting section share a significant amount of musical material, implying that the environment it portrays is more or less the same as before. While the two formulas seem incompatible, Mahler deals with this difficulty in various ways in his five ternary *Wunderhorn* ballads,[6] sometimes utilising ternary form as a plot device to demonstrate that even after a series of events has occurred, life is not so different after all.

'Des Antonius von Padua Fischpredigt' tells a fantastic tale of a priest's sermon being told to a group of fish (Fig. 2.2). The original poem features nine stanzas, and Mahler made few changes to the text in order to create this particular lyric, primarily altering his stanzaic structure through repetition or omission of lines. The song begins with a narrated passage, describing Antonius's trip to the river and his initial reception from the fish. A contrasting section sets lyrical poetry, providing detailed descriptions of the various aquatic creatures that arrive on the scene. The recapitulation reports on the inefficacy of Antonius's sermon, using essentially the same music that Mahler used to describe the circumstances before the saint's arrival.

Bearing a strong resemblance to a flute and clarinet passage in Smetana's tone poem *Vltava*, the flowing sixteenth-note passages passed between the clarinets, flutes, oboes, and violins create the musical image of a flowing river (Ex. 2.5). The fish themselves are depicted with staccato eighth notes in the low winds and bass, and the triangle and birch brush mark the surfacing of their heads from the water.

Mahler depicts the futility of Antonius's sermon (Ex. 2.6) in bars 52–62 and again in bars 87–98 with a modal section that sounds distinctly like a klezmer melody, marked with the performance directive *mit Humor* (with humour). The irony of this clearly Jewish melody appearing in a song about a Christian clergyman is striking, and it indicates the impossible task that Antonius has set before himself. The fish are no more likely to learn and benefit from the sermon than the humans who have failed to attend Mass. The klezmer motive fails to return in the recapitulation, latently indicating Antonius's ultimate failure, as if the motive served as a warning to the priest, and its absence as an unspoken voice claiming, 'I told you so.'

Mahler utilises arch form in 'Antonius' for two distinct purposes. The structure creates a kind of narrative frame, distinguishing the action of the opening

Des Antonius von Padua Fischpredigt (Boxberger)	Des Antonius von Padua Fischpredigt (Mahler setting)

Antonius zur Predig
Die Kirche findt ledig;
Er geht zu den Flüssen
Und predigt den Fischen.
  Sie schlagn mit den Schwänzen,
  Im Sonnenschein glänzen.
	Antonius zur Predigt
	die Kirche find't ledig!
	Er geht zu den Flüssen
	und predigt den Fischen!
	  Sie schlag'n mit den Schwänzen!
	  Im Sonnenschein glänzen,
	  Im Sonnenschein, Sonnenschein
	glänzen, sie glänzen, sie glänzen, glänzen.

Die Karpfen mit Rogen
Sind all hierher zogen,
Habn d'Mäuler aufrissen,
Sich Zuhörens beflissen.
  Kein Predig niemalen
  Den Karpfen so gfallen.
	Die Karpfen mit Rogen
	sind all' hierher zogen;
	hab'n d'Mäuler aufrissen,
	sich Zuhör'n's beflissen.
	  Kein Predigt niemalen
	  den Fischen so g'fallen!

Spitzgoschete Hechte,
Die immerzu fechten,
Sind eilend herschwommen,
Zu hören den Frommen.
  Kein Predig niemalen
  Den Hechten so gfallen.
	Spitzgoschete Hechte,
	die immerzu fechten
	sind eilends herschwommen,
	zu hören den Frommen!

Auch jene Phantasten,
So immer beim Fasten,
Die Stockfisch ich meine,
Zur Predig erscheinen.
  Kein Predig niemalen
  Dem Stockfisch so gfallen.
	Auch jene Phantasten,
	die immerzu fasten,
	Die Stockfisch ich meine,
	zur Predigt erscheinen!
	  Kein Predigt niemalen
	  den Stockfisch so g'fallen!

Gut Aalen und Hausen,
Die Vornehme schmausen,
Die selber sich bequemen,
Die Predig vernehmen.
  Kein Predig niemalen
  Den Aalen so gfallen.
	Gut' Aale und Hausen
	die Vornehme schmausen,
	die selbst sich bequemen,
	die Predigt vernehmen.

Auch Krebsen, Schildkroten,
Sonst langsame Boten,
Steigen eilend vom Grund,
Zu hören diesen Mund.
  Kein Predig niemalen
  Den Krebsen so gfallen.
	Auch Krebse, Schildkroten,
	sonst langsame Boten,
	steigen eilig vom Grund,
	zu hören diesen Mund!
	  Kein Predigt niemalen
	  den Krebsen so g'fallen!

Fisch große, Fisch kleine,
Vornehm und gemeine,
Erheben die Köpfe
Wie verständge Geschöpfe:
  Auf Gottes Begehren
  Antonium anhören.
	Fisch' große, Fisch' kleine!
	Vornehm' und Gemeine!
	Erheben die Köpfe
	wie verständ'ge Geschöpfe!
	  Auf Gottes Begehren
	  Die Predigt anhören!

Fig. 2.2 'Des Antonius von Padua Fischpredigt', Poem and Song Text

Die Predig geendet,	Die Predigt geendet,
Ein jedes sich wendet:	ein Jeder sich wendet!
Die Hechte bleiben Diebe,	Die Hechte bleiben Diebe,
Dir Aale viel lieben.	die Aale viel lieben,
Die Predig hat gfallen,	die Predigt hat g'fallen,
Sie bleiben wie alle.	sie bleiben wie Allen!
Die Krebs gehn zurücke,	Die Krebs' geh'n zurücke,
Die Stockfisch bleiben dicke,	die Stockfisch' bleib'n dicke,
Die Karpfen viel fressen,	die Karpfen viel fressen
Die Predig vergessen.	die Predigt vergessen, vergessen!
Die Predig hat gfallen,	Die Predigt hat g'fallen, sie bleiben
Sie bleiben wie alle.	wie Allen!
	Die Predigt hat g'fallen, hat g'fallen!

Fig. 2.2 Continued

Ex. 2.5 'Des Antonius von Padua Fischpredigt', bars 16–24, flowing river

and closing stanzas from a lengthy lyrical description of the fish appearing at the sermon. At bar 107 the B section begins, and the music changes drastically, becoming softer and more legato, leading one to believe that a miraculous transformation may have actually taken place and the fish that have emerged from the water to hear the sermon may forever be changed by the saint's words. This lengthy descriptive section holds listeners in suspense as they wait to learn whether the fish will prove any more receptive to Antonius's message than his human congregation.

Unfortunately, we know this to be impossible, and in bar 159 the initial musical material with its bouncing rhythms and sounds of flowing water returns. By the end of the song, when the fish simply swim away completely unaffected, the music fades off into the distance and we learn that nothing has changed; fish will be fish, just as people will be people. The return of the musical language heard at the beginning of the song serves to underline the apothegm of

Ex. 2.6 'Des Antonius von Padua Fischpredigt,' bars 52–57, klezmer melody

this final stanza, as the lack of musical change emphasises Antonius's inability to impact the salvation of those who hear his words.

Bar Forms

The nature of bar form tends to imply a substantial change mid-story, so that the final segment of the narrative and music differs markedly from what came before. Mahler utilised bar form for three of his *Wunderhorn* ballads, and the circumstances that confront the characters in these three stories are remarkably similar.[7] All three protagonists are facing a tremendous loss, and once their circumstances have played out, their lives will never be the same.

The first of Mahler's military songs to take seriously the sorrows facing lovers separated by war is 'Nicht Wiedersehen!' (Fig. 2.3). Mahler dramatically

Nicht wiedersehen (Boxberger)	Nicht Wiedersehen! (as set by Mahler)
"Nun ade, mein allerherzliebster Schatz! Jetzt muß ich wohl scheiden von Dir Bis auf den andern Sommer; Dann komm ich wieder zu Dir."-	Und nun ade, mein herzallerliebster Schatz! Jetzt muß ich wohl scheiden von dir, von dir, bis auf den andern Sommer; dann komm' ich wieder zu dir! Ade, Ade, mein herzallerliebster Schatz, mein herzallerliebster Schatz!
Und als der junge Knab heimkam, Von seiner Liebsten fing er an: "Wo ist meine Herzallerliebste, Die ich verlassen hab?"-	Und als der junge Knab' heimkam, von seiner Liebsten fing er an: "Wo ist meine Herzallerliebste, die ich verlassen hab'?"
"Auf dem Kirchhof liegt sie begraben, Heut ist's der dritte Tag; Das Trauern und das Weinen Hat sie zum Tod gebracht."-	"Auf dem Kirchhof liegt sie begraben, heut' ist's der dritte Tag! Das Trauern und das Weinen hat sie zum Tod gebracht!" Ade, ade, mein herzallerliebster Schatz, mein herzallerliebster Schatz!
"Jetzt will ich auf den Kirchhof gehen, Will suchen meiner Liebsten Grab, Will ihr alleweil rufen, Bis daß sie mir Antwort giebt.	Jetzt will ich auf den Kirchhof geh'n, will suchen meiner Liebsten Grab, will ihr all'weile rufen, ja rufen, bis daß sie mir Antwort gab!
Ei, Du mein allerherzliebster Schatz, Mach auf Dein tiefes Grab! Du hörst kein Glöcklein läuten, Du hörst kein Vöglein pfeifen, Du siehst weder Sonn noch Mond!"	Ei du, mein allerherzliebster Schatz, mach' auf dein tiefes Grab! Du hörst kein Glöcklein läuten, du hörst kein Vöglein pfeifen, du siehst weder Sonne noch Mond! Ade, ade, mein herzallerliebster Schatz, mein herzallerliebster Schatz! Ade!

Fig. 2.3 'Nicht Wiedersehen', Poem and Song Text

alters the form of the original poem to create his lyric, changing five short stanzas into three larger verses with a refrain adapted from the opening line of the poem. Mahler utilises bar form to express the tragic events faced by a young man who leaves to perform his military duty. Upon his return, he learns that his beloved has died of a broken heart, only days earlier. Still, he goes to her resting place, and their reunion is marked with a substantial, albeit heart-rending, change in musical setting.

'Nicht Wiedersehen!' makes the anguish experienced by this young soldier obvious from the first notes of the introduction, a lonely melody that echoes the tragedy to come. From the very outset, the slow, quiet theme informs the listener that all is not well, and in bar 3, when the soldier addresses his love for the first time, a low-pitched descending fourth appears in the piano (Ex. 2.7).

Ex. 2.7 'Nicht Wiedersehen!', bars 1–4, tragedy beckons

This motive recurs five times more throughout the song and soon becomes as-sociated with the maiden's death, gradually taking on the symbol of church bells ringing to signal her burial as noted by the marking 'Wie fernes Glockenläuten' (like the distant ringing of bells). A brief respite from the sorrow takes the form of an epic narrated section in bars 16–20, in which we learn that the soldier has returned and immediately looks to find his love, only to discover that she has died. This section has a lighter accompaniment and lacks the dragging tempo found in the earlier parts of the song, providing a detached, more neutral point of observation. This brief passage also contracts the time that the soldier has been away into an instant, allowing the accompaniment to assume the role of narrator. Only a quaver rest separates the soldier's final words before parting and the narrator's announcement that he has returned. If not for the lightening of the texture and the return of the church bell motive, it would be easy to overlook the fact that his tour of duty has passed by in the story so quickly.

The bar form in 'Nicht Wiedersehen!' is conventional, comprised of two *Stollen* and an *Abgesang*, each containing the refrain, created through repetition of the opening poetic lines, 'Ade, mein Herzallerliebster Schatz' ('Farewell, my heart's beloved'). Mahler's *Stollen* are nearly identical, except for the added doubling of pitches in the bass at the lower octave. This new arrival signals to the young man and the audience that the young woman has only recently died, and these low pitches lend a sense of heaviness and sorrow to the scene, as if the echoes of the tolling bells from her burial still hang in the air. They remain throughout the entire second verse, while the young man absorbs the knowledge of his love's death and subsequently vows to wait by her graveside until she 'gives him an answer', presumably to his proposal of marriage, though that is never made clear.

A significant change in the mood of the music occurs at bar 52, the begin-ning of the *Abgesang*, when the key changes from minor to major (Ex. 2.8). The soldier has at last gone to the graveyard to address his beloved directly.

Ex. 2.8 'Nicht Wiedersehen!', bars 55–59, a hopeful reunion

Du hörst kein Glöcklein_ läu - ten, du hörst kein Vöglein_ pfei - fen, du

The shift from C minor to its parallel major brings a sense of comfort, as though even under the dreadful circumstances, the soldier is relieved to at last be reunited with his love. He asks her to 'open her deep grave' so she can hear bells and singing birds. During this passage, the church bell motive heard earlier in the song continues relentlessly, as if the accompaniment is speaking directly to the young man, trying to convey to him the fruitlessness of his pleas. Finally he realises that what is done cannot be undone, and he says his final goodbyes to his beloved, the tragedy of reality reveals itself, and the final refrain returns to C minor.

Free Forms

Free-form songs offer unique approaches to musical storytelling, allowing the music to grow and expand dramatically along with the storyline. Mahler only abandoned traditional song forms toward the end of his engagement with *Des Knaben Wunderhorn*, in what many consider to be among the greatest of the *Wunderhorn* ballads, 'Revelge' and 'Wo die schönen Trompeten blasen'. The intermingling of dialogue, epic description, and narrative distance lends these songs qualities of the *scena*, an operatic episode featuring a combination of recitative and aria-like singing, that gives rare glimpses into Mahler's dramatic compositional abilities within the context of song.

Among the last of the *Wunderhorn* songs to be composed for 1898 publication, 'Wo die schönen Trompeten blasen' (Fig. 2.4) displays some of Mahler's most sophisticated Lieder compositional techniques, in part due to his creation of the song's text from two distinct poems, 'Bildchen' and 'Unbeschreibliche Freude'. Each exemplar poem is made up of stanzas of the same length, rhythm, and rhyme scheme, but Mahler's resulting lyric uses none of these features in quite the same way; lines are mixed and matched and expanded and contracted so as to leave their sources practically unrecognisable. He also abandons the final stanzas of both poems, leaving the focus and ultimate conclusion of his story quite different from those of his sources.

Unbeschreibliche Freude (Boxberger)	Bildchen (Boxberger)	Wo die schönen Trompeten blasen (Mahler setting)
	Auf dieser Welt hab ich keine Freud: Ich hab einen Schatz, und der ist weit; Er ist so weit, er ist nicht hier. Ach, wenn ich bei meim Schätzchen wär!	
	Ich kann nicht sitzen und kann nicht stehn, Ich muß zu meinem Schätzchen gehn; Zu meinem Schatz da muß ich gehn, Und sollt ich vor dem Fenster stehn.	
Wer ist denn draußen und klopfet an, Der mich so leise wecken kann? „Das ist der Herzallerliebste Dein. Steh auf und laß mich zu Dir ein!"	„Wer ist denn draußen, wer klopfet an, Der mich so leis aufwecken kann?" - „Es ist der Herzallerliebste Dein; Steh auf, steh auf und laß mich 'rein!" -	Wer ist denn draußen und wer klopfet an, der mich so leise, so leise wecken kann? Das ist der Herzallerliebste dein, steh' auf und laß mich zu dir ein!
	„Ich steh nicht auf, laß Dich nicht 'rein, Bis meine Eltern zu Bette sein. Wenn meine Eltern zu Bette sein, So steh ich auf und laß Dich 'rein." -	

Fig. 2.4 'Wo die schönen Trompeten blasen', Poem and Song Text

„Was soll ich hier nun Länger stehn?
Ich seh die Morgenröth aufgehn,
Die Morgenröth, zwei helle Stern;
Bei meinem Schatz da wär ich gern."

Da stand sie auf und ließ ihn ein;
Sie heißt ihn auch willkommen sein.
Sie reicht ihm die schneeweiße Hand;
Da fängt sie auch zu weinen an.

„Wein nicht, wein nicht, mein
    Engelein!
Aufs Jahr sollst Du mein eigen sein.
Mein eigen sollst Du werden gewiß;
Sonst Keine es auf Erden ist.

Das Mädchen stand auf und ließ
    ihn ein
Mit seinem schneeweißen
    Hemdelein,
Mit seinen schneeweißen Beinen.
Das Mädchen fing an zu weinen.

„Ach, weine nicht, Du Liebste mein!
Aufs Jahr sollt Du mein eigen sein;
Mein eigen sollt Du werden,
O Liebe auf grüner Erden!"

Fig. 2.4 Continued

Was soll ich hier nun länger steh'n?
Ich seh' die Morgenröt' aufgeh'n,
die Morgenröt', zwei helle Stern'.
Bei meinem Schatz da wär ich gern'!
Bei meinem Herzallerliebe!

Das Mädchen stand auf und ließ ihn ein,
sie heißt ihn auch willkommen sein.
Willkommen trauter Knabe mein!
So lang hast du gestanden!
Sie reicht' ihm auch die schneeweise
    Hand.
Von ferne sang die Nachtigall,
da fängt sie auch zu weinen an!

Ach weine nicht, du Liebste mein,
ach weine nicht, du Liebste mein!
Auf's Jahr sollst du mein Eigen sein.
Mein Eigen sollst du werden gewiß,
wie's Keine sonst auf Erden ist!
O Lieb auf grüner Erden.

Unbeschreibliche Freude (Boxberger)	Bildchen (Boxberger)	Wo die schönen Trompeten blasen (Mahler setting)
	Ich zieh in Krieg auf grüne Haid; Grüne Haid die liegt von hier so weit. Allwo die schönen Trompeten blasen, Da ist mein Haus von grünem Rasen.	Ich zieh' in Krieg auf grüne Haid; die grüne Haide, die ist so weit! Allwo dort die schönen Trompeten blasen, da ist mein Haus, mein Haus von grünen Rasen!
	Ein Bildchen laß ich malen mir; Auf meinem Herzen trag ich's hier. Darauf sollst Du gemalet sein, Daß ich niemal vergesse Dein."	
Ich wollt, daß alle Felder wären Papier Und alle Studenten schrieben hier; Sie schreiben ja hier die liebe lange Nacht, Sie schrieben uns Beiden die Liebe doch nicht ab.		

Fig. 2.4 Continued

Mahler utilises a flexible, through-composed structure for the story of a young woman's late night visit from her beloved soldier. 'Wo die schönen Trompeten blasen' is made up of three basic sound worlds: the militaristic environment that begins the song, the contrasting *Ländler* passage, and the relaxed, duple-meter middle portion in which the maiden greets her lover. These three soundscapes are alternated in a fashion not unlike a rondo form, but each recurrence of the general musical environment is so widely varied that the rondo structure ultimately collapses.

Marked *Verträumt, leise* (dreamily, quietly), the opening bars feature a muted passage in the horns played *pp*. The thirty-second note motive in the first three bars of the passage mimetically represents a knock on the door (Ex. 2.9), which then evolves into a muted trumpet fanfare at the fifth measure of the passage.

This motive tells the listener that a war is taking place, but it is far off in the distance, as are the young female protagonist's thoughts. This distance remains until bar 19, when the fanfare plays at a louder dynamic. Suddenly the war comes closer to home.

The militaristic music heard in this opening sequence then goes on to accompany the opening words, sung in a lyrical manner by the young woman. The maiden's attention has been divided between her duties at home and her concern for her beloved. She acts as if stirred from a deep slumber and asks 'Wer ist denn draußen, und wer klopfet an?' ('Who is outside? Who is knocking?'), but before she can even say the words, the clarinet has answered her question with its own version of the fanfare. While these fanfares provide a glimpse into the young woman's mindset, I do not believe that she actually 'hears' them, due to her preoccupation with the knocking. Her hesitance to open the door and welcome her lover inside indicates that she does not suspect that it is him waiting outside, despite the musical cues that accompany her, creating a distinction between the diegetic music that can be heard by the maiden and that purely mimetic music which she cannot.[8] Only when the

Ex. 2.9 'Wo die schönen Trompeten blasen', bars 15–20, a knock at the door

Ex. 2.10 'Wo die schönen Trompeten blasen', bars 36–43, *Ländler* motive

soldier identifies himself does the maiden's militaristic music give way to the romantic *Ländler*-inspired theme that symbolises their love (Ex. 2.10).

The rustic, folk-like nature of this dance also identifies the protagonists as innocent, rural people whose destinies have become entangled in political turmoil beyond their control, one of many subtle commentaries on the tragedy of war embedded in Mahler's *Wunderhornlieder*.[9] At this crucial point, the metre changes from duple to triple, the key shifts from D minor to D Major, the notes become more sustained, and the winds give way to the strings. This musical contrast emphasises the gender reversal that points to the mental preoccupations of the protagonists. The maiden, physically at home, thinks only of the soldier, and thus her musical space is filled with masculine, militaristic imagery. The soldier's concern is not on the battlefield, but with his sweetheart, and as such, his primary melodies take the form of the gentle, romantic, *Ländler*. The narrator serves to transition the story back and forth between the disparate sonic spaces of the two protagonists, bringing back the declamatory rhythms of the opening and returning to the key of D minor, associated in this instance with militaristic music and serving as a reminder to the audience that the young man is first and foremost a soldier.

Ex. 2.11 'Wo die schönen Trompeten blasen', bars 169–73, the soldier's military theme

Mahler separates physical locations and past and present events through musical means, using instrumentation to create two of the song's distinct sound worlds. The winds represent the war and events that take place in some other, far-off imagined space of the past, whereas the strings accompany events taking place in the present moment being narrated, that is, the maiden's home and her conversation with the soldier. Only at the end of the song, when the soldier finally speaks in a somewhat declamatory fashion of his military responsibilities (Ex. 2.11), does his accompaniment eliminate the strings in favour of brass, taking on the militaristic tropes previously only heard in the distance of the maiden's thoughts and the passages spoken by the narrator. This shift points the audience's attention to the words he speaks and lends them added significance while at the same time subtly indicating that these thoughts dwell on remembrance of past events rather than the present moment.

In addition to his blending two separate poems from *Des Knaben Wunderhorn* to create the text for 'Wo die schönen Trompeten blasen', Mahler also added one completely original line, which occurs after the maiden has welcomed her beloved soldier into her home. The line reads 'von Ferne sang die Nachtigall' ('In the distance, a nightingale sang'). Upon the mention of the bird's song an oboe enters, playing not the expected call of a nightingale, but a militaristic melody first heard in bar 5 (Ex. 2.12).

In this unusual moment, the story is being narrated by two voices at once: the epic narrator of the text and the allusive narrative voice contained within the music, which appears in place of the silenced nightingale, and what they are have to say is not entirely the same.[10] The nightingale song described by the narrator is overridden by the military fanfare. The maiden hears only the nightingale, long associated with lament, which merely warns her of an impending misfortune, but the fanfare heard by the audience transforms what she fears may occur in the future into her present reality, telling the audience

Ex. 2.12 'Wo die schönen Trompeten blasen', bars 5–8, premonition from a nightingale

that the young man who has appeared at the door is not actually the maiden's lover, but his ghost, come to inform her that he has died in battle and to indicate that she, too, will soon join him in death, stating 'Within a year, you will be mine.' The revenant soldier eventually confirms the tragedy by claiming that he must return to his 'house of green turf', that is, his grave. The complex exchange of recitative, lyrical singing, dialogue, and accompaniment portrays this mysterious ballad more engagingly than would be possible using any conventional song form and offers us a small glimpse into what Mahler might have been able to accomplish in a dramatic medium, had he brought his early attempts at composing an opera to conclusion.

Mahler's use of formal structure as a narrative device in his ballads from *Des Knaben Wunderhorn* points to his keen sense of musical storytelling. The constructions of these ballads share a strategic process that uses music to clarify and portray specific elements of the stories being told, such as physical and temporal context, issues of narrative point of view, and the logical sequence of events. Mahler chose *Wunderhorn* texts that tell their stories with varying degrees of clarity, but in all cases, his musical choices serve to make those stories more visceral for the listener. These ballads emerged from a complex process of simultaneous manipulation of pre-existing material and creation of new musical ideas. In each case, the musical form shapes the story and reveals things about the situations and the characters beyond what is said in mere words.

This unusual approach to narrative offers scholars the opportunity to examine Mahler's narrative processes from an entirely new angle and invites similar studies in his other song output as well as explorations of other subtextual methods of storytelling utilised by the composer. Greatly overshadowed by the symphonies in terms of scholarly attention, Mahler's songs, and those based on texts from *Des Knaben Wunderhorn* in particular, offer a fascinating glimpse into the veritable kaleidoscope of musical soundscapes he could create. These songs serve as far more than mere steppingstones to future symphonic compositions, but as subtle commentaries on Mahler's cultural and political environment.[11] Exploring Mahler's nuanced techniques in portraying the tales of the *Wunderhorn* reveals potentially endless layers of hermeneutic meaning that could occupy the scholarly community for years to come. This can only help us to find deeper levels of meaning in Mahler's music, both vocal and symphonic, leading to an even greater understanding and appreciation of this endlessly fascinating repertoire.

Notes

1. Freitag, *Ballade*, 36.

2. Examples include Lake, "Hermeneutic Music Structures", Oltmanns, *Strophische Strukturen*, and Roman, "Structure as a Factor in the Genesis of Mahler's Songs".

3. Alma Mahler, *Erinnerungen und Briefe* [1971], 120 'Es käme ihm auch immer wie Barbarei vor, wenn Musiker es unternehmen, vollendet schöne Gedichte in Musik zu setzen. Seien keine vollendeten Gedichte, sondern Felsblöcke, aus denen jeder das Seine formen dürfe'.

4. 'Um schlimme Kinder artig zu machen', 'Starke Einbildungskraft', 'Der Schildwche Nachtlied' (features paired verses), 'Verlor'ne Müh'!', 'Das irdische Leben' and 'Lied des Verfolgten im Turm' (features paired verses).

5. Berger, "Diegesis and Mimesis", 424–25, Abbate, *Unsung Voices*, 55.

6. 'Ich ging mit Lust', 'Scheiden und Meiden', 'Trost im Unglück', 'Des Antonius von Padua Fischpredigt', and 'Rheinlegendchen'.

7. 'Zu Straßburg auf der Schanz', 'Nicht Wiedersehen', and 'Der Tamboursg'sell'.

8. See Abbate, *Unsung Voices*, 124–25, and Berger, "Diegesis and Mimesis".

9. See Breckling, "Narrative Strategies", 237–41, 256–71.

10. See Johnson, "The Breaking of the Voice".

11. See Breckling, "Narrative Strategies" for further discussion of these contexts.

3

The Earliness of Mahler's Late Romanticism

The Poetics of the 'Deceptive Perfect Cadence' in the Ninth Symphony and *Das Lied von der Erde*

Mark Summerfield

It is a common observation that Mahler's musical language lies somewhere between those of Wagner and the Second Viennese School. In terms of musical theory this idea has a long history, which might retrospectively be considered to stretch as far back as Schoenberg's posthumous dedication of his *Harmonielehre* to Mahler. By 1951, this frame of reference was clearly in place when Hans Tischler emphasised Mahler's influence on Schoenberg in his discussion of Mahler's part in the 'crisis in tonality.' For Tischler, Mahler had a 'direct impact' on Schoenberg, but he still describes Mahler's technique as prefiguring those of a range of later composers such as Hindemith, Stravinsky, Bartók, and Strauss.[1] Nine years later though, in the most influential argument for this relationship (musicologically at least), Theodor Adorno defined the historical location of Mahler's technique purely in terms of the 'New Music' of the Second Viennese School.[2] In both accounts Mahler's cadence treatment is used as evidence for this historical positioning. Tischler notes that an important feature of Mahler's harmonic techniques is its 'avoidance of the usual classical cadences' which results in 'cadence-less' tonality and modulation.[3] Even Adorno, whose concerns are much more wide ranging, makes important points about the effect of an 'almost vanishingly insignificant' element of mixture in a cadence or the way that 'the cadence [loses] itself entirely' at the end of the Ninth Symphony.[4]

In his discussion of Mahler's deceptive cadences, John Williamson offers a corrective to Tischler's description of Mahler's avoidance of 'the usual classical cadences', noting that 'there are enough perfect cadences in Mahler to provide a generalisation in the opposite sense'.[5] More recent discussions of Mahler's cadence formation place less emphasis on harmony and instead situate Mahler's cadences within discussions of the nature of closure. Though this represents newer musicological concerns, Adorno's influence is still clearly apparent. Robert Hopkins relegates Mahler's harmonic practice from occupying a key role in relation to closure,[6] whilst John Sheinbaum, attending to Williamson's points, has noted that Mahler's conventional cadential harmonies are 'complicated' by their discontinuous modernist orchestration.[7] In these accounts, the harmonic conventionality of Mahler's cadences is unimportant, since his musical technique demonstrates its contemporaneity and thus its historical place through non-harmonic, 'secondary' parameters such as timbre. In the discussion which follows, I want to question this idea that the contemporaneity of Mahler's practice and aesthetic are neatly convergent by looking at some interesting cadences found in the Ninth Symphony and *Das Lied von der Erde*. Using this close reading as a starting point I intend to widen the terms of this debate in two particular ways. Firstly, I want to show how Mahler's music does include cadences that are unconventional from the perspective of 'the usual' common-practice, classical cadences. Secondly, I will show how these cadences, which at first might suggest the contemporaneous modernist aesthetic of Mahler's technique, can be more productively understood through reference to the aesthetics of the early romantics.

Mahler's Hybrid Cadences

The idea of a progression that combines elements of the perfect and deceptive cadences is not new. Kofi Agawu has described 'enrichment processes' in Mahler's harmonic syntax and cadences, such as the 'conflation' of perfect and deceptive cadences.[8] In Agawu's example the deceptive cadence is used to modulate, and the final cadential chord, the VI or ♭VI chord, is treated as a tonic on its arrival (see Ex. 3.1).[9]

Key to Agawu's conception of 'conflation' is that the VI chord is in first inversion and thus retains the bass progression of a perfect cadence. It is possible to see this particular cadence as an instance of a broader phenomenon in Mahler's music, the modulating deceptive cadence. As in Agawu's example, the progression establishes a new key, but a more common example has the bVI chord in root position, establishing the new key more firmly. An example of this can be seen in *Das Lied* (see Ex. 3.2) where it, too, is used to modulate from a major tonic to its flattened submediant. This sudden modulatory shift could be related to the suggested drunkenness of the protagonist, and the instability of the preceding initial tonic certainly supports this. However, this cadence is also found in Mahler's earlier music in a quite different context. In the 'Adagietto' of Mahler's Fifth Symphony the same cadence is used to create a sideways motion where an anticipated modulation to B♭ shifts to G♭ instead (see Ex. 3.3).

Even earlier than this, there is a modulation from B♭ to G♭ using a deceptive cadence in bars 13–14 of Schumann's Lied 'Meine Rose' from the *6 Gedichte und Requiem*, op. 90. This clear example of a modulating deceptive cadence, described by Jon Finson as 'striking', shows that this technique cannot be considered a Mahlerian innovation.[10] This type of modulation can be traced back even further to the dramatic, yet brief appearances of VI that are found in

Ex. 3.1 Agawu's 'conflated' cadence: Ninth Symphony, first movement, bars 53–54

Ex. 3.2 Modulating Deceptive Cadence: *Das Lied von der Erde*, 'Der Trunkene im Frühling', bars 6–8

Ex. 3.3 Modulating Deceptive Cadence: Fifth Symphony, 'Adagietto', bars 45–47

Beethoven's music. For example, in the first movement of the String Quartet in F minor, op. 95 there are elaborations of the final VI or ♭VI chords of a deceptive cadence (bb. 37–38 and bb. 106–7), whilst the first movement of the Piano Sonata in E♭, op. 81a (bb. 7–8) briefly emphasises ♭VI through deceptive cadence content.[11] However, there are crucial differences as well. In Schumann and Mahler, the deceptive cadences are both at the end of a phrase, and the final ♭VI is unambiguously taken up as a new tonic in the music which follows.

That this is not always the case is shown by other examples of hybridity that do not clearly move from one key to another. Instead, a combination of perfect and deceptive cadence features can be used to maintain an ambiguous tonal centre. In bars 225–30 of 'Das Trinklied vom Jammer der Erde' from *Das Lied von der Erde*, a phrase ends with the harmonic sequence A♭–E♭[7]–C[5]–Fm (see Ex. 3.4). This progression can be read as a weak perfect cadence in F minor if the C[5] is seen as an incomplete dominant of F minor, but it can also be seen as a deceptive cadence in A♭, if the C[5] is considered an interpolation between the E♭[7] dominant and the final submediant F minor chord. What makes this reading particularly viable is the absence of a third in the C chord. The presence of E♭ or E♮ would confirm one reading conclusively and the absence of such a decisive feature is crucial to maintaining that ambiguity.

V–VI–I Cadential Sequences

The modulating deceptive cadence is not the only cadence which combines elements of the deceptive and perfect cadences. In both *Das Lied von der Erde* and the Ninth Symphony there are 'conflated' cadences which combine elements of the deceptive and perfect cadence, but in a more linear manner. In these cases

Ex. 3.4 Hybrid Cadence: *Das Lied von der Erde*, 'Das Trinklied Jammer der Erde', bars 225–30

there are recurrent phrase-ending progressions which use some form of the harmonic sequence V–VI–I. Since this cadence is effectively a perfect cadence containing elements of the deceptive cadence within it, I refer to it as the 'deceptive perfect cadence.'

Simple Deceptive Perfect Cadences

The linear progression of chords V–VI–I at the end of a phrase is the simplest form of the deceptive perfect cadence. 'Von der Jugend' from *Das Lied von der Erde*, contains two such examples, the first at the end of the second stanza (bb. 22–25), and the second (bb. 107–11) when the music of the first two stanzas returns at the end of the movement (b. 97). These can be seen in Ex. 3.5 and Ex. 3.6. Whilst the opening music did feature a perfect cadence (in bb. 12–13), in the return of the music at the end of the movement only the deceptive perfect cadence reappears. This has the effect of making the return seem less

Ex. 3.5 *Das Lied von der Erde,* 'Von der Jugend,' bars 22–25

substantial, perhaps appropriate given that the text of these stanzas returns us to the pavilion and bridge first presented in the opening stanzas, but now viewed as reflections.

A more complex example comes from bars 429–32 of the second movement of the Ninth Symphony (Ex. 3.7). Here the sequence creates a fleeting sense of deflection prior to the tonic arrival. Interestingly, the violin continues as if the tonic had never arrived, starting the next phrase as if supported by a ♭VI chord from a conventional deceptive cadence.

Modulating Deceptive Perfect Cadences

The V-VI-I sequence is also used to establish new key areas such as in Ex. 3.8, bars 147–53 of 'Das Trinklied Jammer der Erde.' This is a modulatory sequence that begins in B♭ and ends in E♭ minor. However, the sequence uses

Ex. **3.6** *Das Lied von der Erde*, 'Von der Jugend,' bars 107–11

Ex. **3.7** Ninth Symphony, second movement, bars 429–32

Ex. 3.8 *Das Lied von der Erde*, 'Das Trinklied Jammer der Erde,' bars 147–53

a clear E♭ minor V-VI-I sequence to accomplish the transition to E♭ minor. This is a useful example of Mahler using an augmented (and so whole-tone) dominant, since the use of prolonged whole-tone dominants is common to both the Ninth and *Das Lied*.[12] In the context of a modulation from B♭ to E♭ minor, this augmentation of the B♭ chord emphasises its new dominant role, but also softens the progression from dominant to tonic as the note G♭ remains in place throughout all three chords.

Chromatic Elaboration and Sparse Textures

The presentation of V-VI-I progressions at the ends of phrases is not always this distinct. In Ex. 3.9, bars 564–70 towards the close of the second movement of the Ninth Symphony, there is a V-VI-I sequence where chromatic slippage between the VI and the I chords produces a blurring effect which is eventually resolved through the simple appearance of tonic fifths. This example

Ex. 3.9 Ninth Symphony, second movement, bars 564–71

demonstrates that the key to identifying whether a cadence is deceptive perfect or deceptive is related to when a phrase ends. Here, the texture of the VI
chord almost collapses, but retains enough coherence to link the opening V-VI
motion to the arrival of the tonic.

In Ex. 3.10a, bars 98–102 from 'Der Einsame im Herbst' from *Das Lied*, the blurring takes place between the V and the VI. Here, a $V\flat^{9/13}$ chord chromatically slides into a $\flat VI^7$ chord whilst the dominant pedal remains. The blurring is particularly evident in the absence of a clear root for the $\flat VI$, though when the pedal ceases, the $\flat VI$ is still dimly present for a measure before the tonic tentatively appears in bar 102. A voice leading reduction (Ex. 3.10b) shows that there is an underlying deceptive perfect cadence sequence in this blurred transition between the dominant and the tonic.[13] One way of looking at the absent root is to consider it an example of what Adorno describes as Mahler's 'tendency towards bass-lessness' [Baßlosigkeit].[14]

Enriched Voice Leading

An even more chromatically enriched example of the progression can be seen in Ex. 3.11a, bars 213–21 from 'Der Abschied'. This extract features the extensive use of appoggiaturas and neighbour notes (a voice leading graph is given in Ex. 3.11b). These appoggiaturas also extend to the VI chord itself. In a sense it is impossible to judge whether the VI is in the natural or flat form, as it could be that the VI, despite lasting five times as long, is merely a harmonic appoggiatura to the 'real' $\flat VI$ chord.

Ex. 3.10a *Das Lied von der Erde*, 'Der Einsame im Herbst,' bars 98–103

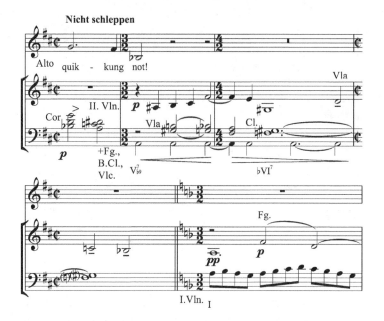

Ex. 3.10b *Das Lied von der Erde,* 'Der Einsame im Herbst,' bars 98–103 (voice leading graph)

Ex. 3.11a *Das Lied von der Erde,* 'Der Abschied,' bars 213–21

Ex. 3.11b *Das Lied von der Erde*, "Der Abschied", bars 213–221 (voice leading graph)

This sequence can also be found with even more complex voice leading. In measures 295–99 of the second movement of the Ninth Symphony (Ex. 3.12a) an A major dominant chord in bar 295 is prolonged through two chords of F and D♭ major prior to the arrival of the VI chord in bar 298. The voice leading graph (Ex. 3.12b) shows how the notes of the harmonies between the dominant and the VI chord can be seen as chromatic passing notes or neighbour notes between the two chords. As such, this interpretation of the voice leading allows bars 295–97 to be treated as a dominant prolongation. There are other reasons for treating the chords found in bars 296 and 297 as continuous, or at least as a further interpolation between the dominant and the VI chord. From a neo-Riemannian perspective, the roots of the sequence A, D♭, and F demonstrate a symmetrical division of the octave and the triads themselves only feature the notes of the hexatonic scale (in this case A, C, C♯, E, F, and G♯). This is not 'maximally smooth' though, since it features only major triads.[15]

Mahler and Digression

These varied examples show that the effects of this cadence can be very different and to some extent depend on whether the VI is flattened or not.[16] To assess the more specific effects of each of these examples, it would be necessary to contextualise them in terms of Mahler's frequent use of 6-5 neighbour progressions, and especially in terms of his use of mixture in relation to the 6.[17] However, rather than considering the individual character of these examples, I want to consider what the aesthetic implications of opening up a musical space between the tonic and dominant might be. This musical opening at the point where a phrase ends is very much in line with Mahler's reported claims for his art: 'A work whose bounds are clearly apprehended, reeks of mortality—and that's just what I can't stand in art!'[18] This is the Mahler who 'can't stand

Ex. 3.12a Ninth Symphony, second movement, bars 295–99

the economical way of going about things; everything must be overflowing, gushing forth continually, if the work is to amount to anything.'[19] And who also notes, 'In my writing from the very first, you won't find any more repetition from strophe to strophe; for music is governed by the law of eternal evolution, eternal development—just as the world, even in one and the same spot, is always changing, eternally fresh and new.'[20] These examples describe an aesthetic which values development and flow over repetition and clearly apparent boundaries. It is possible to relate this more directly to Mahler's cadential technique by considering Theodore Spiering's description of the effect of Mahler's revisions of Bruckner's Fourth Symphony. Spiering notes that '[through] a whole series of very skilfully worked-out cuts he relieved the work of its jerky, periodic nature; and he achieved a logical unity which brought out the work's many beauties to an unimaginable degree.'[21] In the context of these comments, the VI can be seen as an excess at a phrase ending or elision, with elements of 'development' or 'overflow' that erode the 'jerky periodicity' provided by direct motion from the dominant to the tonic.

Ex. 3.12b Ninth Symphony, second movement, bars 295–99 (voice leading graph)

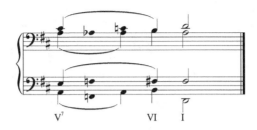

Though referring to some of the same elements, this is a different role to that found in Williamson's discussion of deceptive cadences in Mahler's Seventh Symphony, where he sees the deceptive cadence as being a 'mediation' between the positive and the 'discontinuous'.[22] What is clear though, is that the cadences identified here (and there are many more modulating deceptive cadences in the late works) cast doubt on Williamson's claim that 'deceptive shifts survive into Mahler's final period with their effect heightened by their sparing deployment'.[23] More useful here is Schoenberg's description of deceptive cadence in his *Harmonielehre* where he notes that 'the deceptive cadence is a strong means by which to introduce a secondary matter: it leads to a digression'.[24] At the foreground then, the VI chord of the deceptive cadence can be seen as a digression within the perfect cadence itself.

Middleground Digressions

In this sense it is interesting to note that there is an example of this internal digression within the cadence being expanded to middleground levels which relates to Kofi Agawu's 'conflated' cadence from earlier (Ninth Symphony, first movement, bb. 53–64). Agawu notes that the cadence introduces a clearly tonicised B♭ major section before returning to D major. As such, it is possible to interpret this section as a middleground V–♭VI–I progression. Effectively, the tonicised B♭ major section acts as a prolongation of a middleground ♭VI (bb. 54–63) between the V (b. 53) and the subsequent return of the tonic in bar 64. As these examples demonstrate, ♭VI[7] is a very common form of the VI chord in the V–VI–I sequences, and the use of B♭[7] in bar 63 to precede the return to D major is particularly telling here. This example is important in relation to Williamson's point that when assessing Mahler's praxis, it is necessary to identify whether his foreground techniques are projected as middleground progressions.[25] However, whilst this extension of Agawu's cadence into a prolonged deceptive perfect cadence demonstrates its potential as a middleground progression, its singular status in Mahler's last two completed works suggests that the transformation of this foreground cadence to a middleground structure cannot be regarded as a normative Mahlerian practice. Nevertheless, in that sense the deceptive perfect cadence is treated much like the perfect cadence in Mahler's late compositions. Though perfect cadences are apparent at the foreground, there are far fewer instances of modulations which reproduce tonic-dominant relationships in the middleground.

Schlegel, the Fragment and Mahler

By associating this cadence with the avoidance of distinct internal boundaries and the concept of digression, this chapter touches on features which previously have been convincingly related to a modernist aesthetic conception of closure.[26] However, both of these features also play a crucial role in the conception of the romantic artwork as described by Wilhelm Friedrich Schlegel, a key figure in early romantic aesthetic theory. Whilst there is no evidence that Mahler read Schlegel's work directly, he had an enthusiasm for writers who either knew Schlegel, such as Jean Paul (writer of *Titan*) or Clemens Brentano (co-editor of *Des Knaben Wunderhorn*), or who were themselves admired by the Jena Romantics, such as Laurence Sterne.[27]

For Schlegel, the earlier classical age had its beautiful unity (*schöne Einheit*), but the modern age to come will have its perfected totality (*vollendete Allheit*). Thus the 'unity of homogeneity' (*Einheit der Homogeneität*) will give way to the 'unity of multiplicity' (*Einheit des Vielfältigen*). In Schlegel's writing this is a somewhat distant, potentially unattainable possibility. But in the interim, this eventual organic whole can be anticipated by use of the 'fragment', which, as well as being a move towards that organic whole, is indicative of the present absence of the eventual organic whole to come.[28] When discussing such artworks, Schlegel, like Mahler, is opposed to clearly defined boundaries and he notes that 'a work is cultivated when it is everywhere sharply delimited, but within those limits, limitless and inexhaustible; when it is completely faithful to itself, [everywhere the same], and nonetheless exalted above itself.'[29] Similarly Schlegel values digression highly. He famously noted that 'Irony is perpetual digression',[30] since irony is an important means by which an artwork can achieve the multiplicity which he values. Irony and Mahler have long been linked, but when Stephen Hefling considered Mahler's relationship with Schlegel's conception of irony he rightly noted that 'it need not be cynical or negative.'[31] As such, this romantic aesthetic of limitlessness and ironic digression can be seen to sit easily with Mahler's own disdain for boundaries and his emphasis on the necessity of change and newness.

There is, however, a potential contradiction present here. In the quote above, Schlegel notes that the work of art should be 'sharply delimited.' This provides an interesting insight in Mahler's case, if we relate it to the end of the musical work. Of the pre-1907 symphonies, the majority have a decisive conclusion, the most notable exception being the Fourth. Mahler's conclusions have often been points of contention for both reviewers and analysts, particularly that of the Seventh Symphony which, as Williamson notes, is often described in terms of a seeming contradiction between the delimitation of end and the profusion of content.[32] Whilst Mahler may not have known Schlegel's thought directly, his comment to Bruno Walter that 'as a whole' the Ninth Symphony (in which 'something is said that I have had on the tip of my tongue for some time') is to be 'ranked beside the Fourth',[33] perhaps indicates his awareness that an aesthetic breach was shared by both symphonies.

A Schlegelian Cadence?

Similar claims for the links between the structures and musical techniques of Mahler's works and Schlegelian aesthetics have been made by a number of authors in recent years: John Daverio has discussed Mahler's use of form in relation to Schlegel's conception of *Mischgedichte* (mixed genre works);[34] Julian Johnson refers to Schlegel when assessing Mahler's use of irony and digression in his musical technique;[35] and Stephen Hefling has catalogued various examples of Mahler's technique and different types of irony.[36] Here, I want to make a similar case for the deceptive perfect cadence, which has features very much consistent with the aesthetics of early romanticism.

Schoenberg's point about the idea of a deceptive cadence as digression is based on the expected return of the perfect cadence which then closes more strongly as a result. Schoenberg's model suggests at the minimum a V-VI-V-I sequence, and from this perspective the deceptive perfect cadence has a fragmentary character since the return of the dominant never takes place.[37] So rather than a fully presented digression which returns to the point of departure (the dominant), the digression instead ends with the return of the deferred tonic itself. This leaves the two outer elements as sharply delimited (the initial V and concluding I), but within these points are layers of deferral (the VI defers the expected I, which when it then appears, defers the expected V) which provide a strong sense of the suspension of (harmonic) boundaries.

Of course, it is tempting to associate these digressions and deferrals with the fractures of modernity. However, these features of the cadence avoid 'jerky periodicity' whilst retaining a sense of continuity, producing a distinctly romantic effect. The linear discontinuities of modernism (such as those found in a work like Stravinsky's *Symphonies of Winds*) often feature jarring shifts of focus. The mode of digression here introduces new material, but still retains a sense of linear harmonic continuity.[38] In this sense, the development and continuity through deferral and digression in this cadence can be seen as a specifically musical way of addressing Schlegel's demands for the artwork to be 'everywhere the same' yet still 'exalted above itself'.

Mahler and the Past

The presence of 'hybrid' elements of the deceptive and perfect cadences as far back as the music of Beethoven suggests the possibility that Mahler's techniques merely reflect their early romantic origin. Mahler's cadential techniques can be related to early nineteenth-century practice, but there are significant differences between Mahler's usage and that of earlier periods. Beethoven's foreground exploitation of deceptive cadence content and Schumann's middleground innovations are not comparable to those hybrids used to maintain tonal ambiguity (Ex. 3.4) or Mahler's extensive use of modulating deceptive cadences. Most importantly, the V–VI–I deceptive perfect cadence has no place in the music of that time.

However, the comparison of Mahler's practice and reported thoughts with the aesthetics of early romanticism demonstrate that it is still possible for these new techniques to relate to the aesthetic of an earlier time, particularly when its artworks are still valued within the later culture. As I noted in the opening of this chapter, there is a long tradition of seeing Mahler's music as a stepping-stone to the Second Viennese School, not least by the members of the school themselves. In contrast, the ideas of Schlegel give us the opportunity to see Mahler's 'discontinuities' not as some subversive modernist practice but as manifesting the fluid multiplicities of an early romantic aesthetic. This is not to say that Mahler's reported comments from ten years prior to the composition of the late works provide the only way that these cadences can be heard. At the least though, these comments, which argue against clearly apprehended boundaries and for constant renewal, need to be addressed when discussing how Mahler's music is constructed at boundaries, whether cadential or otherwise. This is especially the case when making correlations between unprepared change and critique or subversion.

Breaking Boundaries

Rather than close on this sharply delimited note, I want to look at one last example which contains a number of features relating to the concepts that have been discussed here but which presents them in a quite different way. This example demonstrates the deceptive perfect cadence in relation to another feature of Mahler's cadential practice: the unfinished cadence.[39] In the first movement of Das Lied, in the passage leading up to what is usually referred to as the recapitulation,[40] it is possible to see a deceptive perfect cadence preparing to modulate to C that breaks off before the modulation is complete (Ex. 3.13). Instead of an arrival in C (which could be major or minor) as the vocal phrase ends, an octave E in the Glockenspiel introduces a chromatically inflected A minor. There are two points of comparison with the earlier cadences which support the idea that this is an unfinished deceptive perfect cadence. Firstly, the whole-tone dominant is reminiscent of the modulating cadence from earlier in the same movement (Ex. 3.7). Secondly, the ♭VI chord which follows the dominant has very similar chromatic descents and ascents to those found in the example from the end of

Ex. 3.13 *Das Lied von der Erde*, 'Das Trinklied Jammer der Erde,' bars 311–26

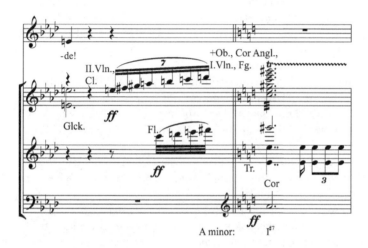

the second movement of the Ninth Symphony (Ex. 3.8). Adorno makes particular note of this whole-tone dominant chord and says that the music 'crumbles away',[41] a description which touches on Adorno's idea of a tonal language that is at its most expressive when it reaches the limits of its expressivity and 'does not finish its utterance'.[42] This is very much in line with early romantic thought and was surely in Andrew Bowie's mind when he described Schlegel's romantic irony as 'deriving precisely from the realization that one cannot say what matters most and can therefore only point to it via the acknowledgement, even as one says it, of the ultimate failure of what one says'.[43]

This deceptive perfect cadence is prevented from completing as a result of the return of the opening material and produces a moment of foreground rupture created by a formal middleground imperative. The rupture itself is no hammer blow and commences with a single toll of a glockenspiel that introduces the return of the horn call which opened the work and will shortly be revealed to be an ape howling on a grave. In Adorno's terms, rather than a breakthrough, where musical material fractures the form,[44] this is recapitulation as negative and yet necessary.[45] Appropriately for this example, Adorno notes that when Mahler 'repeats past material for formal reasons, he does not sing its praises or those of transience itself'.[46] The character of this unfinished deceptive perfect cadence ensures that the recapitulation is introduced without the 'jerky periodicity' of a conventional cadential progression. Despite this, Mahler has still constructed a 'clearly apprehended' boundary that 'reeks of mortality'.

Notes

1. Tischler, "Mahler's Impact", 119–20.
2. Paddison, *Adorno's Aesthetics of Music,* 256. Further direct examples can be found in Adorno, *Mahler,* [German edition] 23, 47, 109, and 154; [English edition] 35, 69, 145, and 199.
3. Tischler, "Mahler's Impact", 113, 117.
4. Adorno, *Mahler* [German edition], 147, 166; [English edition], 190, 215.
5. Williamson, "Deceptive Cadences", 90.
6. Hopkins, *Closure and Mahler's Music.*
7. Sheinbaum, "The Artifice of the 'Natural' ".
8. Agawu, "Prolonged Counterpoint", 233.
9. Due to the fluidity of Mahler's orchestration in the late works, the instrumentation given in this example (and all others) is indicative rather than comprehensive.
10. Finson, *Robert Schumann: The Book of Songs,* 204.
11. In his writing on classical cadence usage, William Caplin directly relates cadential function to phrase ending, noting that the presence of cadential content (such as cadential chord progressions) at the start of a phrase does not indicate cadential function (Caplin, "The Classical Cadence", 82–85). Seen in these terms, the 'deceptive cadence' in the opening movement of the 'Les Adieux' sonata only has cadential content, whilst the Schubert and Mahler examples have both content and function.
12. Nixon [now Summerfield], *The Construction of Closure and Cadence,* 112.
13. The voice leading graphs use minims for tonic chords, crotchets for prolonged consonances, quavers for prolonged dissonances and stemless notes for passing or neighbor notes.
14. Adorno, *Mahler* [English edition], 115. I am indebted to Peter Revers for this astute observation.
15. Cohn, "Maximally Smooth Cycles".
16. I am grateful to Seth Monahan for raising this point.
17. John Williamson's interesting points about the frequent use of this sequence in Mahler's music would provide a useful starting point for such a discussion ('Prolonged Counterpoint', 258).

18. 'Ein Werk, bei dem man die Grenzen sieht, riecht nach Sterblichkeit, was ich in der Kunst absolut nicht vertragen kann!' Bauer-Lechner, *Recollections [Errinerungen]*, 171 [163].

19. 'Ich kann das Sparsystem nicht leiden, das muß alles im Überfluß da sein und ohne Unterlaß quellen, wenn es was heißen soll.' Bauer-Lechner, *Recollections [Errinerungen]*, 29 [7].

20. 'Bei mir findest du von allem Anfang an keine Wiederholung bei wechselnden Strophen mehr, eben weil in der Musik das Gesetz ewigen Werdens, ewiger Entwicklung liegt—wie die Welt, selbst am gleichen Ort, eine immer andere, ewig wechselnde und neue ist.' Bauer-Lechner, *Recollections [Errinerungen]*, 130 [119].

21. Spiering, "Zwei Jahre mit Gustav Mahler", 227.

22. Williamson, "Deceptive Cadences", 96.

23. Williamson, "Deceptive Cadences", 95.

24. 'Ebenso ist der Trugschluß ein starkes Mittel zur Einführung einer Nebensache: er schafft den Anschluß für eine Abschweifung'. Schoenberg, *Theory of Harmony [Harmonielehre*, 2d ed.], 119 [144].

25. Williamson, "Prolonged Counterpoint", 249.

26. A recent example is Barry, "In Search of an Ending".

27. Barham, "Mahler the Thinker", 133–34.

28. Armstrong, *Romantic Organicism*, 42–43.

29. *Athenäum Fragmente* 297 [1798]: 'Gebildet ist ein Werk, wenn es überall scharf begrenzt, innerhalb der Grenzen aber grenzenlos und unerschöpflich ist, wenn es sich selbst ganz treu, überall gleich, und doch über sich selbst erhaben ist.' Schlegel, *Philosophical Fragments [Charakteristiken und Kritiken]*, 59 [215]. I have changed the original translation so that 'überall gleich' is rendered as 'everywhere the same' rather than 'entirely homogenous'. This is a simpler rendering, but avoids introducing the concept of 'homogeneity' to describe a modern art work when, as I note earlier, Schlegel sees this as a characteristic feature of artworks of antiquity.

30. "Die Ironie ist der Permanente Parakbase". Schlegel, *Philosophische Lehrjahre*, 85.

31. Hefling, "Techniques of Irony", 101.

32. Williamson, "Deceptive Cadences".

33. Martner, *Selected Letters*, 341.

34. Daverio, *Nineteenth-Century Music*, 5–7.

35. Johnson, *Mahler's Voices*, 270.

36. Hefling, "Techniques of Irony".

37. Though the nature of the deceptive perfect cadence means that the tonic implied by the V-VI returns, it is interesting that Mahler's use of deceptive cadence in the late works avoids the implications that Schoenberg refers to here. In the Ninth Symphony and *Das Lied*, no deceptive cadence is followed by a confirming cadence in that key. This transformation of deferral into a form of unfulfilled longing also has resonances with early romantic aesthetics (see Bowie, *Aesthetics and Subjectivity*, 52).

38. The continuous G♭ in Ex. 3.7 provides a very literal example of continuity in voice leading terms.

39. Nixon [now Summerfield], *The Construction of Closure and Cadence*, 135.

40. Hefling, *Das Lied von der Erde*, 82–92.

41. Adorno, *Mahler*, 148 [19'].

42. Adorno, *Mahler*, 146–47 [189].

43. Bowie, *Aesthetics and Subjectivity*, 288.

44. Buhler, " 'Breakthrough' ", 129–30.

45. Buhler, " 'Breakthrough' ", 135–37.

46. Adorno, *Mahler*, 94 [128].

4

'Pedester ist der Musikstoff, sublim der Vortrag'

Mahler's Scherzos as Impulses for the Evolution of Musical Language

Mathieu Schneider

In 1960, to mark the centenary of Mahler's birth, Adorno published his *Mahler: A Musical Physiognomy* that aimed to re-evaluate the composer's position within the artistic context of his era. By highlighting the striking and innovative aspects of his musical language, Adorno, the champion of avant-garde music, portrayed Mahler as a resolutely forward-looking composer. Fifty-one years later, in celebrating the centenary of his death, we can say that the importance of Mahler in the history of music is no longer in doubt. Why return then to a subject that seems already well charted? Is it really still necessary to show the modernity of Mahler's language? These days, the question finds its locus at another level.

This chapter aims to develop further the idea of how, in Mahler's hands, compositional techniques and musical styles clearly belonging to the language of the nineteenth century were suddenly able to adopt a modern mantle. It is precisely this connection between the past and future that I would like to explore here using as a basis the specific genre of the scherzo, whose roots and development are strongly entrenched in nineteenth-century Viennese culture. Mahler's scherzos are part of this tradition which they conspicuously assert but which the composer subverts on several levels.

It would be futile to make an exhaustive analysis of the eight scherzos composed by Mahler, but basing my argument in particular on the Scherzo of the Ninth Symphony, I hope to show how Mahler, by a caricatured composition of two Ländler and a waltz placed in an unexpected form, broke with Viennese tradition and anticipated what the following generations of composers after him would later put into practice.

Even a cursory glance at the literature shows that the Scherzo of the Ninth Symphony has received less analytical attention than the other three movements. Since the 1966 analysis by Erwin Ratz,[1] for whom the Ninth Symphony posed a serious problem of form in post-romantic music, many studies have been made of this work. Such studies have covered a range of approaches, from traditional analytical methods (Andraschke),[2] models based on narratology and semiotics (Newcomb),[3] to harmonic analysis from a Schenkerian perspective (Lewis).[4] Very often, it is the first movement that has been the focus of study (Leclerc),[5] or even the structure of the symphony as a whole. The scherzo, with its more rustic feel and readily transparent plan, has exercised musicologists to a lesser degree. On the other hand, the scherzos by Mahler that have intrigued musicologists tend to be those that relate to the Lied (such as that in the Second Symphony).[6] Nevertheless, there have been several interesting studies dedicated to the scherzos in Mahler's symphonic output. A case in point would be Wolfram Steinbeck's article showing that on the whole, and despite their unquestionably modern elements, they respect the formal framework of the scherzo.[7] Whilst this needs to be qualified in the case of the Ninth Symphony, the idea put forward is correct. Nevertheless, the innovations in this scherzo are not found at the outset at a macro-formal level but rather in the detail of its compositional technique. Thus I will first consider the form and composition of the first Ländler of the Scherzo, before dealing with more general comments about the movement's overall form.

The first thing to be said about this Ländler—and this is something that has not been sufficiently highlighted—is that the appearance of a Ländler at the beginning of a scherzo is very unusual. If we consider the Viennese scherzo before Mahler, we notice that when a Ländler is included in a scherzo movement, it is always in the trio section, and not in the opening scherzo. The six op. 33 string quartets of Haydn, historically considered as the earliest examples of the genre, include two Ländler: one in op. 33/2 in E♭ major, characterised by glissandi on an arpeggiated theme in strongly marked 3/4 time; the other in op. 33/3 in C major. In both cases, the Ländler is placed in the trio section. The scherzo sections themselves in these six quartets are to be considered either as stylised minuets, that is, dance-like themes with strong metric accentuation on the first and third beats and which therefore betray close ties with the minuet, or as clearly athematic sections based simply on a melodic unit of two or three repeated notes which would go on in the nineteenth century to constitute what we might call the 'scherzo style'. The latter was used by Haydn in this period with much audacity in the scherzo of op. 33/3 in C major, and this work alone justifies the claim which Haydn made for all of these quartets: of having been 'composed in a new and special way'.[8]

With Beethoven, the scherzo style initiated by Haydn became established. Although only three of Beethoven's symphonies have a scherzo, these movements are clearly drawn from the minuet tradition. The third movement of the Eroica Symphony extends the experimentations of Haydn's op. 33/3: the theme of the scherzo itself is built on the at first irregular, then regular, repetition of the cell b–c, which generates a strictly rhythmic theme totally at odds with the melodic themes of a minuet. It is once again the trio that will oppose the melodic abstraction of the scherzo with a more rustic arpeggiated theme in the horns. Even Beethoven's Sixth Symphony, with its third movement that serves as a scherzo in all but name and which describes the 'Merry gathering of country folk' (*Lustiges Zusammensein der Landsleute*), offers a lively theme in D major played by the violins and solo flute, and which has the vague feel of a Ländler. But its entry there is still deferred by a typical scherzo motif (a rapid succession of falling thirds and rising seconds played in unison by the strings) in bars 1 to 9. The list of scherzos without an initial Ländler can be extended to include, for example, Schubert's Sixth Symphony (the only one along with the Ninth to have a scherzo) or most of the scherzos in the symphonies of Bruckner. The Brucknerian scherzo almost always begins with a short repeated motif in the spirit of the 'scherzo style'.

When Mahler decided to begin the Scherzo of his Ninth Symphony with a 'leisurely Ländler' (*ein gemächlicher Ländler*), he broke openly with the tradition of the genre. There are at least two reasons for this. First, Mahler himself had already bent this rule in the second movement of his First Symphony, whose initial theme in A major also has the character of a Ländler, with its regular ternary rhythm and octave leaps in the violins and violas that recall the glissandi of the Ländler in Haydn's op. 33/2 (see Ex. 4.1).

Secondly, we can find another explanation in the link the composer's symphonic style generally maintained with folk music. To take just the scherzos alone, we should mention those of the Second and Third symphonies, based on Lieder of the *Knaben Wunderhorn* that Mahler transformed into symphonic movements. More generally, many of Mahler's symphonies use folk music themes, from dances like the Moravian Hatscho in the First Symphony to the trio section of the Scherzo in the Fifth Symphony whose Czech folk song quotation has been pointed out by Karbusicky.[9] In this context, there is finally nothing very surprising about how Mahler's scherzos make use of the Ländler, given that the composer's symphonic style draws heavily from sources of central European folk music and that this dance was present in the Viennese trios and scherzos from their beginnings.

On the other hand, the appearance of a Ländler right at the beginning of the movement does not seem to be a progressive element of language; it seems instead to be a retreat. In fact, historically the scherzo with Haydn and Beethoven had become uncoupled from dance by turning its back on the minuet, even

Ex. 4.1 The octave leaps in the scherzo of Mahler's First Symphony renouncing the idea of a melodic theme and thereby making the scherzo an essentially rhythmic movement. Mahler, for his part, came back to it and re-established the melody, the regular ternary metre, and even-numbered phrases. But as we all know, appearances can be deceptive: the Mahlerian scherzo, and especially the one in the Ninth Symphony, deploys the Ländler as nothing more than an empty frame, a sort of 'mask' that keeps up the appearances of music whose tonal structure and formal coherence has in fact broken down.

Of all the Mahler scherzos, the one that begins the second movement of the Ninth Symphony is probably the most authentic, and perhaps the most carica-tured. At the entry of the actual theme (Ex. 4.2), at the upbeat to bar 10, Mahler specifies its 'ponderous' or 'clumsy' character (*schwerfällig*) and how the second violins should play it 'like a fiddle' (*wie Fiedeln*). This insistence on the rustic and crude character of the theme is even more visible in the musical notation itself: the melody in the violins begins *fortissimo* and Mahler notates the first two notes of the anacrusis (G and A) as down-bows, thus making its rendition considerably more ungainly. In the same way, in the next bar, the composer calls for three 'down-bows' on the descending quavers G–E–D and only an 'up-bow' on the final C. Futhermore, the *sforzando* on the second beat of each bar renders the theme unstable and clumsy since its natural accent, which is here emphasised by the double basses, is on the first beat. Last but not least, the open-fifth drone (C–G) of the basses adds to the heaviness, and consequently to the overall rustic feel, and unambiguously evokes its folk-like style.

Even so, taking a closer look, this Ländler is stillborn: it is nothing more than an external element to which the form of the movement fails to give life. To start with, the theme itself only lasts four bars. The 'cheeky' (*keck*) entry of the principal horn inhibits and impedes it from continuing. In a classical thematic structure, the initial four bars would have called for a second sym-metrical four-bar period. This does not in fact happen, probably because the melodic swing between C and B in the violins has returned to the tonic C (bar 13) and also because in this context it is hard to imagine an answer to an al-ready concluding subject. Mahler therefore can only add a bar of confirmation and repetition of the pseudo-cadence. In bar 15, this is followed by a short pas-sage leading to the clarinets' initial motif. To put it another way, the theme of the Ländler only lasts over a period of 4 + 1 + 1 bars. When this same theme is repeated with richer orchestration, with doublings in the woodwinds at the upbeat to bar 20, it also fails to extend itself beyond these six bars. The trans-position an octave higher gives it more brilliance, but this makes its failure to exist melodically and harmonically only more bitter.

Peter Oswald, in the aftermath of Adorno, thought of this theme as a 'mon-tage', meaning a sort of external element to the tonal and motivic progression.[10] This comment needs qualifying: the Ländler is a negative element that prevents the form from being deployed rather than being simply a neutral and exter-nal theme. A harmonic reduction of the Ländler's entire first section clearly

Ex. 4.2 The Ländler-theme in the scherzo of the Ninth Symphony (bb. 9–16, reduced to strings, horn 1 and clarinet 1)

Ex. 4.3 Harmonic reduction of the first Ländler's entire section in the Scherzo of the Ninth Symphony

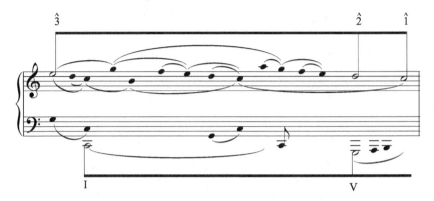

shows this tendency (Ex. 4.3). In the movement as a whole, we do find several dominant-to-tonic cadential progressions: the first occurs in bar 4, the moment when the motif is first presented by the clarinets in the introduction. But if we take into account thematic and registral questions, the real tonic of the movement is stated by the cellos in bar 10 on C^1, the moment the Ländler theme enters. On several occasions the clarinets' motif articulates a dominant that then resolves onto the tonic, but always in a register an octave higher than the cellos, and never on a statement of the main theme. The C^1 is only heard again at each return of the Ländler theme, especially when this theme is taken up by the basses (in bars 40, 49, and 58). Three times the double basses' line reaches the dominant which is resolved onto the tonic at the end of the theme's statement, but never melodically, as this resolution does not coincide with an end of the melodic phrase on a C. At bar 44, there is not really any melody; at bar 53, the violins play an E and the melodic line is not completed; the same goes for bar 62 where the violins play an A, the appoggiatura of G. At the end of the passage, the repeated phrases of the theme's anacrusis in the double basses lead either to a return of the clarinets' motif on an E in the higher part, or do not round off the G–A–B melodic gesture with the expected C in the bass.

Returning to this section's reduction, we notice therefore that the C–G–C progression in the bass never coincides with a concluding melodic movement. The Ländler's great self-confident theme is therefore destabilised and continuously wrong-footed by a static harmonic structure that is unable to provide closure to a banal passage towards the dominant and return of the tonic. This analysis corroborates the thesis by Francesca Draughon, who sees (in the scherzo's different themes) stereotypes, or fixed, almost quotational structures that she reduces in her analysis to social symbols.[11]

Turning now to the movement as a whole, it seems hard to identify it as a form that is immediately related to nineteenth-century symphonic scherzos.

It is true that in his scherzos Bruckner profoundly modified and extended the classical outline we find in Beethoven and Schubert, with its tripartite structure that alternates the scherzo and trio. Mahler continued down this path by giving significant expressive and architectonic weight to the trio section, especially in his Third Symphony, where the episode with the posthorn makes it the focal point of the entire movement. In the Scherzo of the Ninth Symphony, Mahler attempts something much more innovative: he starts the movement with the trio. Indeed, the introductory nine bars of the movement call for only a small orchestra—the violas, two of the four bassoons, the bass clarinet and two of the three clarinets (in other words, barely fifteen musicians out of a total of at least eighty). The statement of the theme scarcely asks for more: the cellos, violas, second violins, two bassoons, and a horn. It is therefore resolutely a 'chamber orchestra' minus its higher and lower string sections (first violins, double basses), whilst the desks called for (bassoons, clarinets) are only partially deployed by Mahler. As we know from the history of the minuet and scherzo, the trio got its name from its reduced number of players. This is true of all trios at the end of the eighteenth and beginning of the nineteenth centuries, and it even applies to Bruckner and the first symphonies of Mahler. In choosing a Ländler, Mahler therefore dresses up his scherzo as a trio, and in doing so falls within the genre's Viennese tradition that, as we have seen, expected the Ländler (if the scherzo has one) to be placed in the trio.

Does this mean as a result that the waltz which follows the Ländler at bar 90 plays the role of the scherzo? The waltz also does not deploy the entire orchestra, but at least it is played by all the strings. The woodwind and brass are quickly added, to such an extent that the texture on average is denser than the texture of the Ländler. It must be mentioned also that scherzos rarely begin with an orchestral *tutti*. The Scherzo of Bruckner's Fourth Symphony begins with a solo horn, and the Scherzos in Mahler's Third and Fourth Symphonies call for only a small part of the orchestra at the beginning. But in these three cases, as in the waltz of the Ninth, we need no more than twenty to thirty bars before the orchestra is used in full.

Beyond the mere question of instrumentation, the waltz section also has the feel of a scherzo because of the thematic and harmonic work that Mahler brings to it and which contrasts with the stasis of the Ländler: the waltz section modulates from E major to F major, passing via Eb major, C major and B major. It is also based on a theme whose Schenkerian reduction clearly reveals a stable harmonic and melodic structure (Ex. 4.4).

The Ländler and waltz seem therefore to have inverted their normative positions in the movement: the waltz as pseudo-scherzo only comes in second position; the Ländler as pseudo-trio opens the movement. Certain writers, such as Draughon,[12] have seen this progression of the Ländler towards the waltz as a form of dialectics between the rural and the urban, and therefore the musical manifestation of the social and historical reality of Vienna at the beginning

Ex. 4.4 Harmonic reduction of the waltz theme at its first appearance (bb. 90–102)

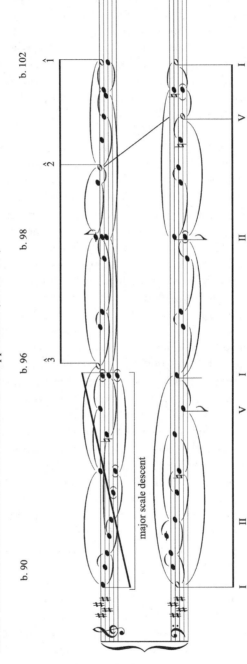

b. 90   b. 96   b. 98   b. 102

$\hat{3}$ $\hat{2}$ $\hat{1}$

major scale descent

I   II   V   I   II   V   I

Ex. 4.5 First bars of the second Ländler (bb. 218–21, reduced to strings)

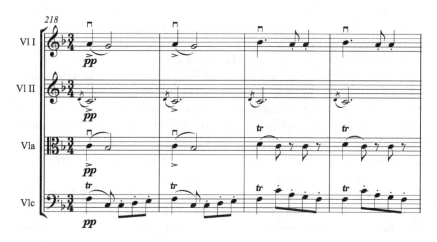

Table 4.1 Structural Outline of the Movement (final version)

A	B	C	B'	C'	A'	B"	A" (+B+C)
C major	E major -> E♭ major -> F major	F major	D major -> B major -> C major	F major (-> E major)	C major	E♭ major -> B♭ major -> G major	C major
EXPOSITION			**DEVELOPMENT**			**RECAPITULATION**	

of the century. I believe we should first understand the Ländler-waltz succession as a gesture toward musical tradition and the history of the scherzo that
Mahler, as an orchestral conductor, knew perfectly well. To do so, we need to
widen once again our viewpoint in order to consider the overall form of the
movement.

To the two Ländler and waltz sections, Mahler adds a third element in the
form of a second Ländler at bar 218, which he identifies with a separate tempo,
marked 'Tempo III'. This justifies considering the second Ländler as an entirely
separate section, even though the ties to the first Ländler are fairly strong, especially because of the presence of a variant of the opening motif of the first
Ländler in the bass (Ex. 4.5).

If A denotes the first Ländler, B the waltz, and C the second Ländler, the sequence of these three elements in the movement can be summarised as shown
in Table 4.1.

In terms of tonality, what should be noted is the astonishing harmonic stability of the two Ländler during the movement, in that they always return in
their initial key. As for the waltz, this arrives each time in a different key and

continuously modulates so as to restore either the tonic or dominant of the following section, without discontinuity. If this reading of the movement reinforces the static role of the first Ländler, already indicated by the tonal analysis of its internal structure, it also allows us to go beyond the conclusion that has so far been drawn by all analysts, which is to say that it is a scherzo form. The fact that the scherzo form begins with a totally static trio would immediately complicate this reading of the form. But taking a closer look, Mahler seems to have constructed its form more on a sonata model than on a rondo form. The two Ländler, A and C, are heard respectively as the tonic and subdominant and are linked to each other by the waltz that by its tonal mobility functions as a transition. Here we can see the classical outline of a two-theme exposition. After this follows a development which is also modulative, thanks to the waltz. This development ends with the return of the second Ländler finishing on the dominant of E. The return to C major of the first Ländler sounds therefore like the beginning of a recapitulation: even Mahler marks it 'like at the opening' (*wie zu Anfang*). The waltz returns as a transition element and leads to G major, which allows logically the second Ländler to return in C major. Instead, it is in fact the first Ländler, which is very similar to the second, that returns and in which elements of the waltz and second Ländler are blended.

It might seem excessive to speak about sonata form, as the relation between the two themes is harmonically and thematically weak: the passage from the tonic to the subdominant, without being exceptional, creates a harmonic slackening instead of tension, and the two themes do not contrast either in their motifs or in their character. We should not forget, however, as Colin Matthews has shown, that the form in the first orchestral score was the one shown in Table 4.2.[13] The double permutation of the first and second Ländler after the first waltz B and before the last waltz B2 changes completely the movement's appearance, which as a result is closer to a rondo, whose refrain would be the waltz rather than the first Ländler.

Table 4.2 Structural Outline of the Movement (draft and score)

Draft	A	B	A'	C	B'	C'	B"	A"
	Couplet	Refrain	Couplet		Refrain	Couplet	Refrain	Couplet

Score	A	B	C	B'	C'	A'	B"	A" (+B+C)
		EXPOSITION			DEVELOPMENT		RECAPITULATION	

The change implemented in the final version is not trivial and Mahler must have been aware of the consequence: the transformation of the scherzo form into a sonata form can therefore be considered a conscious act.[14] The point of departure for the trio imposed this on him. At the same time, the sonata form reflects the internal structure of the first Ländler: it is an empty shell that uses the different sections as no more than 'labels' and which juxtaposes them as completely 'watertight' external elements.

To conclude, this movement should be placed in the context of scherzos from Mahler's other symphonies. Apart from the First Symphony, which contrasts the initial scherzo with a real trio that still has very classical tonal articulation, the scherzos in the symphonies that followed often tend to mark out the trio as a contrasting and tonally static element: the lilting theme of the trumpets in E major of the Second Symphony initiates this tendency with a very long tonic pedal and very static texture that contrasts with the agitation of the scherzo. Here, Mahler has still not sacrificed tradition, as the episode is very short. However, in the following symphony the trio becomes an autonomous episode: this is so both spatially, as the posthorn should sound 'as if from afar', and in terms of character, tonality, and texture. This process is echoed in the Scherzo's central horn episode of the Fifth, or, more vaguely, in the 'altväterisch' section of the Scherzo in the Sixth. The Scherzo of the Ninth can therefore be interpreted in terms of an evolution that aims to make the trio an element that is outside of symphonic time. Certain commentators, such as Dieter Schnebel, have spoken about 'collage'.[15] I prefer to speak of an 'element out of time': for if the Ländler was 'stuck on' (*collé*), it would not take part in the form. It is one of the main articulations (as a first theme), but, importantly, it is not subject to the time that it structures. As a static and banal element (Adorno said *'pedester'*) suddenly placed at the outset of the movement, it induces an unexpected formal process: a pseudo sonata form— that is to say, a sonata form in name only. The banality of its structure with its abrupt contrasts of tempo and tonality, cruelly throws light on the disappearance of the element that had structured all tonal music since Monteverdi: syntax, or to put it another way, 'the art of movement'. Was not the first title of this Scherzo 'Minuetto infinito' (infinite minuet)? Mahler therefore openly incorporated stasis in music. With him, tonality dies because it freezes. Schoenberg and Webern would later kill it by replacing it with another system. Mahler, by not renouncing tradition but by depriving it of its vital sap, revealed himself as one of the most modern composers in the early part of the twentieth century.

Notes

1. Ratz, "Zum Formproblem bei Gustav Mahler".
2. Andraschke, *Gustav Mahlers IX. Symphonie.*
3. Newcomb, "Narrative Archetypes and Mahler's Ninth Symphony".

4. Lewis, *Tonal Coherence in Mahler's Ninth Symphony*.

5. Leclerc, *Analyse formelle du premier mouvement de la Neuvième symphonie de Mahler*.

6. Maurer-Zenck, "Technik und Gehalt im Scherzo von Mahlers Zweiter Symphonie".

7. Steinbeck, "Gustav Mahler und das Scherzo".

8. 'auf eine ganz besondere neue Art'. From a letter of 3 December 1781 to Swiss writer Johann Caspar Lavater.

9. Karbusicky, *Gustav Mahler und seine Umwelt*, 60–61.

10. Oswald, *Perspektiven des Neuen,* 119.

11. Draughon, "Dance of Decadence", 394.

12. Draughon, "Dance of Decadence," 394.

13. See Matthews, "Mahler at Work".

14. This reading of the scherzo's form does not fundamentally contradict other interpretations that have so far been made and that have often aimed at presenting this movement as a succession of formal vestiges—Stephen Hefling has spoken of the 'vestiges of the scherzo-trio plan and of the old waltz suite' ("Aspects of Mahler's Late Style", 211)—but seeks rather to offer an explanation for their presence and their organisation. The significance of this change has already been studied by several writers (Draughon and others) and is therefore not the subject of the present study.

15. Schnebel, "Mahlers Spätwerk als Neue Musik", 78.

5

Forming Form through Force

Bruckner, Mahler, and the Structural Function of Highpoints

Alessandro Cecchi

One reason that led some scholars to deny the historical connection between Bruckner and Mahler in the aftermath of the Second World War was the understandable reaction to the Nazi regime's cultural politics, which imposed a remarkable distance between the two composers: while Mahler's 'degenerate' music was banished, Bruckner's music flourished because it was turned to political use.[1] There is an echo of these events in the beginning of Theodor Adorno's influential 1960 monograph, where the names of Mahler and Hitler occur together and, one page later, we find the claim that Mahler's 'incommensurable presence ... defies ... the bald historical derivation from Bruckner'.[2] The distance between Mahler and Bruckner created by the Nazi regime is thus basically maintained in Adorno's contrary evaluation. On the other hand, he was too intent on depicting Mahler as the composer who paved the way for the 'new music' to accept the idea of a contiguity with the late-romantic Bruckner.[3]

Historical distance enables us to understand the dynamics of this reception and revise these evaluations. Among the few scholars who have returned to the connection between Mahler and Bruckner after Adorno, the work of Peter Revers stands out. He discusses some 'aspects of a phenomenology of Bruckner's and Mahler's composition' in order to 'test their comparability' and 'question the possibility of a reception of Bruckner in Mahler's oeuvre'.[4] In the close examination that follows, he focuses on three research directions, highlighting analogies and differences in the 'construction of time', the tendency to 'clarification' of structures in subsequent versions of the same work, and the 'construction of highpoints'.

In this chapter I take up this third direction, developing a different perspective: on the one hand, I move the focus from the 'construction' to the 'function' of highpoints in the formal organisation of a symphonic movement; and on the other hand, I adopt a criterion of historical contiguity, offering a comparison between two symphonic movements that from the point of view of

The author wishes to thank Federico Celestini for his helpful comments on an earlier draft of this chapter.

compositional process can be considered contemporary: the first movements
of Bruckner's Ninth and Mahler's First symphonies.[5] The fact that any direct
influence between these works must be excluded serves the purposes of my
examination: I do not intend to support the thesis of a 'filiation' but rather
to compare the compositional strategies of the late Bruckner and the young
Mahler in order to draw connections in the light of the historical music milieu
they shared: the post-Beethovenian Austrian symphonic tradition.[6] Toward
the end of the nineteenth century, this took the course Adorno referred to in
the concept of 'nominalism':[7] a process of increasing individualisation of musical artworks, which gradually broke away from genres and formal conventions.

To do this I rely on a theoretical-methodological framework that derives
from an interaction of perspectives. I pose the problem by referring to the
debate concerning the role of 'climax' in music during the last sixty years, and
complete it by taking up the 'energetic' theory of musical form proposed by
Ernst Kurth in his 1925 Bruckner monograph. From his discursive examination of the first movement of Bruckner's Ninth Symphony, I derive a model of
analysis that I then apply to the first movement of Mahler's First, while using
diagrams that are in fact alien to Kurth's sensibility. In this application I refer
to Adorno's idea of a 'material theory of musical form'[8] as a key to understanding Mahler's music. In fact, Kurth and Adorno give a similar answer to the
hermeneutic question which emerges when traditional forms, intended as abstract typologies, are reduced to an inert state: when, that is, they are present
and recognisable but no longer able to justify the concrete formal organisation
of a composition by supplying its 'meaning'.[9] Such theoretical imbrication encourages a revision of the verdict on the connection between Bruckner and
Mahler: Kurth's positive evaluation of late romanticism offers a corrective to
Adorno's opposite view, opening the path to less unilateral positions. Moreover,
Kurth's approach has the advantage of defining the level of formal organisation to which analysis has to be oriented to highlight analogies between the
compositional strategies of the two symphonic movements. The recognition of
such analogies will enable us to circumscribe the differences ascribable to the
more 'nominalist' character of Mahler's compositions, limiting the thesis of
incommensurability so as to support the idea of gradual historical evolution.

Climax in Music: Theoretical Perspectives

Though confined to a small group of scholars, the theoretical debate on the
role of 'climax' in music conducted over the last sixty years provides interesting points for discussion. One point on which scholars agree is that climax
meets the requirement of integration, yet their arguments concern different
structural levels. While William Newman intends such integration in terms
of general aesthetics by claiming that 'the concept of a single climax within
a single curve of force is possible only in a completely integrated art form',[10]

Leonard Meyer deals with basic syntactic unities, investigating the possible functions of climax in musical themes with a periodic structure.[11] And while Kofi Agawu chooses relatively short compositions involving the intoning of a poetic text,[12] Richard Kaplan investigates 'the sense of climax' as a possible strategy 'for achieving structural integration' by observing 'coherent musical processes or relationships in the large dimension of the piece as a whole'.[13]

A second point is the connection between the discussion of climax and the stylistic distinction between classical and romantic music. Newman claims that classical art only can be taken into consideration in order to achieve a 'valid generalization', given that 'the location of climax in a romantic style may very well depend on subjective reaction to emotional expressions'.[14] Nevertheless, when he underlines the 'romantic' variability in the location of climax, he implicitly claims its more prominent structural importance—for instance, when he identifies in Wagner's *Tristan und Isolde* examples 'of the long postponed climax'.[15]

On this point Meyer offers a more articulated examination. He derives from compositions of the cassical age an 'archetypal structure':[16] the abstract scheme of a period with 'syntactic climax' intended as the 'turning point' of a process of 'reversal . . . shaped by the primary parameters of melody, rhythm, and harmony'. To this Meyer opposes a 'statistical climax' or 'apotheosis' obtained through 'a gradual increase in the intensity of the more physical attributes of sound' to a 'tensional "highpoint," followed by a usually rapid decline in activity . . . to quiet and closure'.[17] On this basis Meyer distinguishes between the classical and romantic style by highlighting 'the increasingly important role played by secondary parameters in the shaping of musical process and the articulation of musical form', matched by 'an increase in the importance of statistical climax . . . relative to syntactic climax in the shaping of musical structure'.[18] In his analytical examination he compares the main theme of a late work by Beethoven which conforms to the 'archetypal structure'—the fourth movement of the String Quartet op. 131 (1826)—with the main melody (*idée fixe*) in the first movement of Berlioz's *Symphonie Fantastique* (1830), where the archetype is 'obscured'[19] by the insertion of a musical process Meyer names 'Sisyphean sequence',[20] that is, an ascending sequence of a descending motivic model, which through intensification leads to a 'statistical climax'. Unlike what happens in Beethoven's theme, in Berlioz's melody there is no coincidence between statistical and syntactic climax. Rather, the first precedes the second, undermining its structural predominance: here the subsequent syntactic climax can only confirm (or repeat) the 'highpoint' in order to lead the melodic and harmonic course of the archetype toward the end and achieve closure. On this basis Meyer concludes that the two works, chronologically close, manifest a radical change in style: 'In Beethoven's theme, syntactic climax dominates apotheosis; in Berlioz's melody, statistical apotheosis dominates syntactic climax.'[21]

Agawu also connects nineteenth-century music intrinsically to the 'structural' importance of 'highpoints', pointing out that this term avoids confusion

with the original meaning of 'climax', which in Greek 'denotes an arrangement of figures in ascending order of intensity',[22] as Newman had previously
noted.[23] The choice of Schumann's song cycle *Dichterliebe* (1840) depends on
the premise that he is 'the quintessential Romantic composer'.[24] In his examination Agawu tries to surpass the limitations of the prevalent theoretical and
analytical models by investigating the role of an undefined number of musical
parameters involved in the shaping of highpoints and adopting the methodological criterion of 'flexibility': the syntax, form, melody, harmony, dynamics,
texture, expressive cues, and even syntactic and narrative processes of Heine's
poems are variously involved in the analysis, and in his closing remarks Agawu
proposes that for nineteenth-century music the rigid hierarchical distinction
of 'structural and ornamental factors' should be abandoned.[25]

    When investigating the Adagio of Mahler's Tenth Symphony (1910), Agawu
seems to return to a more traditional conception, insofar as he claims that
the famous chord in the 'climax' of the movement 'performs both rhetorical
and structural functions, rhetorical because it uses such so-called "secondary
parameters" as timbre, dynamics, and register in a big way, and structural because it presents the ultimate conflict between the primary key system . . . and
a subsidiary one'.[26] For the overlapping of 'structural and rhetorical functions'
to be considered significant, the two attributes must be clearly distinguished in
theoretical terms, and here they are distinguished precisely by relying on the
usual hierarchy of musical parameters, which Agawu has recently reasserted.[27]

    In his systematic study dedicated to the role of secondary parameters in
processes of 'closure', Robert Hopkins starts from a persuasive definition of the
concept of 'parameter' based on the criterion of independence.[28] On this basis
he specifies and reinforces the distinction between primary and secondary
parameters. From the former he excludes 'rhythm', which depends on other
parameters,[29] while the latter are reduced to four independent parameters: 'registral pitch', 'dynamics', 'duration', and 'timbre'.[30] In the analytical section of
his book, Hopkins offers a systematic examination of the different forms of closure in Mahler's oeuvre, highlighting the role of secondary parameters—taken
individually and in their interaction—in four basic strategies: 'dissolution',
'collapse', 'fragmentation', and 'subsidence'.[31] The introduction of a terminology suitable for the description of the modalities of interaction of the secondary parameters must be stressed: secondary parameters, actually, can be more
or less 'synchronized' and/or 'congruent'.[32] In his investigation of 'closure'
Hopkins takes into consideration strategies of 'abatement', yet his terminology
can be easily applied also to strategies of 'intensification'.[33]

    The role that climax plays in Mahler's symphonies has been investigated by
Kaplan, who referred to the concept of 'fusion' in two different perspectives. In
terms of the chord of the climax in the Adagio of Mahler's Tenth Symphony,
Kaplan identifies a process of fusion by explaining its harmonic structure as
the overlapping of dominant chords of two distinct tonalities at the basis of the

movement,[34] while when it comes to the peculiar narrative function of 'sections' in Mahler's works he focuses on relations of 'reminiscence' and 'foreshadowing' which prove to be established among quite remote places in the score. In this case he observes that the proximity of the climax tends to produce forms of coalescence of the two temporal directions, defined as 'temporal fusion'.[35]

The whole debate tends to concentrate either on the first half of the nineteenth century or on the works Mahler composed in the twentieth century, thus focusing on the extremes of a historical development. This shortcoming is partly remedied by Wolfgang Krebs, who proposes the idea of an interaction between musical syntax and the construction of highpoints in Wagner and Bruckner. Krebs identifies a new kind of syntactic typology he names 'energetic' or 'dynamic period with highpoint effect', shortened as 'culmination period',[36] in an attempt to give a syntactic guise to processes involving relaxation of syntax. For the rest, his examination is wholly based on Kurth's treatises, to which I will refer directly, in order to set them in the light of the discussion on climax.

Kurth adopts the framework of Vitalism, relying on one hand on the philosophical tradition (Schopenhauer) and, on the other, on the *Lebensphilosophien* emerging and consolidating, in polemic with Positivism, around the turn of the century (Dilthey, Bergson). Within this framework he proposes a metaphysical perspective, based on the idea of a 'force [*Kraft*]' (noumenic principle) that assumes a spatial-temporal (phenomenic) form through an act of 'coercion [*Bezwingung*]'.[37] The philosophical concept of form has in Kurth a dynamic structure, defined through the tension between the 'force' and its 'consolidation [*Festigung*] in the phenomenic world'.[38] Similarly, the concept of musical form results from the 'interaction between the force and its coercion in outlines [*Umrissen*]'.[39] Relying on this definition, Kurth introduces a stylistic distinction between 'classical' and 'romantic' formal principles, depending on the different relation established between 'outlines' and 'force'. To Kurth, the composers who conform to the classical style deliberately highlight the 'outlines' of their works, that is, syntactic articulation, symmetries, regularity of accents, melodic lines, and formal partitions, while those conforming to the 'romantic' principle shape and structure their works predominantly through 'forces', that is, energetic configurations which relax syntax in favor of processes based on tensions, polar attractions, intensifications, accumulations, involutions, and so on.

The principle Kurth names 'romantic' does not refer to the composers that we today consider equally representative of musical romanticism, but only to a specific evolutionary line. This starts from Berlioz, evolves in Liszt, finds its full realisation in Wagner's *Tristan*, and is transferred by Bruckner to symphonic music. The other evolutionary line—though involving romantic composers such as Schubert, Schumann, Mendelssohn, and Brahms—is to Kurth still anchored in the principles of classicism, derived from the classical style of Beethoven. Kurth develops his theory in order to underline such difference and at the same time contrast the *Formenlehre* that still dominated didactics and academic treatises of his period, founded by Adolf Bernhard Marx in the mid-nineteenth century and relying on classical models. For Kurth, this theory of form is unsuited to confronting the stylistic changes that emerged in the romantic authors of the first line.[40] In order to overcome such limitations, Kurth defines the morphology of Wagner and Bruckner using the concept of 'wave of force [*Kraftwelle*]',[41] through which he underlines the incomparably greater value and importance assumed by 'forces' relative to the 'outlines' and particularly by the cumulative principle building to 'highpoints [*Höhepunkte*]'.

By combining Kurth's perspective with Meyer's reflection it becomes plausible to hypothesise that during the nineteenth century there was a progressive extension of the role of the musical processes based on secondary parameters: while in Berlioz these served to 'obscure' the archetype, in Wagner and Bruckner they broke free from traditional syntactic structures and became all-pervasive. The processes Kurth talks about under the term 'intensifying waves [*Steigerungswellen*]' are based on ascending modulating sequences of prevalently descending motives (like Meyer's 'Sisyphean sequence'). He explains such processes as energetic configurations in tension toward 'highpoints' defined in statistical terms. What Kurth names *Steigerung* is thus none other than a process of intensification based on the 'congruent' and 'highly synchronized' increase of Hopkins's secondary parameters, though Kurth would prefer using 'melodic curve' in the place of 'registral pitch', and 'density [*Dichte*]'—which highlights the quantitative aspects of instrumentation—in the place of 'timbre'. And it is the convergence of all the secondary parameters that Kurth refers to when he claims the primacy of the 'symphonic course [*Verlauf der Symphonik*]' over melody.[42]

Relying on the previous discussion I can now formulate with enough clarity the thesis that in the late nineteenth-century Austrian symphonic tradition the highpoints gain a peculiar structural relief not by virtue of the correspondence with syntactic, harmonic, or formal turning points, but exclusively as configurations of force, that is, in the 'statistical' value emerging from the congruent and synchronised increase of all the independent secondary parameters, whose convergence undermines the structural predominance of the primary ones.

Energetic Deployment and Formal Organisation in Late Bruckner

The first movement of Bruckner's Ninth Symphony offers a heuristic model of Kurth's treatise; he considers it as the last result of evolution within Bruckner's symphonic oeuvre, where he sees an increasingly wider role of the energetic deployment in the concrete formal organisation. This is the reason we can find analytical cues both in the paragraph dedicated to this movement[43] and in the systematic sections of Kurth's monograph.[44]

The strategy of presentation of the main thematic configuration is revealing: unlike the other initial movements of Bruckner's symphonies, the exposition of the theme does not coincide with the beginning of the piece. Kurth considers the first ninety-six bars[45] as a coherent process whose integration relies not on a well-established syntactic structure but on the fluctuation of secondary parameters, resulting in a symphonic 'wave' articulated in energetic phases. The 'preliminary development [Vorentwicklung]'[46] (bars 1–26) begins with a string tremolo—which to Kurth is in general the 'stirring of force more than of sound'[47]—joined by woodwinds in the lower register (bar 3) accompanying for a while the entrance of the horns (bar 5). These offer simple motivic configurations insisting on the basic intervals of the D minor triad (third and fifth). To Kurth such intervals are 'striving' for the octave, establishing a tension that is not resolved at this point; a 'turn [Wendung]' follows (bars 19–26), characterised by harmonic modulation and deployed as a little wave within the bigger wave, with its own culmination.[48] From the harmonic point of view the little wave begins in E♭ major with seventh (D♭) in the bass, reaches the culmination on the C♭ major triad and arrives at A♭7 (with a suspension of the fourth to the third scale degree) before dispersing.

The lengthy 'intensification [Steigerung]' (bars 27–62) that follows is based on the principle of a modulatory sequence and articulated in three phases (bars 27–38, 39–50, 51–62), the last of which is characterised by a remarkable ascent of the melodic curve and synchronised increase of dynamics, orchestral density, and motivic acceleration, all building to the 'highpoint' (bars 63–75). This is the main event (D minor) of the wave, the result of the tension triggered in the first bars, which Kurth sees as corresponding not to the 'exposition' of the main theme but rather to its 'outburst [Ausbruch]'.[49] Completing Kurth's analysis, we can investigate the detailed construction of the theme in order to underline energetic as well as syntactic aspects of its articulation. Therein, a periodic structure is quite recognisable: the first part (bars 63–70) is an antecedent [A] based on melodic descent: chromatic from tonic to dominant, diatonic from dominant to 'Neapolitan' scale degree (E♭), harmonised as C♭ (the tonality of the culmination in the 'turn'). After a pause, the second part (bars 71–75) represents a consequent [B] starting from E minor (as resolution of C♭ major, enharmonically equivalent of B), ascending at first gradually and then in rapid scales to B♭, on the seventh chord on the second scale degree of D minor with G in the bass. The highest note (B♭) (bar 74) is the melodic highpoint which leads to the final cadence [C]—a simple descending fifth of the dominant on the major tonic (bars 74–75).

The last phase of the wave (bars 77–96) is to Kurth the energetic consequence of the highpoint, that is, a reverberation of the outburst causing an 'after-tremor [*Nacherschütterung*]', and corresponds only superficially to a transition to the second theme.[50] I would make this point more precise by saying that the passage conserves the 'function' though not the 'character' (the traditional features) of a transition. Kurth interprets the *pizzicato* which dominates this passage both as a symbol of the rebounding of the energy in descending figurations to the complete dissipation, and as the expression of a 'state of tension';[51] the last bar prepares, in fact, a new event through the dominant of A major.

In this first articulated formal process emerge two striking configurations of force: the first is perceived as primary or 'structural', for the highpoint corresponds to the tonic key, to a defined syntactic structure (basically periodic), and to the formal function of exposition of the main theme; the second is perceived as secondary and 'episodic', for the motivic configuration of the 'turn' represents something preliminary, playing an undefined formal function, offering a loose syntactic construction, avoiding fundamental tonalities (even if the culminating chord is then included in the main theme) and following a modulatory and fluctuating course. Yet the primary configuration does not merely 'underline' or 'reinforce' the theme; rather it identifies it as the outburst of a force that previously was only latent. I would define this as an energetic 'translation' of a structural function.

The exposition continues with two thematic waves, each with a less prominent highpoint. These follow a more linear course, corresponding to a second theme in A major, whose character is that of a typical *Gesangsthema* (bars 97–152), and a third theme (*Unisono*) initially unfolded in D minor (bars 167–226) after a short preparation (bars 153–66). The subsequent development is to Kurth a single great evolutionary process, though initially divided up into short sections.[52] The first two (bars 227–52, 252–76) combine the preliminary horn motives (bars 5–11), respectively, with the retardation at the end of the 'turn' (bars 24–5) and inverted fragments of the second theme, concluding in short intensifications (bars 245–52, 256–76) based on the 'turn' (bars 19–25). The third (bars 277–301) develops motivic materials from the 'after-tremor', combined with materials of the second theme. The accompaniment motive of the subsequent section (bars 303–20) also relies on the inversion of the first part of the *Gesangsthema* (bars 97–98, violins), developing a gradual intensification based on the principle of the ascending modulating sequence. This motive accompanies the restatement (in fact, identical) of the last phase of the lengthy intensification of the first symphonic wave (bars 321–32), building to the first highpoint of the development.[53]

This could be the beginning of the 'recapitulation' of the main theme in D minor. Yet the antecedent [A] is restated, only to be elaborated through melodic sequences (bars 333–54) that touch tonal regions recalling that of the 'turn' (E♭ minor, G♭ minor, E♭ major). A 'march'[54] in A♭ minor follows (bars 355–66), returning to elaborate the initial horn motives (treated with motives from the antecedent of the main theme) that subsequently become predominant (from bar 367). With the emergence of a new motive in the violins (bars 367–80), in obsessive repetitions and sudden changes of tonality, the march episode leads to a sudden 'concentration [*Verdichtung*]'[55] on harmonies of B major to F minor, building to a second highpoint (bars 387–91). This ends in a forceful collapse, with repeated rebounds of the F minor chord, to the exhaustion of all the residual energy (bars 391–7). What follows (strings only) is an episode based on augmentation of the descending triplets from the main theme, over a lengthy dominant pedal (bars 400–20). This serves two functions: one of energetic compensation for the previous highpoint, the other of concluding the development and preparation of the recapitulation of the *Gesangsthema* in D major.

The whole passage from the first highpoint of the development to the recapitulation of the second theme is to Kurth 'a twofold formal event [*formales Doppelereignis*]': the 'restatement' of the main theme is completely 'woven into the development'[56] while the traditional character of the reprise as formal fulfillment has been transferred to the second theme (bar 421). However, its restatement is shortened (bar 458) or rather broken off by a sharp caesura and is followed by a shorter recapitulation of the third theme (bar 459). Instead of reaching a relative culmination, as in the third wave of the exposition (bar 210) and moving to closure, the theme becomes a modulating ascending sequence that through powerful concentration leads to a third highpoint (bars 493–503)—harmonically a polytonal passage combining B♭ minor and E♭ minor chords. A 'chorale'[57] follows (bars 505–16) modulating toward the dominant but also producing energetic compensation after the highpoint.

An extremely lengthy intensification begins once again (from bar 518) on the tonic pedal, at first based on motives from the antecedent [A] of the main theme. After a while, the restatement of the consequent [B] of the main theme enters in the horns (bars 531–41), repeated several times (bars 542–7) in exact correspondence with the chord of the culmination of the main theme, to build a powerful cadence [C] to D minor (bars 548–50) as the fourth highpoint. Here we find a process that Kurth elsewhere names 'over-intensification [*Übersteigerung*]',[58] continuing the culmination and expanding it to a fifth and more powerful highpoint (bar 551). At this point the head of the 'turn' enters in the trumpets at its proper pitch level (bars 553–55), yet over the tonic pedal, and is heard repeatedly (bars 557–62) until it resolves on D as an open fifth (bar 563). After a descending fifth in the trumpets (bars 563–5), the rebounding of the bi-chord in the horns concludes the movement.

To interpret the location of these highpoints I draw on a criterion that can be connected to the concept of 'formal tension [*Formspannung*]',[59] though this does not receive a univocal definition in Kurth's treatise. I refer to the idea of 'formal events in tension toward the . . . final result'.[60] As in the single symphonic wave, the highpoint is the main event towards which what precedes is oriented in terms of tension, so in the whole organisation of a symphonic movement the succession of highpoints establishes a field of forces relying on a web of tensions; these, on one hand, orient the formal organisation and, on the other, help to show the 'meaning' of the symphonic process as a whole. The highpoints are thus in tension with one another. Completing Kurth's indications, it could be said that in the first symphonic wave the tension between the initial horn motives and the highpoint establishes a 'primary' line of force (see Fig. 5.1).

From this highpoint radiates a formal tension to two other highpoints: the first and the fourth (counting from the beginning of the development). Though Kurth does not take into consideration here the thematic-motivic relations, I notice that the first highpoint of the development corresponds to a recapitulation of the antecedent of the main theme [A]. This means, on one hand, that its structural value is crippled and, on the other, that it has to be completed to achieve integration. The fourth highpoint is preceded by intensification, restating the consequent of the main theme [B] while broadening the cadence from the end of the theme [C]. The first and fourth highpoints are also involved in the first line of formal tension, establishing a process of motivic-thematic completion.

In fact, Kurth focuses his attention on another line of tension ('secondary'). This is established starting from the 'turn' and is all the more important, on the one hand, because it makes it possible to 'explain' the particular shaping of the development and all the events following the reprise of the second and third themes, and, on the other hand, because its possible 'structural' meaning is exclusively established by forces and tensions. Kurth touches on this point when he describes the second highpoint of the development. He does not rely on primary parameters but notices a tension that he names 'preparation of the end'.[61] Subsequently he describes the recapitulation of the second and third themes as 'interruption', identifying the third highpoint (as continuation of the third theme) as the decisive 'resumption'[62] of such tension toward the end of the movement. Concerning this 'end', Kurth is aware that the final motivic configuration in the 'over-intensification' following the final cadence in the fourth highpoint restates the initial motive of the 'turn', but he does not clarify the relation between this last climactic passage and the highpoints (second and third) enclosing the reprise. By failing to make such a relationship explicit, his analysis is compromised on this point. A closer motivic analysis shows that both highpoints offer a combination of fragments from the themes (the first and the third, respectively) with a motive consisting of an octave leap, divided into two intervals of fifth and fourth: in the second highpoint it is the motive in the violins (from bar 381); in the third it is the most prominent motive (bars 493–500, violins and woodwinds), though apparently a derivation from the third theme. In this sense, both highpoints 'prepare' the end of the movement, even if only the powerful collapse at the end of the second highpoint (bars

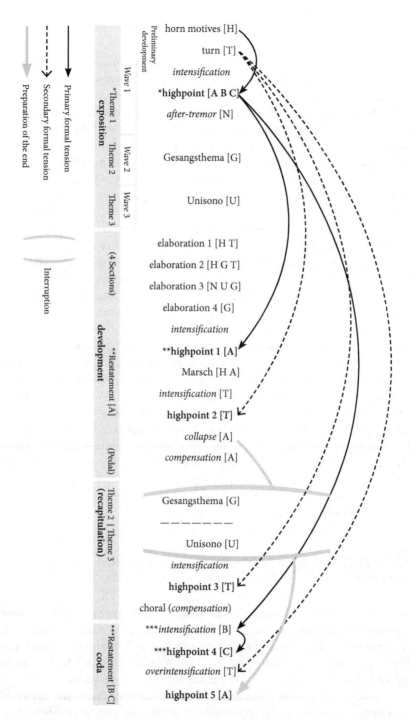

Fig. 5.1 Diagram of formal tensions in Bruckner's Ninth Symphony, first movement

391–95) offers a rather catastrophic prefiguration of the very end of the piece (bars 563–67, trumpets).

My interpretation of this double formal tension—helping to achieve in-tegration on the energetic level—touches on the hermeneutic aspects of the question: the energetic course 'explains' what from the point of view of sonata form theory would be rather difficult to understand, that is, the broad and articulated development including the partial restatement of the main theme, but also the peculiar construction of the coda.[63] Moreover, I underline a rather unusual function of highpoints in late Bruckner. These can no longer be con-sidered 'episodic' or 'rhetorical'. By means of secondary parameters, Bruckner seems to transform structural moments into configurations of force (primary line of tension), while non-structural elements gain a new structural meaning thanks to their forceful significance (secondary line of tension). Consequently the two lines of formal tension come to be assimilated on the strictly ener-getic level, with repercussions for the organisation of the movement. The con-figuration of the coda, where the fourth highpoint (the cadence) is surpassed through over-intensification while the 'turn' is restated, announces, as it were, a 'trans-valuation of values': the secondary tension overwhelms the primary one through its constitution of force. At the same time, the conclusion of the movement offers an interactive overlapping of the two tensions (with relative motivic contents), revealing the structural meaning of both. Thus, highpoints as statistical configurations based on the articulation of secondary parameters become structural markers of a formal organisation that is predominantly based not on abstract typologies relying on sonata form theory, but rather on the concrete energetic deployment: the movement is in fact characterised by continuous alternation of intensification processes building to highpoints and zones of compensation. Compared to this, the traditional formal 'charac-ters' move into the background: though present and still recognisable (mostly as formal 'functions'), they are no longer able to convey the 'meaning' of the formal organisation; on the contrary, they hinder it.

Material Theory of Form and Energetic Organisation in Mahler

While Kurth resolves the question of formal organisation in Bruckner from an energetic point of view, Adorno proposes a 'material theory of form' with recourse to 'the deduction of formal categories from their meaning [*Sinn*]' as a key to understanding Mahler's music. What Adorno claims for Mahler could equally apply to Bruckner: 'The usual abstract formal categories are overlaid with material ones; sometimes the former become specifically the bearer of meaning; sometimes material formal principles are constituted beside or below the abstract ones, which, while continuing to provide the framework and to support the unity, no longer themselves supply a connection in terms of musical meaning.'[64]

The material categories proposed by Adorno—including 'suspension', 'fulfilment', 'breakthrough', and 'collapse'—are not far from Kurth's vocabulary, and it is perhaps no coincidence that in his discussion of the first movement of Mahler's First Symphony Adorno focuses his attention on the relation between the fanfares in the introduction (bars 9–15, 22–26, 36–38, 44–47) and their extraordinary explosion in the development (bar 352).[65] To Adorno it is reductive to think of this passage as reaching a 'climax'; rather, 'the music has expanded with a physical jolt', and there is a 'rupture . . . intervening from outside'. It is a 'breakthrough' that 'affects the entire form'. Subsequently, the 'recapitulation . . . shrinks to a hasty epilogue', while 'the memory of the main idea drives the music swiftly to its end'. In this sense, the outburst 'dictates the entire structure of the movement'.[66]

The analogies with some of the previous remarks on Bruckner's movement are evident. Yet, by interpreting Mahler's movement in Kurth's energetic perspective, the connection to Bruckner becomes more striking. The introduction corresponds to a phase of 'preliminary development' (bars 1–62) where some motivic figures prepare the theme (the fourths) while others quite 'out of context' assume the narrative function of 'foreshadowing'.[67] I refer particularly to the third fanfare (bars 36–39) on the D major triad, while the first (bars 9–12) develops the same semitone harmonic relation (B♭ on A pedal) as the 'turn' (E♭ after D) and the conclusive event (E♭ on D pedal) in Bruckner's movement.

Considering the theme that follows (bars 63–162), it is not so much a quotation as a symphonic re-formulation of the second song of *Lieder eines fahrenden Gesellen* 'Ging heut' Morgen über's Feld'. Its character of 'montage', involving rearrangement of the components through permutation of the original order and combination with elements from the introduction, is the prominent aspect at the narrative level.[68] At the energetic level the main point is rather the comprehensive course with which it conforms, established through the deployment of secondary parameters. In addition to dynamics, instrumental density, and melodic curve, tempo too cooperates in structuring the whole thematic complex in the form of a wave. Mahler indicates '*Tempo-Steigerung*' in the score (from bar 110), but the passage builds a *Steigerung* even in the sense used by Kurth, involving gradual intensification and concentration with a highpoint almost at the end of the exposition (bar 151) corresponding to a motivic derivation [X] that is not present in the original song. In the symphonic re-formulation the highpoint is a 'syntactic climax' (employed as reversal to closure) that coincides not only with the 'statistical climax' but also with a 'tempo-culmination' (bars 151–59). It is particularly these aspects that in Mahler mark the aesthetic and structural distance between the symphonic idea and the strophic conception of the Lied.

Given that Mahler prescribes repetition of the whole theme (a traditional character of exposition), what follows (from bar 163) can only be seen as development. Tempo, timbre, density, dynamics, durations denote a 'material' continuity with the introduction. Mahler lingers on this development, where proper elaboration is confined to the motive [X] in the flutes in combination with the fourth intervals of the introduction (from bar 165). What emerges is rather the gradual entrance of the 'new theme',[69] or rather new 'motives' in a germinal state (bars 167–202, cellos), with insertions where fragments from the introduction concentrate and overlap one another (bars 189–98). The return of the initial tempo of the theme (bar 207, *Sehr gemächlich*) suggests an aspect of 'recapitulation', but the movement still maintains the character of a development, into which hints of a recapitulation are 'woven' in more radically when compared to Bruckner. The 'new motives' evolve in two directions: from the last elaboration in the cellos (bars 201–2) derives a 'new fanfare' which includes the descending fourth (bars 209–16, horns), while the major 'variant' of the motive (bars 220–24) develops a counterpoint within the texture of the Lied theme, which appears in a new permutation, giving place, at times, to the 'variant', that undergoes further development (from bar 257). With the return to the minor (from bars 304–6), the 'new theme' proper combines with more vigorous melodic figurations (bars 310–16) anticipating the main theme of the Finale. Through haunting motives based on an octave leap (from bar 317) the movement becomes a preparation for a climactic restatement, not of the main theme but of the third fanfare from the introduction: this appears the first time in D♭ major (bars 323–25), followed by a more accurate prefiguration of the main theme of the Finale, here developed as a further variant of the 'new theme'. A sudden *pianissimo* represents what Mahler himself indicates in the score as '*Beginn der Steigerung*' (bar 338). Melodic values are here virtually unaltered and the deployment of this intensification relies on secondary parameters through dynamic *crescendo* and instrumental concentration, while the timbral quality of massed horns accompanies the last phase of the *Steigerung* with repeated triplet notes (bars 348–51). The resulting highpoint is the apotheosis (Adorno's 'breakthrough') corresponding to the restatement of the fanfare from the introduction starting in D major (with A in the bass) and continuing, *accelerando*, to the dominant chord (bars 352–57) which resolves on the restatement of the 'new' fanfare [NF] from the development (bars 358–63).

This double highpoint is followed by elaborations based on the 'new theme' (bars 364–69) and fragments of the Lied theme, until a short intensification corresponding to an ascending modulating sequence (bars 378–83, woodwinds) establishes a high level of dynamics (from bar 383) that will be maintained until the end of the movement. Therein the main theme in D major appears in the trumpets and then in the woodwinds and strings. Even the last wave is characterised by '*Tempo-Steigerung*', but starting from a faster tempo than in the exposition. Now the modular components of the theme that preceded its culmination in the exposition are restated in the same order, but tempo and secondary parameters do not permit the syntactic reversal to achieve closure (bars 431–36), involving it in a further intensification (from bar 436), until the theme undergoes its peculiar 'liquidation' (in Schoenberg's terms)[70] through reduction to the fourth interval. In the timpani this becomes a peremptory gesture of quieting (bars 436–40). Twice the movement attempts to escape, only to be silenced by the timpani strokes in two striking general pauses (bars 443–47), until it succeeds, reaching the last cadence with the fourth interval (now ascending) in the bass (bars 449–50).

It is not difficult to identify the role of energetic organisation in Mahler's symphonic movement, based on the location of highpoints along tension lines establishing a field of forces. By mapping such tensions, the connection with the strategies adopted in Bruckner's movement can be further defined. Here too, the preliminary development is the point of departure for two different tensions (see Fig. 5.2).

The first ('primary') is triggered by the initial fourth motives and prepares the theme, which develops a symphonic wave reaching the highpoint near the end of the process. The second ('secondary') emerges in the series of fanfares, appearing as rather episodic and is to some extent 'doubled' by the new fanfare in the development. Such secondary tensions have their goal in the climax of the development, combining the apotheosis of both fanfares into an uncommon 'cadence of highpoints'.

The tension of the main theme interacts, then, with the entrance of the 'new theme' in the development. Before the highpoint, the 'restatement' of the Lied theme is confined to some modular arrangements of its components, with insertions where the new theme is in relief. After the highpoint the 'new theme' is still combined with the Lied theme; this becomes predominant only when the tension toward its true culmination is reactivated. Retrospectively, this culmination at the end of the exposition can be characterised as a 'preparation of the end'. Yet the impetus triggered by the 'breakthrough' combines with the tension of the theme to its highpoint, adding up its force. This is the reason that now the theme cannot achieve closure: the increased force involves the motives of the 'closure' in a rush, with a tempo acceleration that only the forceful gesture in the timpani can counteract.

Once the analogies have been identified, it is possible to clarify the extent to which Mahler's composition emerges, right from the outset, as more radically nominalist than Bruckner's less traditional sonata movement. The fact that motivic and embryonic thematic materials proliferate in the 'preliminary development' as well as in the development proper (though derived from rather homogeneous musical material) gives the decisive impetus to the dissolution or at least to the weakening of primary thematic centres. Moreover, the shaping of tempo, through its true articulation, does away with regularity, still predominant in Bruckner—with the exceptions of *ritenuto* before highpoints are

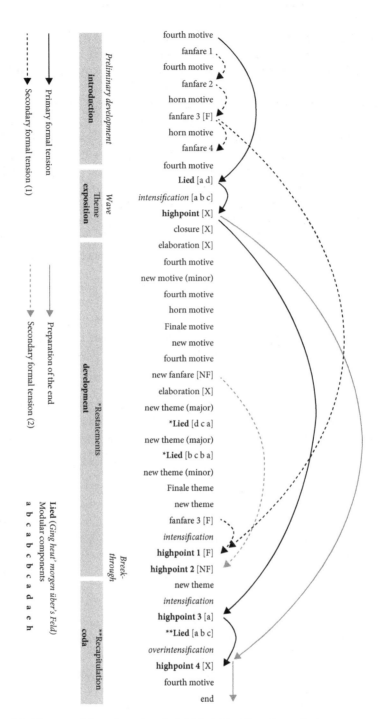

Fig. 5.2 Diagram of formal tensions in Mahler's First Symphony, first movement

reached (Ninth Symphony, first movement, bars 61–62), and gradual *accelerando* in lengthy episodes of intensification (bars 325–32). More generally, secondary parameters come radically to the fore, emphasising the secondary and episodic thematic centres over the primary ones through deployment of configurations of force. Adorno too connected the category of 'breakthrough' first of all to the fact that the fanfare explodes 'quite out of scale with the orchestra's previous sound or even the preceding crescendo'.[71] In fact, the instrumentation represents the most significant innovation of Mahler's symphonies, giving the main highpoint the effect of a shock with the outburst of statistical values (density and dynamics) being enforced by the quality of timbre—a parameter that in Mahler assumes an uncommonly constructive role. Yet the structural meaning of the highpoint in terms of formal tension can be fully explained only by evaluating the comprehensive energetic organisation of which it is the statistical turning point.

Referring to the second (although he mistakenly speaks of the 'first') movement of Mahler's Fifth Symphony (1902), Meyer claimed that it is difficult to identify a 'single decisive syntactic climax' in the 'succession of more or less equal, and local, syntactic turning points', while 'the main statistical climax' can be easily recognised, because Mahler indicated '*Höhepunkt*' in the score.[72] I would ask whether the presence of such an indication does not rather suggest the opposite conclusion: that Mahler's First and Fifth symphonies are different steps in an evolution. While late Bruckner takes the direction of nominalism by means of energetic strategies, Mahler initially conforms to the same principle only to develop it further and expand the sphere of its influence. The First Symphony, with the prominent climax in the first movement, represents an early phase. Subsequently Mahler will surpass the predictability of the energetic course that is so peculiar to Bruckner, moving toward an increasingly greater compositional freedom. Yet the deployment of the energetic organisation will remain a decisive element until the Adagio of the Tenth Symphony. A greater attention to these aspects would be crucial to historicise Mahler's symphonic oeuvre.

Notes

1. See Gilliam, "The Annexation of Anton Bruckner"; Solvik, "The International Bruckner Society and the N.S.D.A.P."; Brotbeck, "Verdrängung und Abwehr", 364.
2. Adorno, *Mahler: A Musical Physiognomy*, 3–4.
3. An opposition between Mahler and Bruckner had already been created by music critics in Mahler's time. See Wandel, *Die Rezeption der Symphonien Gustav Mahlers*; Celestini, "Der Trivialitätsvorwurf an Gustav Mahler".
4. Revers, "Gustav Mahler und Anton Bruckner", 265.

5. See Cohrs, "Vorwort", VII; Wilkens, "Vorwort", V.

6. Bekker, *Die Sinfonie von Beethoven bis Mahler*, 20.

7. Adorno, *Mahler*, 62.

8. Adorno, *Mahler*, 44.

9. I use this term to refer to the idea of a logical and coherent organisation of the musical work. Adorno always used the term '*Sinn*' so as to avoid the idea of 'reference', which is unequivocally expressed in '*Bedeutung*'. For an in-depth discussion of this problem see Borio, "Über Sinn und Bedeutung in der Musik".

10. Newman, "The Climax of Music". 284.

11. See Meyer, "Exploiting Limits".

12. See Agawu, "Structural 'Highpoints' in Schumann's *Dichterliebe*".

13. Kaplan, "Temporal Fusion and Climax in the Symphonies of Mahler", 215.

14. Newman, "The Climax of Music", 285–86.

15. Newman, "The Climax of Music", 292.

16. Meyer, "Exploiting Limits", 184.

17. Meyer, "Exploiting Limits", 189.

18. Meyer, "Exploiting Limits", 194.

19. Meyer, "Exploiting Limits", 191.

20. Meyer, "Exploiting Limits", 188, 195.

21. Meyer, "Exploiting Limits", 199.

22. Agawu, "Structural 'Highpoints' in Schumann's *Dichterliebe*", 160.

23. Newman, "The Climax of Music", 283.

24. Agawu, "Structural 'Highpoints' in Schumann's *Dichterliebe*", 160.

25. Agawu, "Structural 'Highpoints' in Schumann's *Dichterliebe*", 176.

26. Agawu, "Tonal Strategy in the First Movement of Mahler's Tenth Symphony", 231.

27. See Agawu, *Music as Discourse*, 61–73.

28. See Hopkins, *Closure and Mahler's Music*, 29–30.

29. Hopkins, *Closure and Mahler's Music*, 29.

30. Hopkins, *Closure and Mahler's Music*, 31.

31. Hopkins, *Closure and Mahler's Music*, 64–155.

32. Hopkins, *Closure and Mahler's Music*, 7.

33. Hopkins, *Closure and Mahler's Music*, 5.

34. Kaplan, "The Interaction of Diatonic Collections in the Adagio of Mahler's Tenth Symphony".

35. Kaplan, "Temporal Fusion and Climax in the Symphonies of Mahler".

36. Krebs, "Zum Verhältnis von musikalischer Syntax und Höhepunktsgestaltung", 33.

37. Kurth, *Bruckner*, 239.

38. Kurth, *Bruckner*, 239.

39. Kurth, *Bruckner*, 234.

40. Kurth, *Bruckner*, 235–36.

41. Kurth, *Bruckner*, 249.

42. Kurth, *Bruckner*, 273–74.

43. Kurth, *Bruckner*, 661–707.

44. Kurth, *Bruckner*, 320–22, 445–46, 450–51, 558–61.

45. I refer to the critical edition: Bruckner, *IX. Symphonie D-Moll*.

46. Kurth, *Bruckner*, 279.

47. Kurth, *Bruckner*, 281.

48. Kurth, *Bruckner*, 682–83.

49. Kurth, *Bruckner*, 685.

50. Kurth, *Bruckner*, 450.

51. Kurth, *Bruckner*, 282.

52. Kurth, *Bruckner*, 689.

53. Kurth, *Bruckner*, 693.

54. Kurth, *Bruckner*, 697.

55. Kurth, *Bruckner*, 700.

56. Kurth, *Bruckner*, 695.

57. Kurth, *Bruckner*, 703.

58. Kurth, *Bruckner*, 410.

59. Kurth, *Bruckner*, 246.

60. Kurth, *Bruckner*, 696.

61. Kurth, *Bruckner*, 696.

62. Kurth, *Bruckner*, 702.

63. For a different but in my opinion problematic formal division of this development see Steinbeck, *Anton Bruckner: Neunte Symphonie*, 80–82.

64. Adorno, *Mahler*, 44–45.

65. I refer to the critical edition: Mahler, *Symphonie Nr. 1 in vier Sätzen für großes Orchester*.

66. Adorno, *Mahler*, 5–6.

67. Kaplan, "Temporal Fusion and Climax", 216.

68. Borio, "Le parole cancellate e le tracce", 23.

69. Adorno, *Mahler*, 13.

70. Schoenberg, *Fundamentals of Musical Composition*, 58.

71. Adorno, *Mahler*, 4–5.

72. Meyer, "Exploiting Limits", 199.

6

Die Meistersinger in Mahler's Seventh Symphony

Anna Stoll Knecht

In November 1899, when Mahler was rehearsing the first uncut production of Wagner's *Die Meistersinger von Nürnberg* in Vienna,[1] he declared to his friend Natalie Bauer-Lechner, 'I tell you, what a piece ["*das* is ein Werk"]! If the whole of German art were to disappear, it could be recognized and reconstructed from this one work. It almost makes everything else seem worthless and superfluous.'[2] These words strongly resonate with Hans Sachs's famous speech at the end of the opera, in which he exhorts the people to 'honor their German Masters', so that 'even if the Holy Roman Empire should dissolve into mist, there would yet remain sacred German art'. And if German art were to disappear, added Mahler, one could reconstruct it from *Meistersinger*, which would make this work the essence of German art.

Wagner's operas held a privileged position in Mahler's conducting repertory, and *Meistersinger* in particular was among the most performed works at the Vienna court opera during Mahler's tenure.[3] His rendition of this opera in Prague in 1885 had been acclaimed. Mahler went on conducting *Meistersinger* each year between 1891 and 1895 when he was in Hamburg, and, shortly after becoming Director of the Vienna Court Opera in 1897, he performed uncut versions of the *Ring* and *Tristan*, followed by *Meistersinger* in 1899.[4]

Yet it is not only as a conductor that Mahler interpreted *Meistersinger* but also as a composer, particularly in his Seventh Symphony. Premiered on 19 September 1908 in Prague under his baton, the Seventh was initially rather well received.[5] It then progressively acquired the status of 'problem child' in the Mahlerian canon, and it seems that the Finale, which openly refers to *Meistersinger*, lies at the core of the Seventh's negative reception.[6] As if to reinforce the perception of this connection, on 7 October 1909 in Amsterdam, Mahler chose to open a concert including his own Seventh with the *Meistersinger* Overture.[7] This was the last time Mahler ever conducted

This chapter is an expanded version of a paper read at the Mahler Centenary Conference held at the University of Surrey, July 7–9 2011. It is dedicated to the late Robert Bailey, with my heartfelt gratitude. I would like to thank warmly Michael Beckerman, Stanley Boorman, Warren Darcy, Julian Johnson, William Kinderman and Richard Kramer for their insights and precious comments.

his Seventh Symphony. It could have turned out to be an even more extensive Mahler-Wagner programme, since Mahler initially intended to include
Wagner's *Faust Overture* and *Siegfried Idyll* as well.[8]

While the *Meistersinger*-like quality of the Finale has been duly noted by
commentators since the Seventh's premiere, the question of the nature and
function of this allusion at the core of the Symphony has not been explored
in depth.[9] This chapter argues two points. First, that Mahler's clear gesture
toward *Meistersinger* in the Finale prompts the listener to hear other elements throughout the Symphony in relationship to Wagner's opera. Second,
the connections between these two works crystallise around the character of
Beckmesser, the pedantic critic who initially claims to know what makes art
meaningful but whose own music is ultimately perceived as meaningless.

Since the subtle echoes of *Meistersinger* in the Seventh are most easily heard
against the backdrop of Mahler's blatant references to Wagner in the last movement, the following section will provide a detailed overview of the Finale.

The *Meistersinger* References in Mahler's Finale

Formally, the ritornello of the Seventh's Rondo-Finale may be heard as a condensed version of the first part of the *Meistersinger* Overture, where the positions of the constitutive elements are inverted (see Fig. 6.1).

The introduction to Mahler's ritornello shows traces of a distant connection with Wagner's theme B (Ex. 6.2); the ritornello theme (MA1 + MA2)[10]
deliberately points towards the *Meistersinger* opening theme (Ex. 6.1); and the
perfect authentic cadence closing the ritornello clearly alludes to the cadence
ending the initial section of Wagner's Overture (Ex. 6.3). I begin by examining some details of the sonic relationship between Mahler's ritornello (MA1 +
MA2, bars 7–23) and Wagner's opening theme.

Mahler's theme shares several characteristics with Wagner's: the same
key (C major), the same metre (4/4), and the same rhythmic progression for
three bars. Moreover, both themes are built on related thematic material: a

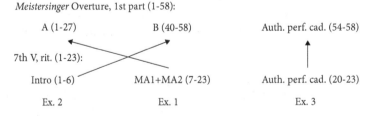

Fig. 6.1 Initial part of the *Meistersinger* Overture (bb. 1–58) and Mahler's ritornello
(bb. 1–23)

Ex. 6.1 Mahler's ritornello theme (MA1 + MA2) framing Wagner's theme (A)

descending fourth (a in Wagner, ma in Mahler); the cells al and mal, whose relationship is revealed when they appear for the second time (MA1, bar 9, lower staff, and A, bar 5); the cells b (A, bar 2) and mb (MA1, bar 8), sharing a similar melodic contour and the same rhythm; and an ascending scale (c [A, bar 3] and mc [MA2, bar 16]).

Each section of Mahler's theme offers a different variation on Wagner's theme. The first section (MA1) contains Wagner's cells a, al, and b—varied to a certain degree—but not the ascending scale c. The second section (MA2) quotes a shortened version of Wagner's theme (where cell b has been omitted), which actually appears, rhythmically varied, in *Meistersinger* Act I, when the congregation begins the chorale 'Da zu dir der Heiland kam' (Ex. 6.1, bottom line). Mahler quotes the theme in a varied form already used by Wagner, but he leaves a trace of this transformation: the omitted cell (b) appears two bars later (MA2, bar 18), in a diminished form, hidden within the ascending scale mc. We should note that here Mahler did not use his own variant of the cell

Ex. 6.2 Wagner's theme B and the introductions to the Seventh's first and last
movements

Ex. 6.3 Perfect authentic cadences in the *Meistersinger* Overture and in Mahler's Finale

b (mb), but instead directly quotes Wagner's cell (b). The Wagnerian mate-
rial is transformed, but the similarity of critical parameters strongly associates
Mahler's ritornello with Wagner's Overture.[11] That this intertextual allusion to
Meistersinger in the ritornello was both intentional and meant to be heard is
borne out by Mahler's decision to perform Wagner's Overture before his own
Seventh in Amsterdam.

At the beginning of the Finale, the ritornello is introduced with a few bars
that may relate to Wagner's theme B in a subtle way (Ex. 6.2). The connection
is barely audible, but these two 'fanfare' motives are actually built on similar

material—a dactylic cell (‒ ˘ ˘) on repeated notes followed by a major ascending arpeggio—and orchestrated in a similar way (brass and woodwinds).

The presence of Wagnerian material can be traced here, but it is radically transformed—which questions the very existence of this connection. Moreover, the dactylic cell opening Mahler's Finale is a rhythmic reminiscence of the dark, funeral-march beginning of the Seventh's first movement (Ex. 6.2, line 3), which could suggest that the referential aspect of the Finale's introduction is only internal. However, I propose to hear Mahler's accelerated and harmonically unstable opening in the Finale as a transformed version of the stable, solemn, and diatonic theme heard in Wagner's Overture, marked *sehr gehalten* and bearing the weight of a long tradition.[12] This connection fits well with Mahler's use, in his Finale, of music associated with the Mastersinger's Guild in Wagner's opera—and I come back to this question below.

Finally, the perfect authentic cadence closing Mahler's ritornello unmistakably evokes the cadence ending Wagner's theme B (see Ex. 6.3).[13] Both cadences arise from an ascending scale (belonging to Wagner's theme A [c] and Mahler's ritornello theme [mc], see Ex. 6.1) followed by its inverted and diminished form. Mahler's descending scale (mc inv.) has the same pitches as Wagner's— except for the F♯—but it is placed differently with respect to the bass motion, and represents different scale degrees. In my previous example, the differences between Mahler's and Wagner's motives were more striking than their similarities. Here, on the contrary, Mahler's gesture towards Wagner is so audible that it almost conceals his transformation of the borrowed material.

These cadences are built on similar material but they do not have the same structural function. In *Meistersinger*, it concludes an important part of the Overture. In the Finale of the Seventh, the cadence appears directly at the end of the ritornello's theme, and its excessively affirmative character, reinforced by accents on each note, seems disproportionate to its position in the musical progression: it comes too quickly to fulfill the need for a strong closing. Besides, this cadence appears so often throughout the movement that it seems eventually to lose its conclusive strength.[14]

Mahler not only alludes to this 'Mastersingers cadence' in the Finale, but, twice in the movement (bars 127/Rehearsal Fig. 239 and 546/Rehearsal Fig. 291), the authentic cadence expected between each section of the ritornello theme (cf. bars 14–15) is replaced by a deceptive motion: the dominant seventh chord in C major moves to a ♯iv 6/5 (or vi + ♯6) half-diminished chord, instead of resolving to the tonic. The first occurrence appears in Ex. 6.4 (bars 127–28).[15]

This progression plays a crucial role in *Meistersinger* Act III: it is part of the harmonisation of the 'Wahn' motive, the first few notes heard in the Prelude to Act III, which eventually become the main motive for Sachs's 'Wahn' monologue (III, 1). This deceptive progression appears in different keys throughout the opera, but it is found in C major—just as in Mahler's Finale—shortly after the end of Walther's

Ex. 6.4 Deceptive cadences in Mahler's ritornello and *Meistersinger* III, 5

prize song (III, 5, see Ex. 6.4).[16] The crowd joins in to urge Walther's victory, and the harmony is founded on a G dominant seventh chord moving to ♯iv7 (here with F♯ at the bass) instead of resolving to the tonic. The harmonic progression is identical in both cases, as well as the trill on the leading tone B resolving to C.

The close relationship between these two passages is clearly audible, but here, again, the Wagnerian material is reinterpreted. In *Meistersinger*, the half-diminished chord interrupts the authentic cadence, but the transition is made softly, *pianissimo, dolcissimo*, and *rallentando*. In Mahler's Finale, however, the half-diminished chord abruptly negates the expected resolution: the *piano* dynamic quickly leads to a *fortissimo* on the ♯iv6/5, marked >. In *Meistersinger*, this deceptive progression is associated with Sachs, and Mahler's use of it in the middle of his own 'Mastersinger theme'—the ritornello—resonates with the idea, suggested in Wagner's opera, that Sachs represents the essence of an accomplished Mastersinger, who acknowledges the value of both tradition and innovation.[17]

What Remains from *Meistersinger* in Mahler's Finale?

The first part of Wagner's Overture mainly exposes themes that will be associated with the Mastersinger's guild throughout the opera (except Walther's theme, which appears only once in the Overture (bars 27–38)). By using this material in his ritornello, Mahler alludes to the traditional side of *Meistersinger*, to the tradition of 'sacred German art'. This tradition is represented by two opposing characters in the opera: on the one hand, Beckmesser, the self-appointed guardian of conventions and rules, who dismisses Walther's song because it is meaningless ('unsinnig'); on the other hand, Sachs, the cobbler-poet, who eventually shows how meaningful Walther's innovative art is because it sounds 'so old, and yet so new' (II, 3). Beckmesser represents the pedantic aspect of tradition and Sachs its wisdom. The idea of tradition in Mahler's Seventh seems to be mostly represented in caricature, and therefore by Beckmesser rather than by Sachs. In fact, even when the latter is evoked, as in the deceptive cadence discussed above, the allusion is made in caricature, 'à la Beckmesser'.

Mahler not only transforms the Wagnerian material itself but also its function in the form. The positions of Wagner's constitutive elements in the musical narrative are inverted in Mahler's ritornello (Fig. 6.1), which thereby alters their original function. We have a similar inversion on a larger scale: in Mahler, a ritornello referring to an operatic Overture is endlessly repeated in the last movement of the Symphony. Wagner's beginning becomes Mahler's ending.

Introductions and cadences, beginnings and endings, constitute the main substance of Mahler's references to *Meistersinger* in his Finale. The ritornello's introduction leads to a theme clearly referring to an operatic Overture (Ex. 6.1), and these two successive openings prompt the expectation that the curtain will rise and that a story will be enacted on stage.[18] Instead, these beginnings lead directly to a strong concluding gesture. In fact, the whole Symphony is characterised by frequent intrusions of these 'rhetorical moments' that seem to announce important structural points in the musical flow, but without really leading anywhere. The main characteristic of these moments is their double function, introductory and concluding at the same time (like the introduction to the Finale's ritornello or the beginning of the second *Nachtmusik*, for example). This blurring of the boundaries between beginnings and endings is puzzling and leads us to question their meaning and function.[19]

With *Meistersinger* in mind, Mahler's play on the use of formal markers in the Seventh evokes Beckmesser's outraged reaction to Walther's trial song in Act I:

> Where to begin, when there was no beginning or end to it? . . . Who might find an end there? . . . I will accuse him only of 'blind meaning'; could a meaning be more meaningless?

And the Masters answer: 'It was completely meaningless! I must admit it was impossible to predict its end'; and later they ask: 'who calls this singing?'[20] According to the Mastersingers, a song must be clearly marked with a beginning and an end—the listener must even be able to 'predict the end'—in order for it to be meaningful. In other words, an artwork must be understandable rationally, and structural markers should function as a guarantee of musical meaning.

Returning to the Seventh, I propose to interpret Mahler's particular use of introductory and concluding gestures in the light of Beckmesser's compositional lesson. It is as if Mahler, by saturating his Symphony with rhetorical markers, was exploring Beckmesser's statement that beginnings and ends can provide musical meaning. But, instead of shaping the musical discourse and making it more intelligible formally, Mahler's use of structural markers questions their traditional function; thereby revealing the limits of Beckmesser's lesson.[21]

I see another parallel between Mahler and Beckmesser. At the end of *Meistersinger*, Beckmesser steals the poem of his rival Walther, thinking that it was composed by Master Hans Sachs, and because of his inability to read Sachs's handwriting, his deficient memory, and alleged lack of poetic talent, he makes slight changes in the initial text that have considerable impact on the global meaning of the poem. The Merker omits a letter here, adds one there, inverts two syllables, does not demarcate the words correctly; and the story of Adam and Eve in Paradise becomes the story of a gleaming man hanging from a tree, looking at a woman who is as pale as a cabbage. We may wonder how Mahler perceived Beckmesser's interpretation of the poem and if the idea that local changes deeply affect the meaning of the whole appealed to him. In a way, Mahler and Beckmesser both 'borrow' material from another composer and radically transform its original meaning. I shall come back to the potential implications of this comparison.

If Beckmesser-the-Critic is a caricature of a traditionalist, the serenade of Beckmesser-the-Composer in Act II (sc. 6) provides the thematic material for the most dissonant moment of the opera, the riot that breaks out on St John's Eve in the streets of Nuremberg, culminating in striking quartal harmony that originates in the melodic fourths of his song, themselves derived from the tuning of his lute.[22] I suggest that Mahler's use of quartal harmony in the Seventh (especially in the first movement), often perceived as one of the most innovative aspects of the work, was—at least partly—inspired by the music performed by the most traditionalist of Wagner's characters.

Quartal Harmony in the Seventh and *Meistersinger*

The First Movement of the Seventh

The cell heard at the beginning of the Seventh, which appears in most themes of the Symphony, is gradually transformed throughout the slow introduction; and just before the Allegro section (bars 45–46), the descending seventh is divided into two symmetrical fourths (x', Ex. 6.5, line 2).[23] At this point, three trumpets enter in imitation, and melodic fourths are gradually stacked over an F♯ pedal, building the chord F♯–B–E–A.

In terms of tonal relationships, this fourth chord (F♯–B–E–A) functions as a dominant seventh chord with a suspended fourth in E minor (B–E–F♯–A, here inverted to F♯–A–B–E), which resolves to B–E–A♯ (bar 48) instead of the expected dominant chord (F♯–A–B–D♯). If we keep the resonance of the F♯ in

Ex. 6.5 The first movement of the Seventh, end of the introduction (bb. 45–50)

the bass—since it is a pedal—this B–E–A♯ could be heard as a V of V in E minor ([F♯]–B–E–A♯), where the suspended fourth (B) would be heard simultaneously with its resolution, the major third (A♯). This B–E–A♯ itself resolves to an E minor tonic chord by simply shifting A♯ to B (already heard in the previous chord), when the main theme of the movement enters (bar 50).

To summarise, this progression (bars 47–50) could be interpreted as a dominant chord with a suspended fourth that does not resolve, moving to an altered pre-dominant chord (V of V) resolving directly to the tonic without passing through the dominant. But at the same time, the 'bass' (or the lowest voice, since there is no real bass here) moves by fourths (F♯3–B3–E4, see trumpet 3 at bars 47–50), which sounds like a pre-dominant – dominant – tonic progression in E. In other words, the bass motion (ii–V–i) contradicts the global harmonic progression (V–II♯ – i).[24]

The contradictory aspects of this harmonic interpretation—expected resolutions diverted, suspensions co-existing with their resolutions—are balanced by the straightforwardness of contrapuntal motions. F♯–B–E–A is a fourth chord produced by the successive entrances of the three trumpets, originating from the melodic activity. At bar 48, A shifts to A♯ and F♯ is no longer held. Two bars later, when the main theme of the movement starts, A♯ resolves to B and a real bass enters on E4 (cellos, bar 50). This particular moment in the introduction is developed throughout the movement, and fourth chords built the same way—arising from chains of melodic fourths—appear at crucial points in the musical form: in the exposition (from bar 105/Rehearsal Fig. 13), in the recapitulation (from bar 456/Rehearsal Fig. 57), and in the coda (from bar 531/Rehearsal Fig. 66). To briefly summarise what happens at these moments, the chain of fourths (deployed harmonically in the exposition and recapitulation, but not in the coda) has F♯–B–E–A as common notes, and it is expanded below to C♯ in the exposition (C♯–F♯–B–E–A), and up to G in the coda (F♯–B–E–A–**D**–**G**).

Meistersinger Act II, sc. 7

The chaotic Finale of Act II is built on the theme of Beckmesser's serenade, used as a cantus firmus. As Robert Bailey has shown, the climax of the riot is marked by successive fugal entries on pitches corresponding to the strings of Beckmesser's lute, E–A–D–G–C (resolving to B, to follow the correct pattern of his lute, E–A–D–G–**B**–[E]) (see Ex. 6.6).[25]

As in Mahler's Seventh, a fourth chord built on an F♯ pedal (F♯–B–E–A–D–G–C), arising from melodic fourths, is eventually resolved to E (major in Wagner, minor in Mahler). But as opposed to what happens in the Seventh, where expected resolutions are denied, Wagner's fourth chord moves to a dominant seventh chord that resolves on the tonic of E major with the beginning of the serenade's theme (C resolves to B, and the suspended fourth E resolves to

Ex. 6.6 *Meistersinger* II, 7 'Auf, schreit zu Hilfe: Mord und Zeter, herbei!'

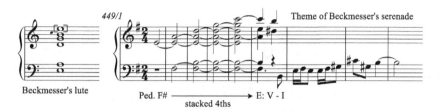

D♯). Beckmesser's serenade may have been a source of inspiration for Mahler's use of melodic and harmonic fourths in the Seventh, but there is no direct allusion to it in the score. In fact, the connection appears more clearly in a sketch that did not make its way into the final version of the Seventh.

Discarded Sketches for the Seventh

The manuscripts with sketches and drafts for the Seventh comprise numerous fragments of unidentified music which have previously escaped scrutiny. One of the main sources is a small pocket sketchbook containing material used in the Sixth, Seventh, and Ninth symphonies as well as a significant quantity of unidentified material.[26] Two pages in the sketchbook show striking connections to Beckmesser's serenade (fols. 5v and 6v). The upper voice on folio 6v (bars 4ff) strongly recalls the odd coloratura that ends each *Stollen* of the serenade (on 'We-e-e-e-er-ben'; see Ex. 6.7).

In the sketchbook, fifths replace the fourths of the serenade, but the melodic contour is the same.[27] We may go further and hear a relationship between the alternation of open fifths, in Mahler's sketchbook, and the prelude that Beckmesser plays on his lute to calm his anxiety before starting his serenade (II, 6; Ex. 6.7, second system).[28] In addition, we may note that this page (6v) starts with the cell found at the beginning of Mahler's ritornello (ma, cf. Ex. 6.1)—but placed here on different scale steps (and not on 1–5–1)—which establishes a relationship between the 'Beckmesser sketch' and the Finale of the Seventh.

Folio 5v begins with a melodic fragment that shares motivic connections with the first movement of the Sixth Symphony, with the Finale of the Seventh and—even if the link may appear tenuous here—with Beckmesser's serenade (see Ex. 6.8).

This fragment was probably not conceived as an inversion of Beckmesser's serenade, but since the presence of this character is so strongly suggested on the following folio (6v, Ex. 6.7), the connection is worth noticing it here as well.

This is not the only case of a sketch for the Seventh pointing towards both the Sixth and *Meistersinger* at the same time. Three folios (1r, 1v, and 2r)

Ex. 6.7 Mahler's sketchbook (6v) and Beckmesser's serenade

Ex. 6.8 Mahler's sketchbook (5v), Beckmesser's serenade, the Sixth and Seventh symphonies

included in a group of five separate leaves show material related to the first movement of the Sixth, to the Finale of the Seventh, and to *Meistersinger*.[29] Close examination of the compositional materials for the Seventh reveals first that its composition was deeply entangled with that of the Sixth; and second that Mahler's project was strongly grounded in a dialogue with works from the past. This referential aspect should therefore be taken as an important key to interpreting the work. The fact that Beckmesserian references are more explicit in the preliminary sketches than in the final version suggests that Mahler, while openly alluding to the Mastersingers Guild theme in the Finale, sought to obscure his interest in Beckmesser's music.

E minor to C major: from St John's Eve to St John's Day in *Meistersinger*

The introduction to the Finale of the Seventh is in E minor (bars 1–6), and leads to the ritornello theme in C major (bars 7–23). This recapitulates the tonal progression of the whole Symphony, which starts with a first movement in E minor (even if the introduction is in B minor), and ends with a Finale in C major. This path from E to C is also found in *Meistersinger*, at crucial points of the dramatic development. Act II ends on St John's Eve with the riot that follows Beckmesser's serenade to Eva. Alone in his workshop, on St John's Day, Sachs reflects upon the causes of this collective madness: 'God knows, how that befell! A goblin ['Kobold'] must have helped: a glowworm could not find its mate; it set the trouble in motion. It was the elder tree: St John's Eve ['Johannisnacht']! But now has come St John's day ['Johannistag']!' (III, 1). Sachs's evocation of the passage from St John's Eve to St John's Day is musically signaled by the modulation from E (major here) to C major (see Ex. 6.9).

This E may be heard as a reference to Beckmesser: it is the lowest string of his lute, and the fundamental of the fourth chord associated with its tuning (E – A – D – G – B, see Ex. 6.6). As noted above, the fugal entries leading to the climax of the riot closing Act II start on E and follow the pattern of Beckmesser's strings. Right after the last fugal entry on B, we hear the serenade's theme at the bass in E major (see Ex. 6.6). Moreover, Beckmesser's leading role in the chaotic events on St John's Eve is recalled in the 'Wahn' monologue by the theme of his serenade, heard when Sachs evokes the 'Kobold' (goblin) that helped cause the riot.[30]

In the final scene of the opera, Beckmesser offers his own interpretation of Walther's poem using much the same melody as that of his serenade to Eva. But whereas this melody was initially sung in G major (II, 6), it is now transposed to E minor. His performance arouses a moment of collective confusion: 'My, what is this? Has he lost his mind? Did we understand correctly? What does this mean?' say the People and the Mastersingers (III, 5). Walther then sings his own prize song properly, in C major, and the crowd is unified by a feeling of enlightenment ('Yes, indeed, I see, it makes a difference if one sings correctly,' and 'What a difference the right words and the proper delivery make!') This shift from E minor to C major evokes the light overcoming the dark night imposed upon the people's spirit by Beckmesser's own interpretation of Walther's poem.

In a Wagnerian context, it is difficult not to mention another work where the shift from E minor to C major has a revealing power—the *Ring*. We hear this shift when Brünnhilde is awakened form her long sleep at the end of *Siegfried* (III, 3), and at the end of *Götterdämmerung*, when Siegfried is dying

Ex. 6.9 *Meistersinger* III, 1 "Wahn, Wahn, überall Wahn!"

Ex. **6.10** *Götterdämmerung* III, 2 and *Meistersinger* III, 5

and remembers Brünnhilde (III, 2; see Ex. 6.10): 'Brünnhilde! Heilige Braut! Wach' auf! Öffne dein Auge!' The E minor to C major progression heard on 'Wach' auf!' is melodically expressed with an ascending fourth, which brings us back to *Meistersinger* (even if the harmonisation is different). In the final scene of the opera (III, 5), the crowd greets Sachs with the motet 'Wach' auf!' using the same melodic cell:

> Awake! The dawn is drawing near; singing in the green grove is a blissful nightingale, its voice ringing through hill and valley; night is receding in the west, the day arises in the east, the morning's ardent red glow penetrates the gloomy clouds. Hail! Sachs! Hail to you, Hans Sachs!

The light of the rising day clears the clouds at the end of *Meistersinger*, and Nuremberg salutes Sachs as Brünnhilde welcomes the sun in *Siegfried* ('Heil dir, Sonne! Heil dir, Licht!' III, 3).

Night and Day in Mahler's Seventh

This is how Mahler described his Seventh Symphony to the Swiss writer William Ritter: 'Three night pieces; bright daylight in the finale. As basis for the whole, the first movement.'[31] At first sight, this path from night to day could be compared to the passage from 'Johannisnacht' to 'Johannistag' in *Meistersinger*, from the chaotic riot following Beckmesser's serenade on St John's Eve to the bright St John's Day in C major that will celebrate Walther's triumph. But what does Mahler's 'bright daylight' really have in common with St John's Day in *Meistersinger*, which transforms chaos into order, confusion into enlightenment, and discord into unity?[32] Wagner's day in *Meistersinger* resolves the conflict between tradition and innovation (since Walther's song 'seemed so old, and yet was so new').[33] But Mahler's ordinary day—marked *Allegro ordinario*—leaves the listener with a feeling that certain expectations, prompted by the presence of strong rhetorical markers, are not to be satisfied. Indeed, the final cadence of the Symphony—the one that 'should' be perfect and authentic—goes wrong at the last minute: instead of the tonic expected after the dominant, the chord is augmented (C–E–G♯), before it is finally resolved on a C major triad. This final pirouette might be interpreted as another wink at Beckmesser—often characterised with an augmented triad in *Meistersinger*[34]—who always goes by the book, but somehow manages to misuse the rules because he misunderstands their true function.

Mahler's Finale alludes to Wagner's day in C major, representing resolution and reconciliation but without providing a satisfying closure. However, the passage from night to day in the Seventh, corresponding to the transition between the second *Nachtmusik* (fourth movement) and the Finale, can be compared to the contrast between the private and the public sphere in *Meistersinger*. William Kinderman recently suggested that the Adagietto and the Rondo-Finale of the Fifth Symphony (which, besides its title, has much in common with that of the Seventh) could represent a shift from a subjective moment of isolation to a collective experience, which he compared with the passage from Sach's 'Wahn monologue' to his collective acknowledgement at the end of the opera.[35] We have a similar contrast in the Seventh, between the chamber-like orchestration of the second *Nachtmusik* (and its potential references to the *Siegfried Idyll*) and the noisy brass chorale opening the Finale, evoking, as Julian Johnson put it, 'the gathering of different groups of characters in an operatic crowd scene.'[36]

While Wagner's intimate moment focusses on the character of Hans Sachs, Mahler's second *Nachtmusik* would be rather Beckmesserian, with its mandolin and guitar instead of a lute. There is even something in the melody of the first theme that recalls the rigid rhythm and awkward melodic contours of Beckmesser's serenade.[37] The fair copy of the Seventh shows that the mandolin is a late addition, since its part is sketched in pencil at the bottom of the page.[38] Therefore, Mahler decided to include the mandolin in the second *Nachtmusik* only after he had composed the Finale, which contains the most obvious references to *Meistersinger*.

Mahler and Beckmesser

The only documentary evidence we have for Mahler's view of Beckmesser is a remark, reported by Natalie Bauer-Lechner, that he was highly dissatisfied with Benedikt Felix's interpretation of this character in the 1899 Viennese production of *Meistersinger*: '"Only *one* person could do it," he shouted—as he said already once about Mime—"*me!*"'[39] Mahler's remarks about Mime are more explicit:

Although I am convinced that this figure [Mime] is the embodied persiflage of a Jew, as intended by Wagner (with all the traits which he gave

him: his petty cleverness, greed, and all the complete musically and tex-
tually excellent jargon), that should not be exaggerated and dished up
so thickly here, for heaven's sake, as it was by Spielmann—especially in
Vienna, at the 'k.k Court Opera', it is clearly laughable and a welcome
scandal for the Viennese! I know only *one* Mime (we all looked at him
anxiously) and that is *me*! You will be surprised to see what lies in the part
and what I could make of it![40]

Did Mahler see, through Wagner's treatment of Mime and Beckmesser, a reflection of his own caricature as depicted by his critics? Mahler's musical allusions to the works of other composers—as well as to his own works—were
often cited by his detractors as demonstrating a supposed lack of originality.[41]
As Karen Painter and K. M. Knittel have shown, this critique, implicitly addressed to Beckmesser in *Meistersinger*, relates to anti-Semitic stereotypes such
as those transmitted in Wagner's *Das Judentum in der Musik*.[42] Pushing further the idea of Mahler's identification with Beckmesser, one could imagine
the Seventh, or perhaps only its Finale, as a symphonic version of Mahler's own
interpretation of Beckmesser's role, as if he was eventually showing us what he
could 'make of it' on stage. In this version of the story, Beckmesser's awkward
fourths contain the germs of future developments in twentieth-century music.[43]
They are used to build a new language which certainly contributed to influenc-
ing Schoenberg's change of attitude towards Mahler's music after he had heard
the Seventh in 1909: 'From now on', he wrote to Mahler, 'I am really wholly
yours.'[44] How Mahler's reading of *Meistersinger* in the Seventh relates to his
interpretations of Wagner as a conductor has yet to be explored. Investigating
this double-sided interpretation—performative and compositional—will tell
us more about Mahler's reception of Wagner, and, by extension, about Mahler's
view of his Jewish heritage, as well as about his relation to German culture.

Notes

1. The conductor Hans Richter had already restored some of the traditional
cuts, but Mahler brought back all the music that was still missing. See La Grange,
Mahler, Vol. 2, 195, fn. 111.
2. Bauer-Lechner, *Recollections of Gustav Mahler*, 137.
3. See Martner, "Mahler im Opernhaus", 191–99.
4. See La Grange, *Mahler*, Vol. 2, 195.
5. See Mitchell, "Reception", in *Gustav Mahler, Facsimile of the Seventh
Symphony*, 31–74; and "Mahler's German-language Critics: the Seventh Symphony",
in Painter, *Mahler and His World*, 267–332.
6. Deryck Cooke considered the Finale as 'too reminiscent of *Meistersinger*'
(*Gustav Mahler*, 90–91). The Austrian critic Robert Hirschfeld described it as 'a

frightful mockery of the Overture to the *Meistersinger*, which infuriates even admirers of Mahler's symphonies' (*Wiener Abendpost* 254 (5 November 1909): 1–3,
cited in Mitchell, "Reception", 61–62.) Comparing the Finale of the Seventh with
the Eighth Symphony, Adorno considered both as an 'identification with the at-
tacker. It takes refuge in the power and glory of what it dreads; its official posture
is fear deformed as affirmation' (*Mahler*, 139).

7. See Martner, *Mahler's Concerts*, 239.

8. See Alma Mahler, *Memories and Letters* (1990), 309; and "Mahler's German
Language Critics", in Painter, *Mahler and His World*, 316.

9. See, for example, Korngold, "Feuilleton. Mahler's Seventh Symphony";
Robert Hirschfeld, *Wiener Abendpost*, 5 November 1909 (in Mitchell, "Reception",
Facsimile, 61–62); Meylan, *William Ritter*, 120ff; Specht, *Gustav Mahler*, 303;
Cooke, *Gustav Mahler*, 91; La Grange, *Mahler*, Vol. 3, 873–80; Floros, *Gustav
Mahler. The Symphonies*, 209 and 337, fn. 45.

10. I label Mahler's themes and cells with the letter M ('M' for themes, 'm' for
cells).

11. Musical examples are labeled as follows: Work ('7th or '*Meist.*') + movement
or Act and scene, and theme (for example: *Meist*. O, A). 'O stands for 'Overture.'

12. This theme goes back to the medieval repertoire of *Meistergesang*. See Mey,
Meistergesang, 166.

13. In this example the upper voices are notated an octave lower.

14. See bars 84–87, 133–36 (quieter variant), 194–97, 366–67, and 551–54.
The cadence at bars 134–36/Rehearsal Fig. 240 uses melodic turns that recall
Wagner's archaicist style in *Meistersinger*, especially when the music evokes the
Mastersingers Guild.

15. I refer to passages in *Meistersinger* Acts I, II, and III with the page
number in the Peters/Dover orchestral score, followed by the measure number on
that page.

16. Walther's Prize song also ends on a deceptive cadence in C major, but on a
V4/3 of V, instead of the half-diminished ♯iv. Since the applied dominant chord is
in its second inversion (4/3), its bass is A, and therefore we have there the same bass
(G moving to A) as in the Mahler example.

17. On cadences in the Finale of Mahler's Seventh Symphony, see Sponheuer,
Logik des Zerfalls, 353–401 (one of the most comprehensive analyses of the whole
movement); Williamson, "Deceptive Cadences"; Scherzinger, "The Finale of
Mahler's Seventh"; and Whitworth, "Aspects of Mahler's Musical Language", Ch.
3. The theme at bars 23–37/Rehearsal Fig.226-2 also presents connections to material associated with the Mastersinger's Guild in Wagner, particularly Kothner's
coloratura in Act I, sc. 3 (189/10ff) and a passage in Sachs's 'Wahn monologue' alluding to the *Meistersinger* tradition (488/3ff).

18. This comparison with the operatic world is particularly appropriate, since
most of the musical references heard in this Finale are taken from the operatic
repertoire (Lehar, *Die lustige Witwe*; Mozart, *Die Entführung aus dem Serail*;
Offenbach, *Orphée aux Enfers*, etc.)

19. The question of structural markers in the Seventh has been discussed in Kramer, "Postmodern Concepts", Johnson, *Mahler's Voices*, 119–24, and elsewhere.

20. This recalls a passage from Hanslick's *Vom Musikalisch-Schönen*: 'We recognize the rational coherence of a group of tones and call it a sentence [*Satz*], exactly as with every logical proposition we have a sense of where it comes to an end" (*On The Musically Beautiful*, 30). Beckmesser's claim that Walther's trial song is 'meaningless' because it has 'no beginning nor end' implies, in a way, that the meaning of music lies in its form, and this can be taken as a caricature of Hanslick's view of musical form as expounded in *Vom Musikalisch-Schönen*.

21. Scherzinger ("The Finale of Mahler's Seventh Symphony", 76) and Jonathan Kramer ("Postmodern Concepts of Musical Time", 34) have shown that, in the Finale, Mahler makes an extensive use of traditional structures only to question their meaning, although neither writer suggests a relationship with the presence of *Meistersinger* in the Seventh.

22. The instrument played by Beckmesser is a particular kind of lute, which is tuned like a guitar but sounds an octave higher. Christopher Williams ("Mahler's Seventh Symphony") proposed *Meistersinger* Act II as a precedent for the use of quartal harmony in Mahler's Seventh.

23. This double descending fourth is derived both from the initial cell x and from the descending fourth ma heard at bar 46. This is why it has two different names ('x' and 'ma expanded').

24. Several elements in the melodic and harmonic texture are contradictory: for example, trumpet 2 has E4–B3 while trumpet 3 has B3–E4 at bar 48. Mahler plays on the double identity of the fourth: while this interval has an atonal potential, it is also strongly associated with tonal motion (D–T).

25. Bailey, "*Die Meistersinger* Act II".

26. Transcriptions of sketches were made from the original manuscript sources. My thanks to Dr. Christiane Mühlegger-Henhapel for allowing me to study Mahler's sketchbook at the Österreichisches Theatermuseum in Vienna (Anna Bahr-Mildenburg's Nachlass, VK 905 BaM). In the first published study of the sketchbook (1997), Stephen Hefling concentrated on the pages containing music that ended up in the Seventh Symphony and did not analyze the unidentified music in detail (see '*Ihm in die Lieder zu blicken*'). A detailed analysis of the sketches and drafts for the Seventh can be found in my forthcoming monograph *Mahler's Seventh Symphony* (Oxford University Press).

27. Except for the second beat of bar 4 in the sketchbook (C6–G5).

28. Moreover, pairs of fifths are stacked together to build the chord C–G–D–A–E (at the end of the system on fol. 6v), which may be heard as an inversion of the fourth chord built on the four lower strings of Beckmesser's lute: E–A–D–G– (and C or B, depending on the context).

29. Bayerische Staatsbibliothek, Munich, Moldenhauer Collection, Mus. ms.22741. Edward Reilly's description of these pages focuses on the music used in the Seventh and does not address the issue of the unidentified fragments. See Reilly, "Gustav Mahler Sketches in the Moldenhauer Archives", 301–12.

30. 494/4. Sachs's ascending fifth on 'Ko-bold' also points towards Beckmesser, since the first syllable of his name is usually reached by an ascending interval (see 116/1, 185/13, 392/5).

31. 'Trois morceaux nocturnes; au *Finale*, le grand jour. Comme base du tout, le premier morceau'. In Meylan, *William Ritter*, 116. It is worth noting that Mahler does not characterise the first movement in terms of light. About night and day in the Seventh, see Floros, "Tag und Nacht", and Davison, "Nachtmusik II", 95–96.

32. Mitchell thinks that Mahler's and Wagner's day have much in common: 'It is well attested that Mahler himself referred to his last movement as "Der Tag" and, as if to emphasize the point, he was known to perform the overture to *Die Meistersinger* as a pendant, so to speak, to his own Seventh, thus unequivocally clarifying the relationship between his concept of light and that of Wagner—in both Wagner's opera and Mahler's symphony, night finally gives way to day, and both affirm C major' ("Reception", 73 (see fn. 6)).

33. Warren Darcy interprets C major in *Meistersinger* as the social order threatened by individuals, and the tension towards the final scene in C major as an attempt to restore this collective order lost in Acts II and III ("In Search of C major", 111–28).

34. See *Meistersinger*, Acts I, 3; II, 6; III, 3 (pantomime) and 5.

35. Kinderman, *The Creative Process in Music*, ch. 4; particularly 130–37. Kinderman's comparison between the Fifth and *Meistersinger* encourages us to think further about the connections between the Fifth and Seventh symphonies, as well as about Mahler's reception of *Meistersinger*.

36. Johnson, *Mahler's Voices*, 119. According to Davison, ' "the contradiction between the personal and public stance is a persistent dualism in Mahler's music' ("The *Nachtmusiken* from Mahler's Seventh Symphony", 19).

37. Peter Revers compares the 'irritating interjections' of Mahler's serenade with the way Beckmesser's serenade is constantly interrupted, either by Sachs's hammering or by Beckmesser's 'own uncertainty' ("Return to the Idyll", 46). Lewis Smoley and Christopher Williams also mention Beckmesser's serenade in the context of the second *Nachtmusik* ("Mahler's Seventh Symphony: Inscrutable Enigma or Obvious Parody", in *Wunderhorn* 4/1 (2005): 3; "Mahler's Seventh Symphony", 10).

38. See Mitchell and Reilly, *Facsimile*, 189, 196, 198, etc.

39. Bauer-Lechner, *Gustav Mahler in den Erinnerungen von Natalie Bauer-Lechner*, 146. This passage does not appear in the English translation; it is found only in the German text. Bauer-Lechner does not mention the name of Benedikt Felix (see La Grange, *Mahler*, Vol. 2, 196).

40. Bauer-Lechner, *Gustav Mahler in den Erinnerungen von Natalie Bauer-Lechner*, 122 (transl. Carl Niekerk's in *Reading Mahler*, 15). This passage appears only in the German text, and it concerns the Viennese *Ring* production of 1898. Mahler's insistence on the need to avoid caricature in representing Mime recalls Wagner's own description of this character in the text of *Yound Siegfried* from 1851: 'Mime, the Nibelung, alone. He is small and bent, somewhat deformed and hobbling . . . There must be nothing approaching caricature in all this: his aspect,

when he is quiet, must be simply eerie: it is only in moments of extreme excitement that he becomes exteriorily ludicrous, but never too uncouth' (Ernest Newman, *The Life of Richard Wagner*, Vol. II: *1848–1860* (Cambridge: Cambridge University Press, 1976), 3460).

41. In her introduction to *Seeing Mahler*, Knittel mentions a Viennese cartoon, captioned 'Mahler's Metamorphosen', dating from 1905—precisely the year of the Seventh's completion—which shows Mahler dressed as several nineteenth-century composers, including Wagner (2).

42. See Knittel, *Seeing Mahler*; and Painter, "Jewish Identity". The idea that Beckmesser's character embodies Jewish stereotypes has been widely discussed since Adorno's *Versuch über Wagner* (1952): 'All the rejects of Wagner's works are caricatures of Jews' (*In Search of Wagner*, 23). For Adorno's followers, see Millington, "Nuremberg Trial", 247–61; Weiner, *Richard Wagner and the Anti-Semitic Imagination*; and Zaenker, "The Bedeviled Beckmesser". For more recent and refreshing takes on this problematic question, see Grey, "Masters and Their Critics", and Vaget, "Du warst mein Feind von je".

43. The German philosopher Ernst Bloch interpreted Beckmesser as a Dadaist artist (see "Über Beckmesser's Preis-Lied Text").

44. Letter from Arnold Schoenberg to Gustav Mahler, 29 December 1909, Vienna, cited in Mitchell, "Reception", 70.

7

Idyllic Masks of Death

References to *Orphée aux Enfers* in 'Das himmlische Leben'

Lóránt Péteri

This chapter presents the hypothesis that Mahler's song 'Das himmlische Leben' includes a rich web of motivic and stylistic references to the 'chanson' of Aristaeus from Act I of Jacques Offenbach's *Orphée aux Enfers* (*Orpheus in the Underworld*)—a work Mahler conducted repeatedly during the early period of his career. On grounds of intertextual and topical connections I wish to reconsider the meanings of the Wunderhorn setting, which played a crucial role in Mahler's various symphonic plans until its final incorporation into the Fourth Symphony. The references to Offenbach's 'opéra bouffon' reveal a remarkably dark irony present in Mahler's song. The allusion can be also interpreted as a generic marker of the song which was originally conceived as a 'Humoreske' by its composer.

The starting point of my argument is the striking resemblance in the musical materials of the two works which, in terms of their genres and cultural backgrounds, lie very far apart from one another. Nevertheless, to define precisely the nature of this resemblance is not an easy task. Clearly it is not a matter of 'literal' quotation, nor is it a free musical thematic allusion. Rather, the two works are related in their musical build or physique. First, I attempt to support this assertion in empirical detail (see Ex. 7.1 and Ex. 7.2).

We can see in both the Mahler and the Offenbach that a defining feature of the musical texture is the grace note falling onto the fifth degree. In both works this ornament may appear in major or minor keys, either as a decoration of a high register sustained note or as an element in a freely moving melodic line, notated as a grace note or as part of the regular rhythm. Of course, in themselves grace notes of this sort are a much too general phenomenon to justify from their appearance alone a connection between the music of Mahler and that of Offenbach. Yet the two composers do make uncannily similar use of the device. It is striking that both Offenbach and Mahler make greatly exaggerated use in their musical texture of an ornament falling from the sixth to the fifth degree. It is not without significance that this figure occurs even more frequently in Mahler's original orchestral version of 1892 than it does in his later orchestration, which the composer in fact prepared when he inserted 'Das himmlische Leben' into his Fourth Symphony in April 1901,

Ex. 7.1 Jacques Offenbach, *Orphée aux enfers*, Act I (1858 version), 'chanson pastorale' of Aristaeus, excerpt from the refrain

and revised repeatedly until 1910/11 when he made his final alterations to the proof Universal Edition provided him.[1] Focusing on the E major conclusion of the song, it seems that Mahler consciously reduced the number of occurrences of the aforementioned ornament. In the E major orchestral interlude of the original version, the figure is performed sixteen times by the cor anglais (bars 123–32), while the same instrument presents it only fourteen times in the corresponding passage of later versions (bars 124–33). A more radical reduction in the number of ornaments can be detected in the cor anglais part of the accompaniment of the vocal line 'Die englischen Stimmen ermuntern die sinnen'. The figure in question occurs nine times in the original score (bars 164–68), six times in the intermediate printed versions, and only three times in the final version of the orchestration (bars 165–69). It is still more striking, however, that the continuous crooning of the oboe and the cor anglais successively, which accompanies the vocal line *'Kein musik ist ja nicht auf Erden'* and includes seventeen occurrences of the ornament, is practically omitted from the finalised score (cf. bars 141–49 of the original and bars 142–50 of the final version). I discuss the underlying motives of Mahler's decisions later in this

Ex. 7.2 Gustav Mahler, 'Das himmlische Leben' (1892 version), entry of the singer. Gustav Mahler, 'Wunderhorn-Lieder für Singstimme und Orchester'. GA Bd. XIV/2: © Copyright 1998 by Universal Edition GmbH, Mainz

chapter. For now I merely emphasise that Mahler's first and original formulation of his musical material was even more similar to Offenbach's 'chanson', than its later versions, reshaped for the purposes of a symphonic cycle.

Regarding the Aristaeus 'chanson', this ornament, which constitutes something of an empty gesture, dominates the musical text in a rather grotesque manner towards the end of the refrain (Ex. 7.1). The voice part repeats the ornament throughout eight bars, during which the written pitch forces the tenor soloist

Ex. 7.3 Gustav Mahler, 'Das himmlische Leben' (1892 version), ending. Gustav Mahler, 'Wunderhorn-Lieder für Singstimme und Orchester'. GA Bd. XIV/2: © Copyright 1998 by Universal Edition GmbH, Mainz

to use 'falsetto' technique. At the same time the instrumental accompaniment is reduced to repeating a figure no less empty: the bass line alternates in a regular rhythm between the tonic and the dominant, the music meanwhile gradually dying away (see especially the passage from the last bar of the second system in Ex. 7.1). This same combination of musical features appears unmistakably in the last seven bars of 'Das himmlische Leben' as well (see Ex. 7.3). The dynamic level sinks from *pianissimo* to quadruple *piano*; the grace note figure is played repeatedly by the cor anglais, during which the regularly alternating tonic-dominant is heard on the harp. In fact this alternating bass figure plays an important role in both Mahler's and Offenbach's scores independently of the passages under discussion. Of course once again we are dealing with something that belongs among the least idiosyncratic features of tonal music. Furthermore this figure crops up with obstinate frequency in Mahler's works from *Das klagende Lied* onwards.[2]

Apart from this, the character resemblance of the 'chanson' and the 'Lied' is strengthened by the scalic motives in regular rhythm which Offenbach notates in quavers in 6/8 time and Mahler notates in triplets in 4/4 time. The orchestration of both works is characterised by a predominance of the woodwinds and a sensitive use of their timbres. We also find points of contact in the area of tonality. Aristaeus's 'chanson' is in G minor, which in the refrain brightens into G major. 'Das himmlische Leben' is in G major, which in the last verse changes to E major. Harmonic archaicisms in the Offenbach reach back to the Baroque, and in the Mahler to even earlier periods of music history. Some of the features mentioned so far reveal a connection with a particular genre. Both Offenbach and Mahler make reference to pastoral instrumental traditions. However whereas Offenbach evokes and parodies the pastoral conventions of the seventeenth and eighteenth centuries in comic textbook fashion, Mahler uses more subtle methods in his song, pointing to other genres as well as the pastoral. It is enough to recall the very different characters of the pastoral sections in Mahler's early symphonies[3] to acknowledge that the connection between 'Das himmlische Leben' and Aristaeus's 'chanson' cannot be restricted to the reference they share to this particular genre.

Having presented what I hope is a convincing argument for the existence of an intertextual connection between the two works, in what follows I try to throw some light on how this connection enriches our understanding of the meaning of Mahler's song.

After its world première in Paris in 1858, Offenbach's operetta *Orpheus in the Underworld* was performed for the first time in Prague and Breslau (today's Wrocław) in the subsequent year, and later, in the year of Mahler's birth, also in Vienna, then with a new German version of the libretto written by the popular Austrian playwright Johann Nestroy. The work gained international fame and continued to attract worldwide productions during the 1860s.[4] Together with other Offenbach operettas (*L'île de Tulipatan*; *Les '66'*; *La belle Hélène*; *La vie parisienne*), *Orpheus in the Underworld* appeared in the repertoire of the Iglauer Stadttheater between 1860 and 1870. As La Grange emphasises, 'Several of Mahler's teachers held posts at the Iglau Theatre and surely procured tickets at reduced prices for him or invited him to their rehearsals, thus enabling him to discover part of the lyric repertoire.'[5] It seems very likely, therefore, that Mahler became acquainted with Offenbach's style during his childhood. All we know about Mahler's repertoire in the small spa theatre of Bad Hall, where he was engaged as a conductor at the beginning of his career, in 1880, is that it consisted of 'the best and most recent operettas, comedies, etc.'[6] However, the fact that various Offenbach works were performed in Bad Hall in the 1870s (*Barbe-bleue*; *La Princesse de Trébizonde*; *Le Mariage aux lanterns*; *Les géorgiennes*; *Orphée aux Enfers*) makes all the more probable that Mahler also conducted the operettas of the Parisian composer during his short employment there.[7]

In the period preceding the composition of 'Das himmlische Leben' Mahler certainly conducted at least eight stage works by Offenbach, among them *Orpheus in the Underworld*: this was a very considerable repertoire (Table 7.1). Although he did not conduct any work by Offenbach during his tenure as the director of the Royal Opera House in Budapest, he promoted a new production of

Table 7.1 The Number of Performances of Offenbach's Theatrical Works Conducted by Mahler

	Laibach (1881–1882)	Kassel (1883–1885)	Leipzig (1886–1888)	Vienna (1897–1907)	Total
Barbe-bleue	1				1
La belle Hélène	1				1
Les contes d'Hoffmann			7	8	15
Lischen et Fritzchen [Französische Schwaben]		1			1
Jeanne qui pleure et Jean qui rit		1			1
Le Mariage aux lanternes	2	4			6
Orphée aux enfers		2			2
La vie parisienne	2				2
Total	6	8	7	8	29

Source: Martner, *Mahler's Concerts*, 369.

Le Mariage aux lanterns in 1890, and also made preparations for an Offenbach cycle which was never realised.[8] Thus Mahler was able to interpret *Orpheus in the Underworld* not in isolation but in a wider context of the musical and theatrical conventions of Offenbach's operettas.

The libretto of *Orpheus in the Underworld* by Hector Crémieux and Ludovic Halévy is rooted in a parody of the classical Greek mythological story. The main source of the humour derives from filling the framework of the sublime immortal myth with prosaic content taken from nineteenth-century bourgeois life, and even saturating it with references to real features of contemporary French social and political life. The humour of the musical setting stems from similar sources. Some of the pithy musical numbers of the 'opéra bouffon' evoke in miniature the atmosphere of operatic forms from the past and the heroic and lyrical moods of the nineteenth-century present, while the rest of them are based upon the most recent popular dance music. Like other operettas by Offenbach, *Orpheus* is full of operatic quotations and allusions, of which the most famous is undoubtedly the reference to the hero's famous aria ('J'ai perdu mon Eurydice') from Christoph Willibald Gluck's opera *Orpheus and Eurydice*.[9]

The character of Aristaeus in *Orpheus in the Underworld* is taken from book IV of Virgil's *Georgics*. In the Virgil, Aristaeus is partly a shepherd, partly a hero of beekeeping, who plays an indirect role in the death of Eurydice. In the operetta we meet Aristaeus as Eurydice's secret lover, his cottage displaying the following sign: 'honey-producer; retail and wholesale, warehouse on the Hymettos hill'.[10] In the 'chanson' which he sings at his entry on stage, found in the operetta's original version of 1858 as well as in the revised version of 1874, Aristaeus lists in encyclopedic detail all the ingredients needed for the shepherd's rural idyll, emphasising the innocence of a shepherd's pleasures. Even so, Aristaeus's naivety feels counterfeit, insincere, and artificial. The reason for this has much to do with the music. The instrumental evocation of a pastoral topos, as discussed above, ends up with the unconvincing mechanical repetition of two motives. Indeed, the seemingly innocent 'chanson' of the shepherd Aristaeus appears in the course of the plot as part of a camouflage. In fact, it is Pluto, the god of the underworld who is disguised as Aristaeus in order to lure Eurydice to her death. In other words, the ironic manner in which the operetta treats the pastoral musical tradition is given a dramatic function: the feigned naivety turns out to be a cunning ruse, the idyll a mask of death. Whether the death is a comic portrait of moral death resulting in a loss of social identity is a further question. Eurydice, who is a respectably married woman, sets off down the steps to the underworld of society, and when she reaches the bottom she is consecrated a priestess of Bacchus—that is to say, she becomes a 'woman of low repute'.

This duality of naivety and chicanery, the lofty and the lowly, appears also in the text of 'Das himmlische Leben'. The words, on the one hand, describe the joys of Heaven from a child's point of view—very much of this world—yet on the other hand, they are full of references and symbols taken from the gospels and hagiography, revealing wide theological knowledge. Mahler found the poem in the anthology *Des Knaben Wunderhorn*, in which it figures as a Bavarian folk song with the title 'Der Himmel hängt voll Geigen' (literally 'Heaven Hangs Full of Violins', and figuratively 'Heaven is brimful of delight'). In origin, however, it is not folk art: the author was Peter (Nikolaus) Marcelin Sturm (1760–1812), a scholar and sometime Augustinian priest. Stephen Hefling cites the poem set by Mahler as an example of *ingénu* irony, 'whereby the ironist creates a naive innocent who lures victims into his ironising: the *ingénu* poses questions or makes comments, the full import of which he or she does not realize'.[11]

As we know, in terms of its genre Mahler's first decision was that 'Das himmlische Leben' would be a *Humoreske*, and according to his original plan of April 1892 the song would have been published together with other *Wunderhorn* settings ('Der Schildwache Nachtlied', 'Verlorn'e Müh', 'Trost im Unglück', 'Wer hat dies Liedlein erdacht?!'), bearing the title *Fünf Humoresken*.[12] This definition of genre derives partly from Robert Schumann and partly from writers like Johann Paul Friedrich Richter (also known as Jean Paul) and E. T. A. Hoffmann who exercised a decisive influence on both Schumann and Mahler.[13] Relevant here is Jean Paul's definition of humour as ' "the inverted sublime" which makes visible the contrast between the finite, everyday world of individual things and people and the infinitude of the world of spirit and ideas'.[14] This idea can just as well be applied to an interpretation of Offenbach's parody of a myth as to the irony of the religious poem of the *Wunderhorn* collection. At the same time, *Humoreske* as a musical genre also has some distinguishing features. Analysing Schumann's *Humoreskes*, Bernhard R. Appel stresses among other things the importance of their 'stubborn repetitions of empty figures'. This is a characteristic, as we have seen, that plays an important role in both Aristaeus's 'chanson' and *Das himmlische Leben*. Moreover, Appel considers one of the sources of musical humour to be 'quotations, reminiscences and allusions'.[15] The role of these in Offenbach's operetta based on parodying opera is fairly clear. The humour of the songs included in Mahler's *Fünf Humoresken* is also strongly linked with the idea and practice of ambiguous quotations.

Donald Mitchell has suggested that the 'exuberant vocal cadenza' of one of the *Humoresken*, namely, the song 'Wer hat dies Liedlein erdacht?!' 'has its roots ... in an "instrumental" vocal style that Mahler would certainly have known from Bach'. Mitchell went even further, claiming that the defining rhythmic and melodic features of Mahler's Ländler-like song are similar to those of a soprano aria in G major ('Ich will dir mein Herze schenken') from J. S. Bach's *St Matthew Passion*.[16] The similarity between the two vocal pieces is also striking in terms of the texture, the harmonic progress, and the orchestration dominated by the oboe d'amore in the Bach, and by the oboe in the Mahler. The simultaneous references to folk dance and passion seem to invite carnival humour as an interpretative framework of Mahler's song. The subversive nature of the allusion to Bach is strengthened by the peculiar parallelism of the texts. While the central topic of the Bach aria is the believer's love for Christ, the Mahler song is based on a poem whose subject is a lad's love for the host's daughter. That poem is labelled as '*mündlich*' (orally transmitted) by Achim von Arnim and Clemens Brentano, editors of the *Wunderhorn* collection. In 1909, however, Karl Bode discovered that the text of 'Wer hat dies Liedlein erdacht?!' was actually manufactured by the editors who 'felt free to take elements from folk poetry and create from them their own unique mix'.[17] That circumstance sheds light on the hidden irony of the text, which formulates a self-referential question: 'Wer hat denn das schöne Liedlein erdacht?' ('Who then has thought up this pretty little song?') The answer, as Johnson puts it, is 'wonderfully self-deprecatory':[18] 'Es haben's drei Gäns' übers Wasser gebracht' ('three geese have brought it over the water'). Although Mahler might regard the text as a piece of folk poetry, it remains probable that, with his allusion to Bach, he wished to respond to the poem's playful question regarding its own hidden author. In doing so, Mahler created an amusing juxtaposition of the noise of the geese and the music of the composer who was regarded as the most elevated creator in the German tradition.

'Das himmlische Leben' generates musical meaning in a very similar way. The humoresque character of the song lies precisely in the presence of the Offenbach reference, which fundamentally subverts the song's possible meanings. To understand this I would like to trace the main directions taken by interpretations of the song so far. Commentators on 'Das himmlische Leben' are divided on the question of whether the song makes use of the rhetoric of certainty or ambiguity. Constantin Floros writes that the song affirmatively presents its eschatological theme, and that as the finale of the Fourth Symphony it provides us with a key to understanding the other movements as well: 'An insider as well as a listener who did not know any of Mahler's explanations could conclude from the text of the Finale that life after death is also the subject of the three previous movements.'[19] Mitchell also sees a similarly fulfilled utopia in 'Das himmlische Leben', but with a different content. In his opinion the Fourth Symphony is simply a 'long journey from Experience to Innocence', and correspondingly in the closing section of 'Das himmlische Leben' there is 'Not Paradise, perhaps, but Innocence Regained'. According to Mitchell, it is

> [a] stroke of genius that an unadorned E should be the very last sound we hear. But not less inspired, surely, is the long-breathed, seamless melody, occupying virtually the totality of the last stanza's available musical space, a quietly rapturous celebration of a music that awaits us when Experience has been purged ... and by reserving that sublime melody for his final act of simplification, by his concentration on melody alone to bear the weight of the ultimate transformation, Mahler seems to return us to an age of innocence in music when (if I may echo Freud) such things were still possible.[20]

However, before this Theodor W. Adorno had already drawn attention to the disturbing contradiction that arises between the words and the music in the last bars of the song. Although the words speak of a joyful awakening, the music gradually fades to the limits of audibility, the orchestral texture is gradually dismantled, and the thematic and motivic activity gradually dies away. As he puts it: 'The phantasmagoria of the transcendent landscape is at once posited by it and negated. Joy remains unattainable, and no transcendence is left but that of yearning.'[21] On the other hand, Raymond Knapp has more recently argued that the deep and weighty meanings, and the 'disturbing ambiguities' which we discover in 'Das himmlische Leben' can be derived from the varying contexts into which Mahler placed the song.[22] As we know, Mahler gave the song a role in his plans for the Third Symphony, as the finale of his originally intended seven movements, with the title 'Was mir das Kind erzählt'—'What the Child Tells Me'.[23] Mahler rejected this plan, but thanks to Paul Bekker another plan of Mahler's survives, whose date is unknown and which lists the movements for a 'Fourth Symphony' with the subtitle *Humoreske*.[24] Its six movements would have included among other things the song 'Das irdische Leben' composed in 1893, and as its last movement Mahler intended using 'Das himmlische Leben'—which later acquired its final position as the finale of the four-movement symphony he really did compose as his Fourth. In Knapp's interpretation, among the various meanings of the song, the motive of the death of a child owes its appearance to the context provided by the ballad of the starving child ('Das irdische Leben') and by the scherzo of the Fourth Symphony with its 'danse macabre' character.[25] At the same time Knapp claims that 'Das himmlische Leben', 'as a stand-alone song . . . projects in the simplest of terms an untroubled scenario involving a healthy child and adult fully capable of transporting the child into comforting sleep.'[26] The stand-alone song therefore in Knapp's opinion is a straightforward lullaby. The ending of the song he interprets as follows: 'We sense that by the end, the child is fully asleep, and that the mother is singing the final chorale phrase in benediction, as much for herself as for the child.'[27]

In opposition to Knapp, I believe that we have no need of the context of the Fourth Symphony or of 'Das irdische Leben' in order to arrive at questions related to death when examining the meanings of 'Das himmlische Leben'. Neither do I think the song is a confirmation of the existence of 'life after death', as Floros claims. In contrast to Mitchell, I do not read the ending of the song as 'innocent'. It is precisely the ending which most clearly refers to Aristaeus's *chanson*, and, furthermore, to the 'self-revealing' refrain with its repetitious motive. It shows a rather dark irony: following the lines about life in heaven and its pleasures we hear the deceptive, manipulative camouflage music of Pluto, the ruler of the underworld. This irony on the one hand brings to the surface the ambiguity latent in the text: after all what sort of idyll and what sort of heaven is it where 'St John lets the lamb go; Herod the butcher marks it well'? On the other hand, the consequences of the Offenbach reference take us still deeper. This reference suggests that the whole idealised heaven seen with a child's eyes is simply a masque, behind which death tempts its victim—namely, the child—into the unknown. It is rather like the gingerbread house seducing Hänsel and Gretel to deliver themselves into the hands of the Witch in Humperdinck's opera, written contemporaneously with Mahler's song. In the last three bars the music of 'Das himmlische Leben' is covered by darkness, and, as it were, goes silent. Thus in vain does the subject of the music look behind the idyllic mask: it cannot share with us what it sees there. In its place it is forced to confront the truth formulated by Ludwig Wittgenstein: 'whereof one cannot speak, thereof one must be silent'. It seems, however, that the fine changes which Mahler executed in the orchestration and the texture of the final version of the song slightly weakened the more direct and straightforward allusion to Offenbach as can be found in the original version. The allusion is doubtless recognisable in the final version also, but its importance is diminished by the new and enormously rich context of a multi-movement orchestral work.

Notes

1. See Zychowicz, *Mahler's Fourth Symphony*, 167.
2. See Mitchell, *"Das klagende Lied"*, 79–80.
3. See Peattie, "In Search of Lost Time".
4. See Lamb, "Orphée aux enfers".
5. La Grange, *Mahler*, Vol. 1, 18.
6. La Grange, *Mahler*, Vol. 1, 76; see also Martner, *Mahler's Concerts*, 365.
7. La Grange, *Mahler*, Vol. 1, 76.
8. Roman, *Mahler és Magyarország*, 161; Tallián, "Intézménytörténet 1884–1911", 100.
9. See Lamb, "Orphée aux enfers".
10. For the purposes of the present research, I have studied the following historical editions of Offenbach's work: a vocal score of the 1858 version, edited by Heugel et Compagnie (Paris, au Ménestrel, rue Vivienne 2 bis); a bilingual vocal score of the 1858 version, edited by Bote & Bock (Berlin), with a German translation by Ludwig Kalisch; and a vocal score of the 1874 version, edited by Heugel in Paris.
11. Hefling, "Gustav Mahler: Romantic Culmination", 306–7.
12. Hefling, "Gustav Mahler: Romantic Culmination", 307.
13. See Johnson, *Mahler's Voices*, 202–3, and 125–34 on Mahler's 'carnival humor'.
14. Johnson, *Mahler's Voices*, 127.
15. Appel, "Humoreske", 455.
16. Mitchell, *Gustav Mahler: The Wunderhorn Years*, 297.
17. Finson, "The Reception of Gustav Mahler's *Wunderhorn* Lieder", 100.
18. Johnson, *Mahler's Voices*, 137.
19. Floros, *Gustav Mahler, The Symphonies*, 131.
20. Mitchell, "'Swallowing the Programme'", 216.
21. Adorno, *Mahler: A Musical Physiognomy*, 57.
22. See Knapp, *Symphonic Metamorphoses*, 13–69; quotation, 17.
23. See Mitchell, *Gustav Mahler: The Wunderhorn* Years, 187–91.
24. Mitchell, *Gustav Mahler: The Wunderhorn* Years, 139.
25. See Knapp, *Symphonic Metamorphoses*, 21–6, 67–9.
26. Knapp, *Symphonic Metamorphoses*, 16.
27. Knapp, *Symphonic Metamorphoses*, 20.

II

STAGE, SCREEN, AND POPULAR CULTURES

8

Mahler and the Myth of the Total Symphony

James Buhler

Music and the Myth of Total Cinema

Mahler once said that 'the symphony must be like the world. It must embrace everything.'[1] Similarly, in a short but influential essay, French film critic André Bazin noted that the development of the cinema has been driven more by the pursuit of an idea, what he calls 'the myth of total cinema', than by the technological inventions and improvements. The inventors of cinema, he suggested, all imagined it 'as a total and complete representation of reality',[2] and innovations such as synchronised sound and colour were neither supplements nor foreign intrusions to the art but means of realising the very origin and essence of cinema. Bazin thereby takes the 'myth of total cinema' as revealing a picture of its real history, and in a related article, 'The Evolution of the Language of Cinema', he sketches phases of a dialectical history based on the 'myth' and the notion that cinema has been divided between 'those directors who put their faith in the image and those who put their faith in reality'.[3] The movement of cinema history passes from symbolic montage in the silent film (c. 1925), to analytical editing in the classic Hollywood sound film (c. 1935) to the long take and deep-focus photography of postwar filmmaking (c. 1945), which Bazin understood as a way to increase the realism of the cinema and to allow it to approach the aims and status of the novel.

Whether or not one is convinced by Bazin's conceptual scheme for explaining cinema and its history, it undoubtedly gives rise to a fruitful metaphorical world, and it is this metaphorical world that I want to explore and extend to Mahler's music. Cinematic comparisons to Mahler are not of course unusual, and they have typically focussed on montage, on the collage-like juxtaposition of disparate material that is often used to relate his symphonies to the aesthetic realism dominant in many of the arts at the turn of the century. For example, Raymond Monelle thinks that Mahler leaves much of his material, especially the musical topics he deploys, in relatively unprocessed form. 'Always the effect is one of *montage*, and the [musical] topics seem to possess a rawness, as though they were meant to speak for themselves instead of becoming part of the composer's language.'[4] Julian Johnson similarly observes Mahler's use of 'horn calls, fanfares, the calls of birds and animals, the summoning of bells ... Such calls construct a complex layering of semiotic activity: their literal quality, drawn from the realities of urban and rural life, seems to suggest an almost theatrical narration.'[5] In fact, Johnson's description seems more appropriate to cinema than to the theatre. Carl Dahlhaus likewise finds that Mahler's music is 'pieced together from heterogeneous elements converging from all directions,' yielding 'a stylistic montage in which snatches of song could be included without any aesthetic compatibility'.[6] According to Dahlhaus, Mahler's compositional principle runs contrary to symphonism, 'the symphonic principle of thematic-motivic working' toward a goal that operated under the 'law of symphonic motion'.[7] Mahler, Dahlhaus thinks, promotes diversity rather than unity, an aesthetic practice with strong ethical implications.

> It is precisely by the act of forcing heterogeneous material to coexist, without glossing over inconsistencies, that Mahler creates a panorama which truly fulfils the claim he made for the symphony: it stands as a metaphor in sound for a world which contains within itself high and low, the sophistication of fine art and artless vulgarity, with complete impartiality and with a sense of reality which is rooted in a sense of justice. In Mahler, the momentum of a deeply felt 'universalism' effortlessly overrides the most extreme incompatibilities between the multifarious contents of the one work ... it is the inseparable accompaniment and condition of a realism which takes hold of everything without distinction, however humble, and entrusts it to the embrace of the symphony, the metaphor for a world.[8]

Montage is evidently the compositional principle (or at least device) that allows Mahler to put his faith in reality and write symphonies that could encompass the diversity of the world and reveal its deep and profound mysteries.

While montage is thus situated as the 'modern' symphonic principle in opposition to the 'classical' symphonic principle of thematic-motivic work and although this opposition has certain interpretive utility and basic historical veracity, the concept of montage deployed—essentially rudimentary cutting and assemblage of tableaux, or in any event of autonomous shots—is elementary when compared to the systems of editing that would develop beginning around 1910. Moreover, the continuity system, based on principles of matching and the analytical breakdown of space, became the dominant system of editing in Hollywood, and in its mature form Hollywood montage actually bears a closer resemblance to classical symphonism than to Mahler's practice, which itself has more affinities with the critical spirit of someone like Orson Welles or Luchino Visconti than with earlier directors such as John Ford, Fritz Lang, or even Sergei Eisenstein, all of whom have certain broad thematic concerns in common with Mahler. At least, this will be my argument: comparisons of Mahler to cinema become more productive when approached through the fundamental category of time.

Two Forms of Musical Time

Aside from the fact that cinema appropriates music as one of its basic components, cinema and music share the basic property of unfolding in time; both are
regularly identified as temporal arts. Though music and film each order time
somewhat differently, the respective orderings do in fact follow similar principles and this similarity allows certain insights to emerge from a comparison.

Raymond Monelle, following narrative theorists who distinguish description from the narration of plot, offers a musical distinction between lyric and
progressive time. Lyric time is the extended present of the musical moment,
the way in which a melody seems to subsist in a present that overrides the immediate present of reflective cognition, the instant propelled by the irresistible
press of time at which future is continually being turned into past. Monelle
understands lyric time as the musical analogue to narrative description, those
passages in a novel where the time of the story seems to congeal and gives way
to the detailed inventory of the narrative world in its spatial existence. The
impression of realism in narrative discourse is often attributed to description
(this attribution is not quite accurate inasmuch as spatial description proceeds,
like a still photograph, by depriving the world of time and movement) and for
Monelle the musical impression of realism resides in lyric time's emotional
verisimilitude that similarly suspends time. He sees lyric time exhibited in
purest form in the relatively closed musical evocations of genre. While the
analogy between description and lyrical time suits Monelle's interpretive demands, it poses a number of difficulties for my purposes here.

First, many argue that films do not describe at all, and that, if films do describe, they do not describe in the way that novels do. A film discloses its world
through the presentation of images and sounds and this disclosure generally
occurs within the basic temporality of the diegesis.[9] Though shots can linger
on objects and attenuate to some extent the unrelenting press of diegetic time,
such lingering never stops diegetic time in the way narrative description in the
novel can and frequently does. Generally, lingering also does not stretch time
the way lyric time in music does. Rather, lingering represents more a decom-
pression of narrative time, which typically advances discontinuously through
elision of dramatically inconsequential or idle diegetic time, a time when nothing of dramatic importance happens. It therefore represents a kind of refusal
of this idle diegetic time to pass tacitly into an ellipsis under the demands of
drama. Lingering animates the idle time, gives it form, and so draws attention to the fraying of real time, to the way narrative ordinarily masters time
by dividing it into essential and inessential, consequential and inconsequential, active and passive, and so organises the world analytically according to
dramatic pertinence, that is, in terms of how the represented time serves the
drama of the story.

Second, understood as subjective introspection, the direct analogue to musical lyric time in the novel (but also film) lies not so much in narrative description per se but rather in appearances of the lyrical mode, that is, interior monologue, indirect discourse, and generalised passages of character focalisation that seem to stretch and bend time beyond the point of cinematic lingering. Moreover, the reflective mood of lyrical introspection means that although it gives the impression of being outside of diegetic time (its perpetual present perhaps out of time altogether) or not bound to the immediate unfolding of plot, the time of subjective reflection appears through just this dislocation of reflection from the moment rather than through the lived experience of the moment.

Monelle's progressive time, by contrast, is the time of musical development, and it accords more straightforwardly with the generalised, abstract time of cognition, which is also the model for normal diegetic time, but also for the time of the plot. 'Natural or "objective" time,' Monelle writes,

> is a condition of life, a 'transcendent form' in the expression of Kant. It is continuous and irreversible, the present always poised between a past and a future. It is an object of cognition; it is 'known' rather than lived. Apparently, natural time flows at a uniform pace in one direction and penetrates all that occupies it. It is thus not dependent on events or change; all events take place *in* time, without modifying it in any way. We think of it as 'clock time,' Susanne Langer's term, but it is not necessarily the time of the clock. It is the time in which events can be placed, the tabula rasa on which temporal forms of life are written.[10]

This time is natural, objective, and universal only in the sense that it is the indifferent time observed by science and so true for the abstract general moment and accessible by reflection of the abstract universal subject. What matters is not its reality (its full conformance to the world or the subjective experience of it) but the reproducibility of its general form (its independence as a variable) and its efficacy for making a sensible analysis of the world, especially with respect to movement. For Henri Bergson, this time is an objective illusion, one that coincides with science's own fundamental misappraisal of time.[11] The cinematic apparatus is, in a sense, a perfected model of this time, with its series of snapshots selected arbitrarily at twenty-four frames per second for sound film, the process then reversed at projection to synthesise movement. As Gilles Deleuze notes, however, though the apparatus conforms to the scientific analysis of movement, its synthesis in projection produces the immediate image of motion, a mobile section rather than an immobile section with movement added,[12] and this shift relates actual movement not immobile sections to any moment whatsoever, the general moment of science.[13] With each moment, something qualitatively new comes into existence insofar as this motion is real. The relevant cinematic distinction for Deleuze is therefore not between the objective time of science and the phenomenological time of subjective experience but between a movement-image based on what he terms 'the sensory-motor schema' of the body and a time-image based in thought and reflection encountering something alien to itself within itself. Deleuze maps this passage from a cinema dominated by the movement-image to that dominated by the time-image onto Bazin's distinction between image and reality, between montage and analytical editing on the one hand and long take and deep-focus photography on the other. The latter techniques, which Bazin associates with cinematic realism, are those that Deleuze finds contribute to the production of the time-image.

Deleuze's taxonomy of cinematic images is helpful in reworking Monelle's classification of musical temporalities. According to Monelle, one of the achievements of musical classicism and the founding principle of sonata form was the management of the play of lyric and progressive time. Progressive time for Monelle is the temporality of the musical plot, the irreversible forward advance that carries music's impression of movement. Progressive time, he argues, is produced by the music of transition and development, and it is characterised by instability, sequence, development, and semantically weak passage work. Its prototype is the transition section of the classical sonata form, which requires dissolving the musical markers of lyrical stability (e.g., monotonality, clear phrase structure, particularised motivic content, texture that sets off melody) asserted by the opening theme in order to dramatise the movement away from the initial lyrical pose and prepare the arrival of another.[14] Though in these terms the form serves ostensibly to contrast the lyrical states or poses captured in the tableaux of tonal settings (and to dramatise the underlying tonal shift that the lyrical poses serve to mark), Monelle suggests that it is actually the appearance of the thematically nondescript progressive time, and not the establishment, refinement, and proper deployment of a rich repertory of thematic poses in tonal space, that allowed sonata form to dramatise subjectivity and to become the musical analogue of the *Bildungsroman*. The drama of sonata form takes place in progressive time rather than in lyrical time or even in tonal space insofar as it is abstracted from considerations of temporality (as the theory of sonata form inevitably does).

Two Forms of Cinematic Action

This is a fine thesis, and it will serve as my basis here for defining the classical conception of the symphony, but we should note that it begins by allying progressive time with the abstractions of clock time in a way that is strange given that progressive time will also become, in this dramatisation of sonata-form temporality, the time of subjective development, that is, precisely a mobile section rather than a set of static poses with motion added. Here, Deleuze's development of Bergson's ideas of temporality for cinema proves particularly useful. Deleuze classifies the movement-image into various types: affection-image, action-image, relation-image, and so forth. What will concern us here is the action-image, the dominant image type of the classic cinema no doubt because, focused on action, it 'has the greatest affinity with narrative.'[15] The action-image also yields two important cinematic forms: the large (S-A-S') and the small (A-S-A').[16] These forms both involve coupling situations (S) and actions (A) in a way that leaves a strong impression of realism, but from two sides, one following an integrative logic that produces a global organic image, the other a differential logic that produces a local fragmented image. As Deleuze states, 'What constitutes realism is simply this: milieux and modes of behavior, milieux which actualize and modes of behavior which embody. The action-image is the relation between the two and all the varieties of this relation.'[17] Musically, milieus can be defined tonally, not just as tonal regions but as the appearance of those regions as constituted in and by musical time. 'Behavior' in this context might be taken on first approximation as the appearance of musical action, that which contracts into musical motion (integrative), but it might also be understood in terms of a musical habitus, a tonal array of conventions, customs and habits that also constitute a musical action (differential). Moreover, for Deleuze,

> the milieu always actualizes several qualities and powers. It carries out a global synthesis of them, it is itself the Ambience or the Encompasser, whilst the qualities and the powers have become *forces* in the milieu. The milieu and its forces incurve on themselves, they act on the character, throw him a challenge and constitute a situation in which he is caught. The character reacts in his turn (action properly speaking) so as to respond to the situation, to modify the milieu, or his relation with the milieu, with the situation, with other characters. He must acquire a new mode of being (*habitus*) or raise his mode of being to the demands of the milieu and of the situation. Out of this emerges a restored or modified situation, a new situation.[18]

The passage is musically suggestive, with its language of forces and powers and the struggle for individual definition within and against a constituted situation. In the large integrative form, the most common in cinema, an action effects a changed situation, and this is the basic ethical model of the spiral quest. In terms of classical sonata form, Monelle's two temporalities of music might be better construed as figuring a similar temporal oscillation between situation and action, the shift representing a contraction into action that bursts forth (progressive time) and the emergence from the explosion of the reconfigured new situation (lyrical time), in which case the large action form also forms the basis of a common musical form.

That the action-image has a second, differential form, A-S-A', suggests that we might look for a musical analogue to it as well. In this so-called small form, 'it is the action which discloses the situation, a fragment or an aspect of the situation, which triggers off a new action ... From action to action, the situation gradually emerges, varies, and finally becomes clear or retains its mystery.'[19] The small form differs from the large in being local rather than global, tracing an elliptical rather than spiral path, being comedic rather than ethical in spirit, and being constructed around events rather than the large encompassing structure.[20] Where the large form posits a gap that must be closed, the small form begins from a small difference and opens a gap from it. The changed action (A') or rather the difference that it illustrates serves as an index to a situation, which if represented is equivocal and if not gives rise to an ellipsis from which we have to infer the missing situation. In the first case uncertainty about initial action leads us to mistake one situation for another; therefore the initial action (A) leads to a further action (A') that clarifies the actual situation to which the action is the index. In the second case, the situation itself is missing, and the action (A') or the difference in a set of paired actions (A–A') serves as an 'index of lack' to an underlying but unrepresented situation.

The large and small forms permeate every level of structure, and attending to their work brings out a strong resemblance between the analytical editing of classic Hollywood sound film, where cuts are based on a logic of matches and psychological motivation that produces the illusion of continuity across cuts, and the standard classical techniques of symphonic form and development in, say, Beethoven. Although montage is often understood in terms of elementary juxtaposition, a whole set of procedures, the syntax of film (or music), exist to allow one image to call forth another logically across the cut; antecedent: consequent; shot (Fig. 8.1a): reverse-shot (Fig. 8.1b); thesis: antithesis. The shots, like basic ideas in musical phrases, play out through montage with a purposive developmental logic. Synthesis: the two-shot (Fig. 8.1c) that frames the relationship, the negative space between the characters representing in the case of this sequence from the end of *Now, Voyager* (1942) a bittersweet distance that can no longer be traversed without rupturing the relationship that traces the thin thread to the stars (small form), although in many romantic situations this last shot represents precisely the distance that is traversed for the kiss that binds the shots, narrative, and world together (large form).

The effect is similar in symphonic technique, not just with the classical phrase structure of the period, where the oppositional structure balances one pose with another only slightly different from it (small form), but also in the more prototypical thematic sentence, where the centrifugal force of the individuating basic idea is attenuated and dissolved in the encompassing consensus of the conventional cadence (large form). In Mahler's Sixth Symphony, the theme of the Andante Moderato presents the small form. This theme does not contract into action and then present a new situation. Instead, the period form of the theme works to disclose a situation. The antecedent (bars 1–5.2) presents a 'mode of behavior' that the consequent

Fig. 8.1 Classic shot/reverse-shot cinematic editing pattern with concluding 2-shot in *Now, Voyager* (1942)

(bars 5.3–10) replicates with a difference—or rather several differences. These differences in turn serve as enigmas, in this case indices of equivocation or distance, notably in bars 7–9, where a shadow passes momentarily across the music.[21] In this theme, it is uncertain immediately whether the action marked out in the antecedent or consequent will ultimately prove decisive (hence the equivocation) or indeed what to make of the difference that the shadow indicates (suggesting that the theme also contains an important index of lack). The main theme of the first movement, by contrast, follows the large form. Here, a drumming accompaniment pattern in the strings serves as a brief introduction (bars 1–5) that builds to an initial thematic statement. The statement itself is forceful but rudimentary, melody with block chords for the first four measures (bars 6–9), becoming somewhat more complicated in the frantic dissolution that concludes the sentential structure, leaving it without firm cadential confirmation (bars 10–13). The answering statement (bars 14–23) gives the impression of passing the main line back and forth between oboes and violins with lower strings drumming underneath and various other figures (trombone, trumpet) weaving in and out of the texture before this statement too dissolves (in somewhat more orderly fashion than the first) rather than coming to a clear cadence. An even more austere variant—almost entirely octaves for the first three measures—appears at bar 25. Further variants appear in bars 32 and 43, the first resembling the answering statement, the second the opening. Overall, the entire thematic complex presents a series of contractions into action, an initial situation confronted and acted upon.

Realism, Automatic Transcription, and the Embrace of the World

Besides the now very quaint-seeming desire to remove the concept of aesthetic realism from the shadow of Soviet Realism under which it had evidently fallen during the Cold War, Carl Dahlhaus's primary argument in *Realism in Nineteenth-Century Music* is that the concept is both somewhat inimical to music (because music is an ideal and so fundamentally unreal art) but also the dominant aesthetic of the nineteenth and early twentieth centuries, and so one that music could hardly avoid confronting in its own way if it wanted to remain a culturally relevant art form.[22] Under the influence of the novel especially, realism, in fact, penetrates to the very core of music, fundamentally transforming even the basic principle of symphonic construction, which must accommodate an expansion of material and means if it is to retain its hard-won capacity to encompass the whole (the principle of the large action form) rather than being resigned to present the 'beautiful' illusion of a whole given in advance and understood in the subjective mood, an 'as if.'

What is curious perhaps is that cinema seemingly traced out a similar path from classicism to its critique in realism, albeit in a tighter circuit. In any event, Bazin discerned characteristics of realism emerging in the post-classical cinema that appeared after the Second World War. Interestingly, Bazin saw a connection between this realism and the novelistic (rather than dramatic) mode. For Bazin, the constructive elements of film, especially the presentation of story through the device of dramatic montage (whether analytical as in Hollywood or dialectical as in Soviet cinema), necessarily undermined the impression of realism because the image was reduced to its dramatic value. What disappeared in this drama was precisely the image of reality, which served to 'disclose the mysteries and epiphanies of lived experience'.[23] Realism, for Bazin, is thus bound up with the ability to capture and allow reflection on the contingent aspects of the world. This explains as well his association of the long take and deep-focus photography with realism: they allow more of the world to appear.

Deleuze takes issue with Bazin's framing of the change in terms of realism, asking whether the issue in fact concerns allowing more of the world to appear as an addition to an image that was apparently less than replete, impoverished to increase the dramatic efficacy. Deleuze proposes instead that there is a more fundamental shift in the very object of the image, which is no longer focused and captured movement of the sensory-motor schema but is now instead extended to thought. And this extension of thought into an object created new images marked by the dissolution of the sensory-motor schema that provided the unity of the old images and created semi-autonomous components in the new one. The crystallisation of these images into time-images—indeed Deleuze calls the most condensed form of the time-image the crystal-image[24]—made narrative more difficult, inducing a crisis of cinematic understanding on a par with the dissolution of tonality in music. The effect of this new image, Deleuze says, is to transform the characters but also the film into observers, seers. 'The character has become a kind of viewer,' Deleuze says. 'He shifts, runs and becomes animated in vain, the situation he is in outstrips his motor capacities on all sides, and makes him see and hear what is no longer subject to the rules of a response or action. He records rather than reacts. He is prey to a vision, pursued by it or pursuing it, rather than engaged in an action.'[25]

Deleuze's observer or seer populates a new cinematic image. The breakdown of the sensory-motor schema means the loss of the world as a place of effective action; action is replaced with a certain passivity that replicates in its own way the mechanisation of the senses in the cinematic apparatus. And the cinematic apparatus was designed in the first instance—that is, as a scientific instrument—not to reproduce motion but to analyze it. This scientific prehistory of the cinema figures the apparatus as a tool of scientific observation, most famously establishing the gait of a galloping horse but also used to analyze and improve the efficiency of work on assembly lines.

According to James Lastra, 'the idea of "capturing" phenomena that were previously fugitive or ephemeral ... definitively shapes the theorization of scientific recording' in the second half of the nineteenth century.[26] The representational technologies that were developed for this purpose—notably the camera and the phonograph—were passive and automatic. The effect of this indiscriminate copying, however, was to disrupt the mental hierarchy that made sense of the world. In creating dictionaries, for instance, linguists sought to discount individual variation in order to abstract the universal form of the word. With phonographic systems, by contrast, properties of sound unrelated to meaning and sense often dominated the recording, and this required a cultural reorientation for these recordings to establish their own value. The more contingency was revealed in the recording, the more it forced subjects into the position of observer: what the observer perceived was not the thing itself but a particular (and particularised) perception of the thing perceived, a perspective determined by the essential fugitive quality of the world that could only be captured and framed rather than positioned in an ideal sense.[27] 'If a passenger on a train failed to notice an object as he hurtled through the landscape, he could not, at will, readjust his framing; his visual experience was determined by forces beyond his control, and at times contrary to his sense of visual importance.'[28] The world simply passes by, allowing no intervention, no ability to assert oneself as agent, as subject. This essentially voyeuristic position presumes to see the world as it reveals itself, an objectivity defined not by an ideal standpoint, but by an arbitrary one.

If cinema offered such objectivity in virtue of the automatic quality of its recording apparatus, the symphony has no direct analogue. Nevertheless, it is telling that romantic ideology sought to reduce compositional labour and so also subjectivity to flashes of inspiration (*Einfälle*) that allowed music to appear to compose itself. As Mahler claimed of his own composing, 'One is, so to speak, no more than an instrument on which the Universe plays, I tell you, in some places it strikes even me as uncanny; it seems as if I hadn't written it at all.'[29] Such automatic transcription serves to ensure the objectivity of the viewpoint, guaranteeing that what the music (or film) records is real rather than an aberration of individual difference. The idea of the cinematograph or phonograph—movement or sound writing itself—allies the recording with the voice of nature. Monelle notes that 'Mahler saw himself ideally as a voice of nature ... [I]n the Mahlerian view of the relation to nature, the composer as subjectivity recedes.'[30] Monelle traces this desubjectification of artistic inspiration to the valorisation of the folk in nineteenth-century German culture,[31] but it has extremely deep roots, relating to the ancient trope of Pope Gregory receiving the chant repertory that bears his name through divine inspiration and indeed the divine inspiration of holy books in general. Music in this respect is constructed not only as the voice of nature but as a form of divine speech. The figure of the recording angel, the desubjectified voice of nature in romantic ideology, is itself a testament that music, too, dreams the myth of the total cinema.[32]

A product of the same era that produced the phonograph and the moving picture, Mahler seems to express a will to the total symphony, to the idea that the symphony will not be complete—will not be true to its idea—until it captures the world in its own image. 'Imagine,' Mahler writes of his Third Symphony, 'such a *great work*, in which in fact the *whole world* is mirrored'.[33] Like the myth of the total cinema, the myth of the total symphony lies in the perceived gap between the existing symphony and the idea: to embrace everything. This embrace is like that of the cinema: the embrace of the world. And the demand of this embrace indicates an idea that likewise serves to guide the symphony to an origin that lies paradoxically in the future and outside itself: the cinema.

Musical Portraiture and the Mirror of Cinema

The idea of music capturing the world in its image leads, inexorably for those aware of the Mahler literature, to the second subject of the first movement of the Sixth Symphony. Alma Mahler wrote a famous little story about this theme. Anyone who has read a set of program notes to the Sixth Symphony undoubtedly knows it, as it is the sort of detail that few annotators can pass up. On the day Mahler completed the first movement of the Sixth, Alma said, he came down from his studio and evidently told her, 'I have tried to capture you in a theme; I do not know whether I have been successful. You will have to put up with it.'[34] It is not important to my argument here as to whether Alma's claim that this theme is a representation of her is actually true. It is perhaps worth noting, however, that her claim to the theme seems to have been tacitly accepted in the Mahler literature. Indeed, it is almost as if critics use the theme to take potshots at Alma on behalf of the composer, as though the theme offered a musical 'photograph' of her apparently 'bombastic and vulgar' soul that the finely attuned recording apparatus of Mahler's artistic subconscious faithfully recorded whatever his conscious intentions.[35] Nevertheless, I do want to ask a question, similar to one that Seth Monahan recently put to the movement: 'What . . . should it mean for our understanding of the Sixth to accept that Mahler was compelled . . . to 'capture' another person in symphonic form (and his new wife, no less)?'[36] Instead of Monahan's question, however, I want to ask a somewhat more literal and less immediately suspicious one: what indeed does it mean to 'capture' someone in a theme? In particular, does it yield a picture? If so, what kind of picture?

Whatever we make of the broader connotations of the term, Mahler's purported use of 'capture' certainly relates by intention to portraiture, making a likeness. Portraiture is evaluated on the basis of resemblance, an iconic correspondence to reality. Almost by default, it demands a hierarchical structure inasmuch as it emphasises the portrait's subject: the setting exists only to be read in terms of that subject. Portraiture also abstracts that subject from a clearly definable space. It is not by chance that soft-focus techniques were largely developed for portraiture nor that the cinematic close-up of the face was modeled on its devices. As Béla Balázs wrote of the cinematic close-up, 'If we see a face isolated and enlarged, we lose our awareness of space, or of the immediate surroundings.'[37]

Because Mahler's portrait is musical, it necessarily unfolds in time; that means it is not a static portrait, like a photograph, but one that must seek to capture the essence of its subject in time. As such, it is more a portrait in motion, a moving picture—one that settles on and captures the characteristic fluctuations of emotion and habitual action that define a being in close-up rather than a pose, an immobile state. The idea of 'capture', however, also doubles in multiple ways. First of all, if we are going to accept the story from which this anecdote comes, making the second theme into a likeness of Alma would also seem to demand that the first theme become a self-portrait of Mahler. These two portraits are then fitted onto a large canvas, or perhaps a screen, the first movement becoming something like the romantic first act of the 'terrifying Symphony Domestica', as sketched by Warren Darcy and filled out with remarkably precise detail by Monahan.[38] Alternatively, we might read it following a somewhat different narrative template as the story of a plucky and vivacious Belle quelling the uncouth raging of the Beast, but a story that will ultimately end, like *King Kong* (1933), in a tragedy of failed assimilation rather than the transformation of the Beast into a fairy-tale prince.

The second theme, in fact, becomes quite uncanny when approached as a portrait, and we attempt to discern what exactly is being captured and reflected in it. The structure of the theme itself is not overly remarkable although it is somewhat under-articulated, using repetition and juxtaposition rather than cadence to mark off units; the theme is perhaps even a little repetitive, and it can easily be described as a ternary form. The opening A section (bars 77–90) is built around a basic statement (Ex. 8.1a) and two variants, each more intense and dissolved than the previous one. Each of these statements is itself subdivided into a longer opening phrase and then two short answering phrases. The second variant of the statement dissolves the two answering phrases through an ecstatic liquidation. The middle B section (bars 91–8; Ex. 8.1b) is a short march-like section, a variant of the opening theme of the movement. The return of the A material (bars 99–115) is again built as a statement and two variants, once again arrayed in increasing intensity. The theme concludes with a strong cadence and a drawn-out codetta (bars 115–22) based on the head motive.[39]

Ex. 8.1a Mahler, Sixth Symphony, I, bars 77–80.

Ex. 8.1b Mahler, Sixth Symphony, I, bars 91–94.

Musically, portraiture seems to encourage a strict melody-and-accompaniment texture, similar to the opening of the Andante moderato movement of the Sixth analyzed briefly above. If in this texture the accompaniment serves to establish a setting and mood—the general function of backgrounds—the lack of distinctive figures in the accompaniment serves both to provide a rather abstract background and to prevent the background from coming forward. The 'Alma' theme does not follow this strategy. Instead, as Monahan notes, Mahler uncharacteristically uses the *alfresco* accompaniment technique of Wagner and Strauss, which has the effect of obscuring the definition of background through busy circles of confusion (the studied production of bokeh), rather than the deep-focus counterpoint or clear melody-and-accompaniment textures that Mahler generally favours. In the more traditionally Mahlerian opening theme of the Sixth analyzed above, for instance, the material is often not easy to parse into discernible layers, and foreground and background figures fluctuate, now one element, now another serving as the point of focus; but the elements themselves are generally distinct throughout the texture. Overall, the effect of the main theme, like most Mahler themes and even the 'Alma' theme when it occurs elsewhere in the movement, is more like having several planes of action, some clearly functional (accompaniment), others less so.

The accompaniment choice here makes somewhat more sense, however, if we distinguish between the immobile still portrait and the mobile cinematic close-up. A close-up, Deleuze says, always provides an image of the face, and the face in close-up delivers what he calls an affection-image that divides into two poles, a surface of 'faceification' and the traits of 'faceicity'.[40] Faceification and faceicity— 'reflecting surface and intensive micro-movements' —correspond to the two questions that Deleuze says we can ask of the face: What are you thinking? What are you feeling?

> Sometimes the face thinks about something, is fixed on an object, and this is the sense of admiration or astonishment that the English word *wonder* has preserved . . . Sometimes, on the contrary, it experiences or feels something and has value through the intensive series that its parts successively traverse as far as paroxysm, each part taking on a kind of momentary independence.[41]

In these terms, the busyness of the *alfresco* technique might be taken less as a means to blur lines and more as a way to provide a trace of the intensive micro-movements of the face, the sound of or musical analogue to faceicity.

Besides its soft-focus *alfresco* technique, the subordinate theme also engages constantly in a play of imitation and pseudo-imitation, especially in the A' section, which calls into question the singularity of the subject. Mirrors appear occasionally in portraiture, where they generally serve as a mark of vanity, and, depending on your view of Alma or your interpretation of the nature of this theme, such a reading is certainly possible in this case. But another interpretation is also possible, one that interprets the reflection in terms of *mise-en-abyme*, the subject caught and split in mirrors (Fig. 8.2). This is in fact a favourite effect of cinema, where it generally serves to destabilise subjectivity, as in a house of mirrors effect. Deleuze calls these crystal-images, and they are a characteristic example of the time-image.

The uncanny reflections of the outer sections of the theme are in fact not its most unsettling aspect. I concur with Monahan's unease with the interior march. He offers three conflicting interpretations of this march without deciding among them: (1) it is unintegrated, (2) it is an intrusion, or (3) it perhaps introduces an entirely new element. He unpacks the last one this way: 'Faced with this bizarre replication of the primary theme . . . could we not imagine ourselves being offered a glimpse of the new addition to the composer's domestic lineup, the progeny that Mahler sought . . . to insure his "immortality"?'[42]

In response, I offer two interpretations of my own, both derived from thinking about affect-images, reflection-images, and the joins among the sections. First, let us consider that march portion, as Monahan does, as separated from the main second subject complex. Each of Monahan's interpretations places considerable weight on the notion of 'capture', on the idea of the representation as being fundamentally determined by the male but also by the protagonist's gaze, whether the representation is one of intrusion or penetration. But who is representing whom here? We can understand this moment not as an intruder per se, certainly not as an intruder controlling the gaze, but rather as the gaze of the other, a focalisation, an affect-image from the pole of faceification (thought) or a reflection-image that transforms the image into an index: in any event, a reflection of the march through the ears of the second subject. We

Fig. 8.2 Cinematic reflections, *mise en abyme* and fractured subjectivity:
a: *The Apartment* (1960); b: *Lady from Shanghai* (1947); c: *Citizen Kane* (1941)

Ex. 8.2 Mahler, Sixth Symphony, I, bars 99–102: dissolve from B to A'.

hear the march as the subject of the portrait hears the march: no longer full of the bluster and drive of the opening but now cutting a slightly comic figure—in this respect, the revision adding the glockenspiel, which 'resonate[s] with echoes of childhood toys',[43] was an exceptionally fine touch. Moreover, if we examine the joins between the march and the outer sections of the theme, we see that they work more by dissolve—sign of a vision or recollection—than by the sort of juxtaposition that would announce an intrusion. Not only does the 'breakaway' portion of the main part of the theme derive, as Monahan neatly shows, directly from the primary theme,[44] but also the march theme continues as accompaniment into the return of the outer section of the theme (Ex. 8. 2), arguably producing the effect of a dissolve at the other join as well. Understood thus, the march theme now appears completely framed by, and so under the representation of the second theme. We might therefore take this section as a recollection-image where time forks: faceification of the affection-image reflects the thought or dream of the figure of the march.

   If we use the under-articulation of the joins as signaling not a dissolve but simply a character movement within a long take, then we must interpret the outer theme and the inner march as reflecting facets of the same time and place. In this case, we cannot take the march as reflecting the gaze of the second theme, that is, its perspective on the march. Rather the appearance of the march now presents a particular relationship of the theme to the march material. Here, the march might be taken more along the lines of what Monahan proposes as an intrusion into the space of the second theme, that is, the march entering the scene; but it might also be revealed as a transformation: in the presence of the theme, the march becomes other than it was. Compared to the opening of the movement, the march seems pacified in the presence of the subordinate theme. If the conception of the second theme area as a long take does not allow us to hear how the theme hears the march, what we gain is that the changes we do hear are now rendered as real rather than as a subjective impression. In any case, we return ambiguity, the unknowability of the other, to the musical setting in order to allow the things of the world to speak.

The World of the Observer

There are a number of ways to interpret the form of the action in the first movement of the Sixth. At the level whole, the movement seems in broad outlines
to be a large form (S-A-S'), with the changed situation dominating, the brooding A minor march gradually yielding over the course of the movement, until
finally swept into the ecstatic whirlwind of the subordinate thematic material.
The prominent anomalies in the movement, notably the unusual transition
material and the passage with the cowbells in the development, suggest that
it is probably a transformed version of the large form, what Deleuze calls a
reflection-image. The opening theme itself chains together a series of rather
fruitless large-form S-A complexes that strike ineffectually against the milieu.
The motto introduces an odd element into the series, what Deleuze calls a
'demark',[45] that belongs properly to what he calls the relation-image. And the
chorale-like transition, with a vestige of the main theme running as counterpoint against it, seems like A', an index of lack (the situation to which it refers is
absent), rather than A, a binomial, the sign of conflict, which has instead been
absorbed into the chain of SAs in the opening theme. This suggests the exposition as a whole is itself structured as a reflection-image, a transformed version
of the large form: S-A'-S'.

The action form of the second theme, by contrast, is more difficult to assess.
On the one hand, if it is taken to be a large form, this also suggests that the
appearance of the march within it is A', an index that in retrospect converts
the exposition into a small form, A-S-A'. The appearance of the march in the
context of the second theme is an index of a changed situation at the level of the
exposition, the changed situation apparently sketched obscurely by the demark
of the motto and the chorale. In this interpretation, on the level of the exposition, the second theme is evaluated primarily for its transforming effects on
the march.

On the other hand, if the second theme is understood as a small form, then
a comparison of the outer 'Alma' sections is decisive, and the return of this
'Alma' material becomes an index to the changed situation of the march. Here
the 'Alma' material would be an index of equivocation. That the *alfresco* technique was earlier interpreted within the affection-image as belonging to intensive micro-movements of faceicity suggests that the equivocation descends not
from the feeling that the face expresses but from the fraught nature of reading
feeling off the face.

This last interpretation adds yet another reflection, and it returns us, by way
of conclusion, to Deleuze's contention that one of the distinguishing elements
of the post-classical cinema is the prominence given to the character of the
observer or seer. The observer is characterised not by a perception-image per
se, but by an image where perception and action do not link up and the status

of the image itself becomes indiscernible. Images become unmoored from the sensory-motor schema. The nature of the observer, the way the observer cannot detach from the world but is caught up in the world's unfolding, makes it the vision of any space whatsoever. A world of any space whatsoever is not a world that belongs to the observer, however, nor is it one over which the observer has any effective control. What is rendered subjectively in the image is affect, how the world feels to an observer from the standpoint of a world not made to order, that has reserved no place for the subject. The world is merely indifferent, consisting of any space whatsoever. If no place is prepared for the observer to occupy as subject, no point whatsoever is barred either—except perhaps the place of the subject itself, which only ever existed out of time as a pose. Any space whatsoever confronts the observer with the reality of desubjectification.

Referring to Italian Neo-Realist cinema, Deleuze wrote:

> Everything remains real in this neo-realism but, between the reality of the setting and that of the action, it is no longer a motor extension which is established, but rather a dreamlike connection through the intermediary of the liberated sense organs. It is as if the action floats in the situation, rather than bringing it to a conclusion or strengthening it.[46]

Mahler's music, too, has moments of such floating action, often signaled by the demark of the cowbells or other prominent intrusions of odd orchestration; and if these remain primarily visionary forks in time in his music, they do nonetheless begin the fraying of the temporal strands that allows his music to encompass a direct image of time.

Notes

1. A comment made to Sibelius dating from 1907, cited in Tawaststjerna, *Sibelius*, 76.
2. Bazin, *What Is Cinema?*, 20.
3. Bazin, *What Is Cinema?*, 24.
4. Monelle, *The Sense of Music*, 184.
5. Johnson, *Mahler's Voices*, 53.
6. Dalhaus, *Realism in Nineteenth-Century Music*, 108.
7. Dalhaus, *Realism in Nineteenth-Century Music*, 107.
8. Dalhaus, *Realism in Nineteenth-Century Music*, 110–11.
9. It is possible to affect the temporality of filmic representation through slow motion or freeze frame. In such cases the filmic temporality differs from the diegetic temporality, though even here the divergence is frequently grounded diegetically as focalisation, the representation of a character's perception, so in the case of slow motion, for instance, it is understood to represent a heightening of a

particular character's perception (even if that character is present in the shot). It therefore has a close association with the lyrical mode.

10. Monelle, *The Sense of Music*, 81.

11. On this point, see Deleuze, *Cinema 1*, 3–8.

12. Deleuze, *Cinema 1*, 2.

13. Deleuze, *Cinema 1*, 7.

14. That the fundamental formal function of the transition is one of destabilisation has long been recognised. See Caplin, *Classical Form*, 125–38; Hepokoski and Darcy, *Elements of Sonata Theory*, 93–116.

15. Bogue, *Deleuze on Cinema*, 85.

16. Deleuze does not deduce the image types from narrative function as is typically done, but in fact derives narrative from the movement-image. 'So-called classical narration derives directly from the organic composition of movement-images [*montage*], or from their specification as perception-images, affection-images, and action-images according to the laws of the sensory-motor schema. We shall see that the modern forms of narration derive from the compositions and types of the time-image: even "readability". Narration is never an evident given of images, or the effect of structure that underlies them; it is a consequence of the visible [*apparent*] images themselves, of the perceptible images in themselves, as they are initially defined in themselves' (*Cinema 2*, 26–7).

17. Deleuze, *Cinema 1*, 141.

18. Deleuze, *Cinema 1*, 141–42.

19. Deleuze, *Cinema 1*, 160.

20. Deleuze, *Cinema 1*, 160.

21. For a thorough discussion of this theme, see Buhler, "Theme, Thematic Process, and Variant-Form".

22. Dalhaus, *Realism in Nineteenth-Century Music*, 1–16.

23. Dalle Vacche, "The Difference of Cinema in the System of the Arts", 148.

24. Deleuze, *Cinema 2*, 68–97.

25. Deleuze, *Cinema 2*, 3.

26. Lastra, *Sound Technology and the American Cinema*, 46.

27. Lastra, *Sound Technology and the American Cinema*, 55.

28. Lastra, *Sound Technology and the American Cinema*, 53.

29. Letter of July 1896 in Martner, *Selected Letters*, 190; cited, transl. amended, in Franklin, *Mahler: Symphony No. 3*, 12.

30. Monelle, *The Sense of Music*, 175.

31. Monelle, *The Sense of Music*, 172–76.

32. On the use of the recording angel as part of the iconography of the phonograph, see Eisenberg, *The Recording Angel*, and Kittler, *Discourse Networks 1800/1900*, 298ff.

33. Martner, *Selected Letters*, 190; cited, transl. amended, in Franklin, *Mahler: Symphony No. 3*, 12.

34. Mahler, *Gustav Mahler. Erinnerungen und Briefe* (1940), 90.

35. The claim that the theme is 'bombastic and vulgar' can be found in Monelle, *The Sense of Music*, 170. Monelle's characterisation is unfortunately far from unusual in the literature.

36. Monahan, "'I Have Tried to Capture You . . .'", 121.

37. Balázs, *Early Film Theory*, 100.

38. Darcy, "Rotational Form," 49; Monahan, "'I Have Tried to Capture You . . .'", *passim*.

39. For a detailed analysis of this part of the movement, see Monahan, "'I Have Tried to Capture You . . .'", passim.

40. Although Deleuze does not explicitly draw the connection, the poles of faceification and faceicity map onto the large and small forms, respectively, of the action-image.

41. Deleuze, *Cinema 1*, 88–89.

42. Monahan, "'I Have Tried to Capture You . . .'", 134, 136, 149.

43. Johnson, *Mahler's Voices*, 70.

44. Monahan, "'I Have Tried to Capture You . . .'", 135.

45. Deleuze, *Cinema 1*, 203.

46. Deleuze, *Cinema 2*, 4.

9

On the British Reception of Ken Russell's *Mahler*

Eftychia Papanikolaou

Ken Russell (1927–2011) followed an idiosyncratic—to say the least—cinematic approach in his early documentary and cinematic renderings of composers. In *Elgar* (1962), *Bartók* (1964), *The Debussy Film* (1965), *Song of Summer: Frederick Delius* (1968), *The Dance of the Seven Veils: Richard Strauss* (1970), and *The Music Lovers* (1970), Russell shaped a largely controversial approach to his subjects, confident in the belief that 'no biographical film can ever capture the authentic essence of an artist's life or work, no matter how faithful it is to the official facts.'[1] Similarly, his 1974 film *Mahler* bears the hallmarks of the director's iconoclastic style. What really sets this film apart, however, lies primarily in its peculiar structure and extravagant modes of presentation. The story unfolds on a train during the last long journey that Mahler and his wife Alma took from Paris to Vienna in the spring of 1911.[2] In the film's narrative, the train's compartment becomes the locus of the diegesis and provides the occasion for a series of reminiscences, during which Mahler's life becomes known to the viewer through several overlapping flashbacks, interspersed with fantasy and dream sequences. By foregrounding the cinematic apparatus, Russell forces the viewer to put together Mahler's life as if in a temporal puzzle, in a non-teleological fashion that comes in sharp relief to the linear progression of time implied by the train's journey. Thus Gustav (Robert Powell) and Alma (Georgina Hale) travel not only literally, in space, but also metaphorically, in time (see Figs 9.1a and 9.1b).[3]

Through the use of flashbacks and fantasy sequences (documenting Mahler's unhappy childhood, his brother's suicide, his conversion to Catholicism, the artistic suppression of Alma, the loss of his child, and Alma's infidelity) Russell reveals 'how [an artist] transcended his own personal problems and weaknesses in creating great art. Showing the personal struggles out of which an artist's work grew', the director continued, 'is more of a tribute to him than making believe that he was some sort of saint sitting quietly in his studio creating masterpieces'.[4] Russell knew Mahler's life exceptionally well and he was, by his own admission, a great fan of his music:

> I was extremely familiar with the subject matter, having absorbed my subjects' lives and art for many years before committing them to celluloid. In the case of the two composers [Tchaikovsky in *The Music Lovers* and Mahler]

Fig. 9.1a Robert Powell as Gustav Mahler. *Mahler,* Image Entertainment, DVD
6305131090, 1998 [1974]

Fig. 9.1b Georgina Hale as Alma Mahler. *Mahler,* Image Entertainment, DVD
6305131090, 1998 [1974]

I took as a starting point their music, which by their own account was
partly autobiographical ... [W]e know that the second subject of his Sixth
Symphony was a musical portrait of his wife, which tells us more in a few bars
than a lifetime's research could ever reveal—not only about the woman, but
also about Mahler himself. That glorious theme is elevated, ravishing, passionate. In the brutal martial music that follows, we experience his jealously
over Alma's many admirers and their threat to his marriage. For as a child,

Mahler lived next door to a barracks and ever after associated bugle calls and military band music with the domestic violence to which he was a frequent and highly distressed witness. And so you gradually put the pieces of this symphonic jigsaw together to end up with a colourful portrait, in which the man's life is seen through the mirror of his music.[5]

Russell makes sure that in *Mahler* the music also tells the story, occasionally with astonishing synchronisation between sound and image. Observations such as those made by Russell about the composer's life and music proliferated for decades, and thus the film mirrors opinions and attitudes about Mahler prevalent at the time. Leon Botstein has rightly claimed that the film's emphasis on controversial biographical content is a result of the state of Mahler scholarship at the time of its creation.[6] It is true that the film serves as a microcosm of reception history after the 1960s eruption of interest in Mahler's life and music, as the body of reception documented in this essay will reveal. At the same time, however, the exorbitant cinematic modes of narration in *Mahler* constitute a critical device for Russell's approach to the composer and his music. Through means that emphasise the ludicrous and absurd in correlation with the level of the protagonist's trauma, Russell chose *not* to give us the conventional, romanticised story of the artist, but rather to speak to the composer's personal and artistic identity in ways that, in reality, entered the convoluted and problematic Mahler reception history only in later years. As a consequence, the film attempts to both uphold and subvert those identities while it functions as an agent that imprints on us the 'memory' of a composer who was in the process of being rediscovered. In this essay I concentrate specifically on the British reception of *Mahler*, particularly in the way it echoes wider issues of Mahler reception.

Mahler in the 1950s and 1960s

Although after World War II performances of Mahler's music were met with considerable acclaim in England (in concert programs, radio broadcasts, and gramophone recordings, as documented by Donald Mitchell),[7] it was the early 1960s that saw the precipitous rise of Mahler's star. The composer had emerged from being 'the subject of a minority cult'[8] to being recognised as worthy of attention and also effective at filling concert halls. At least that was Peter Heyworth's reluctant admission in 1962 in a thoughtful review of a performance of the Sixth Symphony with the BBC Orchestra under the direction of Norman del Mar: 'What an enthralling score this is! Grand and generous in conception, overwhelmingly rich in melody, daringly resourceful in harmony, cornucopian in invention and, at any rate in part, startlingly original in sound . . . Yet a doubt persists. Is it also a great work?'[9] Less than a month later,

Heyworth's earlier declaration of Mahler as 'minority cult' was firmly heralded as a 'growing cult' in the title of a 1962 review for the *Guardian*. Its author, J. H. Elliott, clearly counts himself among those who had been proselytised to Mahler's music:

> The comparatively recent emergence of Mahler on the British musical scene has been due to one of those phenomenal changes in the artistic atmosphere which, thirty years or so ago, could hardly have been foreseen ... In the meantime, there is a good deal of propaganda still to be done, in spite of the efforts of advocates among conductors. We may pat ourselves on the back once again, for Barbirolli has been notable among them.[10]

Sir John Barbirolli's contribution to the Mahler 'cult' is indeed remarkable. Between 1954 and 1970 he performed in concerts all of Mahler's works except for the Eighth Symphony,[11] and Neville Cardus, the influential music critic and high priest of Mahlerites, counted him among the 'most illuminating Mahler conductors'.[12] Two more Mahlerian conductors, Jascha Horenstein and Maurice Abravanel, rightly share credit for their enormously pioneering programming of Mahler's music during the 1950s and 1960s—indeed, Horenstein's performance of the Eighth (his only one) with the London Symphony Orchestra at the Royal Albert Hall in 1959 is said to have ushered in the Mahler obsession in Britain.

The rise of LP recordings undoubtedly helped Mahler's music be 'swallowed in large doses'.[13] In the United States, Dimitri Mitropoulos's pioneering programming of Mahler's music and subsequent recordings with the New York Philharmonic in the 1950s were soon followed by the adventurous Leonard Bernstein, who 'in effect ... built his own legitimacy as a serious conductor around his identification with Mahler'[14] and galvanised an essentially Mahlerian obsession. As is widely known, the 1960 Mahler centenary celebrations on both sides of the Atlantic precipitated a virtual avalanche of interest in Mahler as well as an unprecedented release of recordings. Between 1960 and 1975, Leonard Bernstein (1960–67), Georg Solti (1961–71), Bernard Haitink (1962–71), Maurice Abravanel (1964–75), and Rafael Kubelik (1967–71) recorded complete cycles of Mahler's symphonies. By 2004, as David Pickett has noted, about two thousand recordings of Mahler's symphonies had been produced.[15]

Another aspect of particular interest concerning the reception of Mahler in England involves the early completion and ensuing premiere in August 1964 of Deryck Cooke's performing version of the Tenth Symphony. Subsequent editions of the Tenth, the publication of the complete works (*Gustav Mahler: Sämtliche Werke*, 1960–) and also additional manuscripts in facsimile by the Internationale Gustav Mahler Society in Vienna elevated Mahler's music to new heights of scholarly endeavor. At the same time, Bernard Haitink's tenure with the London Philharmonic Orchestra from 1967 to 1979 proved to be of considerable influence. Haitink offered the British audiences a healthy dose of Mahler's music on his programmes, and it is probably due to that proximity and familiarity with his concerts that Ken Russell chose Haitink's recordings with the Amsterdam Concertgebouw as the soundtrack for *Mahler*.

British critics and the public continued to embrace Mahler's music with obsessive enthusiasm throughout the 1960s. On 19 June 1967 Edward Greenfield reported enthusiastically: 'When Mahler fever remains so high, nothing could be more opportune than the discovery of a "new" movement from a Mahler symphony.'[16] Greenfield of course referred to Donald Mitchell's discovery of the discarded 'Blumine' movement of the First Symphony and its first twentieth-century performance conducted by Benjamin Britten at the Aldeburgh Festival the day before. Mitchell's advocacy of Mahler had already resulted in a pioneering monograph, *Gustav Mahler: The Early Years*, published in London in 1958 (later revised and edited by Paul Banks and David Matthews).[17] Additionally, Kurt Blaukopf's *Mahler oder der Zeitgenosse der Zukunft* was translated by Inge Goodwin and published simply as *Gustav Mahler* in 1973. Several book reviews from 1973 and 1974 brought attention to this scholarly work, mainly on the grounds of its academic outlook. Neville Cardus hailed it as the 'most closely and profusely documented biography of Mahler' to that date.[18]

Alma Militans

This proliferation of books, concerts, recordings, and information available to the public would have done little to stimulate curiosity about Mahler as an individual had it not been for the publication of Alma Mahler's memoirs.[19] Basil Creighton's translation was reprinted in 1956 and later revised and edited by Donald Mitchell.[20] By the time Russell set out to film *Mahler*, a third edition of Alma's memoirs had been published.[21]

Mitchell himself had commented in the first edition that Alma Mahler's book constituted a record of 'a remarkable love affair between a man of genius and a woman of outstanding gifts'.[22] Alma's memoirs received considerable press early on, as evident in Cardus's book review in the *Guardian*. A writer with an unabashedly targeted mission to make Mahler and his music better known to wider audiences, Cardus praised Mitchell's effort to rehabilitate Mahler among British writers who had been critical of Mahler's music in the past. Alma's memoir (whose accuracy he questioned) presented just an excuse for Cardus to claim with characteristic boldness midway through the review: 'Whoever thinks that Mahler's mind, musical or other, was second-rate should have his own cerebellum attended to.'[23]

Almost all of the events dramatised or alluded to in *Mahler*'s flashbacks and
fantasy sequences may be traced to passages from Alma's memoirs. Russell
never denied his reliance on her writings. In fact, this literal devotion to Alma's
word might have served as a measure of assurance to her daughter, Anna, that
the film would be as faithful to her father's legacy as possible. Russell had asked
for Anna's permission to make the film, and eventually received it.[24] The third
edition of Alma's book (published December 1973) instigated yet another
review by Cardus. Typical of his advocacy and wit, the opening paragraph is
worth quoting in full:

> Over each year during the past decade Mahler's music has been omnipresent,
> in concerts, over the radio, on records. Even in Vienna, where, as director of
> the State Opera, he shortened his life—and the life of others—by his fanati-
> cism for perfection, even in Vienna his music is being rediscovered. Another
> sign of the Mahler obsession is the constant stream of additions to his criti-
> cal and biographical literature. A third edition is published by John Murray
> of Alma Mahler's 'Memories and Letters,' edited with truly comprehensive
> scholarship and pertinent allusion by Donald Mitchell.[25]

The following quotation, an open endorsement of Alma's authority, clearly encapsulates the public perception of the composer on the eve of the release of
Russell's *Mahler*:

> The 'Memories and Letters,' put together by Alma Mahler, are, I think, neces-
> sary to anybody hoping to get right into the mind and metabolism of one of
> the most psychologically complex of all composers. He was vain and modest,
> at the mercy of his nerves, violently impulsive, yet he had one of the keenest
> brains of his period. He submitted himself for examination to Freud; and,
> I imagine, after the examination Freud probably needed to consult another
> psychoanalyst. The more I read of Alma Mahler's memories of her genius
> husband, the more I know that into his music Mahler put the whole of him-
> self, without inhibitions.[26]

The year before the film's release had also seen the publication (in addition to
Blaukopf's book) of the first volume of Henry-Louis de La Grange's *Mahler*,[27]
a work that was aptly praised in the British press. Just ten days after the film's
opening, Michael Ratcliffe published a review of both La Grange's and Blaukopf's
books for the *Times*. In this essay, titled 'The Pattern of Mahler's Existence',
Ratcliffe acknowledged Mahler as 'one of the most glittering and influential artists of the twentieth century', noting that La Grange's volume is 'required reading for all Mahlerians, musical or (such is the nature of Mahler's current fame)
otherwise'.[28] He acknowledges that 'Baron de la Grange is determined to retrieve
every piece of documentation available and tap it into place; in so doing, he has
established, for the first time, the pattern of Mahler's existence. He has made
order where there was only chaos and it is a very considerable achievement.'

By the end, however, he finds the 'Baron's' approach lacking in focus, whereas Blaukopf's book 'has a proper Mahlerian sharpness to it'. Ken Russell also makes a cursory appearance; without referring to the film by name, Ratcliffe admits that the director is 'correct to say that, for all his nervous sensibilities and transparent feeling, Mahler was a formidably tough survivor'.[29] In another fascinating review of La Grange's *Mahler* (also discussed later), Peter Heyworth declared, 'La Grange's massive biography will satisfy even the most avid Mahlerians' thirst for information.'[30] By the early 1970s, the Mahler 'minority cult' he had reluctantly acknowledged in 1962 had turned into a veritable religion.

The Film, *Mahler*

In spite of the overwhelmingly successful revival that Mahler enjoyed in the 1960s, one may still wonder: what did average audiences *hear* and *see* in Ken Russell's *Mahler* in 1974? Given the amount of publicity that concerts, recordings, and books about Mahler enjoyed (as even this cursory look at the press of the time has revealed), what was the popular image that the average moviegoer had formed about Mahler's life and music? Similarly, how much did the film do to uphold or subvert that reception? In an effort to answer these questions one needs to look not only at Mahler's image in the press (which emphasised his Jewish roots, unconventional compositional approach, erratic temperament, and marriage to Alma) but also at the reception of Russell's film itself.

The newspaper advertisement for the film's release on 5 April 1974 (see Fig. 9.2) speaks volumes.

Readers must have been intrigued by the image of Mahler in a coffin—on one level, an easy allusion to the composer's fixation with loss and death (of childhood, of his siblings, and of his own daughter). Audiences of the film, however, would also later recognise it as part of the film's fantasy sequence in which Mahler is cremated alive (see Fig. 9.3).

The scene shows Mahler's face in agony screaming through a coffin's little window while Alma and a group of Nazi-dressed soldiers/pallbearers march the coffin to cremation to the non-diegetic sounds of the first-movement 'Trauermarsch' of his Fifth Symphony. This is admittedly one of the most disturbing dream sequences and it is certainly not a coincidence that its imagery was selected to advertise the film. Just as the film's Mahler (inaudibly) screams from inside the coffin in order to be spared a certain death, so the advertisement's Mahler struggles to be rescued from the often clichéd and sentimental image he had acquired over the decades.

The advertisement is explicit in summarising what audiences already knew about Mahler, as the first half of its narrative informs us: 'Throughout his life,

If Mahler's life story isn't about his life, then what is it about?

Throughout his life, Mahler was preoccupied with death.

His childhood was desperately unhappy.

Five of his brothers and sisters died in infancy.

His father was a bully.

His brother, Otto, shot himself.

He set music to Friedrich Ruckert's poems 'Songs on the death of children.'

Soon after which his own child, Maria, died.

Yet this obsession with death drove him to write some of the most beautiful music composed this century.

He has now been recognised as a direct influence on Schoenberg, Britten and Shostakovich.

And now Ken Russell has made a film about him.

Starring Robert Powell as Mahler and Georgina Hale as Mahler's wife, Alma.

It opens today in London at the Odeon, Haymarket.

But please don't go along expecting to see a life of Mahler set to music.

Ken Russell's film isn't about the composer's life, so much as his mind.

And, of course, his music.

Fact, fantasy and dream flow together throughout the film to form an image of Mahler's mind.

At times that image is serene. At others, downright frightening.

'Mahler' is like no other Ken Russell film before it.

We urge you to see it.

Today onwards.

Ken Russell's

MAHLER AA

A GOODTIMES ENTERPRISES PRODUCTION Starring ROBERT POWELL GEORGINA HALE, Executive Producers DAVID PUTTNAM SANDY LIEBERSON. Produced by ROY BAIRD Written and Directed by KEN RUSSELL. Mahler Symphonies conducted by Bernard Haitink and played by the Concertgebouw Orchestra, Amsterdam.

ODEON HAYMARKET

Fig. 9.2 Advertisement for *Mahler* in *The Guardian*, 5 April 1974, 11

Mahler was preoccupied with death.' The rest, however, seems to be cautionary about what this film is *not* saying about Mahler:

> But please don't go along expecting to see a life of Mahler set to music. Ken Russell's film isn't about the composer's life, so much as his mind. And, of

Fig. 9.3 Mahler alive in the coffin. *Mahler*, Image Entertainment, DVD 6305131090, 1998 [1974]

course, his music. Fact, fantasy and dream flow together throughout the film to form an image of Mahler's mind . . . *Mahler* is like no other Ken Russell film before it.

The film is replete with sequences and flashbacks that explore and document Alma's bitterness, Gustav's obsession with his music, his unhappy childhood and family life, his demanding—bordering on neurotic—personality and, of course, his conversion to Christianity. But Russell would rather probe the inner aspects of Mahler's mind and psyche than give us a straightforward narrative. *Mahler* is intended to be about who he 'really' was rather than what he actually did.

Russell contra Visconti

This type of apophatic advertising purposefully seems to subvert what was probably the most popular image that audiences had acquired about Mahler at the time—namely, the constructed image of Mahler in Luchino Visconti's *Morte a Venezia* (*Death in Venice*). This film had been released three years earlier, in 1971, and Visconti had unabashedly turned the hero of Thomas Mann's novella *Der Tod in Venedig* (1912) into a musician, complete with a soundtrack that famously utilises the Adagietto of the Fifth Symphony.[31] Gustav Aschenbach, the writer in the novella, had often mistakenly been viewed as loosely based on Mahler—partly due to a 1921 letter in which Mann admitted that he gave his hero the 'first name of the great musician' as well as his 'physical description' as an homage to the composer who had died just a year before *Death in Venice* was published.[32] If Mann's Aschenbach (played in the film by Dirk Bogarde)

Fig. 9.4 Allusion to Visconti's *Death in Venice. Mahler,* Image Entertainment, DVD 6305131090, 1998 [1974]

had provoked oblique connections with Mahler, Visconti's use of Mahler's music throughout the film (and the fact that he turned the protagonist into a musician bearing Mahler's resemblance) had sealed the identification.

Undoubtedly, Russell felt compelled to respond to the Viscontian rendering. In an unforgettable mise-en-scène, only five minutes into *Mahler,* Russell's Mahler looks outside the train window only to see the hapless hero of Thomas Mann's novella and the young Tadzio, the object of his infatuation. They appear in stunning imitation of Visconti's cinematic portrayal: Aschenbach sits on a bench at the train station's platform, while Tadzio, dressed in his iconic navy suit, swings around the station's poles (see Fig. 9.4), in a stark replication of the famous beach sequence in *Death in Venice.* The scene in *Mahler* is appropriately accompanied by the Adagietto and culminates in an enigmatic smile on Mahler's face. Russell's intertextual commentary, by visually and aurally alluding to Visconti's cinematic adaptation, also raises a paradoxical point. In the film's narrative, Mahler cannot possibly have a vision of these images on the train platform. Russell the auteur has implanted them in Mahler's mind and they serve early on as reminders to *us,* the audience, that what we are about to see is a different Mahler. Russell thus acknowledges a (misrepresented) popular image of Mahler while he manages to manipulate Mahler's and the audiences' (that is, *our*) expectations. It also allows momentarily the character of Mahler 'to stand outside time and survey the full reception history and influence of his oeuvre, past and future', as Arved Ashby has insightfully surmised. '[Mahler's] smile betokens full knowledge of the Visconti film and the influence it will have'.[33]

A large amount of press following the release of Visconti's cinematic *Death in Venice* identified Gustav Aschenbach with Gustav Mahler.[34] The anonymous film reviewer for the *Guardian* in 1971 did not hesitate to state that in Visconti's film 'Gustav Aschenbach is really a code name for Gustav

Mahler.'[35] Published soon after the release of Russell's *Mahler* in April 1974, Heyworth's review of La Grange's *Mahler* leaves no ambiguity about the state of fascination with the composer at the time: 'Twenty years ago a performance of a Mahler symphony was in itself an event; today it is a recipe for an all sold-out house. Even the cinema has muscled in on the act.'[36] As he put it, 'Visconti brashly transformed the hero of "Death in Venice" into Mahler himself. And more recently Ken Russell has followed up with another of his fantasy lives of the great composer.' He goes on, however, to delineate the shortcomings of both films: 'If books [such as La Grange's] have lagged behind [in popularity] that is because, unlike Mr. Russell, they are beholden to facts, a commodity that has not hitherto been in ample supply, considering the fact that Mahler died no less than 63 years ago.'[37] Obviously, *Mahler* did not rise to the level of authenticity desired of a subject's cinematic biography. Russell's advertised warning against such expectations seemed to have gone largely unnoticed.

During the same month as the film's release, several critics chose to take the high ground and instead concentrate on the scholarly investigation of Mahler. In a long article that appeared in the *Guardian* on 22 April 1974, Tom Sutcliffe wrote a sweeping appreciation of the composer based on La Grange's book. The essay's opening, however, is also revealing of Sutcliffe's frustration:

> Gustav Mahler's doom may have seemed sealed these last weeks. It's not so long since Visconti made his sally against the composer in 'Death in Venice', and now Ken Russell, with biographical details culled we are told from the internal evidence of the music has done his worst. Tchaikovsky could perhaps take it, yet Mahler—to judge from the telly advertisements—was destined to become a pseud's delight . . . Henry-Louis de La Grange, the French-American whose 15 years of research will set the record straight, wrote to Russell when he got wind of the film and offered his knowledge. That was in autumn 1972, and Russell wrote back in his own hand that the film was not about to be made. De La Grange's offer was not taken up and the rest, as they say, is history.[38]

None of the available literature has been able to substantiate whether Russell indeed received or wrote any such letters. In his, now multi-volume, biography of Mahler, La Grange has remained taciturn on the topic of the composer's cinematic adaptations. As an afterthought to the final volume (Appendix 3Af: 'Mahler Mythomania'), La Grange admits that Ken Russell's *Mahler* 'does offer a number of authentic details', but he asserts, 'The manner in which people and events are portrayed recalls the schematized world of the cartoon film.'[39] Although hardly an endorsement, it nevertheless speaks to a general reluctance until recently to consider this and other cinematic portrayals of the composer as valuable links in the chain of reception history.

Mahler à la Russell

As has been evident thus far, the reception of Mahler's image in the film also has to do with the reception of the film itself. On 4 April 1974, one day before the film's official opening, the *Guardian* published a review of *Mahler*, provocatively titled 'Alma's Martyr' (a play on the words *alma mater*). Keen on striking a balance by pointing out some of the film's redeeming aspects, the reviewer, Philip Hope-Wallace, also found 'a great deal meretricious, lurid, even offensive'. In the end, he viewed certain scenes as 'flawed, pretentious, and regrettable'.[40] In a similarly polemical review, John Coleman of the *New Statesman* called the film Russell's 'largest aberration to date: almost a dare'.[41] And, in an article titled 'The Murder of Mahler', Hollis Alpert of the *Saturday Review* described the conversion scene (discussed below) as 'one of the more sickening spectacles created for the film medium'.

Indictments such as these might even be considered kind compared with those penned by David Robinson. His review for the *Times*, which appeared on the day of the film's opening, bore the suggestive title 'Poor Mahler gets the Russell Treatment'. Robinson largely acknowledges the popularisation of Mahler's image through Visconti but openly begrudges Russell's approach to his subject:

> Poor Gustav Mahler, out of copyright protection these last dozen years or so, has fallen prey to the film-makers. First Visconti (with very little justification as it proved) identified him with the Aschenbach of Thomas Mann's *Death in Venice* and used the Third and Fifth Symphonies as a musical score. Now the composer comes in for a Ken Russell working-over in *Mahler*.

Like Hope-Wallace before him, Robinson finds of 'appalling taste' two specific sequences that have troubled many critics ever since: Mahler's live cremation with Alma's striptease dance on his coffin (see Fig. 9.5) and the conversion

Fig. **9.5** Alma dances on Gustav's coffin. *Mahler,* Image Entertainment, DVD 6305131090, 1998 [1974]

fantasy sequence. He calls the first 'a Freudian ballet of Mahler's vision of his own death' and the latter a 'Monty Python-cum-*Top of the Pops*'[42] approach— both insightful commentaries given Russell's penchant for cynicism and parody.

The conversion scene operates on a symbolic level and has been viewed as the most outrageous fantasy sequence in the film. It unfolds following Mahler's calculated decision (at least as portrayed in the film) to convert to Catholicism. It focuses the fervent opposition of Mahler's nomination to the directorship of the Vienna Opera on the character of Cosima Wagner—an instance of an overblown Alma story taken out of context.[43] This momentous event furnishes the opportunity for a fantasy sequence whose narrative implicates the viewer in a phantasmagoria that ranges from the subtly nuanced to the downright kitsch. Presented as a silent film, complete with intertitles, it is accompanied by non-diegetic music from Mahler's Ninth Symphony.

The first intertitle reads 'The convert, starring Cosima Wagner with Gustav Mahler' (see Fig. 9.6), followed by 'Valhalla: Shrine of the Goddess of Music, Cosima Wagner'.

Wearing a costume that, anachronistically, resembles a Nazi uniform, Cosima Wagner (the actress Antonia Ellis) appears as an S.S. storm trooper with a curious dominatrix complex (Fig. 9.7).

At the beginning of the sequence Mahler is dressed as an Orthodox Jew, in black suit and wide-brimmed hat, who has to go through a series of trials to renounce Judaism (including the slaying of a dragon, an overt allusion to Siegfried's similar predicament in Fritz Lang's *Die Nibelungen* (1922–24)). At first Mahler throws a Star of David into the fire, and with a hammer, like another Siegfried, forges a sword (see Fig. 9.8).

Fig. 9.6 Intertitle for the beginning of the conversion fantasy sequence. *Mahler*, Image Entertainment, DVD 6305131090, 1998 [1974]

Fig. 9.7 Cosima Wagner as Nazi dominatrix. *Mahler*, Image Entertainment, DVD 6305131090, 1998 [1974]

Fig. 9.8 Mahler as Siegfried. *Mahler*, Image Entertainment, DVD 6305131090, 1998 [1974]

 Still in silent-mode presentation, he willingly accepts Cosima's offer to drink milk and eat pork (literally, a boar's head) in a grotesquely exaggerated manner. The combination of diegetic silence and non-diegetic music amplifies the visual dimension of the scene, whose narrative is thus encapsulated in its aural component. The return of diegetic sound coincides with the end of the conversion process, and is announced by another intertitle: ' . . . and then came the talkies'. Sitting on either side of an inverted sword (an item that, conveniently, also serves as an image of the cross—see Fig. 9.9), Gustav and Cosima celebrate their victory by singing satirical limericks to the music of Richard Wagner's 'Ride of the Valkyries':

> No longer a Jew boy
> winning strength through joy[44]
> you're one of us now,
> now you're a goy.
>
> Don't throw it all
> When on you I smile
> Dictator of opera
> Mahler, Sie heil!

Fig. 9.9 Robert Powell as Gustav Mahler and Antonia Ellis as Cosima Wagner at the end of the conversion fantasy sequence. *Mahler*, Image Entertainment, DVD 6305131090, 1998 [1974].

G: You've made me a star
C: You've gone very far
G: My passage to Heaven, that's what you are
C: No longer a dog
G: You've got me the job
Together: Now we're on the marquee, thanks be to God!

Film critics have viewed this disturbing sequence as the most problematic and least successful part of the film. Russell apparently believed that Mahler's conversion was a betrayal but that it was a necessary career move in an unabashedly anti-Semitic culture.[45] Leon Botstein rightly considers the rendering of Mahler in the film as a 'victim striving for acceptance and deformed by his environment' as 'ludicrous'.[46] I argue that far from the established view as a victim, Mahler emerges as a symbol of resistance that in the early 1970s would have resonated with a number of social and political upheavals on both sides of the Atlantic. Rather than criticising Mahler's conversion, Russell (a convert to Catholicism himself) sheds a sympathetic light on the composer's identity crisis. This fantasy sequence speaks to Mahler's conversion in absurd and disturbing modes of presentation but, in this case, exaggeration facilitates identification and valorisation. The silent-film mode of diegesis adds an important layer of commentary: after the suppression of his Jewish identity, Mahler has found his 'voice' again.

In his review of La Grange's first biographical volume, Heyworth offered what at the time were perhaps the most intricate observations on the British appropriation of Mahler's music:

> Mahler was unmistakably part of the tradition that he seemed at once to venerate and hold up to mockery. Hence, the more apparent his links with it ... the greater the offence given by the sarcasm and nostalgia, anguish and irony that are the hallmarks of his idiom. That idiom embodies an amalgam of emotions that has no precedent in music ... and by means of it Mahler touched an exposed nerve in the decaying corpse of the Habsburg Empire. That, no doubt, was why his music aroused such resentment in the Central Europe of his day, and why it did much the same in post-war Britain. Twenty years ago the British musical establishment, like many other organs of British life, was engaged in an elaborate charade, designed to persuade us that things were as they always had been, that after a century and a half of industrialisation our rural society was still intact and impregnable ... [H]is anguish gave expression to what we today describe as alienation ... In short, Mahler shattered illusions. No wonder he awakened such animosity; no wonder that now that we have shed a few illusions, the truthfulness of what he has to say has become so strikingly relevant.[47]

In sum, Heyworth locates Britain's fascination with Mahler's music in the way it provoked cultural and political identifications in the country that were analogous to those Mahler reflected and critiqued in his own times. The view that the tumultuous 1960s offered fertile ground for the popularisation of Mahler's music has been shared by a number of writers ever since. Mahler's 'soul-searching symphonic dramas', in Lewis Smoley's words, 'seemed to new audiences to be a quintessential expression of their world-view that sought redemption from tyranny, bigotry, pseudo-sophistication and corrupt hedonism'.[48] Interestingly enough, these same qualities have remained at the heart of Mahler reception ever since and, curiously, as Russell admitted, 'Mahler's "bombast" as well as "music that was brutal, vulgar, grotesque, macabre" are the self-same qualities for which he himself is most frequently criticized'.[49] Russell's cinematic language, with its persistent emphasis on the episodic, also reflects back on key Mahlerian compositional traits, such as the obsessive cohabitation of the tragic and the trivial, and the ambivalent disposition of moods. Where Mahler juxtaposes marches with chorale tunes, the film's flashbacks and dream sequences stand for analogous narrative and aural disruptions. Botstein's assertion that 'Mahler's music became the voice of the individual per se as suffering outcast and victim'[50] may be equally true of Russell's cinema.

Camera Futura

When Russell died on 27 November 2011 the press was quick to valorise his contribution to the world of cinema and celebrate his achievements while it simultaneously dissected the visual vulgarity of his work and underscored his innumerable eccentricities. In his obituary for the *Guardian*, film critic Peter Bradshaw brought the discussion full circle to the cultural and political scene of the time. Russell's 'adventures were a rebuke to British parochialism, literalism and complacency', he argues. 'It was as if Russell looked around at the stupefying dullness of Britain in the Heath/Wilson era and thought: what can I do to shake this lot up?'[51] Although it might be an exaggeration to attribute Russell's extreme cinematic viewpoint to the towering figures of Harold Wilson and Edward Heath, who together monopolised British politics for over a decade,[52] their tenures did coincide with the Mahler revival, cult, and obsession of the 1960s and early 1970s. It is possible that the cultural identifications implied by Heyworth in 1974 run a lot deeper than previously acknowledged—or than this essay can address.

Ken Russell's legacy, nonetheless, remains apparent in the next generation of directors who have attempted to bring composers' lives to the big screen. Bernard Rose, the director of *Immortal Beloved* (1994), has admitted that the film was inspired by Russell's aborted Beethoven project. In it we detect a similar concern with 'the struggle of the artist to create, the courage it requires to devote one's life to art, and the tragedy that often results'—that is, qualities that Rose admired in his idol's films.[53]

In spite of its aesthetic and historical idiosyncrasies, *Mahler* is among Russell's most rewarding composer 'biopics'. Over the decades, various historiographic trends have dictated and influenced the ways we perceive Mahler

the composer, which in turn have had an effect on the popular image created. Russell's *Mahler* conveys a snapshot of the reception of Mahler's life and
music at that particular point in time. Through the excessive and exorbitant
cinematic re-telling of the composer's life, however, Russell also delivers a
powerful commentary on that reception. Instead of it being a study in myth-
making, *Mahler* encapsulates the reception of the Mahler myth by often sub-
verting its popular status. To put it simply: the film provides a microcosm of
Mahler reception up to that time, but it also itself becomes part of reception
history by virtue of the ideologies it creates. As is evident throughout, *Mahler*
fulfills the expectation of who Mahler would become rather than just who he
was; and in that respect, Russell seems to have filmed *Mahler* for us, for the
future.

Notes

1. Phillips, *Ken Russell*, 47.
2. In reality, Mahler was too sick to even stand up or walk during that trip.
Alma gives a moving description in her memoirs: 'Chvostek [famous Viennese
doctor who had been summoned to Paris for consultation] and I accompanied him
in the ambulance and then he was carried to the train on a stretcher ... It was
horrible to see him manipulated into the train on a stretcher along the narrow
corridor. He went straight to bed, and Moll, Chvostek and I took turns in watching
through the night ... Journalists came to the door at every station in Germany and
Austria for the latest bulletin, and so his last journey was like that of a dying king'.
Alma Mahler, *Gustav Mahler: Memories and Letters* (1969), 199.
3. All stills were captured from the DVD edition of the film: *Mahler*, dir. Ken
Russell, Image Entertainment, DVD 6305131090, 1998 [1974]. See my "Trauma as
Memory in Ken Russell's *Mahler*" for further discussion of issues of remembrance
and nostalgia raised by the film.
4. Phillips, *Ken Russell*, 43.
5. Ken Russell, *Directing Film*, 32.
6. See Botstein, "Whose Gustav Mahler?"
7. See Mitchell, "The Mahler Renaissance in England".
8. Heyworth, "Mahler and the Lost Generation".
9. Heyworth, "Mahler and the Lost Generation".
10. Elliott, "The Growing Cult of Mahler".
11. Smoley, "Mahler Conducted and Recorded", 252.
12. See Cardus, "Glorious John".
13. Cardus, "Mahler, Warts and All".
14. Draughon and Knapp, "Gustav Mahler and the Crisis of Jewish Identity", §6.
15. Pickett, "Mahler on Record: The Spirit or the Letter?", 371.
16. Edward Greenfield, "Richter and the New Philharmonia at the Aldeburgh
Festival", *Guardian*, 19 June 1967, 7.

17. Mitchell, *Gustav Mahler: The Early Years* (1980).

18. See Cardus, "More of Mahler".

19. Alma Mahler, *Gustav Mahler: Erinnerungen und Briefe* (1940) and *Gustav Mahler: Memories and Letters* (1946).

20. Alma Mahler, *Gustav Mahler: Memories and Letters* (1968).

21. Alma Mahler, *Gustav Mahler: Memories and Letters* (1973). Theodor W. Adorno's *Mahler: Eine musikalische Physiognomik* was published in 1960, but the first English translation did not appear until 1992 (*Mahler: A Musical Physiognomy*). It is probable that wider audiences (and Russell too) would not have been familiar with Adorno's work at the time of the film's making.

22. Alma Mahler, *Gustav Mahler: Memories and Letters* (1968), 369.

23. Cardus, "Alma's Mahler".

24. Phillips, *Ken Russell*, 122.

25. Cardus, Review of 1973 edition.

26. Cardus, Review of 1973 edition.

27. La Grange, *Gustav Mahler*, Vol. 1.

28. Ratcliffe, "The Pattern of Mahler's Existence", 7.

29. Ratcliffe, "The Pattern of Mahler's Existence".

30. Heyworth, "Catching Up with Mahler".

31. *Death in Venice*, dir. Luchino Visconti, Warner Home Video, DVD 08539288812, 2004. Visconti was the favorite to win the main prize at the Cannes festival in 1972. Instead, the award went to Joseph Losey for *The Go Between* and Visconti was given a special conciliatory prize that the committee had just come up with: the 'Twenty-Fifth Annual Prize'. See Young, "Gavin Young Takes It Extremely Easy in the South of France".

32. Mann was also careful to add that 'I wanted to be certain that in the case of such a casual and hidden correlation one would not be able to talk at all about recognition on the part of the readership' (*Death in Venice*, 99).

33. Ashby, *Absolute Music, Mechanical Reproduction*, 242.

34. See Melly, "A Triumph of Seduction" and Langley, "Passion in an Ornate Period Frame".

35. Anon., Review of Visconti's *Death in Venice*.

36. Heyworth, "Catching Up with Mahler".

37. Heyworth, "Catching Up with Mahler".

38. Sutcliffe, "Mahler Record".

39. La Grange, *Gustav Mahler*, Vol. 4, 1677.

40. Hope-Wallace, "Alma's Martyr".

41. Coleman, "A Load of Symbolics".

42. *Top of the Pops* (1964–2006) was a UK BBC TV music-chart programme.

43. In her memoirs, Alma provided the following assessment: 'The Jewish question touched Mahler very closely. He had often suffered bitterly from it, particularly when Cosima Wagner, whom he greatly esteemed, tried to bar his appointment in Vienna because he was a Jew. He had had to be baptised before he could aspire to such a high position under the Royal and Imperial exchequer' (Alma Mahler, *Gustav Mahler: Memories and Letters* (1990), 101).

44. David Huckvale hears 'straight' instead of 'strength' in this line. ('The Composing Machine', 122).

45. Phillips, *Ken Russell*, 126.

46. Botstein, "Whose Gustav Mahler?" 8–9.

47. Heyworth, "Catching Up with Mahler".

48. Smoley, "Mahler Conducted and Recorded", 254.

49. Cited in Tibbetts, *Composers in the Movies*, 194.

50. Botstein, "Whose Gustav Mahler?" 9.

51. Bradshaw, "Ken Russell", accessed 30 November 2011.

52. The Labour-Party politician Harold Wilson served two terms as prime minister (1964–70 and 1974–76), and Edward Heath was the leader of the Conservative Party between 1965 and 1975, and prime minister during 1970–74.

53. Rose, "Hi Ken, Sorry I Stole your Movie", accessed 30 November 2011.

10

Popular Music and the Colloquial Tone in the Posthorn Solos of Mahler's Third Symphony

Timothy Freeze

The idea to set this folk tune abruptly and without artistic finish as the trio of a symphonic scherzo [was] as strange as it was daring. But the risk succeeded . . . Memories, fantasies are awakened, and the posthorn tune effusively develops them further in a folk tone.[1]

As much as any passage in Mahler's works, the posthorn episodes of the Third Symphony's third movement serve as conduits for remote domains of expression and music-making. Their diatonic simplicity, bewitching orchestration, and overt sentiment pose a striking expressive and musical contrast to the rondo refrains. And the spatial remove of the soloist, directed to play 'as if from afar', further enhances the impression of music emanating from a realm beyond the symphony.

Just what kind of realm this is, however, has split critical and scholarly opinion ever since the symphony's première in 1902. There are two basic interpretative traditions of the posthorn solos, each rooted in a different notion of their stylistic origins. According to the first, the episodes are utopian visions. Whether imbued with a rural and historical aspect (in the views of some writers),[2] or an immaterial and timeless one (for others),[3] the idyllic interludes depend for their effect on the vivid re-creation of a folk song style and on the sound of functional posthorns. The second tradition, in contrast, hears the solos as an amalgamation of artless simplicity and romantic nostalgia, a combination that runs counter to imperatives of originality and high-mindedness in an Austro-German symphony of the late nineteenth century. The apparent aesthetic breach perpetrated by Mahler in the use of this sort of music has drawn both censure and praise from writers, but in either case it implies a distinct stylistic influence: popular music. Hence scholars have described the solos as 'poor man's music . . . without shame or inhibition'[4] and 'a deliberate vulgarization [with] almost kitsch, sentimental melodies'.[5] Most famously,

I am indebted to Stephen Rodgers, Daniel R. Melamed, and Scott Southard for their helpful comments on earlier versions of this chapter.

Adorno used the episodes to illustrate Mahler's 'provocative alliance with vulgar music' and predilection for 'shallow popular songs, street ballads, hits'.[6]

The posthorn episodes thus hang in an interpretational balance poised between mutually exclusive alternatives: rural and urban, past and present, metaphysical and material, the epitome of beauty and vulgarity. Lending credence to the one side, scholars have long adduced parallels to nineteenth-century folk songs and posthorn music as represented in anthologies and organology treatises.[7] This chapter shows that Mahler's episodes draw on specific conventions of popular music, too. The early reception of the Third Symphony reveals that these devices, especially as filtered through two famous pieces, were at least as salient to Mahler's contemporaries as were affinities to folk songs and functional posthorns. Mahler's episodes are thus richly associative, weaving together many disparate references. Moreover, the more general colloquial tone that arises from this referential multiplicity functions within the Third Symphony both structurally, as a means of linking sections of the first and third movements, and semantically, as a powerful metaphor for the earthly existence that the symphony seeks to transcend.

When Mahler composed his Third Symphony in the summers of 1895 and 1896, the posthorn loomed large in the public imagination mostly on account of its frequent evocation in popular culture. The instrument originally signaled the arrival, departure, and distress of carriages conveying mail and passengers across Europe. It became a musical topic connoting distance and longing as early as the seventeenth century. Bach, Telemann, Handel, Mozart, Beethoven, and Schubert all incorporated or made stylistic references to posthorns in their works. By the mid nineteenth century, however, the instrument's appeal had become more specialised. As the gap between art and popular music widened beyond repair, the posthorn topic flourished at band concerts and in the theatre, dance hall, and salon; composers of art music all but abandoned it.[8] In the closing decades of the century, the expansion of railroads gradually rendered postilions obsolete, and functional posthorn signals gradually disappeared from the everyday. But they continued to proliferate in popular music, where the instrument's evocation of an irretrievable past became all the more potent. Ernst Challier's *Großer Liederkatalog*, a comprehensive list of all German-language songs with piano accompaniment, contained just over one hundred songs with posthorn-related texts in 1885; by 1900, the number had swelled to over 150, buoyed by a wave of salon and popular songs.

Throughout the nineteenth century, the posthorn topic continued to be rooted in signals and characteristic titles. But composers of popular music also developed a distinctive mode of stylisation. As improvements in the posthorn's design increased its capacity for lyrical expression, the instrument developed a dualistic character aptly captured in the couplet: *Posthornklang, Posthornklang!/Bald Geschmetter, bald Gesang!* ('Posthorn sounds, posthorn sounds!/Now a blast, now a song!').[9] The new popular stylisations incorporated both aspects of the posthorn within a single melody. One early example, from 1841, is Adolf Müller Sr.'s salon setting of Nicolaus Lenau's 'Der Postillon' for voice, piano, and posthorn. The poem, a sentimental depiction of a ride in a postal carriage whose driver stops at a cemetery to pay tribute to a deceased comrade, inspired many song settings and, as recounted by Mahler in a letter to the Austrian critic Ernst Decsey, the solos of the Third Symphony, too.[10] Throughout Müller's song, staccato signals are juxtaposed with legato, lyrical phrases (see Ex. 10.1a and Ex. 10.1b). As the postilion halts the carriage, the posthorn enters softly, marked *dolce*. The second phrase rapidly builds to a dramatic signal and lingers briefly on the highest tone before descending and regaining its lyrical character. Such mixture of signals and lyricism within a continuous melody distinguished the popular posthorn topic not only from functional signals, but also from stylisations of the instrument in art music, and from the contents of posthorn anthologies marketed to hobbyists.[11]

The lyrical aspect of the posthorn's dual character was related to a broader phenomenon in popular music: the sentimental trumpet solo. Originating with the greater melodic facility of the newly invented flugelhorn, the genre became established in both the salon and at outdoor concerts by the 1830s

Ex. 10.1a Adolf Müller Sr., "Der Postillion", mixture of signals and lyrical phrases

Ex. 10.1b Adolf Müller Sr., "Der Postillion", tune at the cemetery

Ex. 10.2 Viktor Nessler, *Trompeter von Säkkingen*, "Behüt Dich Gott" (excerpt)

and continued to grow more popular with the rising prominence of military bands in musical life.[12] In 1853, Victor von Scheffel immortalised this new breed of musician by making a trumpet soloist the main character of his rhymed epic *Der Trompeter von Säkkingen*, which surpassed 250 editions by century's end. The composer, critic, and pedagogue Ferdinand Hiller surely had both Scheffel's *Trompeter* and actual trumpet soloists in mind as he complained,

> The perfecting of brass instruments, highly problematic in many ways, has brought to life deafening, not to mention farcical, figures. The most prominent—one has already become entirely used to it—is the *sentimental trumpeter* [who] devotes himself to the cantilena with the full depth of his soul and the entire sweetness of his brass . . . The trumpet languishes, cries plaintively, trembles upon his lips.[13]

A number of composers used Scheffel's poem as the basis for writing music containing sentimental trumpet solos. By far the most famous was Viktor Nessler's *volkstümliche* opera *Der Trompeter von Säkkingen* (1884). The Trumpeter's Song 'Behüt' Dich Gott', a veritable hit, was often performed in instrumental arrangement at band and beer garden concerts (see Ex. 10.2). Such was the influence of the opera on popular music in Vienna that Ernst Decsey, also a biographer of Johann Strauss Jr., dubbed the late 1880s the *Nesslerzeit*, during which the Waltz King struggled in vain to regain the limelight with his newly composed operettas.[14]

Although not identical, the posthorn topic and sentimental trumpet solo were complementary, both musically and expressively. The court trumpeter of Nessler's opera functions as a reminder of days gone by, and his solos mix signals and lyrical melodies much as a stylised posthorn might. In a speech in 1899, a German congressman, lamenting the demise of the postilion, exclaimed:

> The day will come when one can get to know the posthorn only in songs, tunes, and perhaps novels, for soon it will vanish into thin air . . . I believe Viktor von Scheffel would never have written his *Trompeter von Säkkingen* if he had not occasionally heard the sound of the postilion's posthorn wafting from the Black Forest.[15]

Ex. 10.3 Mahler, *Blumine*, trumpet theme

Mahler was at the vanguard of composers bringing sentimental trumpet solos to the concert hall. *Blumine*, the second movement in the original version of the First Symphony (1889), features a saccharine trumpet theme and simple accompaniment (see Ex. 10.3). The movement possesses more than general stylistic and textural connections to popular music. Mahler originally composed the piece in Kassel in 1884 for a stage adaptation of Scheffel's *Trompeter*. Commissioned just weeks after the success of Nessler's opera in nearby Leipzig had become apparent, the music that would later become *Blumine* initially accompanied the poem's well-known Rhine Serenade.[16]

The posthorn episodes of the Third invoke conventions of popular music in even greater detail. Countless German-language critics of Mahler's day, friend and foe alike, acknowledged such connections, often with reference to one of two specific works. The Czech critic Richard Batka, a staunch advocate of Mahler, was one of many who heard echoes of Nessler's *Trompeter*: 'a flugelhorn, fiendishly recalling Säkkingen, disrupts the comfortable pleasure' of the movement.[17] Indeed, as discussed below, Mahler's posthorn episodes bear striking parallels to Nessler's 'Rhine Serenade', the very scene that *Blumine* had once set. These similarities could not have been lost on Mahler, who conducted Nessler's opera thirty-one times in the late 1880s.[18] Max Vancsa, a critic for Vienna's weekly *Neue Musikalische Presse*, recognised similarities to another piece: 'The mawkish sentimentality of the flugelhorn solo in B-flat, played from outside the hall, fatally recalls that notorious programmatic piece of the promenade and beer-garden concerts, "Die Post im Walde" "with obbligato cornet solo".'[19] Originally for men's chorus but most often heard in instrumental arrangement, this work by the German composer Heinrich Schäffer was probably the most famous rendering of the posthorn in German-language musical culture in the half century before World War I, all but guaranteeing Mahler's familiarity with it.[20]

Mahler's solos share with these pieces a constellation of traits indicative of popular stylisations of the posthorn. Most telling is the mingling of signals and lyrical phrases, as in Exx. 10.4, 10.5, and 10.6. In each case, the soloist usurps the musical proceedings with a flurry of signals whose final pitch lingers and eventually yields to a lyrical melody. A nascent form of this gesture, marked as the *lyrical turn* in the musical examples, introduces the cemetery scene in Müller's salon setting of 'Der Postillion'. Each composer enhances the effect

Ex. 10.4 Heinrich Schäffer, 'Die Post im Walde'

*Note: This example is derived from an arrangement by the Austrian military band con-
ductor Franz Joseph Wagner (Österreichische Nationalbibliothek Mus.Hs.20771). Made
in 1877, it represents a version that Mahler could plausibly have heard. The metrical
deviations in the closing measures are transcribed directly from the manuscript.*

of the lyrical turn. Schäffer introduces a modal shift, and both Nessler and
Mahler reduce the texture to soft, shimmering strings that provide an ethereal
backdrop to the folk song–like melodies that ensue.

In addition, each of the solos contains passages marked by flexible decla-
mation and improvisatory character. In 'Die Post im Walde', all the trappings
of a concerto cadenza—dominant pedal, unaccompanied solo culminating in
a sustained tone (either trilled or flutter-tongued in performance), and *tutti*
reprise of the main theme—belie its being a literal quotation of the Prussian
signal for the arrival and departure of the express mail carriage.[21] Nessler and
Mahler, on the other hand, rely on flexible treatment of melody and rhythm.
The second and third phrases of Nessler's solo contain chromatic embellishments and varied note lengths, and, later in the scene, an entire phrase is

Ex. 10.5 Viktor Nessler, *Trompeter von Säkkingen*, no. 13 (excerpt)

Note: This example is based on the piano-vocal score (Leipzig, 1884). Orchestrational cues are based on the printed orchestral score (Leipzig, 1884; Österreichische Nationalbibliothek OA.1295). Vocal parts have been omitted to conserve space.

repeated with a hint of improvisational ornaments. Mahler also uses chromatic embellishments, but more important are the *tenuto* articulations and such performance instructions as *frei vorgetragen* and *Zeit lassen!* Shortly afterward, in a gesture reminiscent of 'Die Post im Walde', Maher's posthorn recedes into the background and begins to trill as the orchestra states the main melody.

A third common element is the closing formula. A series of signals ascend higher and higher, until the soloist reaches and dwells on the highest note. In Schäffer's piece, the solo ends here, as befitting the close of a popular song. (In

Ex. 10.6 Mahler, Symphony no. 3, third movement, first posthorn episode (excerpt)

the military band arrangement that serves as the basis for the score example, it is followed by an additional tone an octave deeper.) In Nessler's and Mahler's works, however, the onstage proceedings that had been interrupted by the solo resume here; their lines descend to a slightly lower resting point.[22]

The use of distance effects constitutes yet another link to both the post-horn topic and sentimental trumpet solos. Spatial separation could be literal or evoked through dynamic shading, muted timbres, and the like. Nessler's 'Rhine Serenade' is played offstage in its entirety. Likewise, comic opera composers going back to the first half of the nineteenth century had placed posthorn soloists in the wings. The first act of Adolphe Adam's *Le Postillon de Lonjumeau* (1836), a work conducted once by Mahler in Kassel and particularly beloved by German-language audiences, closes with an offstage posthorn signal set against a blanket of sustained strings. Many Viennese operettas had similar gestures. At the end of the prologue of Leo Fall's *Der fidele Bauer* (1907), the posthorn calls even progress through gradations of distance, their performance instructions—*Posthorn entfernter klingend* and *Wie aus grosser Entfernung*—closely resembling those used by Mahler in his first episode. Mahler's more concrete directions for the second solo—*in weiter Entfernung* and *in weiter Ferne*—indicate that the soloist should be placed offstage, but modern performances typically do so for both episodes.[23] It is not clear when this performing tradition began, but it might easily have taken root quite early. In Mahler's lifetime, distance effects were often added as a matter of performance practice in band music involving the posthorn topic or trumpet solo. Robert Hirschfeld, one of Mahler's most perceptive yet viciously antagonistic Viennese critics, alluded to this practice in his review of Mahler's symphony in 1904:

> Then [comes] the Rondo with the posthorn solo that swiftly became famous. It intones once from the distance, once from closer. At this point, one can gladly concede that the military band conductors do not have access to the masterful technique of Gustav Mahler when they use the same effects in their outdoor concerts. Finally, a brilliant artist has come across 'Die Post im Walde.' Perhaps it really was in need of reform.[24]

Hirschfeld's sarcastic contrast between military band conductors and the 'brilliant artist' emphasises the strangeness that the posthorn episodes possessed for many of Mahler's contemporaries. In topic, style, and distance effects, the solos' connections to urban popular music were palpable, even blatant. But the similarities to Nessler's and Schäffer's pieces do not constitute quotations or even univocal references. They are merely allusions. And for each review tut-tutting about such likenesses to popular music, another extolled the spirit of old-fashioned folk song that Mahler had created. This alternate view of the solos' origins was also rooted in compelling musical evidence. The fleeting similarities to numerous folk melodies uncovered by later scholars suggest the convincing recreation of a folk song idiom without the quotation of one song in particular. From such competing and well-grounded accounts of stylistic origins, one can only conclude that the posthorn solos do not make reference to one melody or compositional type to the exclusion of all others. They contain a multiplicity of musical references, alluding to many different sources without being reducible to any one of them.

Ex. 10.7 Posthorn signals of the Deutsche Reichspost with closing gesture paralleling *Abblasen*

  (a) No. 1, Für Estaffeten
  (b) No. 2, Für Kuriere
  (c) No. 3, Für Extraposten
  (d) No. 5, Für Güterposten
       Source: Hiller, *Das große Buch vom Posthorn*, 80–82.

Even the trumpet fanfare that abruptly cuts off the first posthorn episode is referentially open-ended in this way (bars 345–47). Identical to the Austrian military signal *Abblasen* (fall out), the fanfare is among the most widely accepted literal quotations in Mahler's oeuvre today, and its sudden and unexpected entrance after a passage of pastoral sentiment suggests to many interpreters Mahler's ironic intention. Yet most of the official posthorn signals of the Deutsche Reichspost ended in the same way, with a decorated descending arpeggiation (see Exx. 10.7a, 10.7b, 10.7c, and 10.7d). For ten of the twelve years leading up to the composition of the Third Symphony, Mahler lived not in Austria-Hungary, but in Kassel, Leipzig, and Hamburg, where he likely heard the Reichspost's signals. Further suggesting a link with the German posthorn, Mahler initially conceived of the first episode and its closing fanfare as being played by a single instrument.[25] Only after completing the orchestral draft score did Mahler entrust the fanfare to a muted trumpet. This change increased the passage's referential layers, at once sharpening its affinity with *Abblasen* and establishing a clear connection with the symphony's first movement, where cheeky fanfares, in one instance played by muted trumpets, similarly interrupt a pastoral passage (bars 237–39).

One of the few commentators to acknowledge that the posthorn episodes contain a diversity of references is the eminent critic and Mahler supporter

Julius Korngold. His perceptive review describes Mahler's symphony in terms of an imagined symphonic protagonist.

> The person apparently comes riding in the postal wagon, and the forest puts him in a romantic mood. A flugelhorn sounds from the distance with a sentimental melody cut in the shape of a folksong; *Des Knaben Wunderflügelhorn*. Mahler knows as well as we that this flugelhorn solo will raise the suspicion that the rider in his postal carriage is related to Nessler's *Trompeter*. He has certainly also heard the expressive 'Die Post im Walde' on a beautiful summer evening at a concert in a beer garden. He is surely only making fun of his sentimental traveler, which seems to be suggested by the brutal trumpet signal that parodically cuts off that outpouring of sentiment.[26]

Although Korngold recognises the presence of both folk and popular models, he does not offer an overarching account that transcends the two blinkered interpretative traditions. His review is firmly situated within the tradition that sees the solos as a kind of aesthetic slumming that, more often than not, can only be legitimated as high art by an appeal to irony.

Ultimately, it is impossible to reconcile the myriad references and stylistic lineages of the posthorn episodes in all their specificity. The ambiguity and associative richness that masquerade behind the immediacy of folk and popular styles likely constituted some of their attraction to the modernist in Mahler, living in an age whose nature, in the words of his contemporary Hugo von Hofmannsthal, was 'ambiguity and indeterminacy'.[27] But the apparent irreconcilability also invites a broader perspective in which such details as origins in folk or popular music disappear from view. Indeed, such an approach not only resonates with Mahler's views about aesthetics but also clarifies essential features of the Third Symphony's overarching structure and semantic project.

Mahler's statements about music suggest that he did not consider folk and popular music to be different in any respect pertinent to their stylistic appropriation in his own works. Although he clearly subscribed to aesthetic hierarchies, the only important distinction for him was between art and non-art. Insofar as he verbally distinguished between different kinds of inartistic musical utterance, as in the following statement about Johann Strauss Jr.'s waltzes, he did so in ways that failed to hierarchise them.

> I do not hold a low opinion of waltzes; I accept them for what they are in all their uniqueness and delightful inventiveness. But you cannot call them art. They have as little to do with art as has, say, the folksong 'Ach, wie ist's möglich denn', no matter how moving it is.[28]

Mahler's choice of songs could hardly have been more revealing. 'Ach, wie ist's möglich denn' was a widely known love song that circulated in the nineteenth and early twentieth centuries as an unattributed 'Thüringer Volkslied'. In fact, the tune was a *Schlager* composed in 1827 by Friedrich Wilhelm Kücken.[29] That

Mahler could consider it a prime representative of *Volkslied* only underscores that he did not subscribe to the common ideology that gave aesthetic distinction to authentic folk song. Nor did he view aesthetic status as an intrinsic property that could be transmitted to his music through stylistic reference.

> I have often heard composers who claim to seek individuality above all things state that they purposely avoid hearing too much music of other composers, fearing that their own originality will be affected. They also avoid hearing the songs of the street or folk-songs for a similar reason. What arrant nonsense! If a man eats a beef-steak it is no sign that he will become a cow.[30]

Mahler's egalitarian attitude toward lowbrow music suggests that he was not primarily interested in these styles for their origin in either the folk or popular sphere. Rather, he seems to have been attracted to a more fundamental trait shared by both: their widespread familiarity from spheres of music-making outside of the concert hall. Hans Heinrich Eggebrecht aptly dubbed this characteristic quality of Mahler's music the *colloquial tone* (*umgangssprachlichen Ton*).[31] Through the assimilation of routine conventions and turns of phrase, the colloquial tone gives the listener a sense of being already acquainted with aspects of Mahler's music even on first hearing. The particular source for the colloquial tone is not as important as its basic sense of originating from without. In this context, a multiplicity of references was an asset. A bundle of stylistic and melodic allusions would more surely elicit associations in listeners than overt melodic quotation or blunt stylistic reference.

The colloquial tone plays an essential role in connecting disparate sections of the Third Symphony and in expressing its general semantic ideas. Mahler touched on the underlying compositional procedures in his correspondence with Max Marschalk, an early advocate of his works, in the months before completing the Third Symphony. 'Even the most experienced and competent listener must first seek and bring together the connections between the individual passages of the work; only then will the significance of the whole reveal itself to him.'[32] Moreover, Mahler saw the semantic content of the symphony's vocal texts as being implicated in the instrumental music through inter-movemental connections: 'The *conceptual* basis [of the Second Symphony] is clearly articulated in the words of the final chorus. The sudden entrance of the alto solo casts an illuminating light on the initial movements.'[33]

The conceptual basis of the Third is dispersed across two song movements. The fourth movement, a Nietzschean meditation on the profundity of human existence, leads directly to a depiction of cheerful angels and distraught sinner taken straight from *Des Knaben Wunderhorn*. Though contrasting on so many levels, the two songs have in common the basic opposition of life and death, of the pain inherent in the material world and the human concern for what resides beyond it. Mahler exports this opposition to the symphony's purely instrumental sections with two interlocking networks of inter-movemental connections.

The primary inter-movemental network consists of cyclical devices readily identified in the literature.[34] It need only be sketched here. The network encompasses those sections tonally centered on D: the first movement's introduction (and two extended interpolations), the fourth movement, and the finale. The funeral march and chorale elements in the introduction to the first movement convey at this early stage a general sense of the work's transcendental concerns. The entrance of the human voice in the fourth movement concretises these impressions, casting its illuminating light not only through the common tonal center but also with overt motivic connections. Most prominently, Mahler weaves the motives to 'Deep is its woe' and 'All desire wants eternity (bars IV/100–101, 119–22) into turbulent passages of the first movement (e.g., bars I/7–9, 83–86), and the former motive erupts in a cataclysmic spasm in the symphony's finale (bars VI/182–97). Through such links, the opposition of distress and solace in the instrumental, outer movements takes on shades of mortal suffering and transcendence.

The secondary inter-movemental network is also rooted in a tonality, F major. But in place of bald motivic links, the other constitutive element, generally overlooked as a unifying device, is its colloquial tone. Above all, these traits bind two large parts of the Third Symphony that have little else in common: the posthorn episodes and the marches of the first movement's sonata form proper. The marches, like their counterpart in the third movement, are nodes of associative richness, their heroic and folk-like melodies treated to a dazzling orchestrational display that recalls the sounds of military bands, operetta, and battle music. To be sure, these marches and the posthorn solos are not the only sections of the symphony coloured by folk and popular styles. Elements of folk song can be traced in the rondo refrains of the third movement and the cheerful marches of the fifth, and the main theme of the finale anticipates the popular song made famous by Bing Crosby, 'I'll Be Seeing You'.[35] But in each of these instances, the colloquial remnants are limited mostly to melodic ideas seamlessly integrated into a musical fabric that does not, on its surface, convey the impression of origin beyond high art. The chorale of the finale is, after all, closer to the spirit of Beethoven and Wagner, with whose works it shares more than mere melodic affinities, than to popular music.

The difference between a colloquial tone and more subtle forms of stylistic influence is ultimately one of degree, but it is nevertheless sufficiently robust to draw the marches and posthorn solos into a common orbit. For a number of Mahler's contemporaries, this was certainly the case. The reviewer for *Die Musik*, to cite but one example, praised the witty ideas in the third movement, 'among which however I do not count the sentimental, self-indulgent posthorn solo so reminiscent of the trivialities of the first part'.[36] Even more telling is Mahler's coordination of the colloquial tone with the symphony's inter-movemental networks and conceptual basis. The formal premise of both the first and third movements is the alternation of a pointedly colloquial tone with sections related to the symphony's primary concern with death and overcoming. The marches of the first movement's F major sonata, at turns light-hearted and rambunctious, triumphant and tender, alternate with the funeral march and chorale elements of the D minor introduction and its extended interpolations. Similarly, in the third movement, the posthorn solos in F major alternate with C minor refrains, an instrumental reworking of Mahler's setting of 'Ablösung im Sommer', another *Wunderhorn* text whose droll, animal allegory also takes death as its central theme.

The fifth movement distils this opposition, but with a twist. The main sections of the unassuming song are built around the same basic tonal and idiomatic premise as the imposing first movement: F major, joyful marches juxtaposed with sudden D major chorale insertions. The texts associated with each section shed additional semantic light on their respective inter-movemental networks. Whereas the D major chorale snippets center on the sinner's guilt and desire to enter heaven, the angels' description of the joys of heavenly life are accompanied largely by F major marches. Yet these marches are clearly distinct from those of the first movement; they lack the blatant connections to popular music.

The colloquial tone thus functions systematically throughout the symphony as a foil to the preoccupation with the otherworldly. Its suitability to this task resides not in being aesthetically low in comparison to the high-minded music that contextualises it. Rather, the distinguishing framework is psychological and experiential. Nearly every listener has had prior contact with such music outside of the concert hall. In the foreign context of a Mahlerian symphony, the colloquial tone sparks an associative mode of reception, inviting the listener to draw connections to her experiences in the material world.[37] Carl Dahlhaus considers this manner of listening a defining characteristic of the reception of 'trivial music'.[38] Characteristic titles, programmatic headings, sound effects, and a vocabulary of musical topics—all common fare in popular music and Mahlerian symphonies alike—derive their emotional efficacy in part from the joy of remembering. Dahlhaus denies that composers of art music ever elicited this mode of listening intentionally; Mahler's music, however, exploits it to the hilt. The posthorn episodes gave a number of his contemporary critics the opportunity to say so. In addition to Paul Bekker, quoted in the opening epigraph, Robert Hirschfeld remarked:

> One can see in entertainment music, how the so-called hit songs always strike upon those turns of phrase to which we have already been made receptive by related melodies or even just the same intervals. Gustav Mahler's music lives by this method. He ingeniously mixes into his creations ... folksongs, the flugelhorn in the rondo of the Third—in short, those things that are already stored in our hearts.[39]

Likewise, Max Graf, drawing on the long-standing trope of the *postilion d'amour*, a figure still common in popular culture in the early twentieth century, described the posthorn solo as

> one of those songs that you start to sing when you are between fifteen and twenty-five and have fallen head over heels in love . . . We start to be moved a bit—not by the melody, but by memories . . . sweetheart and springtime; forest reveries and sentimental country walks.[40]

What the critics largely missed, however, was how the colloquial tone provides Mahler the ideal metaphor for earthly existence. Whatever veiled references the marches and posthorn solos might contain to classical forebears, and regardless of the specific sphere of music-making they are thought to invoke, they are above all marked by the residue of everyday experience. The joy of remembering that they induce is inextricably bound to the phenomenal world. The marches of the first movement, for example, may elicit memories and emotions bound to military band parades and outdoor performances. The associations open up the listener's frame of reference—and Mahler's symphony along with it—to include the world of sensuous experience, far removed from the metaphysical contemplation that constitutes a primary preoccupation of the Third Symphony and which, for a century, had been the aesthetic goal of the symphony as a genre.[41] These associative impressions are focused into a metaphor for earthly life by virtue of both the tonal links to the idealized marches that set the cheerful heavenly scene in the fifth movement, and, in the opening movement, the opposition of the marches with sections musically connected to the fourth movement's meditation on mortal suffering. The metaphor returns with the colloquial tone of the posthorn solos in the third movement. Their lingering and nostalgic expression is strikingly different from the first movement's optimistic romp. Rather than an affirmation of earthly existence, they constitute a bittersweet remembrance of it, as much a leave-taking as a longing for what can never be regained.

Among the most important functions of the colloquial tone, then, is to bind the marches and posthorn solos into a single semantic and musical network. The sense that the sections encapsulate a single idea is further enhanced by the similarity of their fates. By the close of the exposition and recapitulation of the first movement, the popular marches have achieved an inexorable, almost intoxicating energy. Their triumphal closure is cut short by a sudden harmonic lurch and violent orchestral outburst reminiscent of the turbulence that had permeated much of the D minor introduction (bars 361f., 857f.). Similarly, in lieu of a final refrain after the second posthorn episode, the orchestra surges forward into a spasm of doubt and desperation, the striking orchestration and Neapolitan resolution making the connection to the first movement unmistakable (bars 529f.). No measure of joie de vivre or loving attachment to mortal life, the music seems to tell us, can overcome our inevitable demise.

The stage is thus set for the last three movements of the symphony. The Nietzschean song of midnight and *Wunderhorn* depiction of heavenly morning concretise the meanings that have until then been only implicit. The transition to realms beyond the material world is as clearly reflected in the absence of the colloquial tone from these movements as it is in the D major tonal fulfillment of the Symphony's *per aspera ad astra* trajectory in the finale. When the cataclysmic figure that terminated the marches and posthorn episode returns one last time in the final movement (bars 220f.), its destructive energy is exhausted, dissolving once and for all in a transcendent close.

Of course, the associations invited by the posthorn episodes are not limited to purely musical forebears but extend to the instrument's depiction in art, literature, and poetry. Ernst Decsey delighted Mahler by invoking Lenau's poem 'Der Postillon' in his review of the Third Symphony. Indeed, both share general features of clichéd representations of the posthorn: the mixture of signals and song, distance effects, and connectedness to nature. And Mahler's inscription above the entrance of the soloist in the autograph score—*Der Postillon!*—may be a direct reference to Lenau's poem. Even more fundamental, however, is the similar function. As in Mahler's symphony, the postilion's solo in Lenau's poem is a tribute to a life lived, a reflection on worldly life tinged with the certainty of its inevitable end.

One wonders if Mahler did not also have another poetic ride in a postal carriage in mind, this one by Goethe, his favorite German-language writer. The poem 'An Schwager Kronos', according to its caption, was written 'in a post chaise on October 10, 1774', the day on which Goethe returned from Frankfurt having dropped off the distinguished poet Friedrich Klopstock, whose *Resurrection Ode* Mahler set in the Second Symphony. The poem casts the ride through the German countryside as a metaphor for life's journey, the coachman at once a postilion—*Schwager* was the familiar name for mail coachmen—and Chronos, the god of time. Like Mahler's symphony, Goethe's poem juxtaposes images of the earthly with the otherworldly. The traveller sees how the 'eternal spirit hovers/cognizant of eternal life' between the mountain peaks; in their shadow cluster all the charms of the material world, among them shelter, a girl, beer. The bucolic scene is abruptly cut off as the traveller's thoughts turn to his mortality. Stricken by the horror of his slow and inevitable decline, he redirects the coach to take him straight to hell. Upon arrival, the traveller commands the postilion to sound his horn. Much as in the third movement of Mahler's symphony, the posthorn's call in Goethe's poem constitutes the final utterance from the material world, made at the cusp of the metaphysical. It will probably never be known whether Goethe's poem informed Mahler's own conception of his posthorn solos. What is clear, however, is the central role that Mahler fashioned for the colloquial tone in the Third Symphony's structure and semantic expression.

Notes

1. Bekker, *Gustav Mahlers Sinfonien*, 126: 'eine ebenso absonderliche wie kühne Idee, diese Volksweise unvermittelt und ohne kunstvolle Verarbeitung als Trio in ein sinfonisches Scherzo zu setzen. Aber das Wagnis ist gelungen ... Erinnerungen, Fantasie werden geweckt, die die Posthornweise schwärmerisch im Volkston.' weiterspinnen." All translations are my own unless otherwise indicated.

2. Krummacher, *Gustav Mahlers III. Symphonie*, 95–120.

3. Eggebrecht, *Die Musik Gustav Mahlers*, 169–97.

4. Schnebel, "Über Mahlers Dritte", 152, 165.

5. Franklin, *Mahler: Symphony No. 3*, 174.

6. Adorno, *Mahler. A Musical Physiognomy*, 35–36.

7. Eggebrecht, *Die Musik Gustav Mahlers*, 181–84. For more on the provenance and implications of the quotation of the Spanish folksong 'Jota aragonese' in an orchestral interlude of the second posthorn episode, see Solvik, "Biography and Musical Meaning", 339–60.

8. The most prominent representations of the posthorn by composers of art music in the six decades that separate Schubert's *Die Winterreise* and Mahler's Third Symphony appear in explicitly programmatic chamber works: Louis Spohr's Duo for Violin and Piano (1838) and Bedřich Smetana's String Quartet *From My Life* (1876). One wonders if, in the summer of 1901, Natalie Bauer-Lechner and Arnold Rosé did not play the Spohr duo for Mahler, who admired the composer's 'elegance and skillful instrumental writing' (La Grange, *Gustav Mahler*. Vol. 3: 361).

9. Gumbert and Thieme, *Posthornschule und Posthorn-Taschenliederbuch*, 16.

10. Decsey, "Stunden mit Mahler", 356.

11. See Maximilian in Bayern, *Posthorn-Klänge*; Scherlein, *Anleitung zum Blasen eines einfachen Posthornes*; Pfistermeister, *Taschenliederbuch*; Gumbert and Thieme, *Posthornschule*; Krekeler, *Anleitung zum Blasen des Signal-Posthorns*.

12. These solos could be played by any number of treble brass instruments, including flugelhorn, cornet, posthorn, and trumpet. The trumpet is a suitable term for the genre because it was associated with some of the most prominent examples, including Nessler's *Trompeter von Säkkingen*.

13. Hiller, *Aus dem Tonleben unserer Zeit*, 12–13: 'Die in mancher Beziehung sehr problematische Vervollkommnung der Blechinstrumente bringt betäubende, aber auch burleske Erscheinungen zu Tage. Die hervortretendste—man ist sie aber schon ganz gewohnt worden—ist die des *sentimentalen Trompeters* ... der sich mit der ganzen Tiefe seines Gemüthes und der ganzen Süßigkeit seines Bleches der Cantilene widmet ... Die Trompete schmachtet, klagt, zittert unter seinen Lippen.'

14. Decsey, *Johann Strauss*, 216–17.

15. Cited in Gumbert and Thieme, *Posthornschule*, 22: 'Meine Herren, das Posthorn wird man nur bald noch in Lieder, Gesängen und vielleicht noch Romanen kennen lernen, in Wirklichkeit wird es aber bald von der Bildfläche

verschwunden sein . . . Ich glaube, daß Viktor von Scheffel seinen 'Trompeter von Säckingen' gar nicht geschrieben hätte, wenn ihm nicht aus dem Schwarzwald heraus so manchesmal das Posthorn des Postillons entgegen geklungen hätte.'

16. See Mitchell, *Gustav Mahler: The Early Years*, 225–29, and Mitchell, *Gustav Mahler: The Wunderhorn Years*, 217–24.

17. Batka, 'Viertes philharmonisches Konzert': 'sogar ein Flügelhorn, das teuflisch an Säkkingen erinnert, stör[t] jeden behaglichen Genuß.'

18. Martner, "Mahler im Opernhaus", 169.

19. Vancsa, untitled review of Mahler's Third Symphony: 'Ein gefühlsduseliges Flügel-Hornsolo im B, außerhalb des Saales gespielt, erinnert in fataler Weise an das berüchtigte Programmstück der Promenade- und Bierkonzerte 'Die Post im Walde' 'mit obligatem Pistonsolo.'

20. The song seems to have entered the repertory of the men's chorus in Iglau, Mahler's boyhood home, in 1875, just weeks before Mahler left for the Vienna Conservatory. It was performed to great enthusiasm in two concerts (*Mährischer Grenzbote* [Iglau], 4 July and 15 August 1875).

21. Hiller, *Das große Buch vom Posthorn*, 260.

22. Mahler's solo ends *just* below its highest pitch, but, after a brief orchestral interlude, it replays the closing gesture with an even lower resting point (bars 321–40).

23. In the autograph manuscript (but not the later published scores), Mahler also indicates that the second episode should be played *hinter der Szene* (Peattie, "The *Fin-de-siècle* Metropolis", 25–26).

24. Hirschfeld, "Konzerte": 'dann das Rondo mit dem rasch berühmt gewordenen Posthornsolo, das einmal ferner, einmal näher tönt. Da will man gern zugestehen, daß den Militär-Kapellmeistern für ihre Gartenmusiken, für den gleichen Effekt nicht die meisterliche Technik Gustav Mahlers zu Gebote steht. Es ist endlich einmal ein genialer Künstler über die 'Post im Walde' gekommen. Möglich, daß diese wirklich reformbedürftig war.'

25. Krummacher, *Gustav Mahlers III. Symphonie*, 35.

26. Korngold, "Mahlers III. Symphonie": 'Er kommt offenbar mit dem Postwagen gefahren, und der Wald stimmt ihn romantisch. Ein Flügelhorn ertönt aus der Ferne mit einer sentimentalen, volkstümlich zugeschnittenen Melodie; Des Knabenwunderflügelhorn. Mahler weiß so gut wie wir, daß dieses Flügelhornsolo seinen Postpassagier der Verwandtschaft mit Neßlers Trompeter verdächtigt. Er hat auch gewiß schon an einem schönen Sommerabend bei einer Biergartenmusik die gefühlvolle 'Post im Walde' gehört. Er macht sich also wohl nur lustig über die sentimentalen Reisenden, und darauf scheint auch das brutale Trompetensignal hinzudeuten, das jenen Gefühlserguß parodistisch abschneidet.'

27. Hofmannsthal, "Der Dichter und diese Zeit", 261: 'Aber das Wesen unserer Epoche ist Vieldeutigkeit und Unbestimmtheit.'

28. Bauer-Lechner, *Recollections of Gustav Mahler*, 128; translation amended.

29. Erk and Böhme, *Deutscher Liederhort*, 2: 373.

30. Mahler, "The Influence of the Folk-Song", 301–2.

31. See Eggebrecht, *Die Music Gustav Mahlers*, 39–79. My definition of the colloquial tone differs from Eggebrecht's in that it stipulates an origin outside of the symphonic tradition; his only criterion is prior familiarity. For him, such clichés of art music as sighing figures can impart a colloquial tone as readily as a military march style. Such an inclusive definition misses the ways that Mahler exploited the sense of foreignness elicited by folk and popular styles in particular.

32. Martner, *Selected Letters*, 173; translation amended.

33. Martner, *Selected Letters*, 172.

34. See Krummacher, *Gustav Mahlers III. Symphonie*; Franklin, *Mahler*; Solvik, "Mahler and the Creative Imagination".

35. See chapter 17 in this volume.

36. Klatte, "Die 38. Tonkünstler-Versammlung", 1764: 'zu denen ich allerdings nicht das sentimental sich ergehende, stark an die Trivialitäten der ersten Abteilung gemahnende Posthorn-Solo rechne.'

37. Karbusicky's *Mahler und seine Umwelt* is an extended exercise in following the associative trains of thought activated in specific passages—he turns to the posthorn episodes for his first example—that he dubs *memory-complexes* (*Erinnerungskomplexen*; pp. 7–8). Karbusicky limits his investigation to tracing connections in just one direction, to the Czech music of Mahler's (and Karbusicky's) youth. Eggebrecht, in contrast, denies the validity of the associative trains of thought. Instead, he develops an idiosyncratic semantic system of Jungian vocables that, in his eyes, correspond to the true, timeless meaning of Mahler's music and its colloquial tone.

38. Dahlhaus, *Nineteenth-Century Music*, 314–15.

39. Hirschfeld, "Mahler und Strauß in Wien", 536: 'Man wird in der trivialen Musik immer beobachten, daß sogenannte 'Schlager' jedesmal diejenigen Stellen treffen, die durch verwandte Melodie oder auch nur gleiche Intervalle bereits empfänglich geworden sind. Gustav Mahlers Musik lebt von dieser Methode. Sein raffiniertes Klangwesen läßt ... Volkslieder, im Rondo der Dritten das bewährte Flügelhorn der Gartenmusik, kurz Dinge, die in unserem Gemüte schon lagern, angenehm mitschwingen.'

40. Max Graf, "Die dritte Symphonie Gustav Mahlers": 'eine jener Lieder, das man anstimmt, wenn man recht eselhaft verliebt ist, zwischen fünfzehn und zwanzig Jahren ... Wir fangen an, gerade ein wenig gerührt zu werden—nicht durch die Melodie, sondern durch Erinnerungen ... Jugendliebe und Frühlingszeit, Waldträumerei und sentimentale Feldwanderungen.'

41. Bonds, *After Beethoven*, 15.

11

Gustav Mahler's Eighth Symphony and Max Reinhardt's Concept of *Massenregie*

Peter Revers

Amongst Gustav Mahler's compositions, his Eighth Symphony has been by far the most polarising one. Even its problematic epithet 'Symphony of a Thousand' strikingly reflects the exceptional rank of the work. The Eighth was recognised, on the one hand, for its tendency towards the colossal and sublime: 'Hang zum Kollosalen und Gewaltigen',[1] and on the other hand as a manifestation of 'the elevating enthusiasms of the festivals of song, reviving *Meistersinger* tones',[2] which Adorno condemned as a 'lapse into grandiose decorativeness'.[3] Analysis of numerous press articles, which covered not only the performances but also the circumstances of its preparation and rehearsals, indicates that the symphony was considered not only an artistic event but also a social one.

Two moments in its genesis reflect the 'public' aspect. First were the dimensions and production of this gigantic event, which can be traced back to the early planning stages. A massive advertising campaign accompanied the production: 'When he arrived in Munich, Mahler . . . had been shocked at this riot of publicity, which everywhere struck the eye'[4] (see Fig. 11.1). As early as March 1910 Mahler expressed his hatred of all '(utterly superfluous) publicity' and the 'Barnum and Bayley [sic] methods' of the organiser Emil Gutmann in promoting the new work.[5] Gutmann did indeed place great demands on establishing a new type of grandiose music festival:

> [he] managed to convince the Munich City authorities . . . to cover the deficit that was bound to occur, by guaranteeing a debt up to 100.000 marks. Tremendous expense had been involved in bringing two big choruses of 250 singers each from Vienna and Leipzig, in covering their board in Munich for the days of rehearsals and concerts, besides the fees paid to the orchestra and the soloists. This of course explains why the publicity could not be kept tasteful. Mahler has resigned himself to this because he was ever a pragmatist and knew that the organizers needed to ensure that everyone in Munich, Germany, Austria and wider Europe, would know of the magnitude and unique nature of the coming event.[6]

Fig. 11.1 Alfred Roller's poster advertising the première of the Eighth Symphony

The second important public aspect of this symphony was Mahler's claim to artistic transcendence in terms of a musical universe. In his letter to Willem Mengelberg, Mahler writes:

> I have just finished my Eighth—it's the grandest thing I have done yet—and so peculiar in content and form that it is really impossible to write anything

about it. Try to imagine the whole universe beginning to ring and resound. These are no longer human voices, but planets and suns revolving.[7]

Both aspects, as much as they might sound contradictory, are related to each other. Reports of the rehearsals and the world premiere on 12 September 1910 referred to the 'public frame', the international audience and the intriguing aura of the rehearsals for the symphony. Furthermore, Mahler took into consideration 'the audience's reception of the work'. In this respect, the 'grouping of his forces' as well as his endeavour to organise the visual aspects of the performance strikingly reflect Mahler's fascinating ability to achieve his overall artistic visions. Emil Gutmann, the organiser of the world premiere, states in his memoirs that even the most extrinsic details had a mental and metaphysical goal, a 'Kunstwirken höherer Ordnung' ['an artistic power of a higher order']:

> Mahler strove to transform the initial diffuseness of his performers into a homogenous whole . . . He fused singers, orchestra, stage into an artistic unity, which was nothing less than the representation of the work of art as an organic whole . . . The organization of a work of art was not over, for Mahler, when he had finished with the performers . . . The grouping of his forces was very important to him, in order to make the unity of the work obvious to the eye as well.[8]

Soon after the first performance, and above all as a consequence of the infamous epithet 'Symphony of a Thousand', the inclusion of a visual component under one unified artistic idea gave rise to critical comments about the 'commerciality' of the work. And so Richard Sternfeld stated in April 1912, 'The ear no longer ruled in musical performances . . . but rather the eye: the persuasion of numbers.'[9] What Mahler had thought of as the epitome of the 'homogeneous artwork' was still regarded with suspicion. Notwithstanding that the byname 'Symphonie der Tausend' was probably first and foremost an advertising strategy on the part of Gutmann, the introduction of the crowd (both in the form of performers and audience) became problematic in a similar way to Nietzsche's significant criticism of Wagner. Nietzsche's demand, at the end of *Der Fall Wagner* [*The Case of Wagner*] that 'the theatre should not become the ruler over the arts' is correlated with his warning about 'the advent of the actor in music'[10] and the vision of a superiority of theatricality as 'something bent into shape, something made up for the masses'.[11]

Nietzsche's criticism concerning a dimension of the artwork that aims at a massed public also raises the question of the performance site. While for him the early festivals at Bayreuth (and especially their hustle and bustle in the context of the first performance of the *Ring* tetralogy) were symptomatic of Wagner's shift to massive effects, he does not deal with the place of activity, the Festspielhaus. In contrast to this, the site of the premiere of Mahler's Eighth—the Neue Musik-Festhalle built in 1907—blasts apart the traditional character of the concert hall, not only in its dimensions but also in its function

Fig. 11.2 Mahler rehearsing the Eighth Symphony

as a multi-purpose hall, and thus opens up space for new kinds of acoustics[12] and visual staging effects to achieve the goal of homogeneity in the mass of audience and performers (see Fig. 11.2). This last aspect was apostrophised by Emil Gutmann as 'the result of unified organization' when he wrote:

> When Mahler stepped onto the podium in the dim light of the huge hall, where the black mass of the audience coalesced with the black and white mass of the performers, everyone sensed that a primordial being, well-organized and capable of life, had just now been given its heart, and that this would begin to beat immediately. At this moment there was no singer, no listener, no instrument and no soundboard, but rather a single body, with many, many veins and nerves, that was only waiting to have the blood and breath of art flow through it. No-one else could have led everyone in complete willingness to art, to the artwork, to the reception of art. The name and purpose of this body was termed: the art community.[13]

The 'art community' as a term for the synthesis of performers and listeners in an idealised massed association also forms an important facet of Max Reinhardt's theatre aesthetics. Perhaps it is more than just coincidence that in the same month as the premiere of Mahler's Eighth, Reinhardt also substantially expanded the space in which theatre productions took place. With the first performance of Sophocles's *König Ödipus* on 25 September 1910 in the Musikfesthalle in Munich he established this arena as the forum for a new kind of synthesis of stage and auditorium.[14] Max Epstein explained this concept in 1918:

> The arena has a spatial advantage that no theatre, no matter how large it is, can replace. This is the close relationship between stage and auditorium after which Reinhardt strives so relentlessly. . . . The massed spectators who crowd

around and above the place where the action takes place are not separated from the stage, but rather sense this stage as being, as it were, part of themselves; they feel that they are being drawn into the middle of the action.[15]

Thereby a stage arena was in fact created in the Musikfesthalle

to cope with a directing concept in which the classical Greek chorus is released from its role as commentator on the action, and with the polyphonic role-bearers—the people— begins the modern way of handling crowds (*Massenregie*). And so, in an exhibition hall that is transformed into a circus-like space for music events, there arises a laboratory for a kind of theatre that—with the socio-political emancipation of the people in the foreground—in the theatrical representation of crowd scenes conceives the masses as the sum of individual physiognomies. The provisional arrangement of the Munich Musikfesthalle, which was the first protagonist in the development of theatre reform that lasted for more than a hundred years, is the starting point for a development of modern theatre design that has not yet been fully discussed nor come to an end even today.[16]

There is evidently a significant parallel here to the establishment of an ideal 'art community' as stated by Gutmann. To be sure, Epstein also recognises that there is a problem of alienation created by such a display being transferred into the huge space (merging, so to speak, all the participants in the art work):

Therein lies the enormous danger of the arena, and one cannot be warned sufficiently about this. As soon as one tries to force crowds upon crowds, one will be reduced over time to dealing with extraneous matters. Large displays and a jumble of equipment will end up being the main issue.[17]

As a matter of fact, Reinhardt was very much aware of this danger and he not only argued for the absolute necessity of individual artistic expression even in crowd scenes but also for the responsibility of each actor for the entire artistic organism (see Fig. 11.3):

Every single individual has to be filled with the conviction that he is an actor with a task to master, upon which the success of the whole depends; that he is a small but important part of a greater organism. Only then will he strive to do the best that he possibly can every evening. When this is achieved, I have succeeded in conveying to this crowd of people the expression of feeling required by the poetry, succeeded in helping it to reveal itself to them as an inner necessity; only then can the dynamic nuances be attempted.[18]

Epstein explains the aesthetic relevance of Reinhardt's arena productions through the efforts it took to establish these as a new form of national theatre:

The majority thinks of a national theatre as being simply a large building in which there is space for several thousand people and where classical tragedies

Fig. 11.3 Max Reinhardt: Sophocles, *King Oedipus* (London, 1912)

can be performed on a grand scale. Max Reinhardt unfortunately also belongs to this majority. . . . The masses must be enticed and satisfied. Now and then pure showpieces replace artistic works, and with time one can do business with the decorative piece.[19]

A little later, Epstein's differentiated and yet thoroughly critical attitude towards Reinhardt's theatrical handling of crowds advanced to a trenchant, polemical critique of this arena theatre in Franz Ferdinand Baumgarten's publication *Zirkus Reinhardt*:

> The circus theatre is the most striking example of the fragmentation of art and culture from which we suffer. Its symptomatic significance lends weight to Reinhardt's undertakings and advertisements that they would not have in and of themselves. We recognize here the typical traits of all periods of decadence, the symptoms of sickness in our time.[20]

Certainly for Reinhardt, the arena stage was on the one hand a revitalisation of the ancient Greek theatre, and on the other hand a popularisation of culture based on the aesthetic idea of 'German Folk-Festivals' (*deutsche Volksfestspiele*) in the early 1910s:

> Reinhardt recognized the main characteristic—the mystery of the ancient theatre—in the extension of space for the dramatic stage, as well as for the auditorium . . . There, in the circus, he had enormous space, which, although not capable of seating thirty thousand as in ancient Athens, still had a capacity of at least five or six thousand audience members; here he had an amphitheatre with ascending seats, serving as a soundboard for a popular echo of the masses.[21]

However, he intended a community of actors and audience within the context of a specific aesthetic experience to act as a visionary counterpart to the increasing fragmentation of modern society:

> Reinhardt's productions of *Oedipus Rex* and *Orestie* succeeded in collapsing dichotomies between individual and community, between mind and body which were deeply rooted in Christian culture . . . This also implied the collapse of another opposition—that between elitist and popular culture. By using the most 'sacred' texts from the cultural tradition of the *elite* on the one hand and, on the other, by performing in a circus which emphasized the body, providing 'thrill' and 'entertainment', Reinhardt bridged the gap between elitist and popular culture. In fact, a new people's theatre was created in which members from all social groups, classes and strata met and formed a community together.[22]

Based on an amalgamation of elitist and popular art, mainly realised in the 'Theatre of the Five Thousand' (Circus Schumann, Berlin), a close interaction of stage design, colour, light, music and sound effects, as well as the bodily movement of the actors, evoked a distinct atmosphere resulting in the primarily sensual reception of the audience.[23]

One important aspect of stimulating these sensual perceptions was Reinhardt's insight that in the 'realization of a performance, two groups are always involved—the actors and the audience—that the performance comes into being from . . . the interactions' and the exchange of energies between the two. Thus 'the performance cannot be understood as the work of one or more artists . . . Rather, it is realized as a game in which everyone takes part.'[24] Without going into more detail here about the theoretical and artistic implications of Reinhardt's concept of the handling of crowds, it is nevertheless germane in many ways not only to the specific organisation of the premiere of Mahler's Eighth but also to the context of its early reception. We should remember first of all that Mahler was responsible for all of the necessary performance details that were required to fulfil the integral claim of the Eighth as a unified work (*Gesamtkunstwerk*). This was so important to him that for the 'external grouping of the crowds'—to use Gutmann's expression—he used the services of the stage designer and scenographer Alfred Roller at the early rehearsals to supervise the arrangement of the soloists and the different groups on the stage, as well as the lighting of the hall. These aspects were considered by neither Mahler nor Roller to be accessory elements to the total artistic effect but rather were the result of a subtle analysis of the interaction between performance and public, which Roller described as follows: 'All of the individual moments in a performance are mutually dependent and reciprocal in their emotional, acoustic and optical effects . . . conditioned by their impact on the audience.'[25]

This comprehensive organisational standard had been in force ever since Roller's appointment to the Viennese Court Opera. From the very beginning he included the whole space in his conception, that is, both the auditorium and the stage. Wolfgang Greisenegger has accurately summarised this as follows: 'A new approach becomes apparent here. Up to now, the designers were only concerned with the stage. Roller thinks about visibility on the part of the audience, and checks the stage action from different vantage points in the auditorium.'[26] Moreover, Roller's innovative ideas about a comprehensive stage design converge in a remarkable way with Reinhardt's theatre work. This has been acknowledged in depth by Hugo von Hofmannsthal: Reinhardt, 'a master in controlling light' needs

> the painter, the musician, the machine operator, the lighting technician, the choreographer—he needs and uses them in a totally different way from any other theatre director; through his demands he raises them far beyond the limits of their powers ... but he uses all of these objects and occupations only in the same carefree manner as he treats his own existence ... he is a visionary—the kind that wants to realize his own visions—and thus an organizer and a man of power like few others.[27]

Many of these attributes can be applied to Mahler's organisation of the artwork, whether in the area of opera or the concert hall. These aspects are no less an integral part of a comprehensive understanding of the symphony as the epitome of community art or—as Paul Bekker argues—of a musical public assembly. The realisation of such public assemblies and of the functions symphonies had within this context was of increasing importance, especially since the late nineteenth century. Adolf Seelig and Albert Gutmann, for instance, made demands for the wider scope of so-called *Volksconcerte* (folk concerts), convinced that 'there might exist musical pleasures which are more intensive and longer lasting than the "Promenade-Concerts" of Eduard Strauss or a visit to the Schrammel-Quartet'.[28] Gutmann described this lack of aesthetic profundity even more precisely: 'the Viennese are lacking dramatic accents' and even 'sometimes the "Maëstoso" that only a symphony can provide'.[29]

Although such ambitions initially met with little response from the public, they resulted in a gradual increase in the sensibility of popular taste as well as a more musically educated audience. With this in mind, Paul Amadeus Pisk sketched out a music-historical perspective of the symphony after Beethoven '[resulting from the effect on the masses and the] need to communicate with a huge group of listeners [through its particularization in different national schools, to a last attempt, finally achieved by Mahler before the war] ... to unite the audience in a sense of community.'[30] However, Mahler's understanding of community ultimately transcends the sphere of reality and sensual

feeling, aiming at 'much deeper spiritual desires—an aspiration which can jus-
tifiably be called "all-embracing" ... sketch[ing] out in his music nothing less
than a symbol of the universe in sound'.[31]

In his frequently quoted letter to Alma from June 1909, Mahler gave a
thorough explanation of the final verses of the *chorus mysticus*, describing
them as

> the peak of the whole tremendous pyramid, a world presented and fashioned
> step by step, in one situation and development after another. All point, at
> first dimly and then from scene to scene ... with growing mastery, to this
> supreme moment, which though beyond expression, scarcely even to be sur-
> mised, touches the very heart of feeling.[32]

However, he was very well aware that—despite the monumentality of the
final bars—it is (at the very end) indescribable. Thus Mahler composes a
vision of a utopian realm, but not a utopia itself.[33] Mahler describes the spiritual development of Faust as a journey 'through the manifold entelechies
of lower and higher degree; he [Goethe] presents and expresses it with a
growing clearness and certainty right on to the *mater gloriosa*—the per-
sonification of the eternal feminine!"[34] In Goethe's *Faust* the mothers are
not only beyond the categories of space and time, but they are incomprehensible: for Mephistopheles there exists 'kein Ort, noch weniger eine Zeit'
('no place, much less a time') for them, and the way to them leads towards
the 'Unbetretene/Nicht zu Betretende/ein Weg ans Unerbetene/Nicht zu
Erbittende' ('Untrodden/Not to be Trodden/a Path to the Unsolicited/Not to
be Requested').[35] The 'mothers' ('Die Mütter'), principally the Mater Gloriosa
as central representation of the eternal feminine, thus belong to another,
transcendent sphere. In Mahler's score this is already clarified with her first
appearance in part II of the Symphony ('Mater gloriosa schwebt einher', bars
780–803), which is suggested exclusively by the orchestra without vocal representation. Nevertheless, the sonority as well as the tonal disposition unfold
a network of references. With regard to the tonal disposition, it is the sphere
of E major. Doctor Marianus's calling on the Mater Gloriosa ('Höchste
Herrscherin der Welt,' bars 639–41) as well as her appearance in bars 780ff.,
take place within this tonality, in the latter case realised—according to the
stage direction—by a soft and floating timbre of the first violins, the harp
and the harmonium, evoking a suggestion of *musica caelestis*, which finds its
final evidence in a segment preceding the *chorus mysticus* (bars 1421–48: here
with the addition of celeste and piano). A similar situation can be found in a
passage where the god-like mercy of the Mater Gloriosa is mentioned (bars
1362–84: 'Jungfrau, Mutter, Königin/<u>Göttin, bleibe gnädig</u>'; 'Virgin, Mother,
Queen ... /Goddess, kind for ever!'). There is again a similar orchestral disposition, although enriched with woodwinds, trumpets, trombones, and low

strings. Adorno insistently pointed out the function of tonality as an important means of representation in Mahler's compositions:

> He does not organize his work through harmony in detail, but uses harmony to create light and shadow in the whole, effects of foreground and depth, perspective. For this reason tonal areas are more important to him than seamless transitions between them, or the fine harmonic articulation of each surface in itself: his harmony is macrological.[36]

Donald Mitchell rightly pointed out that E major 'is Mahler's visionary, heavenly key ... that introduces the "new world" ... into the Eighth, as forcefully as it did in the Fourth'.[37] In both cases a theatrical moment comes into effect: a well-calculated theatrical production of the E major tonality, as it were, functions in the calm third movement of the Fourth as if 'a dream's long-heralded desire for bliss is finally fulfilled, a dream which is then expressed in words in the following song [the final movement of the Fourth]'.[38] Thus the E major sonority opens up in the Fourth as well as in the Eighth a vision of a transcendent world, which is 'staged' by virtue of a distinct musical dramaturgy where sonorities function as actors in an imaginary plot. In a similar way, light functions as a theatrical means in Reinhardt's productions of *King Ödipus* in Circus Schumann in Berlin:

> The chorus acted synchronously ... in order to heighten the effect of an emotionalized crowd. Spotlights, which picked out individual groups from the darkness, increased the effect still further. With his production of *Oedipus*, Reinhardt initiated a trend-setting development as far as new spatial dimensions and the accompanying style of production and presentation were concerned.[39]

The confluence of these manifold aesthetic visions in a state of highly sensitised inspiration provides a further parallel between the composition of Mahler's Eighth and Reinhardt's visions of stage production. Just as Mahler described the process of composition as 'a lightning vision—suddenly the whole thing stood before me and I simply had to write it down, just as if it had been dictated to me',[40] so Reinhardt explained his creative process in his 'Autobiographical sketches: The promptbook' as follows:

> One reads a play. Sometimes it inspires one with enthusiasm immediately. While one is reading one has to pause from sheer excitement. Visions follow in rapid succession ... One can see every gesture, every move, every piece of furniture, the light, one can hear every nuance of tone, every enhancement, the musicality of the phrases, the pauses, the various tempi ... The effect of the light. And then one writes them down, those perfect optical and acoustic visions, like a musical score. One can hardly get it all down, so powerfully does it rush into one's brain, and it is, in fact, something mysterious, without thought, without effort.[41]

As Christian Wildhagen rightly points out, Mahler retains ties to the symphonic tradition but also includes elements of compositional strategies influenced by Wagner's concept of the *Musikdrama*. Thus, his characterisation of Mahler's Eighth as a 'Prototyp eines "unsichtbaren Theaters"' ('prototype of an "invisible theatre"')[42] is hardly conceivable within the traditional limits of the genre. Rather, it reflects a striking amalgamation of different genres whose traces nevertheless remain present. As a special case of a symphonic type of *Gesamtkunstwerk*, Mahler's Eighth is certainly one of the most prominent, influential and original examples within the entire tradition of the symphony: a ' "theatre of the mind", of the spirit, which was surely how the great poet must have imagined the second part of *Faust*'.[43] In this regard Mahler was a visionary for a new concept of the symphony just as Reinhardt was for a new concept of the theatre.

Notes

1. Korngold, "Mahlers III. Symphonie," 2. Unless otherwise indicated, all translations are the author's.

2. Adorno, *Mahler* [English edition], 140.

3. Adorno, *Mahler*, 142.

4. La Grange, *Gustav Mahler*. Vol. 4, 953–54.

5. Blaukopf, *Mahler's Unknown Letters*, 74.

6. La Grange, *Gustav Mahler*. Vol. 4, 942 and 958.

7. Martner, *Selected Letters*, 294.

8. Gutmann, "Gustav Mahler as Organizer", 85 and 87.

9. Sternfeld, "Symphonie der Tausend", 444, cited in Wildhagen, *Die Achte Symphonie von Gustav Mahler*, 116.

10. Nietzsche, *Der Fall Wagner*, 39 and 37.

11. *Nachschrift zu Der Fall Wagner* (in Nietzsche, *Der Fall Wagner*), 42.

12. See Wildhagen, *Die Achte Symphonie von Gustav Mahler*, 131, fn. 364 and the surrounding discussion.

13. Gutmann, "Gustav Mahler as Organizer", 88 (translation amended; see Gutmann, "Gustav Mahler als Organisator", 91.

14. See Huesmann, *Welttheater Reinhardt*, 91.

15. Epstein, *Max Reinhardt*, 195: 'Die Arena hat einen räumlichen Vorzug, den kein noch so großes Theater ersetzen kann. Das ist die innige Beziehung zwischen Bühne und Zuschauerraum, nach der Reinhardt unablässig strebt . . . Die Massen, die rund um und über der Stelle sich drängen, wo eine Handlung sich abspielt, sind nicht getrennt vom Schauplatz, sondern empfinden diesen Schauplatz gleichsam unter sich, sie fühlen sich mitten in diese Handlung hineingezogen.'

16. Huesmann, *Welttheater Reinhardt*, 22: 'zur Bewältigung einer Regiekonzeption, in der sich das Chorelement der griechischen Klassik aus seiner Zwischenaktkommentierung löst und mit dem polyphonen Rollenträger Volk

moderne Massenregie beginnt. Damit entsteht in einer zum Zirkus entfremde-
ten, für Musikveranstaltungen umgerüsteten Ausstellungshalle der Laborraum
für ein Theater, das im Vorfeld der sozialpolitischen Emanzipation eines Volkes
in der szenischen Darstellung von Massenverhalten Masse als Summe individuel-
ler Physiognomien begreift. Das Provisorium der Münchner Musikfesthalle, erster
Protagonist einer mehr als hundertjährigen Entwicklung des Reformtheaters,
bildet den Ausgangspunkt für eine bis heute weder ausdiskutierte noch abge-
schlossene Entwicklung des modernen Theaterbaus.'

17. Huesmann, *Welttheater Reinhardt*, 196: 'Darin liegt die ungeheure Gefahr
der Arena, vor der nicht genug gewarnt werden kann. Sobald man versucht die
Massen durch Massen zu zwingen, muß man notwendiger Weise ins Äußerliche
verfalle. Großes Gepränge Ausstattungskram wird schließlich zur Hauptsache.'

18. Reinhardt, "From an interview with Max Reinhardt", 76: 'Jeder und
jede einzelne muß von der Überzeugung erfüllt sein, daß er eine darstellerische
Aufgabe zu bewältigen hat, von der das Gelingen des Ganzen abhängt; daß er ein
kleines aber wichtiges Glied in dem großen Organismus ist, Nur dann wird er an
jedem Abend das Beste, was er vermag, zu geben trachten. Ist dies erreicht, ist es
mir gelungen, den von der Dichtung geforderten Gefühlsausdruck auf diese Masse
zu übertragen, ihn auch ihr als innere Notwendigkeit offenbar werden zulassen,
dann erst kann die dynamische Abschattierung versucht werden.' (Fuhrich and
Prossnitz, *Max Reinhardt, Die Träume des Magiers*, 76; English edn., 76).

19. Epstein, *Max Reinhardt*, 296: 'Die Mehrzahl denkt sich bei einem
Nationaltheater einfach ein großes Haus, in dem ein paar tausend Menschen Platz
haben, und wo die klassische Tragödie großen Stils eine Stätte finden kann. Zu dieser
Mehrzahl gehört leider auch Max Reinhardt . . . Die Massen müssen angelockt und
befriedigt werden. Ab und zu werden reine Schaustücke die Kunstwerke ablösen,
und mit der Zeit wird man nur mit dem Ausstattungsstück Geschäfte machen.'

20. Baumgarten, *Zirkus Reinhardt*, 82: 'Das Zirkus-Theater ist das augenfäl-
ligste Beispiel der Kunst- und Kulturzertrümmerung, die wir erleiden. Die symp-
tomatische Bedeutung verleiht dem Reinhardt-Unternehmen und seiner Reklame
ein Gewicht, das sie für sich allein nicht hätten. In diesem Spiegel erkennen wir
die typischen Merkmale aller Niedergangszeiten, die Krankheitssymptome
unserer Zeit.'

21. Düsel, "Dramatische Rundschau", 782–83, cited in Marx, *Max Reinhardt*,
109: 'Reinhardt erblickte das Hauptcharakteristikum, das Geheimnis des antiken
Theaters in der Raumdehnung, sowohl durch den dramatischen Spielplatz wie für
den Zuschauerkreis . . . Da [im Zirkus] hatte er den gewaltigen Raum, der, wenn
nicht dreißig-, wie im alten Athen, so doch fünf- oder sechstausend Zuschauer zu
fassen vermag; da hatte er das Amphitheater mit den aufsteigenden Sitzen, was
allein den Resonanzboden für einen volkstümlichen Massenwiderhall abgibt.'

22. Fischer-Lichte, *Theatre, Sacrifice, Ritual*, 64.

23. See Fischer-Lichte, "Sinne und Sensationen", 24.

24. Ibid., 23f: 'dass am Zustandekommen einer Aufführung immer zwei
Gruppen beteiligt sind—Akteure und Zuschauer—dass sie . . . aus der Interaktion

zwischen ihnen ... aus den Energien, die zwischen ihnen ausgetauscht werden,' entsteht. 'Die Aufführung ist also nicht das 'Werk' eines oder mehrerer Künstler zu verstehen ... Vielmehr ereignet sie sich als ein Spiel an dem alle beteiligt sind.'

25. Roller, "Bühne und Bühnenhandwerk", 1930, 145: 'Alle die einzelnen Momente einer Aufführung sind in ihren seelischen, akustischen und optischen Wirkungen voneinander abhängig und gegenseitig ... in ihrem Ausdruck auf den Zuschauer bedingt.'

26. Greisenegger, "Alfred Roller", 276: 'Hier wird eine neue Einstellung sichtbar. Die Ausstatter kümmerten sich bisher nur um die Bühne. Roller denkt an die Sichtverhältnisse des Zuschauers, überprüft das Bühnengeschehen von verschiedenen Punkten des Zuschauerraumes aus.'

27. Hofmannsthal, "Reinhardt bei der Arbeit", 298–99: Reinhardt, 'ein Meister in der Beherrschung des Lichts', braucht 'den Maler, den Musiker, den Maschinenmeister, den Beleuchter, den Choreographen—braucht und verbraucht sie in einem ganz anderen Maße als irgendein anderer Theaterchef, steigert sie durch seine Forderungen weit über die Grenzen ihrer Kräfte ... aber er verbraucht alle diese Materialien und Existenzen nur so, wie er auch unbekümmert seine eigene Existenz verbraucht ... er ist ein Visionär und ein solcher, der seine Visionen realisieren will, und als solcher aber ein Ordner und ein Kraftmensch wie wenige.'

28. Seelig "Die Wiener Orchesterfrage", 64: 'daß es noch nachhaltigere musikalische Genüsse gibt, als ein Promenade-Concert von Eduard Strauß oder ein Besuch bei den Schrammeln.'

29. See also Max Kalbeck, "Feuilleton. Das populäre Concert": 'The need to hear serious music is not a general one in Vienna, indeed it is hardly even to exist.' ('Das Bedürfniß, ernste Musik zu hören, ist in Wien kein allgemeines, ja, es ist so gut wie nicht vorhanden.') For the significance and historical development of the *Volksconcerte* in the context of an ideology of the symphony see Notley, "*Volksconcerte* in Vienna", 444–49.

30. Pisk, "Zur Soziologie der Musik", 186; partially cited in Notley, "*Volksconcerte* in Vienna", 451 fn. 108: '[ausgehend von einer Wirkung auf die Massen und dem] Zwang, sich einer großen Hörerschaft mitzuteilen [über deren Partikularisierung in verschiedene nationale Schulen zu einem schließlich mit Mahler erreichten] letzten Versuch vor dem Krieg ... die Hörerschaft zu einer Gemeinschaft zusammenzufassen."

31. Wildhagen, "The 'Greatest' and the 'Most Personal'", 131.

32. Alma Mahler, *Gustav Mahler. Memories and Letters* (1990), 320.

33. 'It is all an allegory to convey something which, whatever form it is given, can never be adequately expressed. Only the transitory lends itself to description ... the intransitory behind all appearance, is indescribable.' Alma Mahler, *Gustav Mahler*, 320.

34. Alma Mahler, *Gustav Mahler*, 321.

35. Goethe, *Faust*, part II, act 1, verses 6223–24.

36. Adorno, *Mahler* [English edn.], 27.

37. Mitchell, *Gustav Mahler.* Volume III, 526.

38. Hansen, *Gustav Mahler*, 105: 'als ob sich ein lang angekündigter Wunschtraum vom Glück endlich erfüllt, ein Traum, der im anschließenden Lied denn auch zur Sprache kommt.'

39. Fuhrich and Prossnitz, *Max Reinhardt*, 54 (English edn., 54): 'Der Chor agierte synchron . . . um den Eindruck bewegter Massen zu steigern. Scheinwerfer, die einzelne Gruppen aus der Dunkelheit herausgriffen, verstärkten die Wirkung. Mit seinen "Ödipus"-Inszenierung hatte Reinhardt eine richtungsweisende Entwicklung bezüglich neuer Raumdimensionen und den damit verbundenen Inszenierungs- und Darstellungsmitteln eingeleitet.

40. Specht, "Zu Mahlers Achter Symphonie", 9; cited in Wildhagen, *Die Achte Symphonie von Gustav Mahler*, 15.

41. Fuhrich and Prossnitz, *Max Reinhardt*, 59 (English edn., 59): 'Man liest ein Stück. Manchmal zündet es gleich. Man muß vor Aufregung innehalten im Lesen. Die Visionen überstürzen sich . . . Man sieht jede Gebärde, jeden Schritt, jedes Möbel, das Licht, man hört jeden Tonfall, jede Steigerung, die Musikalität der Redewendungen, die Pausen, die verschiedenen Tempi. . . . Der Einfluß des Lichtes. Und dann schreibt man es nieder, die vollkommenen optischen und akustischen Visionen wie eine Partitur. Man kann kaum nachkommen, so mächtig drängt es an, eigentlich geheimnisvoll, ohne Überlegung, ohne Arbeit.'

42. Wildhagen, *Die Achte Symphonie von Gustav Mahler*, 224.

43. Mitchell, "Mahler's Eighth Symphony", 453.

III

VARIETIES OF HISTORICAL AND AESTHETIC EXPERIENCE

12

The Particularity of the Moment

Julian Johnson

Ex. 12.1

In the moment that it happens, how do we make sense of this astonishing viola gesture (Ex. 12.1) in the Finale of Mahler's First Symphony? More a physical spasm than musical material, it erupts from within the orchestra, isolated and without metrical or syntactical context. It tears the surface of the music like a kind of protest against the structural limbo at which the Finale has arrived—its rawness all the more shocking because heard in an orchestral voice usually far less demonstrative. And yet, as the gesture begins to make sense of itself over the next few bars, it becomes the key to unlocking the temporal stalemate of the entire work: physical tremor becomes musical motif and then the basic unit in a piece of overt constructivism, as Mahler rebuilds formal momentum through imitative counterpoint. The viola section, it seems, has saved the day (Ex. 12.2).

How should we understand this unprepared assertion of radical particularity? Richard Strauss famously considered that Mahler had made a structural error in introducing the affirmative and apparently conclusive breakthrough (Rehearsal Fig. 34) only then to allow it to collapse and have to be re-approached all over again.[1] The arbitrary quality of the viola gesture that initiates the process of rebuilding may well have been his evidence that Mahler had here written himself into a structural dead-end. Strauss's sense of good narrative form can hardly be called into question but it represents the symphonic order which Mahler's Finale stages, only to subvert. Mahler's reply to Strauss's criticism stresses that his concern was precisely with the precariousness of the affirmative ending, undercut at the very moment of its assured success. In the face of the logical certainty of symphonic form, Mahler introduces a bewildering element of contingency, such that the affirmative closure of the whole is no longer the outcome of the authoritative system but the result of a fragile moment of particularity—here, in the (un)heroic voice of the violas.

Ex. 12.2 Mahler, First Symphony, Finale, bars 519–35

* Erster Eintritt übertreibend stark, und wohl auf die Abstufungen achtend

It is a moment that signals, right at the beginning of Mahler's symphonic career, a tension that the rest of his work would explore, the simultaneity of what Berthold Hoeckner summarised as 'the clash of two aesthetics'—the aesthetics of the particular, which Hoeckner associates with Adorno, and the aesthetics of the whole, associated with Hegel.[2] Invoking an idea of the resistance of the particular to the system of the whole suggests that we might hear the viola gesture as an instance of the Adornian *Augenblick*, characterised by Daniel Chua as 'a superhuman act that seemingly overcomes the material limitations of space and time by making the particular universal and the ephemeral eternal'.[3] Utterly contingent and of the moment, the superhuman act of the violas in Mahler's First Symphony certainly seems to resist the temporal logic of the whole while at the same time redeeming it. Put more strongly still, it might exemplify what Heidrun Friese characterises as the 'liberation from alienation and mere semblance' by means of 'the moment of choice, the dangerous moment, which has to be carried and endured in responsible action, the moment in which the singular human being chooses himself in his specific existence'.[4]

But that is to get ahead of ourselves. In the first instance, the viola gesture breaks the harmonic fixity of the C-pedal which has held the music in a kind of trance for the last eighty-four bars of slow tempo (more than three minutes in performance). The return of the slow introduction from the first movement (after Rehearsal Fig. 39) and the strings' lyrical response to it (Rehearsal Figs. 41–44) are both heard over this interminable pedal, a sideways step from the D-pedal which intitiates the return of the first movement introduction (Rehearsal Fig. 38) but a distantly remembered dominant of the Finale's F minor opening.

Only with the viola gesture does the C-pedal finally give way to F as the root of the harmony and progression gets under way once more. But the triple fortissimo entry of the violas is not heard primarily in harmonic terms; before all else, it strikes the listener in terms of its physicality, as a violent bodily gesture that refuses to be placed either metrically or in relation to its orchestral voicing (only gradually is it subsumed into a clearly defined metre and orchestral function). The rude physicality of the gesture is thus a mark of resistance to the system, its refusal of form, periodicity, and musical grammar.

This moment (*Augenblick*) appears without preparation, inducing a palpable sense of shock through its suddenness (*Plötzlichkeit*). The German term, in its adjectival form *plötzlich*, appears frequently as part of Mahler's performance directions and characterises his music even when not stipulated—just as the Finale of the First Symphony, like its model in Beethoven's Ninth, opens with a gesture of extreme suddenness after the quiet close of the preceding slow movement. It points to a key aspect of Mahler's method of proceeding, in which the smooth unfolding of long-range musical structures is frequently intercut by sudden interruptions or unprepared changes of tempo. Karl Heinz Bohrer underlines that the category of *Plötzlichkeit*, with its origins in German romantic literature, signals a kind of authorial self-awareness breaking the surface of the text. He cites two key essays—Friedrich Schlegel's 'Über die Unverständlichkeit' ('On Incomprehensibility') of 1800 and Heinrich von Kleist's 'Über die allmähliche Verfertigung der Gedanken beim Reden' ('On the Gradual Completion of Thoughts while Speaking') of 1805–6—suggesting that they have in common an 'understanding of cognitive acts as an event—an event that suddenly becomes aware of itself'.[5]

Mahler's fascination with the literature of German romanticism is well known, but he had no need to look beyond music for striking examples of sudden moments of self-awareness, breaking the smooth continuity of the system. Beethoven's music, contemporary with the work of Schlegel and Kleist, is of course founded on this tension (albeit one often neutralised by an approach to music analysis that dissolves away moments of rupture in a concern to demonstrate the mastery of the system). The focus of this essay is Mahler's inheritance of this defining and constitutive tension of Beethoven's music—between the claims of the particular and the logic of the whole—and the manner in which his symphonic music stages a kind of terminal exacerbation of this tension within the Austro-German symphony. In this, Mahler's music continues to differentiate itself from that of Schoenberg for which it has so often been heard as a precursor. Among the Schoenberg circle perhaps only Berg fully grasped this aspect of Mahler's music, a deep-seated similarity which accounts for the fact that neither composer sits easily in the prevalent taxonomies of modernism.

Mahler's symphonies, then, are marked by sudden intrusions, moments of self-awareness that imply reflection upon the symphonic discourse which they interrupt. This is a matter of musical form and material process, but it is thereby also a matter of temporality—that is to say, of the subjective construction and experience of time. Such reflection upon time is not simply an activity provoked in the listener, but is also one staged by the music. Mahler's marking *'wie nachhorchend'* ('as if listening', or 'overhearing'), in the third movement of the Third Symphony (Rehearsal Fig. 28), comes close to this idea, pointing to a music that attends to the manner in which it constructs the passing of time. One outward sign for such displacements, from enactment and narration to moments of self-reflection, is the simple musical comma or *Luftpause*, which Michael P. Steinberg suggests is 'the indicator of a first person musical voice taking stock of itself' in which 'music stops to think'.[6] Put another way, the Mahlerian comma signals a gap that exposes the fictive nature of the activity either side of it, 'as, in a theatre, the lights are extinguished, for the scene to be changed with a hollow rumble of wings, with a movement of darkness on darkness', to borrow T. S. Eliot's resonant metaphor.[7]

The First Symphony foregrounds this idea in overt and striking ways, establishing early in Mahler's career the capacity of his music to present, simultaneously, a narrative of experience and a self-reflection upon that experience. The first movement does this through interpolated returns of the initial slow introduction. At the start of the development (Rehearsal Fig. 12) the cello's dialogue with the flute constitutes a highly self-conscious review of the musical progress, implicitly calling into question the apparently unproblematic and sunny purposiveness of the Allegro by recalling the stasis of the opening. The viola gesture in the Finale, discussed above, signals a way out of the long suspension of forward motion initiated by a further, more distant return of the first movement material (Rehearsal Fig. 38). The slow introduction has no business here in the Finale except as an extreme case of structural self-reflection, underlining that the real subject of this symphony is the generation of temporal progress itself. The reappearance of the slow introduction, 'out of time' in terms of the temporal world of the Finale, offers a kind of lateral reflection upon the progress of the piece as a whole; it does not simply present a repeat of the first movement materials but comments upon them. This is particularly acute in the passage between Rehearsal Figures 39 and 40, in which the sounds of nature (in the woodwind) elicit a lyrical response and commentary (in the strings). A series of pauses and hold-ups in the tempo mark these out as reflective gestures, suspended on a thin ridge of the present, looking back to a timeless nature one way and lamenting the lack of a forward-oriented temporal purposiveness the other. For all the attempts to urge the music forward, it simply dissipates into temporal stasis—until the viola gesture.

In the First Symphony, the *Augenblick* interrupts, as a sudden moment of radical self-awareness, what is otherwise an extended performance of symphonic purposiveness. But in the case of the Fourth Symphony this equation is effectively reversed: structural forms of directed motion are here deployed as the material of a pervasive self-reflection. The distinction is enabled by Mahler's foregrounding of a classical sonata allegro, framed in such a way that content and comment are clearly distinguished. The sonata form serves as a staging of classical temporal direction and purposiveness, while Mahler's inflections and exaggerations constitute a kind of commentary, from the held-back anacrusis in bar 3 (italicised by the glissando) to the later interpolation of unrelated and oddly rustic material (Rehearsal Fig. 4). Instead of the classical flow of one section to the next, Mahler separates his sections with commas and caesuras and has one section start at a tangent to the previous one. The overt promise of the musical surface to deliver forward motion is undercut by a draining away of energy. The recapitulation, which should affirm temporal progression through a sense of structural arrival, is here an unrelated and contingent event (see Ex. 12.3); instead of the smooth logic of return, the caesura on the double bar line at Rehearsal Figure 18 marks a temporal rift between the end of the development and the start of the recapitulation. This short silence, a mere breath between the truncated end of one phrase and the unprepared start of another, thus represents not just a structural caesura, a break in time, but also a historical chasm—separating the promise of classical form and an ironic commentary upon that form a hundred years later.

But perhaps the most exposed instance of temporal self-reflection in this movement occurs in the coda. The point of re-arrival is undermined by a withdrawal of energy over a tonic pedal, as the texture separates out into transparent layers (*Ruhig und immer ruhiger werden*, seven bars before Rehearsal Fig. 24). The reflective reminiscence of the symphony's opening phrase is extended by a solo horn, with a freedom of tempo that constitutes a commentary 'out of time', its subjective time, pushing forward and holding back, being foregrounded against a haze of suspended time in the strings. The gentle ticking of pizzicato strings, a distant reminder of clock time, adds a third element (*Langsam*, nine bars after Rehearsal Fig. 24; see Ex. 12.4). The violins introduce a wistful fragment of the main theme (marked 'extremely held back') but whose distance from the present tense is further underlined by the E in the bass which reharmonises the keynote. The brief jubilant allegro that follows, as a theatrical 'curtain down', merely emphasises the extent to which the foregoing music was elsewhere and elsewhen.

Whereas the outer movements of his symphonies often retell their own past in order to arrive at the precarious moment of the present—witness the Wagnerian retellings of the past in the outer movements of the Second Symphony—Mahler's middle movements are often more concerned with recalling pastness through particularity. Viewed from the perspective of the whole work, the middle movements are parenthetical to the drama of the outer movements, a change of mode which can be understood as part of a larger self-reflection on the temporal drama of the outer movements. The contrast between the two is often extreme, causing Mahler anxiety on more than one occasion and which he tried to ameliorate, in the case of the Second Symphony,

Ex. 12.3 Mahler, Fourth Symphony, first movement, bars 237–41

by directing the conductor to leave a pause of several minutes between the first
and second movements.[8] But what Mahler was trying to cover up here was
less a symphonic misjudgment of the kind Strauss suggested and more a social
and historical disjunction between two modalities of temporal experience; the

Ex. 12.4 Mahler, Fourth Symphony, first movement, bars 330–37

extended comma between Mahler's first two movements is a perfect example of Adorno's contention that 'his fractures are the script of truth'.[9]

The slow Ländler of the Second Symphony could not be more different to the vast eschatological drama of the first movement. It signals pastness by means of a set of exaggerated stylistic particulars—the reference to a Schubert dance, the over-slow tempo, the clipped upbeat, the overfull texture, the use of glissandi in melodic lines, the twist to the minor mode. But the proposition of this movement is not so much a simple evocation of pastness as a foregrounding of the act of recollection. Divided up by returns of its contrasting dance materials, it draws out the gaps between these divisons in highly self-conscious moments of reflection. After the interpolated episodes of contrasting, quicker music, the Ländler is literally recalled by a lingering on a repeated note—the D♯ of the previous section changes into the E♭ of the Ländler, acting as a neat symbol for the change of temporal perspective (Rehearsal Fig. 5). At its second return (Rehearsal Fig. 12) the material is further distanced by being heard pizzicato; the counter-melody, originally in the cellos, is now in the violins, providing a kind of commentary whose temporal distance is emphasised by means of tell-tale glissandi (after Rehearsal Fig. 14). The performance markings *'nicht eilen'* ('don't hurry') and *'gehalten'* ('held back') are outward signs of Mahler's construction of musical memory; combined with the intensity of string tone, the use of glissando, and the characteristic falling figures, reminiscence is here overdetermined as deliberate sentimentality.

Mahler's music is full of such foregrounded moments of self-reflection. In the central dance movement of the Fifth Symphony, a chorus of echoing horns, calling into the distance, suspends the temporal direction of the movement (Rehearsal Figs. 10 and 28). The exchange of call and echo, separated by pauses, and the recurrent holding up of the tempo creates a kind of parenthesis within the movement as a whole. Whereas the particular gesture of the violas in the Finale of the First Symphony breaks through the structural stasis to deliver forward motion, here the solo horn suspends the headlong rush of the collective dance and opens up a parenthetical moment of self-reflection. The horns' particularity is underlined by the performance direction that they should be played 'bells up', thereby ensuring a rawness of tone that emphasises the 'natural' origin of the instrument, somewhat at odds with the smooth, cultivated tone of its orchestral descendant. Its particularity is further underlined by the independence of its slower tempo, which acts as a brake to the entire orchestra. The effect of Mahler's alternation of the solo horn's reflection and the orchestra's rushing forwards is to create a juxtaposition of two different kinds of musical time and space. The fracture in the principal temporal mode of the movement is marked by the air of unreality in the slow waltz (with pizzicato strings), separated from the rest of the music by a caesura at either end.

The peculiar potency of Mahler's interruptive moments—and indeed, interruptive movements—is in direct proportion to the symphonic ordering of time which they suspend. It is not just that they step out of what one might call the temporal purposiveness of the symphony with its overriding sense of directionality and progression but that, in tangential ways, they call the latter into question. And it is here, in the self-critique of symphonic time, that the larger historical import of Mahler's symphonies becomes apparent. Had Immanuel Kant been more musical, he might have realised that the new instrumental

music of the later eighteenth century offered a rich example of what he designated the 'formal purposiveness' of art—in other words, the sense that while
they had no external purpose, artworks are shaped *as if* they were purposive
and thus significant.[10] Formal purposiveness in music is of course the result of
directed temporal motion, nowhere better demonstrated than in the instrumental sonatas and symphonic works of the classical era. While this model
was part of Mahler's cultural inheritance, so too was the essentially divided
and plural nature of romantic time. If nineteenth-century music often seems
enthralled to the forward orientation of Hegelian historicity, it also critiques
that idea and often simply ignores it. To say that Mahler's symphonies draw
on Beethoven *and* Schubert is to remind ourselves that at the century's end,
his work exacerbated the temporal contradictions of the century's beginning.
That is to say, nineteenth-century music is as much concerned with temporal
byways and dead-ends as it is with hurtling along like the musical equivalent of
the new railways; more precisely, this music is preoccupied by the disjunction
between the two.

By the late 1880s, Mahler's self-conscious re-engagement with the Beethovenian
symphony was obviously problematic—as his critics were keen to remind him—
but all the more so because he dared to restate the aspiration of the symphony in
conjunction with music that frequently uncoupled the coaches from the engine
and derailed the inexorable forward progress of symphonic logic. Far more than
any representational content, it was the bewildering mix of different temporalities that lay behind the accusation that Mahler was writing a *'sinfonia ironica'*. It
is surely telling that Mahler makes thematic the idea of temporal purposiveness
in the first movements of his first three symphonies. In each case, an increasingly pronounced sense of temporal direction is generated from beginnings that
are variously static, spatial, heavy, and directionless. Yet, by their closing bars, all
three movements rush forward with unstoppable energy. Of course, there was
nothing new about generating energetic allegros out of slow introductions, but
these movements of Mahler's are differently constructed, taking the notion of
end-orientation to a kind of extreme, by shaping the entire movement towards
its closing section. In all three cases, Mahler deploys distance effects as a means
of achieving a temporal representation of converging upon the present moment.
The whooping horn calls at the cursory recapitulation of the first movement of the
First Symphony (Rehearsal Fig. 26) reach all the way back to the horn duet heard,
in the distance, in the slow introduction.

Reinhold Brinkmann, in his reflection on the 'time of the *Eroica*', reminds
us that in the years following the upheavals of the French Revolution, the movement of historical time was often experienced as a headlong rush, as an overwhelming 'torrent' or 'surging flood'. In Friedrich Schlegel's words of 1828,
'Never before was there a time so deeply, so directly, and so exclusively and
universally directed toward the future as ours.'[11] The time of the *Eroica* is thus
the time of revolution, of pressing forward with a force that sweeps all before

it, and therefore the time of modernity, the sense of being caught in a historical flow inexorably accelerating towards the future. But it also has to do with the bewildering proximity of what Reinhart Koselleck called 'the noncontemporaneousness of diverse, but in the chronological sense, simultaneous histories'.[12] Which brings us back to Beethoven and Schubert—the time of the *Eroica* is also the time of the Unfinished Symphony, or the *Winterreise*—and also back to Mahler, in whose music the juxtaposition of different temporalities offers a reflection upon the unresolved disjunctions of time in modernity.

If Mahler's first movements *generate* temporal purposiveness, his finales are conceived as a *return* to that idea after the parenthetical function of the middle movements. As in Beethoven's Ninth, Mahler's obvious model for such a self-conscious gesture, the idea of having to reforge temporal progress anew in the Finale is often dramatised by a catastrophic opening, framed as a temporal abyss that threatens to swallow human progress (the opening to the finales of Mahler's Second and Sixth symphonies provide powerful examples). But in first and last movements, Mahler displays an astonishing complexity of temporal form, the result of taking up the narrative structures of the Beethovenian symphony but in a self-reflective and self-critical context which repeatedly undermines them. This can be heard on the musical surface in the manner that Mahler's music is tugged in opposite temporal directions. One moment it presses forward urgently, the next it seems to drag heavily or lingers in the moment. Consider some of his most frequent tempo directions: '*schleppend*' ('dragging', but also 'heavy', 'wearisome', 'sluggish'); '*zurückhaltend*' ('holding back', but also 'withholding', 'delaying'); '*Zeit lassen*' (literally, 'allowing time', or 'taking one's time'). But on the other hand one frequently encounters the ubiquitous '*Vorwärts drängend*', or just '*drängend*' ('pushing forward', but also 'driving', 'urging', 'hurrying'). In the Andante of the Sixth Symphony (Rehearsal Fig. 102) Mahler uses the marking '*auf und abwogend*' ('surging and ebbing')—one that might sum up the experience of his music as a whole. A generation later Anton Webern compressed this temporal contour into a series of tiny accelerando/ritardando markings, signs of a vestigial lyrical subjectivity, like his hairpin dynamics. In Webern, this temporal gesture has become introspective and compressed, but in Mahler it is boldly written on large symphonic canvases, projecting the ambivalence of modern time as a matter of social, collective, and historical experience.

Mahler's symphonies confront the disjunction between the compulsion of objective historical time and the experience of freedom in the organic pliability of internal, subjective time—a rift that Schiller identified, as early as 1794, as a key problem for 'us moderns' and one he considered it was the role and responsibility of art to heal.[13] Mahler's music addresses this in the way that objective social forms are opened up, interrupted, and critiqued by an insistence on the subjective nature of musical time. Mahlerian digressions, caesurae, parentheses, and episodes are all the result of this fundamental tension; their mark is the particularity which refuses, however momentarily, to be subsumed into the logic of the whole. In the Funeral March of the First Symphony Mahler presents the most ironically empty form of objective collective time. The march genre stands as a kind of default mode for temporal purposiveness but Mahler frequently uses it to go nowhere (as in the first movement of the Sixth) or, in the case of the Funeral March, to expose the vanity of any ambition of progress. The end of temporal purposiveness, the Funeral March seems to say, is utterly empty time in which the subject has no authentic presence. In the Funeral March of the First Symphony, the exposed, mechanical ostinato of the timpani presents the building blocks of tonal motion reduced to the static rocking of an idiot. The opening section is constructed as a round—a paradox of successive entries indicating cumulative progress but adding up to something merely circular. The implied song text is of course about waking Brother Martin so he can ring in the new day, but no bells will sound here, presumably because he is dead. The promise of the new—*implied* by the march form—is thus grotesquely inverted.

The newness that arrives in its place is the 'shocking' (Jewish) particularity of the street music that interrupts this solemn round (Rehearsal Fig. 5)—the mordant expressiveness of the oboes and trumpets, and the gratingly upbeat jollity of the E♭ clarinets that follows (Rehearsal Fig. 6), accompanied by bass drum amd cymbals to underline its provenance in the music of itinerant street musicians. But it is this bewildering moment of particularity that interrupts the empty time of the Funeral March and introduces a wholly new element of movement and also expressive comment (witness the violins after Rehearsal Fig. 8). In turn, this protest of particularity leads to the utterly parenthetical construction of idyllic time at Rehearsal Fig. 10—the dream-image of a fulfilled time which forms the polar opposite of the return of the Funeral March at Rehearsal Figure 13.

Moments of particularity mark the failure of the symphonic whole to deliver the temporal purposiveness it promises. They draw attention to the points at which the latter fails. This is surely the root of the hostile contemporary reception of Mahler's symphonic works—that they present the symphonic quest for the affirmation of the whole in counterpoint with a bewildering degree of particularity which resists its overarching logic. The tension between the two is partly contained in the relation between the inner movements and the outer ones, but also in those moments of structural failure in the outer movements, such as the manner in which moments of recapitulation serve not as affirmative points of arrival but as *negative* returns which merely underline the absence of any temporal progression. In doing so, they articulate an unspoken anxiety of sonata form, a ghost in the Hegelian machine, that return would be exactly that and no more—not, after all, a musical enactment of the subject expanding through negating its own self-alienation, but rather, merely an empty repetition, an annulment of the promise of linear time. This is exactly what happens in the first movements of the Sixth and Seventh symphonies, where all the heroic striving of symphonic discourse comes to nothing as the moment of recapitulation simply restores the grim heaviness of the opening bars.

Elsewhere, particularity erodes structural unity from within. The rondo last movements of the Fifth and Seventh symphonies are beset with constant changes of direction by heterogeneous materials that refuse the unity implied by symphonic finales. The Finale of the Seventh, for example, suggests a confident sense of temporal purposiveness by means of its opening fanfare and march materials only to be suddenly cut off mid-stream—its C major ending (fortissimo) has apparently no point of contact with the section in A♭ (pianissimo) that follows (three bars before Rehearsal Fig. 230). The structure that unfolds in this way is a sequence of separate sections, each of them presenting purposive and directional music but together constituting no more than a collage. What is implied teleogically by each section is denied by the fragmentation of the form as a whole. The same kind of erosion of temporal purposiveness through particularity is found in Mahler's scherzos. Whether given in genial or acerbic tone, these all have a kind of mechanical quality that foregrounds an essentially repetitive and empty temporality. Their ironic tone arises from the presentation of superficial busyness but which is essentially without purpose or direction, as in the scherzo of the Second, in which the music cycles in quasi-mechanical perpetual motion that is pleasant but pointless. Adorno related such movements to the Hegelian *Weltlauf*; Henri Bergson, writing at the same time as Mahler, described a parallel loss of self-possession ('living outside ourselves, hardly perceiving anything of ourselves but our own ghost') in an external time in which 'we "are acted" rather than act ourselves'.[14]

It is, however, in the Finale that these problems come to a head; this is where Mahler stages his most dramatic enactments of the failure of temporal purposiveness as a kind of catastrophic blockage of time. Of course, this is part of the rhetoric of directed motion, derived from Beethoven, where overcoming a barrier to progression enhances the re-affirmation of the musical subject. Mahler's narrative dramas hinge also on such a play between purposive progression and an opposing force that threatens to stop it in its tracks —like the angel in 'Urlicht', wanting to block the path of the soul yearning for heaven. But elsewhere time is blocked without any apparent outlet, as in the Finale of the Sixth Symphony in music that rages violently without resolution. This is subjective time expressed with the greatest urgency but deprived of any effective direction or points of arrival. Such blockages constitute moments of temporal catastrophe, forcing the music into super-dense passages that seem to hold up time by verticalising it, as in the great dissonant chord Mahler was to deploy in the Tenth Symphony, or the hammer blows in the Finale of the Sixth, extreme examples of blocked time condensed into a single gesture of violence that categorically deny the possibility of forging temporal progression. This is why the

Finale of the Sixth is objectively too long. Mahler forces the orchestra to enact the failure of progressive time repeatedly, staging a deliberate misjudgment of form, exceeding the proportions of dramatic representation in order to negate the promise of the heroic symphony. By the time Thomas Mann's fictional composer Adrian Leverkühn came to revoke Beethoven's Ninth, Mahler had arguably already revoked Beethoven's Third.

It is not that Mahler displaces symphonic affirmation and temporal purposiveness in favour of something essentially negative, but rather that his music presents multiple temporalities that cut against any simple unity; this, after all, is the composer who sometimes instructs individual players to deliver their part 'without regard to the tempo'. The drama of Mahler's musical novels exhibits patterns we have come to know well: the battles of objective and subjective time, punctuated by points of collapse and suspension, anticipation and breakthrough, recall and reminiscence, linear developments and *non sequiturs*. The temporalities of the march and dance are interspersed with those of the idyll. These disjunctions are key to the specific modernity of Mahler's music, but also to its self-reflection upon that modernity, and its attempt to find within it an authentic temporal home. It is not insignificant, in that regard, that Mahler's *Lieder eines fahrenden Gesellen* and the First Symphony are contemporary with an emblematic statement of modernity, Ferdinand Tönnies's *Gemeinschaft und Gesellschaft* (published in Leipzig in 1887, coincidentally when Mahler was a conductor at the Stadttheater there). It is a key text in the history of sociology, setting out in theoretical terms the very division that Mahler's music explores—between the memory of a recollected and idealised community and the present social relations of modern urban life. It is perhaps too neat a parallel that Mahler's *Gesellen* cycle should chart the progressive alienation of the wandering apprentice who fails to find a home in the industrialised world in which he is forced to seek his living. Many of the *Wunderhorn* settings are similarly predicated on the same rift between lost *Heimat* and current alienation.

The specific insight of Mahler's music is that this alienation is experienced as a *temporal* displacement. The soldiers of the *Wunderhorn* songs occasion the development of Mahler's march forms as hollow, social objective time, while the alternating strophes of their distant lovers are couched as gentle Ländler, evocations of the lost time of their idealised *Gemeinschaft*—paradisial, as Proust famously reminds us, precisely because it is lost. The history of the nineteenth-century novel repeatedly retells that tale, of a lost, generally rural past in counterpoint with making sense of the urban present. Mahler's parallel story has its own musical origins of course, not least in Beethoven's *Pastoral* Symphony which, as Richard Will has shown, plays out the tension between idyllic and historical time.[15] But the parallel with literature is nevertheless instructive—from Balzac's *Comédie humaine*, with its proliferation of heterogeneous life caught between the image of a utopian pastoral past and the encounter with new urban modernity, to Flaubert's cutting back and forth between public and private time and to Proust, who like Mahler, makes time his principal theme.

Thomas Peattie has underlined the difference between memory and recollection in Mahler's music,[16] the first being involuntary and the second an active process, and it is the shared sense of an active search for lost time that most closely binds Mahler to Proust (Proust's word is *'recherche'*—an investigation, no less, into lost time). Both share with their contemporary Henri Bergson an exploration of the temporal experience of modernity—specifically, the sense that the more social life is shaped by historical time, the greater role the particularity of individual memory must play in the preservation of self-identity. The faster time passes and the greater the disjunctions between different kinds of temporal experience, the more memory is required as a way of binding fragmentary experience together. The present moment, stretched between the contradictory pull of future-oriented progress and the weight of the past, becomes increasingly thin, fragile, and precarious.

One of the reasons Mahler remains contemporary to our own age, while reaching back into the cultural concerns of the late eighteenth century, is that he takes up the problem of post-Enlightenment temporality as an unsolved problem. What one might call the central aporia of modernity—how to reconcile an abstract totality with individual particularity—is fundamentally a temporal one, played out in Mahler's music in the relationship between symphonic structure and the momentary particularity of gesture and voice. Proust's great self-discovery concerns the absolute significance of the particular, the contingent, individual, ephemeral, subjective, and momentary experience. The writer's task—or indeed the composer's—is precisely to redeem the significance of the passing moment and the particular impression. It is here that Mahler comes closest to Proust, not just because, for both, the intrusion of sensual particularity occasions the digression from the linearity of the narrative but because, for both, it is precisely through those digressions that the larger narrative whole is redeemed. *Le temps retrouvé*, the final volume of *A la Recherche du Temps Perdu*, concludes with redeeming the particularity of the moment from mere contingency by affirming its absolute significance. By contrast, Proust asserts in the final volume, it is the merely logical that is arbitrary.[17] Mahlerian 'readers' are familiar with the same tension; just as the Proustian narrative is suddenly redirected by unprepared moments of particularity—the smell of varnish on the staircase at Combray or petrol fumes in Paris reminding him of trips with Albertine near Balbec—so too is the Mahlerian symphony caught up in the tension between 'the immediate, dogmatic injunction to form ... [and] the contingent, meaningless, potentially fatuous detail'.[18] Mahler too allows the particular detail to speak, even at the expense of the demands of the form, which makes his music, for all the charges of monumentalism, far more concerned with 'the density of the experience of fragility'.[19]

In the Finale of the First Symphony, the particularity of the viola gesture was subsumed into the constructive activity of the ensuing fugato, albeit after five motivic instantiations (at Rehearsal Fig. 45), each of them testing out a different rhythm and metrical accent as a kind of compositional thought process preserved in the finished score. Twenty years on, Mahler's late works were less inclined to build an affirmative ending by such constructive sleight of hand. And yet, the violas' insistence on the particularity of voice persists. In the closing bars of the Ninth Symphony it is once again the violas that keep the music alive by insisting on physical motion, however attenuated. The drawn-out turn figure, circling the same A♭ that was so prominent in the viola figure in the First Symphony, has by this stage become almost a reflex action, a bodily movement, a slow winding down of the corporeal machine (see Ex. 12.5). Its earlier rhetorical power, as the sign of a heightened subjective lyricism, has by now virtually drained away and contracted to a mere vocal murmur.

But a more telling parallel with the figure in the Finale of the First Symphony is found in that of *Das Lied von der Erde*. The first entry, in 'Der Abschied', of the alto solo (the vocal equivalent of the viola) is heard over a sustained low C-pedal (Rehearsal Fig. 3). The only other component is the unmeasured 'birdsong' of the solo flute until this passage, out of time, gives way to the regularity of the slow march (Rehearsal Fig. 4). The rhythmic figure in the clarinets traces out, in inversion, the same trichord as the violas in the First Symphony (A♭-G-F). The prominent outer pitches of the circling oboe figure above are B♮ and D: this is exactly the same harmonic stasis that forms the background to the viola eruption in the First Symphony (see Ex.12.6). In the case of the First Symphony, the D alternates with its neighbour note E; here, in 'Der Abschied',

Ex. 12.5 Mahler, Ninth Symphony, final movement, bars 180–85

Ex. 12.6 Mahler, 'Der Abschied' from *Das Lied von der Erde*, reduction of bars 27–32; First Symphony, Finale, reduction of bars 511–20

the E♮ appears as the momentary breakthough of the vocal line to the light of a C major triad.

The parallels between the two passages, separated by twenty years, are certainly striking—the same held C-pedal, the same harmonic complex above, the unmeasured flute solo, and the same insistence on the F-G-A♭ figure in the middle register. But the passage in the First Symphony represented a collapse of the dramatic energy of the Finale whereas, in the case of *Das Lied von der Erde*, it is the opening of the final movement, a reflection on the entire work beginning outside the usual temporal frame. In the latter, the establishing of some semblance of symphonic temporal order and direction is achieved only by the slow Funeral March (Rehearsal Fig. 4), but this is soon contrasted with a radically different kind of motion (Rehearsal Fig. 7)—an asymmetric flowing of time, unregulated by the symmetrical periodicity and metrical order of the march. The solo oboe, then flute, elaborates a melodic line striking for its apparent a-periodicity, its only accompaniment a simple rocking figure heard initially in the harp and clarinets, then taken up by the violas. A simple alternation of two notes a third apart, the accompaniment figures descends from A-C, to G-B♭, before the violas take it up on F-A. Heard in the same register as the gesture from the First Symphony, the earlier violent restart to productive forward motion is here transformed into a gentle oscillation of duple and

Ex. 12.7 Mahler, 'Der Abschied' from *Das Lied von der Erde*, bars 166–71

triple rhythm, going nowhere, the minor third now smoothed out to a major third, contingent and unschematic, like a kind of humming to oneself.

This passage anticipates the astonishingly new quality of temporal motion with which *Das Lied von der Erde* will eventually end its meditation on time, first introduced at Rehearsal Figure 23 (see Ex. 12.7). Its definitive expanding motif is heard not in the viola but the flute, and the eruptive violence of the violas' earlier gesture is here replaced by music of great tenderness and fragility. Its 'orientalism'—the result of a striking use of the mandolin and the flute's pentatonicism—is merely the familiar label for a radical particularity, a quality of voice hitherto unheard in this music. The ascending gesture presented by the flute, beginning from a simple three notes, expands to the octave before handing over to the violins (Rehearsal Fig. 24). The accompaniment is given in two harps and mandolin, but doubled with second violins and violas playing a remnant of the oscillating dyad, over an interval of a third, heard earlier at Rehearsal Figure 7. It may not be entirely fanciful to hear this as a distant transformation, twenty years on, of the violas' gesture of protest in the First Symphony. It too, in a progressive, additive expansion becomes the turning point of the entire Finale—an opening out of a temporal freedom that, previously, symphonic music had barely imagined.

Notes

1. Blaukopf, *Gustav Mahler—Richard Strauss Correspondence*, 37.
2. Hoeckner, *Programming the Absolute*, 12–15.
3. Chua, "The Promise of Nothing", 23.
4. Friese, *The Moment: Time and Rupture in Modern Thought*, 7.
5. Bohrer, *Suddenness*, 10.
6. Steinberg, *Listening to Reason*, 45.
7. Eliot, "Four Quartets", 180.
8. His anxiety over the order of the Scherzo and Andante of the Sixth Symphony provides a further example.
9. Adorno, *Mahler* (English edn.), 166.
10. See, for example, "On Purposiveness in General", (§10 of *Critique of Aesthetic Judgment*).
11. Brinkmann, "In the Time of the Eroica", 5–7.
12. Koselleck, *Futures Past*, 237–38.
13. Schiller, *On the Aesthetic Education of Man*, 33.
14. Bergson, *Time and Free Will*, 231.
15. Will, "Time, Morality and Humanity", 317.
16. Peattie, "In Search of Lost Time",
17. Proust, *Finding Time Again*, 188.
18. Adorno, *Mahler* (English edn.), 67.
19. Adorno, *Mahler* (English edn.), 147.

13

Gustav Mahler and the Aesthetics of De-Identification

Federico Celestini

Aesthetic experience and, more specifically in this context, musical composition, performance, and listening, can be analyzed as the experience of a shift in the relationship between Self and Otherness. This is a broad topic that is somewhat neglected in current musicological discourse, which focuses mainly on music as an agent for endowing cultural identities. In the framework of the present chapter, I restrict this investigation to the music of Gustav Mahler. In order to achieve a real connection between musical 'text' and cultural and social 'context,' my approach combines the systematic work of aesthetics and analysis with a historical glance over past discourses by introducing analytical categories derived from Friedrich Nietzsche's aesthetic thoughts and the discussion about identities in the context of Viennese modernism.

Accordingly, the first part of the chapter is concerned with Nietzsche's theory regarding aesthetic experience as an experience of de-individuation and its transformation into the aesthetic of de-identification. Since Nietzsche himself defines his position as 'reversed Platonism,'[1] Plato's thoughts on the same topic, that is, de-identification in experiencing arts, are a good starting point. Throughout the paper, Nietzsche's implicit aesthetic of de-identification provides the principal interpretative tool for approaching Mahler's music. A further level of analysis focuses on the aesthetic idea of de-identification in the context of the multi-national, multi-cultural and multi-lingual state of the Habsburg monarchy at the turn of the nineteenth to the twentieth century, when Nietzsche reception was intense and extremely productive.[2] Finally, some compositional aspects of Gustav Mahler's music will be analyzed from the perspective of aesthetic de-identification. A short consideration of the reception of Mahler's music during his lifetime will underline how strongly the aesthetic experience of de-identification can emphasise the issue of cultural identity in music.

Plato and Nietzsche

An approach to the arts from the point of view of identity has a long tradition, beginning with the philosophy of Plato. According to him, aesthetic experience

destabilises both the subjective identity and the social order. Taking the example of a rhapsodist, Plato (using the voice of Socrates) explains in the dialogue
Ion that artists must be out of their senses to produce poems. Therefore, artistic
creation cannot be considered as a *techné*, but something like a divine inspiration, which is not ruled by rational laws:

> For all the good epic poets utter all those fine poems not from art, but as
> inspired and possessed, and the good lyric poets likewise; just as the
> Corybantian worshippers do not dance when in their senses, so the lyric
> poets do not indite those fine songs in their senses, but when they have
> started on the melody and rhythm they begin to be frantic, and it is under
> possession—as the bacchants are possessed, and not in their senses, when
> they draw honey and milk from the rivers—that the soul of the lyric poets
> does the same thing, by their own report ... For a poet is a light and winged
> and sacred thing, and is unable ever to indite until he has been inspired and
> put out of his senses, and his mind is no longer in him: every man, whilst he
> retains possession of that, is powerless to indite a verse or chant an oracle.[3]

The rational constitution of the poet is subverted by divine possession.
Furthermore, as the poet must empathise with people and situations, his or her
subjective identity is seriously compromised. In the third book of the *Republic*,
Plato is concerned with the social consequences of this subversion of identity.
After having confirmed his aversion to mixed genres and imitations, Plato's
Socrates says:

> 'And is this not the reason why such a city is the only one in which we shall
> find the cobbler a cobbler and not a pilot in addition to his cobbling, and the
> farmer a farmer and not a judge added to his farming, and the soldier a sol-
> dier and not a money-maker in addition to his soldiery, and so of all the rest?'
> 'True,' he said.
> 'If a man, then, it seems who was capable by his cunning of assuming every
> kind of shape and imitating all things should arrive in our city, bringing with
> himself the poems which he wished to exhibit, we should fall down and wor-
> ship him as a holy and wondrous and delightful creature, but should say to him
> that there is no man of that kind among us in our city, nor is it lawful for such
> a man to arise among us, and we should send him away to another city ... [4]

The philosophical as well as the political motivations for Plato's rejection of
poetry are based in its mimetic character. According to Plato, poetry imitates
reality, which is itself a copy of ideas. As an imitation of an imitation, poetry
is far removed from the ideal truth and thus rates very low on Plato's scale of
values. At the same time, artists practicing mimesis subvert the social order.
Here, mimesis appears to be a change of identity, which thus loses its binding
character. A changeable identity is actually an antilogy, particularly for Plato,
who regards change and Becoming as attributes of the illusory appearance,
that is, the valueless opposite of the Truth of Idea (*Timaeus*).

Nietzsche's Musical Thinking

A study of Nietzsche's earliest writings (dating in part back to his school days in Pforta) shows that thoughts about the Tragic idea and in particular, the role of music in the Tragic, are among his earliest deliberations. An extensive investigation of these writings sheds new light on his first book, *The Birth of Tragedy out of the Spirit of Music* (1872), which no longer appears to be the point of departure for Nietzsche's reflections on Greek tragedy. Rather, this is the amalgamation and systemisation of a body of astonishingly early thoughts on the topic. If one considers the whole body of Nietzsche's early essays, notes, and records, his view of the tragedy emerges as the attempt to valorise the cultic, multi-medial, and performative context in which the Greek tragedy took place, against the Aristotelian reduction of the Drama to a mere text for silent reading.[5] This perspective highlights the actuality of Nietzsche's opposition to the traditional hermeneutic fixation on the written text and demonstrates the cultural-philosophical implications of this transformed view of Antiquity.

In an early text ('Das griechische Musikdrama') Nietzsche adopts platonic arguments about the arts, but completely reverses the conclusions: Becoming and De-Identification are constitutive principles of the idea of the Tragic. In *The Birth of Tragedy* (1872), Nietzsche describes the process of a cultural transfer in which the Dionysos Cult, originating in Asia, 'storms' to Greece and begins to interact with the art forms there, which had previously been characterised solely by Apollo.[6] In Nietzsche's view, the figure of Dionysos represents not only an Asian cult and thus an instance of cultural difference; rather, as the god of the pre-individualised world and of plurality, Dionysos represents a type of human existence which is completely different to that of the Self. The Dionysian is not merely a different Self but represents the Otherness of the Self, and as such, a paradigmatic principle of Otherness. Nietzsche derives his 'thoughts of the Tragic' from the 'historic' phenomenon of the encounter between the Apollonian Self and the Dionysian Other, namely, the view of the Tragic as the violation of the border between Self and the Otherness of Self. An important aspect here is that this violation can be represented by an aesthetic phenomenon, namely, in the Greek Tragedy.

According to Nietzsche, the Dionysian does not endow identity. On the contrary, it is a principle of De-Identification. However, the *Birth of Tragedy* contains explicit 'identifiers' of a German nationalistic culture, which stem from Richard Wagner. Nietzsche's ambivalence may be described as follows: on the one hand, Nietzsche enthusiastically supports Wagner's attempt to revive the Cultic in musical-theatrical forms. In 1872, this attempt was already in an advanced stage of realisation, and there was no doubt about its nationalistic identity-laden character, based on 'German music' and 'German mythology'. On the other hand, Nietzsche presents the theory that the Tragic is a breach of the Self. Here, an examination of constitutive and productive moments of culture through the continual questioning of established forms and identities leads to the development of a cultural theory that represents the greatest possible contradiction to Wagner's attempt. This ambivalence is partially resolved after the rift with Wagner and the repeated explicit rejection of any German nationalistic positions in Nietzsche's late works.

The eighth main section of *Beyond Good and Evil* (1886) has the title 'Peoples and Fatherlands'. This contains an aphorism that warns of the dangers of 'German music'. Here, the contrast between northern and southern music is ambivalent, on the one hand reflecting the experiences of Nietzsche's own travels. On the other hand, this metaphoric speech also has a symbolic meaning. Through Nietzsche's evocation of exotic worlds and characteristics, it becomes increasingly clear that a centrifugal movement towards cultural diversity is intended, rather than a particular musical or stylistic direction. Even if Nietzsche's 'southern music' wears the mask of Mozart, Rossini, Bizet, or Pietro Gasti, respectively, one should not forget that these are indeed masks whose game defies classification. To 'overcome' one's own cultural identity, it is evidently necessary to turn toward the Other, which must not however be stylised into being 'foreign'. For hypostasised Otherness is merely a construction of the Self.

Vienna at the Turn of the Century

Today we consider heterogeneity, fragmentation, and plurality to be characteristic elements of post-modernity. But the loss of holistic concepts, which Nietzsche addresses in his famous sentence about the death of God, had already happened at the end of the nineteenth century. At that time, growing fragmentation, pluralism in social environment as well as frequently changing referential systems in cultural life raised the question of individual and collective identities. This question was particularly evident in the urban centers of the Habsburg monarchy, where immigration from many different areas caused an extreme population growth in the space of only a few decades, radically changing the social and cultural profile. In 1870, Vienna's population was 840,000 growing to more than 1.9 million in 1910. While the population in the central district increased by 80 percent, the growth in the suburbs was 253 percent. The consequences of this expansion were poverty, unemployment, and social dissent, bringing about widespread uncertainty and disorientation.[7] This aspect, which the Austrian historian Moritz Csáky called 'vertical differentiation', is a common phenomenon of European modernity. Vienna and central Europe were additionally characterised by a peculiar ethnic, cultural, and linguistic heterogeneity, a 'horizontal differentiation', which augments the vertical one and thus strengthens the perception of fragmentation and disorientation.[8] 'For instance, whereas in Paris, the "foreign rate" amounted to only

6.3%, it was up to over 50% in Vienna including immigrants from Bohemia, Moravia, countries from the Hungarian Crown, Galicia, Bukovina and the nowadays Austrian federal states.'[9] In 1883, the geographer Friedrich Umlauf described the Habsburg monarchy as the most diverse mixture of peoples in Europe, totalling twelve different nationalities and five religious denominations.[10] Of course there had been awareness of national and linguistic plurality in the Habsburg monarchy since the late eighteenth century. But the urbanisation process during the nineteenth century resulted in a cultural and religious diversity that was concentrated in the dense area of the city.

The fact that many artists and intellectuals in Vienna had an immigrant background—for instance, Jewish origins—seems to confirm the thesis that marginal groups possess an enhanced creative potential. Such individuals had a plural cultural memory at their command and could alternate between different communicative spaces. They were able to mediate between different cultures, combining differing, even contradictory elements in an unpredictable way.[11] For instance, Gustav Mahler was a German-speaking native of Moravia with Jewish origins. According to Stuart Hall, such representatives of cultural hybridity must give up any ambition to re-discover lost cultural purity and ethnic absolutism.[12] For this exact reason, a variety of languages, religions, and cultures was not only a positive factor for artistic and cultural creativity but also caused conflicts of various kinds, on both an individual and a collective level.

It is not surprising that there was a strong reception of Nietzsche's aesthetic concept of de-identification in Vienna at the turn of the century. For in Vienna, the problem of the Self, its fragmentation, or even its dissolution was the core of a discussion that resounded in the fields of philosophy, literature, and depth psychology. According to the Austrian philosopher and physicist Ernst Mach (1838–1916), 'Thing, body, matter, are nothing apart from the combinations of the elements—the colours, sounds, and so forth—nothing apart from their so-called attributes.'[13] Similarly, 'that complex of memories, moods, and feelings, joined to a particular body (the human body), which is called the "I" or "Ego"' is 'as little absolutely permanent as are bodies'.[14] Neither objects nor the Ego can be considered as Cartesian substances. Therefore, the 'supposed unities "body" and "ego" are only makeshifts, designed for provisional orientation and for definite practical ends'.[15] In more advanced scientific investigations, Mach continues, such terms should be abandoned as 'insufficient and inappropriate'. The 'antithesis between ego and world, between sensation (appearance) and thing, then vanishes'.[16] The result of this analysis can be considered as the paradigmatic expression of the crisis of identity in Viennese modernism: 'The ego must be given up.'[17] It is significant that Mach himself explained some of the political consequences of his investigation: As 'the boundaries of bodies and of the ego do not admit of being established in a manner definite and sufficient', so similarly 'class-consciousness, class-prejudice, the feeling of nationality, and even narrowest-minded local patriotism may have a high importance, for certain purposes. But such attitudes will not be shared by the broad-minded investigator, at least not in moments of research.'[18]

The philosopher and historian Volker Munz studied the reception of Mach and his theories in the literary and artistic environment of Vienna at the turn of the century. His results are noteworthy in our context.[19] In 1908, in a discussion with the literature critic and leader of the artistic group 'Jung-Wien' Hermann Bahr and the Hungarian-Austrian anatomist Emil Zuckerkandl, Mach explicated his idea of the 'unsaveable I' once more. In this context, Mach points out the aspect of eternal movement in particular. He suggests that our so-called 'I' crystallises in this 'game of phenomena', being in permanent motion from birth unto death. Bahr's response refers to some of Hugo von Hofmannsthal's essential ideas centered around the 'I': for instance, that the ego is formed from the outside to the inside. Hofmannsthal visited Mach's lectures in summer 1897 and was obviously quite familiar with his work, since several remarks that either explicitly or at least implicitly remind the reader of Mach's philosophy; for example, ideas Mach expressed in the introduction to the *Analysis of Sensations* in 1886, can be found in Hofmannsthal's diaries and published works. Hofmannsthal's famous fictitious letter from Lord Chandos to Francis Bacon is just one example. Hofmannsthal's description of everything falling apart is certainly connected with Mach's theory of perception. Hofmannsthal's letter is clearly more than an expression of the crisis of language, as it has often been understood. The reduction of the ego to disparate sensations of an empirical experience is a radical expression of an individual identity crisis that begins when the physiological constituents of subjectivity are undermined.

Hoffmansthal was not the only writer in whose works Ernst Mach's ideas were reflected. For instance, Robert Musil wrote his Ph.D. thesis on Mach's philosophy. Arthur Schnitzler's novelette called *Ich* contains basic elements of Mach's theory. Hermann Bahr argued that Schnitzler can be seen as the literary ancestor of Freud's psychoanalysis, and, according to one of Freud's letters to Schnitzler in 1922, Freud himself emphasises that he saw many of the presuppositions and results of his own research in Schnitzler's work. Freud, too, stresses the fictional character of a supposedly consistent 'I': 'normally there is nothing more secure for us than the feeling of our Self, our own I. This I appears to us to be autonomous, uniform and well delineated from everything else . . . this appearance is a deception.'[20] Freud's insight into the fictional unity of the ego is, obviously, a consequence of his massive revaluation of the unconscious in psychology. Indeed, it is only possible to believe in a consistent and stable 'I' for as long as the disruptive instance of the unconscious in human behaviour and psychic life is repressed. Hence, it is no coincidence that Freud's depth psychology stimulated the contemporary theory of cultural difference in an extremely productive way. Homi Bhabha, for example, refers to Freud when considering the unconscious as the instance of Otherness in the human mind.[21] This is a central argument for Bhabha's thesis that Otherness is not external to and separated from the Self but resides in its very internal core. It is worth noting that the obscure and uncanny force of the unconscious is a central topic in Viennese modernism, particularly in the music of Gustav Mahler.[22]

Gustav Mahler's Music

In the social and cultural life of fin-de-siècle Vienna, the belief in stable and consistent identities appears to be seriously questioned. Rather than being a mere representation of this heterogeneous world, Mahler's music can be considered, irrespective of the real intention of the composer, to be a desperate opposition against the logic of identity. With tragic determination, it contradicts the unifying and leveling tendencies that Stephen Toulmin and Zygmunt Bauman describe as the powerful and repressive side of political modernism.[23] At the same time, Mahler's music 'remains partially complicit with that which it seeks to critique',[24] giving expression to contrasting attitudes toward the different worlds he evokes in his symphonies, like nostalgia for a pre-modern way of life with simple and stable categories and values, or a sort of Dionysian inebriation in the face of the experience of de-identification, a belief in the metaphysical transcendence of the limited human existence, or a deep-felt empathy for the tragic destiny of the individual in the world of restless becoming and changes. The way in which this kind of criticism becomes manifest is the radicalisation of the aforementioned aesthetics of de-identification, with which Mahler was familiar, particularly through his enthusiastic reception of the music philosophy of Schopenhauer and of Nietzsche's early writings. In the following, I propose analytical categories able to serve these aesthetics in Mahler's music and briefly discuss some of their most important consequences.

Tragic Breakdown of the Musical Subject

The first occurrence of de-identification in Mahler's work that I wish to address is the symphonic breakdown, or 'Zusammenbruch', which Mahler stages with terrifying effectiveness in most of his symphonies. These are catastrophic points of culmination in which the orchestra strikes extremely loud dissonant chords, only to implode within a few bars. The implicit poetic of such instances is directly connected to Mahler's reception of Schopenhauer, Nietzsche, and Wagner, namely, the tragic collapse of the subject.[25]

Since Adorno's book on Mahler from 1960, breakdown has been considered one of the standard interpretative tools for the study of Mahler's music from a compositional point of view. Suspension, breakdown, and its dialectic counterpart, breakthrough (*Durchbruch*), are occurrences in which extra-musical meaning and formal function meet together to form an ambivalent union. Adorno stressed the importance of these categories for the novel-like character of Mahler's symphonic work.[26] Indeed, these are essential elements in Mahler's symphonic narratives.[27] The first instance of a *Zusammenbruch* in Mahler is at the beginning of the Finale of his First Symphony. Here, not only the compositional working but also the structural placement clearly refers to Beethoven's Ninth Symphony. In the case of Mahler, one can speak of *Zusammenbruch* because this dissonant explosion proceeds from the third movement's death march and provides a narrative connection to the apotheosis-like *Durchbruch* that follows. In a letter to Max Marschalk dated 20 March 1896, Mahler explains that the beginning of the Finale is 'simply the outcry of a deeply wounded heart, which is preceded by the eerily and ironically brooding sultriness of the death march'.[28] In the Second Symphony, the *Zusammenbruch* already occurs in the third movement (Scherzo), in the reprise after Rehearsal Figure 50. Adorno comments on this section as follows: 'The musical I, the We, that emanates from the Symphony, caves in.'[29] In the first movement of the same Symphony, powerful orchestral eruptions (bars 291ff and 325ff) anticipate the effect of the *Zusammenbruch*, while a mildly varied repetition of the same passage opens the Finale of the Symphony. In the Third Symphony, too, the *Zusammenbruch* occurs in the Scherzo (at Rehearsal Fig. 31). The narrative of the Fourth Symphony is quite different, as not only the suggestion of a *Zusammenbruch* but also the *Durchbruch* that follows are both in the slow movement (after Rehearsal Fig. 3 and at the end of the movement, respectively.) In the Fifth Symphony, there are occurrences of *Zusammenbruch* in the first two movements. The *Zusammenbruch* in the Finale of the Sixth Symphony is endowed with a new sound quality through the addition of hammer blows.

Grotesque Destabilisation

It is no coincidence that in the first three of Mahler's symphonies, breakdown occurs as the negative culmination of a process in which the traditional symphonic idiom is increasingly dissociated and distorted. Here, Mahler re-works the well-known narrative scheme, *per aspera ad astra*, meaning 'to the stars through difficulties', which he directly imported from Beethoven's Fifth and Ninth symphonies. The technique of grotesque distortion was introduced by Berlioz in the *Symphonie Fantastique*, a work that Mahler conducted several times. Mahler developed this technique to an extremely high degree, affecting not only sound and form but the whole symphonic idiom.[30] Here, it is worth noting that in the grotesque, deconstruction of objectivity and destabilisation of subjectivity represent both sides of the same aesthetic phenomenon. In a symphonic context, deconstruction of objectivity results from the rupture of the stylistic, idiomatic, and formal norms that constituted the socially and culturally recognised genre of the symphony at the end of the nineteenth century. From a Freudian point of view, the grotesque reverses the sublimation process of individual drives, a process which leads to the establishment of collective cultural institutions. The disruption of symbolic forms releases psychic energy and affects the recipient emotionally. In this way, he or she experiences an uncanny feeling, which, according to Freud, arises by no means from the unknown but from the resurgence of the repressed, internal alien, namely, the unconscious. This is to say that in experiencing the grotesque in Mahler's music, we experience that we are strangers to our own Self.

The Plurality of Voices

In his book on *Mahler's Voices*, Julian Johnson comments with reference to Guido Adler's defence of Mahler's eclecticism, that 'for Mahler himself, the plural and heterogeneous is a counterpart to the idea of a unitary voice that claims an authenticity in the face of the carnivalesque'.[31] Johnson stresses, however, that the carnivalesque disintegration of the symphonic idiom is an irreversible process: it is impossible to subsequently restore the prior status or to reach a higher order.[32] I would like to add just one further consideration to this discussion. Mahler's aim to evoke transcendence as an absolute unifying instance in the finales of the First, Second, and Third symphonies has the opposite effect, heightening the tragic awareness of its irreparable loss. Here, Mahler's deployment of early romantic humour has an unexpected effect. In the same way in which, according to Jean Paul,[33] humouristic focus on a particular detail evokes the opposite outcome, that is, the idea of the infinite, the symphonic staging of transcendence makes manifest the very death of God which it is desperately trying to hide. If Jean Paul defined humour as the inverted sublime, here the tragic appears as inverted humour.

In the reprise of the third movement of the First Symphony (from Rehearsal Fig. 16 onwards) there is an impressive example of the irreducible plurality of voices in Mahler's music. Here, a minor-key version of the *Frère Jacques* canon, a Czech marching band with echoes of klezmer music, and a self-quotation from the fourth of the *Lieder eines fahrenden Gesellen* sound together in astonishing polyphony. This section brings cultural hybridity audibly to life, as all of the 'components' of Mahler's cultural identity sound simultaneously.

Mahler's engagement with romantic irony, a further product of his interest in Jean Paul, is well known.[34] An ironic utterance is not simply the addition of an alternative meaning to the literal one but a real subversion of any attempt to definitively locate meaning. Ironic expressions escape from the control of the addressing subject and confront the addressed person with an intrinsic polyphony of meanings, namely, a polyphony that originates from a single voice.

Although irony is a special case in the process of verbal communication, it allows us to understand a common property of speech: irony demonstrates that meaning is mobile and escapes fixation.

Metamorphosis and Mimesis

In his *Aesthetic Theory*, Adorno considers art to be a refuge for mimetic behaviour. According to him, mimesis is the artistic procedure in which the subject exposes itself to its Other.[35] Through mimesis, the division between subject and object is undermined.[36] The formal equivalent of mimesis is metamorphosis. Both are traditional agents of de-identification in art, and it is not surprising that both are found to a large extent in Mahler's works. In the Scherzo of the Fourth Symphony, the transition from the main section to the trio (bars 65–73) presents an example of Mahler's motivic metamorphosis. A horn motive in a Phrygian-coloured C minor opens the macabre main section and recurs unmodified at its end. The motive leads over into the trio and, with only a few cosmetic modifications, forms the beginning of this new section. The clarinet takes up the repeated-note figure of the macabre section with its final trill, and transforms it into a flowery, *galant* phrase (around Rehearsal Fig. 3). It is astonishing how easily a gruesome motive is given a pleasing character.

In the Scherzo of the Fifth Symphony, four thematic characters alternate and interact, transforming themselves from one into another: the rural Ländler dance, the fugato, the waltz, and the cantabile (Lied). In the second Trio a pizzicato episode occurs, in which the metamorphosis reaches a spectacular level (bars 308–36). Here, the cantabile melody of the *obligato* horn is transformed into a ghostly waltz. Cellos and second violins start with the typical accompaniment formula of this dance in pizzicato, while the first violins pluck the horn melody, slightly varied. After the bassoon has played part of the melody in *diminuendo* and *ritardando*, the violins repeat this melody in the waltz rhythm of the first trio. The metamorphosis is completed with the entrance of the oboe, which now plays the waltz theme directly. In the Rondo-Finale of the same Symphony, the chorale melody is seized by metamorphosis and is transformed into the profane, in the form of a quick dance. Toward the end of the Finale, the apotheosis of the chorale represents an impressive example of the breakthrough discussed above. This is followed by the coda, a large Rossini-like orchestral crescendo that begins with the blasphemous transformation of the chorale melody into the dance (Rehearsal Fig. 34 until the end).

Thematic Instability

Mahler's thematic variants demonstrate a vagueness that is peculiar to musical memory. Adorno writes that the technique of variants is the compositional element that determines the novel-like character in Mahler's symphonies.[37] It enables the establishment of a correspondence to that which Henri Bergson called 'un être à la fois identique et changeant' ('a being at once identical and changing').[38] Unlike variations, which are related to an original version, 'the' theme, variants are not. As variants are not ordered hierarchically, variability itself emerges as the constitutive quality of Mahler's thematic process, which eschews any particular 'original' theme or idea as a reference point. Hence, thematic instability is an evident and pervasive compositional formulation of the aesthetic of de-identification, demonstrating that in music, fixed and stable identities are not even possible.[39]

Ex. 13.1 comes from the fourth of the *Songs of a Wayfarer* and shows how closely Mahler's variant technique is related to the oral tradition of music transmission.

The dotted rhythm typical of a funeral march characterises both the melody and the accompaniment, establishing the basic character of the song. Memory is aroused through melodic properties. In a similar way to Mahler's construction of this song text, built up using word repetition, his musical setting is a continual variance of smaller 'cells', namely, a manner of progression which is based neither on the 'logic' of motivic development nor on the 'mechanics' of literal repetition but is borne by the imprecise workings of the memory. Each new line sounds like a reminiscence of the previous one.

Hybridity of Genre and Form

One of the most characteristic elements of Mahler's work is his mixture of popular and high styles. Mahler's usage of music from the popular sphere in his symphonies is itself ambivalent because he adapts popular styles using a complex, artificial technique. If we examine the aforementioned quotation from the fourth of the *Songs of a Wayfarer* in the third movement of the First Symphony (Rehearsal Figs. 10–13), we can observe a typical example of this ambivalence. The refined instrumentation produces a differentiated and constantly changing sound. Muted violins, first divided into three groups, then into four, are joined by two further unmuted solo violins. Cellos, flutes, and clarinets are also divided into groups. Chromatic figures like those in the first solo violin and in the oboe (bars 97–100) also demonstrate clearly that this is a retrospectively constructed impression of the folk tradition. Here, the folk tune is evoked by means of very sophisticated instrumentation and sound shaping.[40] The resulting hybridisation between folk tune and symphonic complexity is a compositional manifestation of 'cultural translation'.

In the Austro-Germanic symphonic tradition, the presence of stylised folk tunes is as old as the tradition itself, if we think of Haydn, for instance. But echoes of urban popular music of the time, like marching bands, songs from operettas, and trivial dances in Mahler's symphonic works constituted a real

Ex. 13.1 Mahler, *Lieder eines fahrenden Gesellen*, no. 4, 'Die zwei blauen Augen'

shock in a music culture in which the symphony was considered to be the highest genre. The transformation of a chorale into a dance, which we hear at the end of the Rondo-Finale of the Fifth Symphony, symbolises Mahler's predilection for the violation of cultural boundaries. Mahler's symphonic hybridity is achieved by importing music that carries the distinctive stylistic brand of the popular sphere but treating it with great compositional complexity and sophistication. Obviously, this aspect is of substantial importance for the question of cultural identity in music.

Hybridity is also an important keyword in regard to form, both on the level of single movements and of whole symphonies. Surely the Third Symphony represents an extreme manifestation of this tendency. But many of Mahler's individual symphonic movements present an interlacing of two or more different formal concepts. In addition, Mahler's whole oeuvre is a hybrid between songs and symphonies, beginning with the so-called *Wunderhorn* Symphonies and culminating in *Das Lied von der Erde*.

The Eclipse of the Author

The critic Leonard Leibling wrote in 1906 for the American journal the *Musical Courier* as follows:

> It will be observed . . . that some critics find in Mahler's Fifth Symphony resemblances to Brahms, Bruckner, Verdi, d'Indy, Strauss and Wagner. The chronicler of the *Evening Sun* calls attention to Mahler's copying of Bach, Tchaikovsky, and Puccini. Harold Bauer says that the slow movement reminds him of Beethoven. The present writer sets down his opinion that the

Ex. 13.2 (a) Mahler, Lieder eines fahrenden Gesellen, no. 4 'Auf der Straße steht ein Lindenbaum'; (b) J. Strauß, 'Eine Nacht in Venedig', 3rd Act, Caramello: 'Ach, wie so herrlich anzuschaun'; (c) Wagner, *Das Rheingold*, 1st Act, 2nd Scene, Loges: 'Die goldnen Aepfel'; (d) Folk song, 'Es wird scho glei dumpa'

scherzo brought memories of Loeffler, Liszt, and Saint-Saens. Is there no one
to say that any part of the symphony sounds like Mahler?[41]

There is no doubt that Mahler's use of quotations, allusions, references to, and
reminders of music of the past represents one of the most striking characteristics of his music. De-identification in Mahler's music does not affect the
aesthetic subject of the symphony alone but involves the authorial subjectivity of the composer too. The borrowed voices, to use an expression of Julian
Johnson,[42] are an essential contribution to the intrinsically plural character of
Mahler's compositional utterance. In contrast to polyphonic passages, such as
the example given from Mahler's First Symphony, in which many voices speak
at the same time, Ex. 13.2 shows a single voice evoking several different subjects.

This pluralisation arises from the memory, and indeed, in many cases from
the *mémoire involontaire* in the sense of Marcel Proust.[43] This example shows
that the relationship between Mahler's melody and the other melodies is similar to the relationship between variants in the case of oral transmission. In this
way, music becomes the resonance of memory, which is transposed into the
collective dimension by intertextual references.

Conclusions

Many music critics of Mahler's time and after were unable to comprehend that
his music demanded new categories for listening and for critical judgment.[44]
Wagner's abominable writings on Jewish music provide arguments for the criticism of Mahler's recourse to intertextual references. Particularly relevant here is
Wagner's statement that Jewish composers lack originality and use the German
compositional language—like the German language itself—as jargon. Both
anti-Semitic critics and Jewish observers such as Max Brod, who also considered Mahler's music to be Jewish,[45] openly attributed his stylistic rupture to the
composer's Jewish origins. Other critics who denounced Mahler's stylistic rupture gave the impression of arguing in purely musical aesthetic terms, but the
anti-Semitic subtext originating from Wagner is still recognisable. Thus, critics
attempted to neutralise the destabilising effect of music that questioned traditional categories by declaring it as not belonging to their own culture and tradition. In this way, Wagner's anti-Semitic discourse was used for a new purpose,
namely, a reaction against modernism, the aesthetic experience of Otherness.

Notes

1. Nietzsche, *Nachlaß 1869–1874*, 198.
2. See Le Rider, *Modernity and Crisis of Identity*.
3. Plato, *Ion*, 533e–534c.
4. Plato, *Republic*, 397e–398b.

5. See von Reibnitz, "Vom 'Sprachkunstwerk' zur "Leseliteratur". See Celestini, *Nietzsches Musikphilosophie* for an extensive study of Nietzsche's musical thinking.

6. See Biebuyck, Praet, and Vanden Poel, "Cults and Migrations: Nietzsche's Meditations on Orphism, Pythagoreanism, and the Greek Mysteries".

7. See Munz, "The Reception of a Philosophical Text: A Case Study", 17ff.

8. See Csáky, "Die Wiener Moderne. Ein Beitrag zu einer Theorie der Moderne in Zentraleuropa".

9. Munz, "The Reception of a Philosophical Text: A Case Study", 18.

10. Csáky, Feichtinger, Karoshi, and Munz, "Pluralitäten, Heterogenitäten, Differenzen. Zentraleuropas Paradigmen für die Moderne", 22.

11. Csáky et al., "Pluralitäten, Heterogenitäten, Differenzen. Zentraleuropas Paradigmen für die Moderne", 19.

12. See Hall, "Kulturelle Identität und Globalisierung", 435.

13. Mach, "Introductory Remarks: Antimetaphysical", § 3. The book was first published in German in 1886 with the title *Die Analyse der Empfindungen und das Verhältnis des Physischen zum Psychischen*. For the philosophical implications of Mach's analysis see Goeres, "Sensualistischer Phänomenalismus und Denkökonomie. Zur Wissenschaftskonzeption Ernst Machs".

14. Mach, "Introductory Remarks: Antimetaphysical", § 2.

15. Mach, "Introductory Remarks", § 7.

16. Mach, "Introductory Remarks", § 7.

17. Mach, "Introductory Remarks", § 12: 'das Ich ist unrettbar', which could be more literally translated as 'the I is unsaveable'.

18. Mach, "Introductory Remarks", § 12.

19. Munz, "The Reception of a Philosophical Text: A Case Study". The following report is based on this study.

20. Freud, "Das Unbehagen in der Kultur", 198. My translation: 'Normalerweise ist uns nichts gesicherter als das Gefühl unseres Selbst, unseres eigenen Ichs. Dies Ich erscheint uns selbstständig, einheitlich, gegen alles andere gut abgesetzt. Dass dieser Anschein ein Trug ist . . . das hat uns erst die psychoanalytische Forschung gelehrt.'

21. See Bhabha, *The Location of Culture*, 136f.

22. See Celestini, *Die Unordnung der Dinge. Das Groteske in der Wiener Moderne*.

23. See Toulmin, *Cosmopolis: The Hidden Agenda of Modernity*; and Bauman, *Modernity and Ambivalence*.

24. Johnson, "Mahler and the Idea of Nature", 34.

25. Mahler's friend Siegfried Lipiner proposed a religious interpretation of the philosophy of the Tragic he derived from Schopenhauer, Wagner, and the early Nietzsche. On this and its relationship to Mahler, see Celestini, *Die Unordnung der Dinge. Das Groteske in der Wiener Moderne*, 59–63. A German version of the following paragraphs was published as Celestini, "Gustav Mahler und die jüdische Moderne".

26. See Adorno, "Mahler. Eine musikalische Physiognomik", 209–29.

27. See Celestini, "Gustav Mahlers Fünfte Symphonie", 4–10.

28. Blaukopf, *Gustav Mahler Briefe*, 170. My translation: 'Es ist einfach der Aufschrei eines im Tiefsten verwundeten Herzens, dem eben die unheimlich und ironisch brütende Schwule des Trauermarsches vorhergeht.'

29. Adorno, "Mahler. Eine musikalische Physiognomik", 155. My translation: 'Das musikalische Selbst, das Wir, das aus der Symphonie tönt, bricht nieder.'

30. In my book on the grotesque in the music of Viennese modernism, I analysed this technique extensively (Celestini, *Die Unordnung der Dinge. Das Groteske in der Wiener Moderne*, 27–109).

31. Johnson, *Mahler's Voices*, 133.

32. Johnson, *Mahler's Voices*, 133ff.

33. Jean Paul, *Vorschule der Ästhetik*, §§ 31–35, 124–44.

34. See Johnson, *Mahler's Voices*, 123–41.

35. Adorno, *Ästhetische Theorie*, 86.

36. Adorno, *Ästhetische Theorie*, 169.

37. See Celestini, "Gustav Mahlers Fünfte Symphonie", 4–10.

38. Bergson, *Essai sur les données immédiates de la conscience*, 75.

39. Mahler himself considered literal repetition to be a 'lie' (*'Lüge'*) (Bauer-Lechner, *Gustav Mahler in den Erinnerungen von Natalie Bauer-Lechner*, 158).

40. See Celestini, *Die Unordnung der Dinge. Das Groteske in der Wiener Moderne*, 157–59.

41. Quoted in Painter, *Mahler and His World*, 262.

42. Johnson, *Mahler's Voices*, 151–63.

43. See Celestini, "The Acoustic Proximity of Temporal Distance". The first three occurrences are presented and discussed in Ringer, "Johann Strauß und Gustav Mahler", 151–52. Ringer does not hesitate to assume that Mahler knew the music concerned. However, this question is irrelevant in the context of my discussion. In my argumentation, this example is not intended to demonstrate influence, rather the special feature of 'speaking' with an indeterminate voice.

44. See Celestini, "Der Trivialitätsvorwurf an Gustav Mahler".

45. See Brod, "Gustav Mahlers jüdische Melodien".

14

Decadent Transitions

Mahler, Modernism, and the Viennese Fin de Siècle

Zoltan Roman

'Decadence'—'transition'—'modernism'—'fin de siècle': these four terms/concepts of differing longevity tend even today to incite normally unexcitable scholars to disagree strongly in some of the humanities. (For other than the versed reader of this chapter, 'Mahler' and 'Vienna' might well be added to the list.) Such variance is demonstrated by the following:

> Turning to the critics for a definition of Decadence is much like listening to the famous orchestra of the King of Siam, where each musician plays the way he wants to and without paying any attention to the score.[1]

> Decadence is a crucial yet often misunderstood aspect of modernism.[2]

> The points of contact between evolution and decadence [will show them to be] synonyms.[3]

> La décadence esthètique, . . . elle est synonyme de jeunesse fringante et de renouvellement.[4] [Aesthetic decadence . . . is synonymous with dashing youthfulness and renewal.]

> Decadence is less a period of transition than a dynamics of transition.[5]

> Advance or decline—these are the only alternatives. Impasse, in which there is . . . only uncertainty, is unimaginable in the logic of decadence.[6]

If such debates are common in, say, literary studies, they are so much more likely to occur in a relatively young discipline like musicology. Thus it is that the first book-length study to tackle the problem in music was published only in 2010, and even in that case the author felt obliged to limit the geopolitical and ethnic areas he could reasonably expect to cover (see fn. 2).

   As the title of that book and the snippets from a wide variety of sources at the head of this study suggest, the true 'worm' among the four concepts is 'decadence'. Those snippets might well encourage a devil's advocate to suggest that the effort needed to link music and decadence is bound to yield disproportionately meagre results. However, this would not be the first time that cross-disciplinary thinking, unpromising at first, has resulted in a degree of acceptance, if not in the complete mastery of a problem. (Having long worked for the inclusion of *Jugendstil* and its relations in the musical discourse, I take pleasure in the headway that has been made since the idea had been dismissed out of hand by such luminaries in the field as Frits Noske and Reinhold Brinkmann.)

In the following, I shall treat the four concepts as the flexible historical and stylistic convolute they are. The availability of Stephen Downes's study largely obviates the need to lay out their essential traits; it also makes it unnecessary to trace the main lines of the interdisciplinary transmission and subsequent transmutation of what were originally historical, literary, or artistic concepts. But as Downes had, perforce, to accommodate a range of concerns substantially broader than mine are on this occasion, I am able to take a potentially rewarding byway less explored in a number of disciplines.

This path allows me to combine and recombine 'decadence,' fin de siècle, and 'transition' with Mahler in the area of religious systems, beliefs, and history. It is useful to start with St. Augustine's (354–430) treatise, *The City of God* (413–26), written during 'one of the most crucial periods of transition in the history of Western culture'. By attributing the human subject's decadence to the Fall, it has deeply influenced both Catholic and Protestant theology. Scholars as unlike as Walter Benjamin and Jacques Derrida maintained that the many and varied accounts of it (and of the Tower of Babel) demonstrate the influence the concept of decadence has had on theology.[7]

From that ideational foundation we may now move forward to the period under consideration. 'Fin de siècle' as term and concept began to gain currency only in the 1880s. It then rapidly evolved in two directions: as an in-vogue expression, it lost credibility; at the same time, it gained substance by echoing Augustine's *finis saeculi*, with its unequivocal reference to the end of the world. Still, search as we might at the level of nation-states for signs of apprehension of an impending 'fall', it is clear that in East- or West-Central Europe, only Austria-Hungary was seen as 'endangered'. It was 'a plurinational empire without unity, a buffer between East and West'. It reified 'the modern fears of the dissolution of boundaries' in every respect (racially, socially, as well as psychologically).[8] Therefore, what was a gradual turn to neo-Catholicism elsewhere (generally under way by ca. 1890) accelerated rapidly in Vienna and in the homelands. At the same time, the majority of converts were found among those who had insufficient faith in scientific progress. Thus, they did not necessarily convert from religious motivation, from a desire to return to the naïve faith they may have acquired in their early years. Rather, conversion answered a need for reassurance—a flight, as it were, to a new type of spiritual 'certainty'.

Mahler's case, however, seems to be an especially complicated one even in a period of rampant ambiguity. On the one hand, his conversion in 1897 did not emulate the typical turn to neo-Catholicism, in that it was not a flight from anything. At the same time, there are unmistakable clues in his life and music which indicate that he did possess, both before and after his conversion, the 'naïve faith' of someone who had naturally grown up with it. Still, whether we see Mahler's conversion as a type of 'homecoming' depends largely on how much credence we give to the widely held opinion that it was merely an act of convenience.

In order to understand fully the multi-faceted and multi-hued world that was the capital city of the Hapsburg monarchy at the turn of the twentieth century, it is necessary to outline the history of 'decadence' and 'transition' as concepts. Moreover, consideration of Mahler's place in that world will also benefit from a selective look at the literary and artistic situation in fin-de-siècle Vienna.

Tracing the history of the Decadent concept is a fascinating, but also a large and exacting task, much of which is not required for present purposes. But it is essential to note the historical juncture (a 'tipping-point' of sorts) at which a theretofore purely negative concept (one of derisive value-judgement) underwent a re-interpretation, a rehabilitation. Thenceforth decline was balanced by a positive side that showed the more or less simultaneous burgeoning of a powerful life force to be equally important. By attacking the use of 'decadence' as a term of denigration in 1857, Charles Baudelaire (1821–67) is said to have pioneered this development.[9]

Although the French poet's revaluation of the concept had not met with universal acceptance, a substantial faction opted thereafter to use the term neither negatively nor positively; in point of fact, they considered its greatest value to lie in its potential for ambivalence. Friedrich Nietzsche, one of the trend-setting if polarising personalities of the age, acted as an unofficial spokesperson for this group when he famously declared: 'While I am certainly a *décadent*, I am also its opposite.'[10]

It seems but a small step from there to thinking in terms of 'fluency', of 'flux'—of 'transition', in fact. For that, we may once again call on Baudelaire, for it was in his work that the possibilities of a commingling, a kind of conceptual fusion of 'decadence' and 'transition' were first revealed, and then in the most striking (and, for most of his contemporaries, incomprehensible) place and manner. Whether one celebrated or reviled him as an essayist, a critic, or a poet, there was general agreement, as there is today, that Baudelaire's magnum opus was his collection of poems published under the title *Les Fleurs du mal*. The final section of the second, enlarged edition (1861) is subtitled 'La Mort', representing an image that, together with the erotic, suffuses the whole of the collection. The closing poem of this section, 'Le Voyage', has eight parts, the last of which consists of these two four-line stanzas:

> VIII
> Ô Mort, vieux capitaine, il est temps! levons l'ancre!
> Ce pays nous ennuie, ô Mort! Appareillons!
> Si le ciel et la mer sont noirs comme de l'encre,
> Nos coeurs que tu connais sont remplis de rayons!
>
> Verse-nous ton poison pour qu'il nous réconforte!
> Nous voulons, tant ce feu nous brûle le cerveau,

Plonger au fond du gouffre, Enfer ou Ciel, qu'importe?
Au fond de l'Inconnu pour trouver du *nouveau*!

O Death, old captain, it is time! Let's weigh anchor!
This country wearies us, O Death! Let us set sail!
Though the sea and the sky are black as ink,
Our hearts which you know well are filled with rays of light!

Pour out your poison that it may refresh us!
This fire burns our brains so fiercely, we wish to plunge
To the abyss' depths, Heaven or Hell, does it matter?
To the depths of the Unknown to find something *new*![11]

By placing 'new' at the end of the poem, and emphasising it as he did (it is italicised in the original text), the poet sent a 'message' to his readers, his spiritual heirs. This was that even a journey as 'decadent' and gruesome as *Les Fleurs*, transiting through the 'abyss', the 'Unknown', and ending in death as all human journeys must, carries with it the promise that there is a distant shore, an 'other side,' where a start towards new horizons is possible.

Again, many nineteenth-century critics and, more indirectly, visual artists either failed to understand or refused to share Baudelaire's vision. Nevertheless, there were many of the latter (especially among turn-of-the-century symbolists) who wished to illustrate *Les Fleurs* as they understood it; we must content ourselves with one striking example. Between 1899 and 1901, the Belgian painter and graphic artist Armand Rassenfosse (1862–1934) produced a series of coloured etchings for the Les Cents Bibliophiles society. His illustration for the last poem of *Les Fleurs* shows Death drawing the last breath from a sinking female figure; the overall design leaves the viewer in no doubt as to Death's supremacy.[12]

To us, the end of Baudelaire's poem reveals a sense of order and a promise of utility that emerges from the chaotic swirl of what, historically, were competing, conflicting, but also potentially reciprocating terms and concepts. This not only answers to the exegetical needs of the historian but also allows the futurist to push beyond the needs of today's critic. It is likely that the avant-garde theorist, Renato Poggioli (1907–63), had this sort of thing in mind when he wrote of 'the modern idea of Decadence' (as he pointedly called it) some fifty years ago. He concluded that it is best defined in terms of those moments 'when the vision of impending catastrophe merges with the expectation that another culture will be built on its ruins'.[13] (Might we not ask: is it possible to describe the Viennese fin de siècle more aptly?)

The concept of 'transition' as one of life's constants dates back to at least the pre-Socratic age. It is fittingly captured in an aphorism attributed to Heraclitus (ca. 540–475 BCE): 'You cannot step into the same river twice.' At the turn of the twentieth century, Mahler's distinguished contemporary, the English philosopher Alfred North Whitehead (1861–1947) was the foremost exponent of the primacy of change, of permanence-as-illusion. This idea provided the foundation for his 'process philosophy'.[14] A couple of generations later, the cultural historian Malcolm Bradbury (1932–2000), while surveying the fin de siècle from the vantage point of the later twentieth century, reformulated Heraclitus's aphorism for the postmodern reader: 'We live in a world of persistent change, where the past is dead and the present is dying; our pressing imperatives are drawn from a temporal location *somewhere between the present and the future.*'[15] Bradbury left the 'temporal location' unlabelled in 1971; today, that ideational discontinuity is seen to accommodate the so-called intermediate states.

The notion of an 'intermediate state' has had a long history as religious doctrine, in Christianity and elsewhere. It is in that 'temporal location' that we envision the 'process of transition' taking place; it is the process that gives rise to one or more 'intermediate states'. It is important to note, though, that while the two ideas are notionally interchangeable on the one level, they appear to be opposed on another. For—and this now reconnects us with Whitehead's view—a *'process of transition'* is a 'fluency', whereas an 'intermediate *state*' is a 'permanence', however fleeting it may be. Again, ambiguity is the overriding characteristic of such a relationship. It allowed Whitehead to conclude that there may only ever exist a 'wavering balance' between 'permanence' and 'fluency' or 'transition.'

Many 'intermediate states' have been proposed and elaborated over the years in various humanistic disciplines. The following list (in no particular order of precedence) is made up of some of those that are relevant to the Viennese fin de siècle and are useful for illustrating 'transitional' traits in Mahler's oeuvre.[16]

1. 'Being somewhere'—An 'intermediate state' between arrival and departure.
2. 'Bridge'—In the present context, this 'intermediate state' is most important as a metaphor.
   a. 'Island'—A compound secondary 'intermediate state'; it may be connected to the shore by a 'bridge'.
3. 'Evening'/'Twilight'—An 'intermediate state' between day and night. It may produce evanescent spectacles of great beauty or render both colours and forms indistinct. It is also the equivalent of the 'dying day', a metaphor for periods of decline. (Bradbury's fin de siècle as 'dying present' is a special case—see also 7 below).
   a. 'Night'/'Darkness'—A secondary state separating periods of day/light.
   b. 'Moonlight'—Although musico-poetically ubiquitous, this is also a secondary 'intermediate state'. As reflection, it is between 'light' and 'non-light' that creates shadows and reduces forms to vague outlines.

4. 'Autumn'—A 'decadent' period, linking vital summer and dead winter. Redolent of mortification, it is also a time of short-lived gifts (colourful wilting flora) and lasting ones (wine).

    a. 'Wilting'—A secondary 'intermediate state'; it links flourishing and decline.

5. 'Inebriation'—A physical state separating periods of sobriety. (See 8 below)

    a. 'Sleep'—An 'intermediate state' between periods of wakefulness. Depending on the context, it may also be a variant or a consequence of the foregoing.

6. 'Illness'—A lesser or greater 'intermediate state' that may separate periods of health, or health and dying.

7. 'Dying'—A state between being and non-being. In an age of upheaval, it may underlie a number of others. In Bradbury's formulation, the 'dying present' itself is an 'intermediate state' at the fin de siècle. (See 3 above).

8. 'Convalescence'—It separates sickness and health and is suggestively similar to 'sobering', the process between intoxication and sobriety. (See 5 above).

9. 'Spring'—A particularly important 'intermediate state' for us: it is the harbinger of renewal (in life or in art), the way out of Winter (the dead past), a promise of the summer to come.

10. Although it is not an emotional or metaphorical idea, another, somewhat unusual 'intermediate state' proposed by Pynsent (see fn.16) may be adapted for our needs. At the turn of the twentieth century, the Decadent critic Arthur Symons (1865–1945) (Mahler's and Whitehead's contemporary) described Sofia as a city of 'a crudity and sordidness which are half-western and half-eastern'.[17] This prompted Pynsent to label it an 'intermediate state' between two civilizations; it readily brings to mind Vienna, as well as specific works in Mahler's oeuvre, such as *Das Lied von der Erde*.

We now need to look briefly at literature and the arts in order to gain a more comprehensive understanding of Mahler's fin-de-siècle Vienna. In art, stylistic trends in Western and Central Europe ranged from outgoing Naturalism to the onset of Expressionism but were centred by the era's quintessential 'transitional movement', Art Nouveau/*Jugendstil*/Secession (the label depending on language and location). As concerns Vienna, we know the views of one of the most erudite eye witnesses of the age, Julius Meier-Graefe (1867–1935). A German art historian, he was described by some later observers as the *Jugendstil* movement's leading critic and first historian. Increasingly disillusioned by developments in Germany, England, France, and Belgium by 1900, he came to hope for the movement's revival in Vienna—in the 'New Vienna', as he styled it in a chapter added late to his magisterial *Entwicklungsgeschichte der modernen Kunst (Vergleichende Betrachtung der bildenden Künste, als*

Beitrag zu einer neuen Aesthetik).[18] He praised Hermann Bahr for his efforts to 'create a new Vienna', and Viennese artists in general for their willingness to support each other; he also foresaw the impending onset of a 'revolution'. But his astute observations made his views controversial even among his own colleagues:

> There were no great personalities who would have been the better for being alone . . . There was nothing to be made of the native domestic art of Vienna . . . [As] there was no serviceable past, the younger men [believed] that there was a present which was longing for a new art . . . They took what seemed useful from every country.

He was wary of the extent to which foreign (including Exotic) influences impacted 'new' Viennese art. But he concluded that this contributed to its strength, which he saw in its evolution 'from an exaggerated complexity of form . . . to the extremest simplicity'.[19]

Our limited purposes will be best served by avoiding the major artists and writers of the Viennese fin de siècle. In the event, in art (aside from architects and applied artists) there was only Gustav Klimt between the historicism of Makart, and the 'extreme simplicity' of the assault launched on 'good taste . . . in the old imperial city' (as Meier-Graefe felt moved to put it) by the likes of Schiele and Kokoschka. At the same time, the Secessionist movement was rich with multiply creative personalities. They often achieved high standards (if not necessarily critical acclaim) in more than one field, thus tacitly affirming the idea of *Gesamtkunstwerk*. Today they are mostly remembered (though often undeservedly) as 'secondary' figures.

Among Mahler's coevals, Ernst Stöhr (1860–1917) stands out as one such personality. A fine violinist, the young Stöhr also composed, wrote poetry and small plays, and built the stage set for one of them. He chose art eventually but continued to refer to the 'instrumentation' of his canvases, and even 'painted' musical works (for example, Mozart's G-minor Symphony, K. 550).[20] Unable to free himself from the outmoded conventions of Viennese painting, Stöhr contributed to the onset of modernity in the graphic arts. He was also a diversely productive founding member of the Secession: his input included prose studies for several issues of *Ver Sacrum*, the Society's journal. A well-deserved honour was bestowed on him in 1899 when his poems and engravings were published in a single-author issue, including his own cover art (vol. 2, no. 12). Among the many striking pieces contributed by Stöhr to *Ver Sacrum*, there is an intriguing illustration of a ubiquitous subterranean current in turn-of-the-century Viennese art and literature: the cult of the femme fatale.[21] The label captures well the concept of misogyny: hate and fear of woman.[22] From the bottomless fund of visual and literary representations of the seductive, potentially lethal dominatrix, the stories and graphic depictions of female vampires stand out, among them the intriguing, multi-faceted ink drawing by Stöhr shown in Fig. 14.1.

Fig. 14.1 Ernst Stöhr's 'Vampire'

Though left untitled by the artist, it unquestionably belongs to the genre of vampire art.[23] And yet, the positioning of the bodies and the highly complex 'lighting' of the scene (to name but two of the salient elements of the design) give rise to much ambiguity. Is a 'story' unfolding here? Where does this 'moment' fit in? Was the action interrupted by the viewer? In Edvard Munch's well-known oil painting (1893–94) the exsanguination is obviously *in medias res*; looking at Ernst Stöhr's drawing, we are unable to decide whether or not it has even commenced. Is 'domination' no longer an unambiguous idea? Is this a sign of 'evolution'? Are the characters somewhere in Malcolm Bradbury's land: does the drawing depict an 'intermediate state'? Or are they in the 'abyss', the 'Unknown,' through which they must transition to reach the 'new', à la Baudelaire's 'Le Voyage'?[24]

Julius Meier-Graefe's observation that fin-de-siècle Vienna's artists 'took what seemed useful from every country' also held true for its writers. Symbolism, in particular, imbued much of their poetry with Baudelaireian ambiguity towards decadence and transition. Curiously, it is again mostly in Austrian poetry of the second rank that the French writer's journey 'through decline to rebirth' reverberates.[25] Still, an unambiguous counterpart for 'Le Voyage' had to await a major figure like Georg Trakl (1887–1914). His mature oeuvre had clearly left the 'dying present' of the fin de siècle behind for that 'other shore' we call modernity. It is in his early work that we find a striking evocation of Baudelaire's 'journey', but even that with a remarkably modern take on the 'unknown'. 'Einklang' ('Harmony') was written during the same period Mahler was at work on *Das Lied* (ca. 1908–9); the last one of its four quatrains reads:

> Wir gehen durch die Tode neugestaltet
> Zu tiefern Foltern ein und tiefern Wonnen,
> Darin die unbekannte Gottheit waltet —
> Und uns vollenden ewig neue Sonnen.[26]

> Newly formed by death, we enter
> Into deeper torments and deeper delights,
> There, where the unknown Godhead reigns —
> And we are made complete by suns forever new.

Given his idiosyncratic stylistic development, practically any one of Mahler's works displays some transitional characteristics, but they are especially pronounced in the Eighth and Ninth symphonies, and in *Das Lied von der Erde*. In order to maximise the available space, I shall restrict my comments to *Das Lied* and the Ninth Symphony—one texted and one untexted work.

Das Lied is a monumental symphonic song cycle that is a true hybrid of concepts, processes, and genres, its style defined by the inseparability of form and content. For present purposes, though, we may regard the work as an overarching 'intermediate state', a metaphorical 'bridge' that links East and West, word and sound, old and new. Mahler wove the 'intermediate states' depicted in the poems into a rich tapestry of text and music. The framing lyrics are linked variously to the other four songs. For example, the recurrent image of 'wine' in the first song is echoed by 'inebriation' in Song 5, 'drinking' in Song 3,[27] and the 'farewell drink' of 'Der Abschied'. Similarly, evocations of 'evening' and the 'moon' in the latter are foreshadowed by 'night' and 'sleep' in Song 5, by the overpowering sense of exhaustion, 'wilting', and 'sleep' in the second song, and by the 'withered gardens of the soul', the descending 'evening', and the highly symbolic 'darkness' that spreads out from the opening song. Representations of the seasons as 'intermediate states' give rise to a striking interplay of physical and emotional conditions in *Das Lied*.

Notably, the two seasons most readily perceived by human sensibility as impermanent are named directly: 'autumn' in 'Der Einsame', and 'spring' in both of the last two songs. As for 'winter' and 'summer' (periods of relative stability), we must infer them from context. While the former is presaged effectively by the gloom and cold emanating from the second song, the only intimation of 'summer' in the cycle arises from an ambiance of happiness and carefree seasonal activities in 'Von der Schönheit'.

Even such a narrow sampling of the texts attests the critical role of the web of poetic 'intermediate states' in the processual interplay. However, the potential inherent in the ancient Chinese poetry, restated in a chain of multi-lingual modern-day interpretations, had to be actualised by the musical facture. By focusing on the stylistic-technical macrocosm of the six songs, we are able to isolate some of the musical techniques and devices Mahler employed (both conventionally and radically reconfigured) in the service of projecting the lyric drama of the life-death-life cycle.

Member of the post-Romantic generation, Mahler was, apparently, unwilling to cast off some of the technical and aesthetic ties that bound him to the past. Thus, he rarely (and then temporarily) strayed beyond the chromatic tonal-harmonic practice of his time.[28] But analysis of his rhythmic language, together with what we know about his exceptional abilities as a conductor, makes it clear that in this parameter, more than in any other, he pointed the way forward for his discerning contemporaries and successors. In the context of Mahler's oeuvre, *Das Lied von der Erde* presents a somewhat ambiguous picture tonally. The forward-looking feature of progressive tonality is well-nigh absent from this sprawling cycle.[29] Moreover, the central key of the opening song (A minor) is mirrored in the A major tonality of the fifth piece, creating the impression that a five-movement cycle has concluded. This is underpinned by the poetic alternation of the seasons (one of the drivers of the transitional process): it seems to culminate here in the arrival of 'spring'.

Not surprisingly, the real 'finale' of the cycle tends to overwhelm the listener's musical-aesthetic sensorium as much as the analyst's rational understanding. 'Der Abschied' is more than half as long as the preceding five songs together. The richness of the orchestral setting far exceeds what was heard before. Should we suspect a tonal 'progression' of sorts in moving from the A major close of the penultimate song to the opening of the last movement in C minor, looking solely at the sequence of the main keys of the cycle (a – d – B♭ – G – A – c/C) makes it clear that this is a superficial impression. In point of fact, the process of 'transition' is actualised in—and the cycle as a whole revealed as an overall 'intermediate state' by—the final prolonged sonority: in terms of its 'period', the unresolved tonic chord with added sixth (C–E–G–A) leaves this grand symphonic song cycle tonally 'open'.[30]

It is in the metric nature of *Das Lied* that true inventiveness becomes apparent at the stylistic-technical level, making the cycle's overarching 'intermediate state' manifestly clear. While the tonal language retains vestiges of a conventional cyclicity, the rhythmic evolution is of nearly uninterrupted continuity, extending from the firm basic beat in 'Das Trinklied vom Jammer der Erde' to the virtual absence of a perceptible pulse for long stretches of 'Der Abschied'.[31]

The *'nearly* uninterrupted continuity' demonstrates Mahler's architectonic mastery: a 'superstructure', articulated as three successive pairs of songs, is superimposed on the whole. Songs 1, 3, and 5 have single time signatures ($\frac{3}{4}$, c, $\frac{4}{4}$),[32] while in the second one of each 'pair' (Songs 2, 4, and 6) time signatures change with varying frequency and effect, but also in an obviously expanding manner, culminating in the rhythmically indeterminate ending of Song 6.[33] And this reinforces what we concluded from the tonal procedures: *Das Lied* is a large-scale, multi-movement work that stops, and yet does not 'end' in the traditional sense.

Summarising the conclusions drawn from a necessarily cursory examination of the tonal and rhythmic characteristics of this pivotal, epoch-making work, we find that they reinforce those that had been drawn from the nature of the poetry and its use by Mahler in the six songs. We may now relate the totality of our textual and stylistic-technical findings to the problem of 'transition' at the turn of the twentieth century, as it is actualised in the 'intermediate states' observable in *Das Lied*. Accordingly, Bradbury's 'dead past' is represented by Song 1. The increasing infirmity of rhythm and tempo from Song 2 to Song 5 tracks the 'process' of a gradually 'dying present'. And 'Der Abschied' crowns it all: more than any other work by Mahler (and, arguably, of its time), it manifests that 'temporal location somewhere between the [dying] present and the future'.

Completed a year or so after *Das Lied von der Erde*, the Ninth Symphony is all too often lumped together with the former as a grand valediction from a sick, broken man ready—perhaps even longing—to depart this 'vale of tears'. Perhaps stimulated by the absence of a text, a rather substantial inventory of self-referential musical reminiscences said to be present in the symphony has been compiled over the years in support of this thesis.[34] What is of far greater interest to us in the present context, however, are the advances Mahler may have made in this work towards modernism in the two non-textual parameters that were found to be significant in this regard in *Das Lied von der Erde*; these are the metric processes and tonal-harmonic manipulation. The openings of the first and third movements provide us with striking examples for both (Ex. 14.1a and b).

The opening six bars of the first movement are usually described in the analytical literature as an 'introduction'. Yet (the discrepancy in size notwithstanding) their function in this music is manifestly similar to that of the opening sixty-one bars of the First Symphony's first movement, readily seen as constituting the integral first section of the exposition.[35] But in the Ninth the compressive effects of a short passage serve to emphasise the 'equality' of

Ex. 14.1 Attack (a) and Accent/duration (b) patterns in Mahler's Ninth Symphony, first movement: a. bars 1–6; b: bars 1–7

(a)

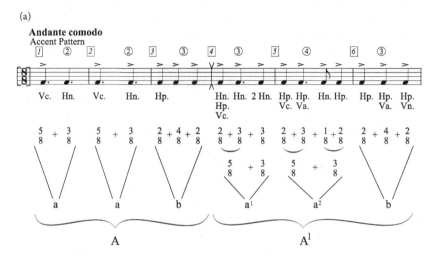

(b)

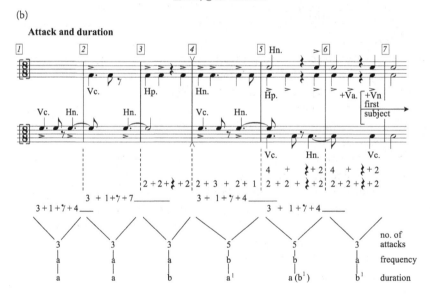

its elements in providing the raw material for the complete motivic and thematic content of this long movement. Because of the quasi-mosaic, threadbare presentation of mostly sub-motivic fragments, the central tonality (D major) remains unclear until the first subject gets under way with the upbeat to bar 7. Mostly for the same reason, but exacerbated by the slow, 'comfortable' tempo

($\frac{4}{4}$, effectively $\frac{8}{8}$), the profusion of seemingly random accents, and ties across the bar line, the opening of the movement is rhythmically indeterminate.

As if his intention had been to create aural confusion of an even higher degree in the third movement, Mahler literally assaults the listener's sensibilities in the opening measures of this fast, 'very defiant [contrary, difficult, awkward]' piece of music titled Rondo-Burleske. The prescribed *alla breve* duple meter is consistently ineffectuated through the random horizontal and vertical regrouping of the material into 'motives' of one, three or four beats (Ex. 14.2). In A minor overall, the movement opens with a surfeit of apparently non-tonal melodic motives and chordal 'clusters', again randomly varied in duration and density. In the event, the home key is first touched on briefly in bar 7 but is established unequivocally (though even then fleetingly) only in bar 11. Thus the opening six bars (replete with a profusion of c♯ and d♯ equivalents) constitute an extended dominant space opening motion.

As it was with *Das Lied*, in the Ninth Symphony, too, Mahler refused to altogether abandon tonality and metric regularity in the end. Notwithstanding, the openings of the first and third movements intimated to his contemporaries, and provide us with unmistakable evidence, that this unexampled master of 'transition' had at least briefly trod on Baudelaire's distant shore of the 'new', where the birth pangs of twentieth-century Viennese musical modernism had already been felt.

If—as Bradbury had it—the 'past was dead', and the 'present' was 'dying' in turn-of-the-twentieth-century Vienna, then surely 'modernism' was the 'future' for prescient members of contemporary society. In his magisterial,

Ex. 14.2 Mahler's Ninth Symphony, third movement, bars 1–7

in toto treatment of the subject, Matei Calinescu described 'two distinct and bitterly conflicting modernities'. The first identifies a historical stage; the second is part of aesthetics and should be understood 'as a crisis concept' in dialectical opposition to tradition, 'to the modernity of bourgeois civilization (with its ideals of rationality, utility, [and] progress)'. According to Calinescu, the latter brought the avant-garde into being.[36] In limiting our attention to the onset of musical modernism in Austria-Hungary, we must not be blinded by the massive presence of Schoenberg and his disciples. In fact, as the process arguably began with their 'rediscovery' of Mahler, it would be helpful to be able to place him in the stylistic evolution from the mid-nineteenth to the mid-twentieth century. But is it possible at all to assign him to an identifiable 'period'? As Julian Johnson observed, no historical label fits his music, as it brings together romantic, modern, and postmodern. Adopting Nietzsche's words, Mahler was an artist 'stretched on the contradiction between today and tomorrow': historicist and modernist culture collided in his music.[37] And Leon Botstein points out that the observer's own chronological position has had a decisive influence on the posthumous estimation of Mahler's place in history. In his concise summary, Botstein identifies three major shifts. In the 1960s, Mahler was broadly seen as a Janus-figure, comparable to Beethoven as a prophet of 'modernism'. With modernism under attack in the 1970s, he was regarded as a 'precursor and model of the postmodern', source and inspiration for restoring 'tonality' and musical expressivity. Finally, since the beginning of our century, 'Mahler has become entirely emblematic of the emancipation from modernism.'[38]

In most cases, we are better able to grasp something elusive if it is circumscribed and delimited. Accordingly, *au fond* we have two simple facts: Mahler's oeuvre encompassed the twilight years of the nineteenth century and the dawning of the New Age, and it was marked by idiosyncratic development. Thus his music may be credibly viewed today as representing the period during which consciousness of the past (even if it was a 'dead' one) regularly clashed with, and gradually yielded to, premonitions of the future. And that marks its creator as the 'transitional' composer par excellence, in a transitional age *sans pareil* in post-Renaissance history. A finely turned passage from the recent *Mahler Handbuch* is eminently fit to conclude this study. In the Introduction, the editor perceptively locates Mahler in a stylistic-historical 'Niemandsland' (no man's land). His elaboration recalls Whitehead's 'wavering balance' between a '*process* of transition' and an 'intermediate *state*':

> Ambivalent, [Mahler's music] incorporates the past in the shape of the entire history of genre, and points to an unknown future, without being wholly identifiable with either; thus it admits of many interpretations. Perhaps it is . . . because of the hesitation between 'departure' and 'arrival,' characteristic of the onset of Modernity, that [this music] remains relevant today.[39]

Notes

1. Van Roosbroeck, *The Legend of the Decadents*, 14.
2. Downes, *Music and Decadence in European Modernism*, i.
3. Arnošt Procházka, 1910. Procházka (1869–1925) was 'an apodistic, polemical, often cantankerous' bank clerk (Pynsent, 'Czech Decadence', 358).
4. Richard, *Le mouvement Décadent*, 259.
5. Weir, *Decadence and the Making of Modernism*, 15.
6. Kuspit, *The Dialectic of Decadence*, 22.
7. Anonymous 'Introduction' to St John, *Romancing Decay*, xii–xiii and xvii. The full title of the treatise is *De Civitate Dei contra Paganos*; known in English as [*Concerning*] *The City of God against the Pagans*.
8. Braun, "Klimtomania/Klimtophobia", 42.
9. Wolfdietrich Rasch singled out Baudelaire in his landmark study, *Die literarische Décadence um 1900*, 23–24.
10. 'Abgerechnet nämlich, daß ich ein *décadent* bin, bin ich auch dessen Gegensatz'; cited in Rasch, *Die literarische Décadence um 1900*, 26 (unless otherwise indicated, all translations are mine).
11. The English translation is by William Aggeler (*The Flowers of Evil*, Fresno, CA, 1954).
12. See Fig. 5 in Haskell, "Illustrations for Baudelaire's *Les Fleurs du mal*", 189 (the associated text is on the preceding page); Haskell dates Rassenfosse's illustrations to 1899.
13. Poggioli, *The Poets of Russia*, 80.
14. Whitehead formulated his 'process philosophy' only after he had moved to Harvard in 1924. See *Process and Reality*, pp. 208–10 for his discussion of ideas of permanence and flux to which I subsequently refer.
15. Bradbury, *The Social Context of Modern English Literature*, 3 (my emphasis).
16. I have adopted some of these from Pynsent, "Conclusory Essay".
17. Quoted by Pynsent from Symons's collection, *Cities*, published in 1903 in London by Dent.
18. The first edition of Meier-Graefe's book was published in three volumes in 1904; internal evidence suggests that "The New Vienna" chapter had been written as late as 1903 or 1904. In the two-volume English edition that served as my source (see *Modern Art*), the "New Vienna" chapter is on 303–9.
19. Meier-Graefe, *Modern Art*, 303, 304, 305, 308.
20. Much of my information comes from the only comprehensive study of the artist (see Bösch, "Die Kunst des inneren Sehens"); see also Stöhr, "Zeichnungen und Gedichte".
21. Alessandra Comini's "Vampires, Virgins and Voyeurs" paints a fascinating picture of time and place; unfortunately, it suffers from instances of misattribution and faulty association.
22. Misogyny is treated exhaustively in Dijkstra, *Idols of Perversity*.

23. This illustration is taken from the original publication (see Stöhr, "Zeichnungen und Gedichte", 8).

24. *Les Fleurs du mal* does include "Le Vampire"; perhaps its early placement (No. 32) reflects Baudelaire's gradual evolution towards the future-oriented conclusion of "Le Voyage" (No. 132).

25. For instance, Anastasius Grün (*recte* Count Anton Alexander Auersperg, 1806–76).

26. Trakl, *Aus goldenem Kelch*, 85.

27. In the sources on which Bethge drew for his rendering of the final text, the drink is identified specifically as 'wine'.

28. Nevertheless, it may be argued that his frequently striking reductions of chromaticism point to Mahler as a forerunner of the development that was to culminate in neo-tonality/neo-Classicism.

29. Although it does play a role in the interior structural articulation, as in the 'strophic' subdivisions of "Das Trinklied vom Jammer der Erde". Perhaps it should be added that the instrumentation also contributes greatly to *Das Lied*'s quiddity as a future-oriented, revolutionary work. However, that discussion belongs to a study of the 'post-transitional' stage of 'modern' music.

30. The chord has additional compositional-structural interest. It is the first inversion of the tonic seventh chords of Songs 1 and 5 (*sans* mode), the framing pieces of the apparent 'cycle' (see above). Moreover, the notes of the closing chord of 'Der Abschied' are identical with the notes of the cycle's extended 'leitmotif' a–g–e (–c), first heard in the violins in bars 5–9 of Song 1, and thereafter ever-present in various guises in each movement. As if to affirm that connection, the last chord of the cycle is voiced with the 'a' as its highest note.

31. Especially towards the end, the very slow tempo, combined with long notes, results in a virtual cessation of 'motion' as that term is applied to the unfolding of music in time. This gives rise to a paradox: the 'fluency' is musically subordinated to a type of 'permanence' (Whitehead), memorably proclaimed in the last words, a sevenfold repetition of 'ewig' (Mahler's addition to the text).

32. Still, the songs are ingeniously differentiated: agogic flexibility in Song 1; *alla breve* of a near-metronomic regularity in Song 3; and a nervously jumpy air in Song 5, foreshadowing the approaching temporal 'dissolution' of the finale.

33. In the slow Song 2, the alternation of three different meters ($\frac{2}{2}$, $\frac{3}{2}$, $\frac{4}{2}$) and the great variety of note values do not create an unsettled sense. But 'Von der Schönheit' was clearly intended to anticipate Song 5. Thus, the alternation of three meters ($\frac{2}{4}$, $\frac{3}{4}$, $\frac{4}{4}$) has a far more telling effect on the three asymmetrically distributed strophes and on the subsidiary structural sections; the trills, and dotted and grace notes foreshadow Song 5, creating a restive impression. Metric and rhythmic restraint is cast aside in Song 6. There are seven double, triple, and quintuple time signatures as well as various groupings of notes that constitute the unmeasured sections of the recitatives. Virtually all subdivisions of a beat (or of note value) between 2 and 14 occur, as do written-out and disguised polyrhythms (for example, bars 288–302). Combined with the variety of note values used in the song (thirty-seconds to dotted

halves tied over several bars), it makes any semblance of conventional rhythmic usage seem little more than accidental.

34. Although my focus there is on *Das Lied*, I argue systematically against the customary, lugubrious interpretation of Mahler's last works in general in my "Between *Jugendstil* and Expressionism".

35. See Roman, "Song and Symphony (I)", 85.

36. Calinescu, *Faces of Modernity*, 41 and 10.

37. Johnson, *Mahler's Voices*, 229.

38. Botstein, "Whose Gustav Mahler?", 4.

39. 'Ambivalent, umfasst [Mahlers Musik] die Vergangenheit in Form der versammelten Gattungsgeschichte und weisst in eine unbekannte Zukunft, ohne dass sie mit dem einen oder dem anderen restlos zu identifizieren wäre, und lässt deshalb viele Interpretationen zu. Vielleicht deshalb, wegen … dieses Zögern zwischen Abschied und Ankommen, das am Anfang der Moderne steht ist [diese Musik] noch heute … aktuell' (Sponheuer, "Einleitung", 11–12).

15

Justine Mahler's *Faust* Notebook

An Introduction

Stephen E. Hefling

The Mahler-Rosé Room at the University of Western Ontario (UWO) in London, Ontario, Canada, has long been known as a splendid repository of primary sources about Mahler,[1] including a large collection of family letters.[2] But among the collection's lesser-known holdings is an item simply designated 'Justine Rosé's *Faust* Notebook.' At present, this 122-page notebook has no title page; it simply begins with commentary on the second part of Goethe's masterpiece (see Fig. 15.1).

Justine (Justi) was Mahler's sister and the wife of violinist Arnold Rosé. The *Faust* Notebook was inherited by the Rosés' son Alfred, a conductor and teacher who arrived at UWO in 1948, bringing Justine's Mahler materials with him.[3] Comparison of the *Faust* notebook to other examples of Justine's writing, such as her 1894 letter to Gustav shown in Fig. 15.2, confirms that the principal hand in the notebook is hers. Clearly, however, the Notebook annotations are not Justi's original observations; both their complexity and the nature of certain corrections in the manuscript indicate that she is copying something—doubtless something unpublished, since Mahler (or Rosé) could easily have purchased any printed *Faust* commentary. The bulk of the manuscript is very neatly written in purple ink, as are most of the (relatively few) corrections. Subsequent sporadic clarifications in pencil are in one or more different hands (see Fig. 15.3); these emendations also indicate a document resulting from careful study. We know that in July 1899 Mahler had Justine make a copy of another long manuscript: Siegfried Lipiner's drama *Adam* (Fig. 15.4).[4]

The last will and testament of Natalie Bauer-Lechner, Mahler's confidante and 'Eckermann' from 1892 through 1901, lists her manuscript entitled 'Commentary to Faust II, according to Lipiner's words, written down immediately after reading, and . . . read by him and praised for its accurate reproduction; therefore <u>nothing</u> is to be altered in it.'[5] From approximately 1876 to 1901, the poet-philosopher Siegfried Lipiner (1856–1911; see Fig. 15.5) was Mahler's closest friend and mentor, one of very few people whom Mahler almost invariably respected. Bruno Walter presents a colorful sketch of their mutual friend:

> Lipiner was by nature an improviser and made to give of himself freely in speech and personal communication . . . it was always the inspired who spoke, the poet, the lover. I never heard a didactic word from the lips of the

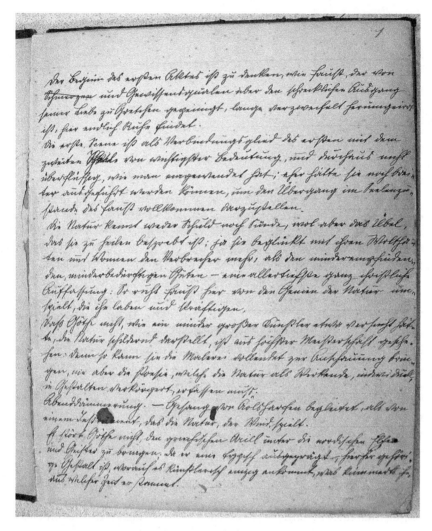

Fig. 15.1 Justine Mahler Rosé's *Faust* Notebook, p. 1. Reproduced by kind permission of the Mahler-Rosé Collection, Gustav Mahler-Alfred Rosé Room, Music Library, University of Western Ontario.

man who was so rich in knowledge, nor a polemic one either, unless he felt like attacking the commentators on Goethe's *Faust*, which he considered his special domain.[6]

Walter also praises Lipiner's 1894 doctoral dissertation, 'On Homunculus: A Study of Faust and Goethe's Philosophy'. And the respected neo-Kantian philosopher Paul Natorp advocated its posthumous publication 'because it traces Goethe's philosophy back to its historical roots and,

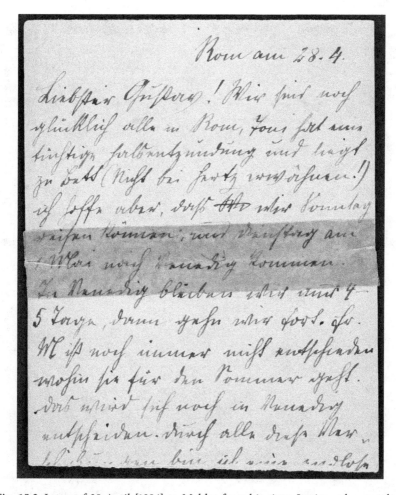

Fig. 15.2 Letter of 28 April [1894] to Mahler from his sister Justine, who was then visiting Rome. Reproduced by kind permission of the University of Pennsylvania Rare Book & Manuscript Library, Mahler-Werfel Papers, Ms. Coll. 575.

one must say, represents it with unified logical coherence for the first time'.[7] Unfortunately, no copies are known to survive today.[8]

Walter also says of Lipiner that 'neither was he lacking in women ... It was natural that Lipiner, a poet so passionately devoted to life, should again and again be taken captive by love.'[9] One such captivatress was Natalie Bauer-Lechner. According to the memoirs of Emma Adler, Natalie divorced her husband (in 1883) because of her passionate love for Lipiner,[10] and Lipiner himself divorced his first wife during this period. Although the Siegfried-Natalie liaison did not last, in her will Natalie states: 'That for which I most thank the Godhead is that in my life it allowed me to encounter these two great

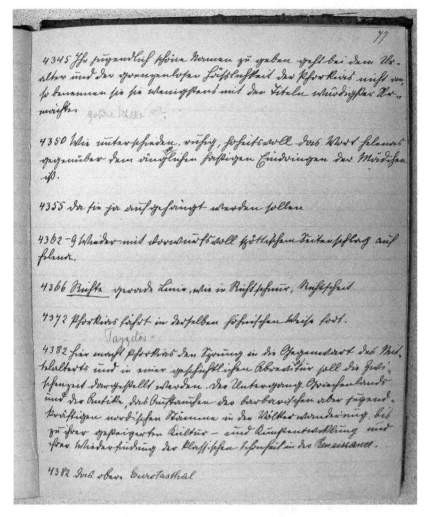

Fig. 15.3 Justine Mahler Rosé's *Faust* Notebook, p. 77. Reproduced by kind permission of the Mahler-Rosé Collection, Gustav Mahler-Alfred Rosé Room, Music Library, University of Western Ontario.

spirits: <u>Lipiner and Mahler</u>.'[11] Lipiner's preoccupation with *Faust*, however, considerably antedates his dissertation: in 1881 he published an interesting feuilleton entitled 'The Artistic Reform in Goethe's "Faust"'. Here he argues that the 'elevated-intimate conversation style [*der erhaben-innige Styl des Gesprächs*]' of *Faust* is the necessary poetic language for the anti-romantic, emphatically realistic orientation of the present times, in which 'erudite elocution [*gebildete Diction*]' has become vapid and meaningless:

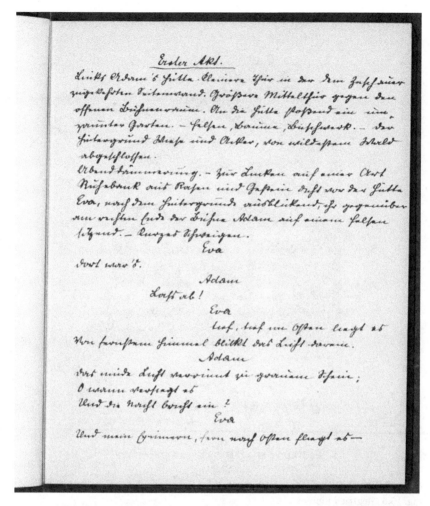

Fig. 15.4 Siegfried Lipiner, *Adam*, manuscript copy in the hand of Justine Mahler [1899]. Reproduced by kind permission of the University of Pennsylvania Rare Book & Manuscript Library, Mahler-Werfel Papers, Ms. Coll. 575.

in 'Faust' one encounters a truly new style. I should like to call it the style of *conversation*, actually the non-declamatory style . . . mostly the language flows with familiar ease . . . it is the language of the often agitated but fundamentally mild disposition, the speech of nature, and in this sense of the people—in short . . . *the German language.*[12]

It was probably during the early to mid-1880s that Natalie and Siegfried read *Faust* and that she compiled her commentary to Part II. And the original source of Justine's *Faust* Notebook must date from 1882 or later because it refers frequently—often unfavorably—to the 1882 edition of *Faust* by the well-known

Nach einer Photographie von Eulenstein
in Leipzig.

Fig. 15.5 Siegfried Lipiner

Goethe scholar, Heinrich Düntzer; many, although not all, Düntzer citations
are marked '(D).' Moreover, similar abbreviations throughout the Notebook—
'Meph' for Mephisto, 'Homunc' for Homunculus, 'G' for Goethe, and so on,
indicate that this copy was for personal use rather than publication. One of the
longest passages discusses Goethe's mysterious 'Mothers', 'the fundamental
sources of all life,'[13] who enable Faust to bring the spirit of Helen of Troy back
to earth: this entry is actually attributed at the end to '(Lipiner)'. That nothing
resembling this discussion occurs in any of Lipiner's published essays would
suggest that he is the source of all but the Düntzer passages in the Notebook
that Justi has copied (probably from Bauer-Lechner's personal manuscript).
Moreover, like Lipiner's 1881 feuilleton, the Notebook emphasises the countless instances where Goethe's use of language is 'never subjective and arbitrary,

but is always drawn out of the true folk-like spirit of the language. Through this freedom his language attains the most powerful immediate expression.'[14]

Many annotations are pedestrian, identifying mythological characters, archaic German usages, foreign terms, and so on. The scope of the commentary is selective rather than comprehensive: this text was probably intended to supplement Düntzer's or some similar annotated edition. The manner of writing is informative yet not pedantic, humane rather than clinically cold; the longer passages might almost be characterised as 'elevated-intimate conversation style'. A number of the comments are simply effusions of enthusiasm: 'How marvelously Goethe has achieved this is entirely out of proportion to the subject'; 'How vividly G has represented such a thing'; 'Marvelous portrait'—and so on (see also Tables 15.1 and 15.2). But the author is also critical of Goethe's text, occasionally suggesting revisions of punctuation and paragraphing, or even emending what he takes to be the poet's oversights. He regularly highlights passages where Goethe seems to ridicule pedantic efforts at understanding, particularly cases in which the exterior, ancient aspect of the situation might be considered more significant than the interior, transcendent meaning. And at one point our commentator seems to mock Lipiner's 1881 discussion about *Faust* and Realism: concerning lines 7279 ff., where Pater Seraphicus takes the blessed boys into himself, the Notebook observes: 'Can one conceive of anything more mystical? And that is the Goethe whom every Philistine dares to play up as "the realist"'.

Portions of *Faust* project panentheistic overtones, which the commentator also underscores. Lipiner had been an enthusiastic student of the scientist and philosopher Gustav Theodor Fechner, famous for advocating that the entire universe is an inwardly alive, spiritual hierarchy. Arguing against contemporary materialism, Lipiner had expanded upon Fechner's viewpoint in his 1878 essay *On the Elements of a Renewal of Religious Ideas in the Present*, which emphasises the interconnection between religion and tragedy: 'We grasp true and serious pantheism only when we see this Nature from within, when the great transformation has proceeded within us, when we have ceased to know and to feel ourselves as individual beings ... and this great transformation is the tragic unfolding, the tragedy.'[15] Concerning the close of Act 3 in Part II of *Faust*, where the chorus begins to dissolve into the four elements, the Notebook declares: 'Therewith Goethe simultaneously achieves something all-important. He shows us the <u>ensoulment, the total spiritualisation</u> of Nature, which was an intuitive belief of the ancients and to which the most advanced conception of Nature must necessarily return, as a living event before our eyes.'[16] This assessment seems more Fechnerian than Goethe's allegorical poetry might suggest. This entry also claims, without specific reference to Goethe's text, that 'What one has become in life he takes with him into the beyond, and according to his higher or lower, more or less distinguished individuality, a higher or lower form of being will be his portion.'[17] This, too, is classic Fechner (albeit that, as

Düntzer notes, Goethe had once made a related observation in a 1781 letter to Carl von Kneben).[18]

An additional clue to Lipiner's authorship of the Notebook is found in an unusual letter he wrote on 12 March 1906 to Alma Mahler: at their first extensive meeting in 1902, she and Lipiner so completely despised each other that Mahler and his longtime friend became estranged for the next seven years. Yet despite their long-standing enmity, evidently in 1906 (the year Mahler composed the Eighth), Alma ingratiatingly requested permission to copy a commentary Lipiner had written on *Faust*, which petition he refused rather scornfully:

> Dear Madam,
> I did not write a commentary on Faust, but rather spoke about it many years ago. You would like to have in hand a transcript that has later been made of it—which I would not have supervised, for the content of which I would have to disclaim merit and responsibility. And whatever in it I was unquestionably accountable for, I would today for the most part reject with mockery: as I now regard life and the world in general so entirely differently, so, too, art, and especially this work of art. That which is central, that which is far and away most important, perhaps what is uniquely, truly greatness in Faust, is in my opinion not understood; and thereby 'my' commentary is also of no help: for when it came about, I also did not understand that greatness!—. Under such circumstances it would not be altogether honorable if I were simply to accept your charming compliment: I do not deserve it. Which of course relieves me of the duty to thank you most sincerely for your so exceedingly friendly words.
> Respectfully sincerely yours,
> S. Lipiner[19]

(Lipiner's apparent disavowal of his earlier thought may be a rhetorical justification for denying Alma's request.)

We cannot here explore all significant aspects of Justine's *Faust* Notebook, but a few observations placing it in the broader spectrum of nineteenth-century *Faust* reception may be made. Although today widely regarded as 'the greatest long poem in modern European literature',[20] *Faust*, and especially Part II, was highly controversial prior to 1870. Significantly, Düntzer was among the earlier commentators to identify Faust's 'unconditional striving towards the highest, noblest, and most beautiful, in the freest manner' as the work's main idea,[21] and he emphasised its overall unity and inherently German nature as well. The 1871 unification of the German Empire (excluding Austria) was concurrent with publication of a widely adopted new edition of *Faust* with extensive commentary by Gustav von Loeper. Thereupon *Faust*, Faustian 'perfectibility', and its attendant ceaseless striving became the national ideology of the *Gründerzeit*. Faust's wickedness and dividedness, and the work's tragic and ironic aspects, were largely swept aside. Indeed, Faust's error and guilt were considered necessary: from them arose heroic greatness. By 1876, *Faust* had been declared the second Bible of the German nation.[22] Both Lipiner and Mahler had been German Nationalist enthusiasts in their student days, and the *Faust* Notebook reflects several of the foregoing viewpoints: (1) Nature knows neither guilt nor sin (although probably evil, which she strives to heal) (p. 1). (2) Mephisto, who constantly laughs both at himself and the world, is fundamentally 'good-natured' (*gutmüthig*) and not possessed of the high-tragic evil and destructive passion of a Lucifer (p. 36). (3) Indeed, the devil is necessary, both for the good and the evil person; both good and evil seriously signify nothing before a supreme power (*vor einer höchsten Macht*) (p. 49). (4) The theme of ceaseless upward striving emerges most clearly in the passages on Homunculus—Goethe's subhuman test-tube creature seeking full humanity. Although only the opening of the Notebook's discussion can be presented here, this is especially interesting since it may represent significant aspects of Lipiner's lost dissertation (pp. 39–40):

> On the *Homunculus* scene: Whereas the archetypes among the Mothers represent the enduring, eternal string of the individual, so in Homunculus Goethe has captured the living, ongoing development [of the individual], his becoming, which the marvelous apotheosis at the end brings to a close, so that this work comprehends life like no other ever, for ever and ever.—
>
> The individual archetype, imagined before its entrance into becoming, into the world of appearance (an abstraction, like the archetypes in general, for a beginning of existence, as well as of its necessary correlates—appearance and becoming—cannot be envisaged) is what Aristotle names _Edos_ [*eidos*], the possibility to become. His ideal concept is confronted by the real: that of the living being, endowed with organs, which has already become, entered into appearance,—the _entelechy_. But it only exists in that it radiates its being, in that it acts, exercises *impact* and also receives it (also an active process), and without activity life is inconceivable. We find this profoundly expressed in the word real, reality, in which to be is combined with action.
>
> Now this essence of being, of activity, requires not only incessant motion, but ever-ascending motion, corresponding to the inherent purposiveness of every nature, against whose goals the individual ultimately cannot contend. Thus we already see in the short span of earthly life a constant higher development of being, which, considered from the perspective of the eternity of essence, constitutes itself as an uninterrupted stepladder of phases of being (of which this life is certainly not the first!).
>
> To bring the force of becoming that is in something that has not become, has not originated, into conception, Goethe created the *Homunculus* (for only thus could it be grasped!). As this half-engendered spirit, having been brought to the life-generating sea by *Proteus* (at the end of the classical

Walpurgisnacht), at last begins the path of development, it is in a distantly
subhuman phase (which, naturally, could only be represented Darwinically
in low forms of earthly life)—following which all intermediate stages up to
humanity and the unending succession beyond it are to be imagined.[23]

The relevance of the notebook to Gustav Mahler's understanding of *Faust* readily
emerges if we compare it to the famous letter of June 1909 wherein Mahler interprets the drama's closing lines for his wife Alma (see Figs. 15.6–15.9). Table 15.1

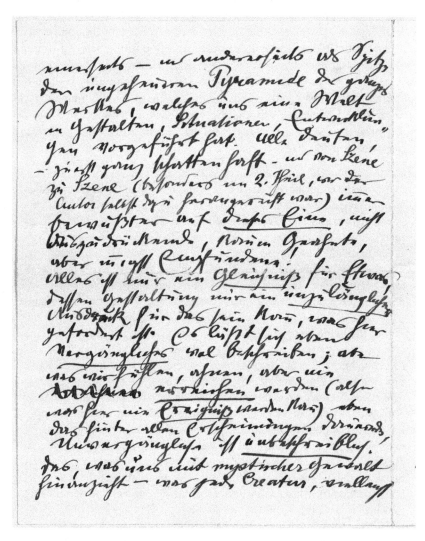

Fig. 15.6 Letter of [22 (?) June 1909] from Mahler to his wife Alma, p. [4]. Reproduced
by kind permission of the Pierpont Morgan Library, New York. Photography by
Graham S. Haber, 2012.

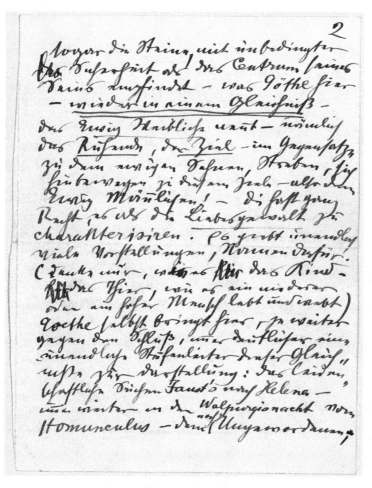

Fig. 15.7 Letter of [22 (?) June 1909] from Mahler to his wife Alma, bifolio 2 (= p. [5]). Reproduced by kind permission of the Pierpont Morgan Library, New York. Photography by Graham S. Haber, 2012.

(pp. 284–289) provides a transcription and translation of the Notebook's entire entry on the *Schlußszene*. By way of introduction, the reader should review three passages of the commentary concerning *das Ewig-Weibliche*: (a) lines 7367 ff., 'Thy secret,' etc: this is where Dr. Marianus, in great rapture, addresses the Mater Gloriosa thus: 'Highest sovereign of the world!/Allow me, in the blue,/Eye-filling heavenly canopy,/to behold your mystery/', and shortly afterward describes her as 'pure in the most beautiful sense'; (b) lines 7385–7401 concerning the penitent fallen women; and (c) lines 7464 ff.: this is the commentary on the concluding Chorus Mysticus.

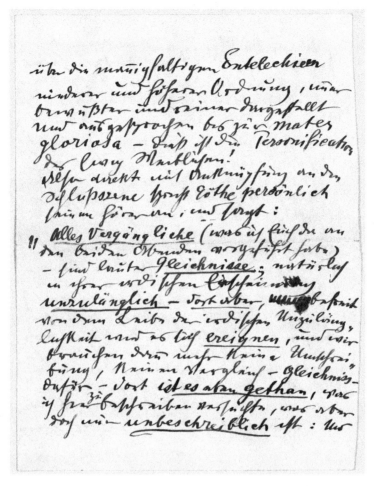

Fig. 15.8 Letter of [22 (?) June 1909] from Mahler to his wife Alma, p. [6]. Reproduced by kind permission of the Pierpont Morgan Library, New York. Photography by Graham S. Haber, 2012.

Table 15.2 (pp. 290–294) presents in four parallel columns, left to right, (1) portions of the German text of the Notebook; (2) the principal passage of Mahler's interpretive letter in German; (3) a translation of the Mahler passage; and (4) the relevant portions of the Notebook in English. The similarity between the two texts is striking: both identify the insufficiency of the allegory to present the indescribable, which is eternal; both characterise the Eternal Feminine in contrast to, yet as the blessed goal of, the eternal masculine striving and struggling to attain the goal of repose. Both allude to Homunculus and entelechy regarding the ascent up the unending stepladder (Stufenleiter) to higher levels of being, culminating in the perfection of the Mater Gloriosa.

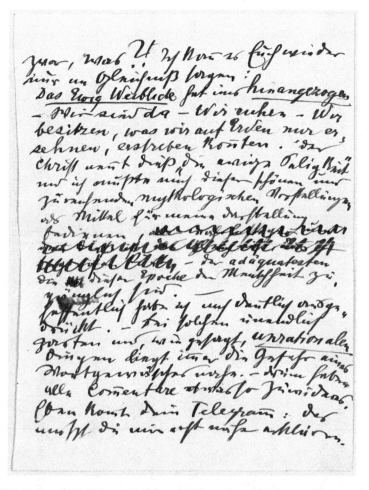

Fig. 15.9 Letter of [22 (?) June 1909] from Mahler to his wife Alma, p. [7]. Reproduced by kind permission of the Pierpont Morgan Library, New York. Photography by Graham S. Haber, 2012.

Both texts interpret Goethe to mean that the allegorical is and ultimately will be attainable. And both allude to the necessity for, and limited adequacy of, Christian symbolism to convey this ineffable vision.[24]

All things considered, the source of the notebook's contents was most probably Siegfried Lipiner. It was probably not Mahler himself, who tells Alma in the same 1909 letter that her own interpretation of the Chorus Mysticus is 'better than those of the distinguished commentators (which I haven't read, but I know that they've been breaking their teeth chewing on this for the past century)'.[25] Understandably, for Alma's sake, Mahler's *Faust* letter does not acknowledge Lipiner, with whom he had probably discussed the Chorus Mysticus

Table 15.1 From Justine Mahler's *Faust* Notebook, pp. 116–22, transl. Stephen E. Hefling and Friedrich Thiel

Bergschluchten Wald etc. Die gewaltige erhebende Gebirgscenerie mit den Gott begeisterten Einsiedlern leitet in großartigster Weise auf die Himmelsglorie zum Schlusse hin.	Mountain gorges, Forest, etc. The tremendous uplifting mountain scenery with the hermits inspired by God leads in the most magnificent way towards the heavenly glory at the end.
Chor und Echo, das in der Wortfolge des Anachoretenchors selbst herrlich gebildet ist, man achte darauf, wie viele *a* außer im viermal sich wiederholendem Endreim in den ersten Zeilen vorkommen, daß es wie oft nachhallendes, langes Echo klingt.	Chorus and Echo, that in the word order of the hermits' chorus itself is marvelously formed, one should take note in it of how many *a*'s occur in addition to the end rhyme repeated four times in the first lines, such that it sounds like a long, reverberating echo.
7214 Am Berge vom Winde bewegt.	Stirred by the wind on the mountain.
7221-2 Nach dem Worte des Herrn bei *Iesaias*, daß der Löwe wie ein Rind Stroh fressen wird, auf dem heiligen Berg Gottes. (D)	According to the word of the Lord in *Isaiah*, the lion will eat straw like a cow on God's holy mountain. (D[üntzer])
7224 Pater *Ecstaticus* (von *Exstasis*), die Kraft der Entzückung soll nach oft wiederkehrenden Legenden, den Ergriffenen schwebend über die Erde emporheben.	Pater *Ecstaticus* (from *ecstasy*), according to frequently recurring legends, the power of rapture is said to raise up floating above the earth the man who is seized by it.
7234 Pater *Profundus* wie der erste im glühenden Entzücken schaut dieser in mächtig tiefem Geiste Gott und die Welt.	Pater *Profundus* like the former [Pater Ecstaticus], in glowing rapture he beholds God and the world in tremendously deep spirit.
7236-43 Herrliches, dreifaches Gleichniss von der Allkraft der Liebe.	Splendid, threefold simile of the supreme power of love.
7244 Es ist um mich her	There is all around me [addition of word to original: "Ist um mich her . . ."]

7257 Die Schranken der beengenden Sinne vergleicht er dem Schmerz scharf angeschlossner [sic] Ketten. Genau heißt: Scharf angeschlossner Kettenschmerz, daß der Schmerz scharf angeschlossen ist, wie es dem von Fesseln bedrückten eigentlich erscheint.

7260 *Pater Serafctus*

In dem Wölkchen ahnt er den Chor seeliger Knaben, die um Mitternacht geboren (wol nach einem Volksaberglauben) gleich die Erde verlassen mußten. Ihre Organe für die Erde sind daher vollkommen unausgebildet, daß sie auf ihr nichts wahrzunehmen vermögen.

Er nimmt sie in sich etc Kann man sich etwas mystischeres denken? Und das ist der Göthe, den jeder Philister als den „Realisten" aufzuspielen wagt.

7280 wie wunderbar das ist!

7300-3 Sie haben von Fausts Ankunft im Himmel gehört und sind gekommen, ihn zu sehen.

7309-11 Schöne Zusammenfassung von Fausts Erettung [sic] und wodurch der zum Werden Bestimmte ihrer theilhaft wird.

He compares the barriers of our senses, which constrict us, to the pain of bitingly locked chains. Sharply locked chain pain means precisely: that the pain is tightly locked, as it actually seems to one who is oppressed by bonds.

Pater Serafctus

In the little cloud he senses the chorus of blessed boys who, born at midnight (probably according to a folk superstition), had to leave the earth immediately. Therefore their organs are completely undeveloped for the earth, with the result that they can never perceive anything on earth.

He assumes them into himself etc Can one conceive of anything more mystical? And that is the Goethe whom every Philistine dares to play up as "the realist."

How wonderful that is!

They have heard of Faust's arrival in heaven and have come to see him.

Beautiful summary of Faust's salvation and how he, the one predestined for becoming, will gain possession of it. [Or: . . . of Faust's salvation and the process by which mortals can attain salvation.]

(continued)

Table 15.1 Continued

7324 Wie er an Fausts Unsterblichen noch haftet. Je kräftiger eine Individualität ist, umso energischer, inniger wird sie sich an das Medium, in den Stoff der bestimmten Entwicklungsform— wir kennen nur die der Erde— gießen, oder wie Göthe sagt: Ihre Elemente an sich heran raffen, sich innigst in sie hinein verwachsen und sie noch festhalten, wenn sie ihre Bedeutung für ihn schon verloren haben, ja ihm hinderlich nachtheilig geworden sind, weil sein Wesen unter ihrer Hülle schon für eine neue, höhere Bildung herangereift ist. Sie von ihm zu trennen vermag nur die göttliche Liebe.	How he still clings to Faust's immortality. The more powerful an individual personality is, the more energetically, fervently will it impose itself upon the medium, upon the substance of the definite developmental form— we know only that of the earth—or as Goethe says: its [spiritual and physical] elements grab each other tightly; they most fervently grow closer together and hold fast, when they have already lost their significance for him, have even become hinderingly detrimental to him, because under their veil his being has already become ripe for a new, higher formation. Only divine love can separate them from him
7348. Die vollendetern [sic] Engel geben Fausts noch erdbeschwerte Seele den niedrigern, minder empfindlichen, seeligen Knaben.	The more perfect angels give Faust's soul, still encumbered by the earthly, to the lower, less sensitive, blessed boys.
7349 Zu steigendem Vollgewinn sei er bis zur Höherentfaltung zunächst diesen gesellt	For [word added] increasing attainment until the higher unfolding, let him for now be joined to them
7552 Puppenstand treffend für die noch untergeordnete Pfase seiner Entwicklung	Chrysalis state appropriate for the still subsidiary phase of his development
7354 Englisches Unterpfand durch den von Engeln ihnen anvertrauten Geist Fausts, hoffen sie selbst empor zu wachsen.	An angelic pledge: through the soul of Faust entrusted to them by the angels, they themselves hope to rise upwards.

7367 dein Geheimniß das religiöse Mysterium der unbefleckten Jungfrau; aber dann auch das Wunder des Weibes überhaupt (nicht wie es sich unvollkommen auf Erden darstellt, sondern in seinem höchsten Idealbild betrachtet) welches in Schönheit und innerer Harmonie, in Ruhe und vollendeter Rundung dasjenige ist, was der Mann kämpfend und werdend, suchend und irrend immerfort anstrebt, dessen Schönheit ihm Ziel und Ansporn, und dessen Erreichen ihm beschlossene Seligkeit ist.

7379 Rein — im schönsten Sinn wie Göthe aufrichtig hinzusetzt, der ja an das Mysterium der unbefleckten Empfängniß nicht glaubt, aber die Reinheit des nicht zu befleckenden (wenn aus wahrer Liebe hingegebenen) Weibes verehrt.

Nach 7382 muß ein Absatz sein, wie auch hier das Versmaß ganz neu einsetzt, ebenso nach 7389

7385 Büßerin[n]en (*Magna peccatrix* etc.) nahen sich in einer Wolke den Füßen Marias, um für Gretchen zu bitten

7390-7401 Daß Wesen, die sich in wahrhafter, innigster, schönster Empfindung dem geliebten Manne hingegeben haben, wie Gretchen, als Sünderinnen, Gnad= und Bußbedürftige betrachtet werden, ist ja absurd und jeder höhern Auffassung entgegen; aber Göthe konnte sich vom Boden der katholisch-kirchlichen Anschauungsweise, auf der er hier fußt, nicht entfernen, und mußte dies daher in seiner Art gelten lassen. Übrigens ist es im Werke selbst im höchsten Sinne ausgeglichen, wenn dasselbe sühnebedürftige Gretchen zur Führerin des Geliebten an den Gottesthron wird.

Thy secret the religious mystery of the undefiled Virgin; but then also the miracle of woman in general (not as it manifests itself imperfectly on the earth, but considered in its highest ideal image), which in beauty and inner harmony, in peace and perfected roundedness, is that which a man, struggling and becoming, seeking and erring, evermore strives towards, whose beauty is to him the goal and incentive, and whose attainment is for him concluded blessedness.

Pure — in the most beautiful sense as Goethe sincerely adds it—he who of course does not believe in the mystery of immaculate conception, but honors the purity of the woman who is not to be defiled (if she surrenders herself out of true love).

After 7382 there must be a paragraph break, since here the meter resumes completely anew; same after 7389

Female Penitents (Magna peccatrix, etc.) in a cloud approach Mary's feet, in order to plead for Gretchen

That beings who in true, most fervent, most beautiful feeling have surrendered to the beloved man, such as Gretchen, should be regarded as penitents, women in need of mercy and repentance, is of course absurd and contrary to every higher conception; but Goethe could not get away from the foundation of the Catholic-ecclesiastical viewpoint on which he is based here, and had to let these notions prevail in his own way. It is, incidentally, in the work itself consistent in the highest sense when the same Gretchen who is in need of atonement becomes the leader of the beloved to the throne of God.

(continued)

Table 15.1 Continued

7401 *mater gloriosa*, schwebt einher — welches Bild!	*Mater gloriosa* floats in— what an image!
7404 Als Führsprecherinnen, Mittlerinnen bei der *mater gloriosa* für Gretchen erscheinen drei Liebessünderinnen (von denen der beiden ersten das *Evangelium*, der dritten die *acta sanctorium* erwähnt) die durch lange heilige Büße sich entsühnten.	As advocates, mediators for Gretchen before the *mater gloriosa*, three fallen women appear (of these, the first two are mentioned in the gospel, the third in the *lives of the saints*). They are absolving themselves through long holy penitence.
Die *magna peccatrix* wie sie Göthe nennt, *Maria Magdalena* (siehe St *Lucä* 7) die *mulier samaritana*, das samaritische Weib (siehSt J IV [sic])	The *magna peccatrix* as Goethe calls her, *Mary Magdalene* (see *Luke* 7); the *mulier samaritana*, the Samaritan woman (see J[ohn] 4)
7415 Der Brunnen, an dem das samaritische Weib *Jesus* zu trinken gab, den Göthe bis in Abrahams, des jüdischen Erzvaters Zeit zurückführt.	The well at which the Samaritan woman gave *Jesus* a drink, which Goethe traces back to the time of the Jewish patriarch Abraham.
7419 Die Quelle, welche sich von dorther nun durch alle Welten gießet, ist nach Christus "sein Wasser" das Wort Gottes, welches zur Ewigkeit führt.	The spring, which from then and there has been flowing through all creation, is according to Christ "his water," the word of God that leads to eternity.
7438 Ungemessen, nicht „angemessen" ist hier geboten zu corrigieren, nach dem unbedingten Erforderniß des Sinnes. (Der Fehler hat sich wahrscheinlich beim Schreiben Riemers nach Göthes Diktiren eingeschlichen).	Unmeasured, not "appropriate," must be corrected here, in accordance with the implicit requirement of the meaning. (The error probably crept in through Riemer's writing from Goethe's dictation.)
7439 klingt an das Gebet Gretchens vor der *mater dolorosa*, im ersten Theile an.	Echoes Gretchen's prayer before the *mater dolorosa* in the first section.
7460-1 Im neuen, hohen Leben erblüht er mit erneuter Jugendkraft.	In the new, elevated life he blooms with renewed youthful strength.

How inexpressibly lofty, holy, and dignified is the treatment of the *mater gloriosa* in the few words that she speaks.

Chorus mysticus the united spirit throngs of heaven.

At whatever stage of being something may be grasped (even in the foremost, most elevated image of the heavenly sphere), it is at best only an allegory in comparison to the final, eternal, divine ~~life~~ essence of all being.

The insufficient (completely opposite to the usual sense); the unattainable, that which extends beyond the boundaries of human understanding, the unreachable, has occurred here (in this scene) before us.

The indescribable, because it is that which is not to be grasped in its truth, but only in simile [or allegory].

The Eternal Feminine: which is to be understood from the above-mentioned antithesis: of roundedness, perfection, harmony, and beauty, as opposed to the unfinished, striving, struggling, becoming [constantly changing], masculine.

A particular sense and weight is therein additionally placed upon the eternal: that this feminine [principle] is under no circumstances the incomplete, earthly-temporal

---

7464-5 Wie unsagbar hoh, heilig und würdevoll die *mater gloriosa* in den wenigen Worten, die sie spricht, gehalten ist.

chorus mysticus die vereinigten Geisterschaaren des Himmels.

7474-5 Auf welcher Stufe des Werdens etwas erfaßt sei, (auch in dem voranstehenden, erhabendsten Bild der Himmelssphäre), es verhält sich nur wie ein Gleichniß zum letzten, ewigen, göttlichen ~~Leben~~ Wesen alles Seins.

7476-7 das Unzulängliche (vollkommen entgegengesetzt dem gewöhnlichen Sinne); das nicht zu Erlangende, das über die Grenzen des menschlichen Verständnisses Hinausgehende, das Unerreichliche hat sich hier (in dieser Scene) vor uns ereignet.

7478-9 das Unbeschreibliche, weil nicht in seiner Wahrheit, nur im Gleichniß zu Erfassende.

7480 das ewig Weibliche, welches aus dem oben bemerkten Gegensatze: der Rundung, Vollendung, Harmonie und Schönheit, zu dem Unfertigen, Strebenden, Ringenden, Werdenden, Männlichen zu begreifen ist.

Ein besonderer Sinn und Gewicht ist noch darin auf das ewig gelegt: das[s] dieses Weibliche eben nicht das Unvollkommene, Irdisch-Zeitliche ist

---

Reproduced by kind permission of the Mahler-Rosé Collection, Gustav Mahler-Alfred Rosé Room, Music Library, University of Western Ontario.

NOTE: Italics are used to indicate the change from Kurrentschrift to Latin script; underlining is reproduced as in the original manuscripts.

Table 15.2 Comparison of 'Schlußszene' passages in Justine's Notebook to Mahler's 1909 *Faust* Letter

Justine's Notebook	Mahler	Justine's Notebook	Mahler
7474-5 Auf welcher Stufe des Werdens etwas erfaßt sei, (auch in dem voranstehenden, erhabendsten Bild der Himmelssphäre), es verhält sich nur wie ein Gleichniß zum letzten, ewigen, göttlichen Wesen alles Seins.	Alles ist nun ein <u>Gleichniß</u>, für Etwas, dessen Gestaltung nur ein <u>unzulänglicher</u> Ausdruck für das sein kann, was hier gefordert ist. Es läßt sich eben <u>Vergängliches</u> wol beschreiben; aber was wir fühlen, ahnen, aber nie erreichen werden (also was hier ein <u>Ereigniß</u> werden kann) eben das hinter allen Erscheinungen Dauernde, Unvergängliche ist <u>unbeschreiblich</u>.	7474-5 At whatever stage of being something may be grasped (even in the foremost, most elevated image of the heavenly sphere), it is at best only an allegory in comparison to the final, eternal, divine essence of all being.	So here everything is an <u>allegory</u> for something whose formation can only be an <u>insufficient</u> expression of what is postulated here. The transitory of course lends itself to description; but what we feel, intuit, yet will never <u>reach</u> (which in any case can here become an <u>event</u>) precisely what is lasting and imperishable behind all appearances, is <u>indescribable</u>.
7478-9 das <u>Unbeschreibliche</u>, weil nicht in seiner Wahrheit, nur in Gleichniß zu Erfassende.		7478-9 <u>The indescribable</u>, because it is that which is not to be grasped in its truth, but only in simile [or allegory].	

(continued)

7367 Thy secret [i.e., of the Mater Gloriosa] the religious mystery of the undefiled Virgin; but then also the miracle of woman in general (not as it manifests itself imperfectly on the earth, but considered in its highest ideal image), which in beauty and inner harmony, in peace and perfected roundedness, is that which a man, struggling and becoming, seeking and erring, evermore strives towards, whose beauty is to him the goal and incentive, and whose attainment is for him concluded blessedness.

That which draws us upwards with *mystical* power— which every *creature*, perhaps even the stones, feels with unconditional certainty as the center of its being—which *Goethe* here— again in a metaphor— calls the Eternal Feminine—namely the resting point, the goal— in contrast to the eternal longing, striving, self-propulsion to this goal— i. e., the Eternal Masculine!—you are quite right to *characterise* it as the love force.

7480 The Eternal Feminine: which is to be understood from the above-mentioned antitheses: of roundedness, perfection, harmony, and beauty, as opposed to the unfinished, striving, struggling, becoming [constantly changing], masculine.

7367 dein Geheimniß [d.h., der Mater Gloriosa] das religiöse Mysterium der unbefleckten Jungfrau; dann aber auch das Wunder des Weibes überhaupt (nicht wie es sich unvollkommen auf Erden darstellt, sondern in seinem höchsten Idealbild betrachtet) welches in Schönheit und innerer Harmonie, in Ruhe und vollendeter Rundung dasjenige ist, was der Mann kämpfend und werdend, suchend und irrend immerfort anstrebt, dessen Schönheit ihm Ziel und Ansporn, und dessen Erreichen ihm beschlossene Seligkeit ist.

Das, was uns mit *mystischer* Gewalt hinanzieht— was jede *Creatur*, vielleicht sogar die Steine, mit unbedingter Sicherheit als das *Centrum* seines Seins empfindet — was *Göthe* hier— wieder in einem Gleichniß — das Ewig Weibliche nennt— nämlich das Ruhende, der [sic] *Ziel*— im Gegensatze zu dem ewigen Sehnen, Streben, sich Hinbewegen zu diesem Ziele— also dem Ewig Männlichen!— Du hast ganz recht, es als die Liebesgewalt zu *charakterisiren*.

7480 das ewig Weibliche, welches aus dem oben bemerkten Gegensätze: die Rundung, Vollendung, Harmonie und Schönheit, zu dem Unfertigen, Strebenden, Ringenden, Werdenden, Männlichen zu begreifen ist.

Table 15.2 Continued

Justine's Notebook	Mahler	Mahler	Justine's Notebook
pp. 39–40: [. . .] so hat Göthe im Homunculus die lebendige Fortentwicklung [des Individuums], sein Werden erfaßt, woran sich zum Ende die herrliche Apotheose schließt, so daß dieses Werk, wie kein anderes je, von Ewigkeit zu Ewigkeit das Leben begreift.— [. . .] die *Entelechie* [. . .] aber ist nur, indem sie ihr Sein ausstrahlt, indem sie *thut*, Wirkung übt und empfängt (auch ein thätiger Vorgang) und ohne Activität ist kein Leben zu denken. [. . .] Nun bedingt dieses Wesen des Seins, der Thätigkeit nicht nur fortwährende Bewegung, sondern immer *aufsteigende* Bewegung, entsprechend der innewohnenden Zweckmäßigkeit einer jeden Natur, gegen deren Ziele das Individuum zuletzt nicht streiten kann. So sehen wir schon im kurzen Erdenlauf eine stete Höherentwicklung des Seins, die, auf die Ewigkeit des Wesens hin betrachtet, sich als eine ununterbrachene Stufenleiter von Werdephasen (deren erste dies Leben gewiss nicht ist!) darstellt.	Es gibt unendlich viele Vorstellungen, Namen dafür. (Denke nur, wie [= written over 'was'] es für das Kind—für das Thier, wie es ein niederer oder ein hoher Mensch lebt und webt)[.] Goethe selbst bringt hier, je weiter gegen den Schluß, immer deutlicher eine unendliche Stufenleiter dieser Gleichniße zur Darstellung; das leidenschaftliche Suchen *Faust's* nach *Helena*— immer weiter in der *Walpurgisnacht* vom *Homunculus*— dem noch Ungewordenen,— über die mannigfaltigen *Entelechieen* niederer und höherer Ordnung, immer bewußter und reiner dargestellt und ausgesprochen bis zur *mater gloriosa*— dieß ist die *Personification* des Ewig Weiblichen! Also direkt mit Anknüpfung an die *Schlußszene* spricht Göthe *persönlich* seinen Hörer an, und sagt:	There are unendingly many of representations, names for it. (Just think how a child— an animal, how a lower or higher person 'lives and moves'). The closer he gets to the end, Goethe himself presents ever more clearly an unending step-ladder of these allegories; *Faust's* passionate pursuit of *Helena*—further onward in the *Walpurgisnacht* by the *Homunculus*— who has not yet come into being— through the numerous *entelechies* of lower and higher order, ever more convincingly and purely represented and declaimed, right up to the *mater gloriosa*— this is the *personification* of the Eternal Feminine! Thus, directly in connection to the final scene, Goethe speaks *personally* to his listeners and says:	pp. 39–40 [. . .] so in Homunculus Goethe has captured the living ongoing development [of the individual], his being, which the marvelous apotheosis at the end brings to a close, so that this work comprehends life, like no other ever, for ever and ever.— [. . .] *entelechy* [. . .] only *exists* in that it radiates its being, in that it *acts*, exercises impact and receives it (also an active process), and without activity life is inconceivable. [. . .] Now this essence of being, of activity, requires not only incessant motion, but ever-ascending motion, corresponding to the inherent purposiveness of every nature, against whose goals the individual ultimately cannot contend. Thus we already see in the short span of life a constant higher development of being, which, considered from the perspective of the eternity of essence, constitutes itself as an uninterrupted stepladder of phases of being (of which this life is certainly not the first!).

7474-5 Auf welcher Stufe des Werdens etwas erfaßt sei, (auch in dem voranstehenden, erhabendsten Bild der Himmelssphäre), es verhält sich nur wie ein Gleichniß zum letzten, ewigen, göttlichen ~~Leben~~ Wesen alles Seins.

7478-9 das Unbeschreibliche, weil nicht in seiner Wahrheit, nur in Gleichniß zu Erfassende.

7476-7 das Unzulängliche (vollkommen entgegen-gesetzt dem gewöhnlichen Sinne); das nicht zu Erlangende, das über die Grenzen des menschlichen Verständnisses Hinausgehende, das Unerreichliche hat sich hier (in dieser Scene) vor uns ereignet.

„*Alles Vergängliche* (was ich Euch da an den beiden Abenden vorgeführt habe)— sind lauter *Gleichnisse*; natürlich in ihrer irdischen Erscheinung <u>*unzulänglich*</u>— <u>dort aber</u>, befreit von dem Leibe der irdischen Unzulänglichkeit wird es sich <u>*ereignen*</u>, und wir brauchen dann mehr keine Umschreibung, keinen Vergleich — *Gleichniss* — *Gleichniss* — dafür — dort *ist es eben gethan*, was ich hier zu beschreiben versuchte, was aber doch nur <u>*unbeschreiblich*</u> ist: Und zwar, was?! Ich kann es Euch wieder nur im Gleichniß sagen:

7474-5 At whatever stage of being something may be grasped (even in the foremost, most elevated image of the heavenly sphere), it is at best only an allegory in comparison to the final, eternal, divine ~~life~~ essence of all being.

7478-9 <u>The indescribable</u>, because it is that which is not to be grasped in its truth, but only in simile [or allegory].

7476-7 <u>The insufficient</u> (completely opposite to the usual sense); the unattainable, that which extends beyond the boundaries of human understanding, the unreachable, has occurred here (in this scene) before us.

"<u>*Everything transitory*</u> (which I have presented to you on both evenings)— is nothing but *allegories*; naturally in their earthly manifestation they are <u>*insufficient*</u>—<u>but there</u>, freed from the body of earthly insufficiency, it will become <u>*actual*</u>, and then we no longer need any circumlocution, any comparison—*allegory*—for it — there *it is really accomplished*, that which I attempted to describe here, but which is just <u>*indescribable*</u>: and what in fact is it?! I can only once again tell you in allegory:

(continued)

Table 15.2 Continued

Justine's Notebook	Mahler	Mahler	Justine's Notebook
7367 [Das Ewig Weibliche] ist, was der Mann kämpfend und werdend, suchend und irrend immerfort anstrebt, dessen Schönheit ihm Ziel und Ansporn, und dessen Erreichen ihm beschlossene Seligkeit ist. 7390-7401 [bez. der Büßerinen] [...] aber Göthe konnte sich vom Boden der katholisch-kirchlichen Anschauungsweise, auf der er hier fußt, nicht entfernen, und mußte dies daher in seiner Art gelten lassen.	*Das Ewig Weibliche* hat uns *hinangezogen*— Wir sind *da*— Wir ruhen— *Wir besitzen, was wir auf Erden nur ersehnen, erstreben* konnten. Der *Christ* nennt dieß „die ewige Seligkeit" und ich mußte mich dieser schönen und zureichenden *mythologischen* Vorstellungen als Mittel für meine Darstellung bedienen [...] der *adäquatesten*, die dieser *Epoche* der Menschheit zugänglich sind.["]—	*The Eternal Feminine* has *drawn* us *upward*— We are *there*— We are at rest— We possess that for which we could only long and strive on earth. *Christ* calls this 'eternal blessedness'; and I had to avail myself of these beautiful and adequate *mythological* ideas as the means for my presentation [...] the most *adequate* that are available to this *epoch* of humanity."—	7367 [The Eternal Feminine] is that which a man, struggling and becoming, seeking and erring, evermore strives towards, whose beauty is to him the goal and incentive, and whose attainment is for him concluded blessedness. 7390-7401 [re: penitent women] [...] but Goethe could not get away from the foundation of the Catholic-ecclesiastical viewpoint on which he is based here, and had to let these notions prevail in his own way.

Mahler's letter is reproduced through kind permission of the Pierpont Morgan Library, New York.

NOTE: Italics are used to indicate the change from Kurrentschrift to Latin script; underlining is reproduced as in the original manuscripts.

well before 1901. And in the spring of 1909, thanks to Bruno Walter, the two had become reconciled[26]— just weeks before Mahler's *Faust* letter; perhaps he and Lipiner had spoken of Goethe's masterpiece only recently.

Mahler's letter has loomed large in discussions of the Eighth Symphony since the twentieth century's second decade. For two recent examples: Christian Wildhagen places it on a plane with the creativity of the symphony itself, whereby it constitutes a suggestive biographical contrafactum scarcely separable from the musical work.[27] And Jens Malte Fischer declares, 'It is an altogether exceptional piece of exegesis, written without any knowledge of existing commentaries or secondary literature.'[28] The close correspondence between Justi's *Faust* Notebook and Mahler's *Faust* letter suggests that future exegesis might further consider that Mahler's interpretation of the *Schlußszene*, verbally and musically, may well date as far back as the mid 1870s, to his earliest encounters with Lipiner, during the multi-faceted discussions of the Pernerstorfer circle, which, we now know, were highly influential upon Mahler's first three symphonies as well as *Das Lied von der Erde*.

Notes

1. The author is grateful to the Mahler-Rosé Collection, the Gustav Mahler-Alfred Rosé Room, the Music Library, the University of Western Ontario, and especially to Music Librarian Lisa Philpott.

2. See McClatchie, *The Mahler Family Letters*; German edn., *'Liebste Justi!' Briefe an die Familie*.

3. See McClatchie, "The Gustav Mahler – Alfred Rosé Collection", 385–86.

4. See Blaukopf, *Gustav Mahler Briefe*, 2nd rev. edn., 263–65.

5. '"Kommentar zum II. Faust," nach Lipiners Worten, unmittelbar nach dem Lesen aufgeschrieben, und . . . von ihm gelesen und über die getreue Wiedergabe gelobt, daher <u>nichts</u> daran zu ändern ist.' In "Natalie Bauer-Lechner: Wunsch und Vermächtnis," typescript, Paris, Médiathèque Musicale Mahler; see also *Gustav Mahler in den Erinnerungen von Natalie Bauer-Lechner*, 11.

6. Walter, *Theme and Variations*, 146–47.

7. Natorp, "Vorwort", 5.

8. As late as 1936 a copy of this work remained in Lipiner's Nachlaß in Vienna, and it is briefly cited in Ida Schein, "Die Gedanken- und Ideenwelt Siegfried Lipiners".

9. Walter, *Theme and Variations*, 146.

10. See Emma Adler, "Biografie Victor Adlers", 1115, and de La Grange, *Gustav Mahler: Chronique d'une vie* I, 327–28. The date of Bauer-Lechner's divorce is confirmed in *Stammbuch des Buchhändlers Michael Lechner* [n.p., n.d.], a copy of which is located at the Médiathèque Musicale Mahler, Paris. Further on the relationship between Bauer-Lechner and Lipiner, see Solvik and Hefling, "Natalie Bauer-Lechner on Mahler and Women", 39–40 and 61–62, fn. 54.

11. 'Denn was ich der Gottheit am meisten danke, ist, daß sie meinem Leben diese beiden größten Geister, <u>Lipiner und Mahler</u>, begegnen ließ . . .'

12. Lipiner, "Die künstlerische Neuerung in Goethe's 'Faust'", 2.

13. '. . . die Urquellen alles Lebens', 27.

14. '. . . die [= Goethes Wort- und Satzbildung] aber niemals subjektivisch und willkürlich, sondern immer aus dem echten volksthümlichen Geiste der Sprache herausgeschaffen sein werden. Durch diese Freiheit gewinnt seine Sprache den kräftigsten unmittelbarsten Ausdruck', 63.

15. 11 (for complete German text, English translation, and commentary, see bibliography).

16. 'Damit erreicht Göthe zugleich ein Allerwichtigstes. Er führt uns die <u>Bese[e]lung, die Allbegeisterung</u> der Natur, welche den Alten unmittelbarer Glauben war und auf welche die vorgeschrittenste Naturanschauung notwendig zurückkommen muß, in lebendigem Geschehen vor Aügen', 92. The Notebook transcriptions presented here use italics where Justine has changed from Kurrentschrift to Latin script; underlining replicates the manuscript.

17. 'Was einer im Leben geworden ist, das nimmt er mit ins Jenseits hinüber und je nach der höhern und niedrigern mehr oder minder ausgeprägten Individualität wird ihm eine höhere oder niedrigere Daseinsform zu Theil werden', 92. Page 14 of the notebook contains a similar observation. Bauer-Lechner, *Fragmente*, 125–26, records a closely related discussion between Lipiner and Bruno Walter, and links it directly to Part II of *Faust*.

18. Heinrich Düntzer, *Goethes Werke, Zwölfter Teil*, 212.

19. '12. März 1906. / Sehr geehrte gnädige Frau! / Ich habe keinen Commentar zu Faust geschrieben, sondern vor langen Jahren über das Werk gesprochen. Sie mögen eine Niederschrift in Händen gehabt haben, die darnach gemacht worden ist, — die ich nicht controlliert habe, für denen Inhalt also ich Verdienst und Verantwortlichkeit ablehnen muss. Und was in ihr unzweifelhaft auf meine Rechnung kommt, das würde ich heute grösstenteils mit Spott abtun: so ganz ander[s] sehe ich jetzt, wie Welt und Leben überhaupt, so auch die Kunst und speciell dieses Werk der Kunst. Das Centrale, das weitaus Bedeutendste, vielleicht einzig wirklich Grosse im Faust wird meines Erachtens nicht verstanden; und da hilft auch "mein" Commentar nichts; denn als er entstand, habe auch <u>ich</u> es nicht verstanden! —Unter solchen Umständen wäre es nicht ganz ehrlich, wenn ich Ihre liebenswürdige Anerkennung ohne Weiteres entgegennähme: ich verdiene sie nicht. Was mich freilich der Pflicht enthebt, für Ihre so überaus freundlichen Worte bestens zu danken. / Hochachtungsvoll ergebenst / S. Lipiner.' Typescript copy, Internationale Gustav Mahler Gesellschaft, Vienna.

20. Boyle, "Goethe, Johann Wolfgang von".

21. Düntzer, *Göthe's Faust in seiner Einheit und Ganzheit*, 15 [and later eds.].

22. See Schwerte, *Faust und das Faustische*, esp. 148–62; Mandelkow, *Goethe im Urteil seiner Kritiker*, xxxiv–xli; and Schmidt, *Goethes Faust: Erster und zweiter Teil*, 312–13.

23. Zur *Homunculusscene*: Stellen die Urbilder bei den Müttern die bleibende, ewige Saite des Individuums dar, so hat Göthe im Homunculus die lebendige

Fortentwicklung, sein Werden erfaßt, woran sich zum Ende die herrliche Apotheose schließt, so daß dieses Werk, wie kein anderes je, von Ewigkeit zu Ewigkeit das Leben begreift.—

Das individuelle Urbild vor seinem Eintritte ins Werden, in die Erscheinungswelt gedacht (ein Abstraction, wie die Urbilder überhaupt, denn es kann ein Anfang von Existens, also auch von Erscheinen und Werden ihre notwendigen Correllate [i.e., Korrelate] nicht vorgestellt werden)—ist, was Aristoteles *Edos*, Möglichkeit zu werden nennt. Seinem idealen Begriffe steht der reale: des bereits gewordene, in die Erscheinung eingegangenen, mit Organen ausgestatteten Lebewesens, die *Entelechie*, gegenüber. Sie aber ist nur, indem sie ihr Sein ausstrahlt, indem sie thut, Wirkung übt und empfängt (auch ein thätiger Vorgang) und ohne Activität ist kein Leben zu denken. Tiefsinnig finden wir das im Worte wirklich, Wirklichkeit ausgedrückt, in welchem sein mit Wirken zusammenfällt.

Nun bedingt dieses Wesen des Seins, der Thätigkeit nicht nur fortwährende Bewegung, sondern immer aufsteigende Bewegung, entsprechend der innewohnenden Zweckmäßigkeit einer jeden Natur, gegen deren Ziele das Individuum zuletzt nicht streiten kann. So sehen wir schon im kurzen Erdenlauf eine stete Höherentwicklung des Seins, die, auf die Ewigkeit der Wesen hin betrachtet, sich als eine ununterbrochene Stufenleiter von Werdephasen (deren erste dies Leben gewiss nicht ist!) darstellt.

Den Werdedrang in einem Ungewordenen, Unentstandenen zur Anschauung zu bringen (denn nur so ließ er sich fassen!) hat Göthe den *Homunculus* geschaffen. Da dieser halbgewordene Geist den Entwicklungsgang, von *Protheus* (Ende der klassischen Walpurgisnacht) ans Leben erzeugende Meer gebracht, endlich beginnt, ist dies in einer weit untermenschlichen Phase (Was natürlich nur in niedrigen Lebensformen der Erde Darwin[i]stisch dargestellt werden konnte)—welcher folgend alle Zwischenstufen bis zum Menschen und die unendliche Reihe darüber hinaus, zu denken sind.

24. This last notion would seem to recall Goethe's admission to Eckermann (6 June 1831) that in the conclusion of *Faust* he resorted to figures and images from Christianity to avoid becoming lost in vagueness; see Eckermann, *Gespräche mit Goethe*, pt. 2, 350.

25. de La Grange and Weiß, *Ein Gluck ohne Ruh'*, 379; de La Grange and Weiß, *Gustav Mahler: Letters to His Wife*, 318.

26. See Walter, "Gustav Mahlers Weg: Ein Erinnerungsblatt" and de La Grange, *Gustav Mahler*, Vol. 4, 440–41.

27. *Die Achte Symphonie von Gustav Mahler*, 159.

28. Fischer, *Gustav Mahler*, 406. Apparently only de La Grange and Weiß (*Ein Gluck ohne Ruh'*, 390; *Gustav Mahler: Letters to His Wife*, 328) have suggested, albeit without specific documentation, that Lipiner's interpretive views may have influenced Mahler's *Faust* letter.

16

Abridging Mahler's Symphonies

A Historical Perspective

Matthew Mugmon

The recent towering edition of Péter Fülöp's (2010) *Mahler Discography* reveals that a hundred years after Gustav Mahler's death, scholars, critics, and audiences have taken for granted their opportunities to hear recorded interpretations of the Austrian composer's symphonies in complete form. The few entries listed in the *Discography* in which conductors have shortened certain movements stand out as oddities against the background of unabridged realisations of these works.[1] Of the more than 150 recordings of the Second Symphony whose timings are included in Fülöp's catalog, for instance, only two are noted as having been abridged.[2] Just as telling as the small number of abbreviated renditions on record are the dates of those that were trimmed down; the most recent version of any Mahler symphony to be publicly available on record with an abridged movement, as performed by a symphony orchestra (and not counting ignored repeats in the First and Sixth symphonies) was a recording of a 1969 concert of the Sixth Symphony conducted by Heinz Bongartz.[3]

When commentators look back at those recordings of Mahler's symphonies that do contain cuts, they tend to do so with bewilderment, derision, and protest against a perceived intellectual crime. In an article on performance practice in Mahler's Fifth Symphony, Paul Banks called one of Hermann Scherchen's infamous performances of the Fifth Symphony in the 1960s, in which the conductor made significant cuts in the third and fifth movements, a 'travesty' and a 'fraud'.[4] In a catalogue of Mahler recordings, Lewis M. Smoley considered Scherchen to have presented 'an abusive reading' of the Fifth Symphony in his 'massacring' of the work, and that the conductor had 'little respect for Mahler's score'.[5] Scherchen indeed had eliminated large sections of

I am deeply grateful to Martin Burlingame, Bridget Carr, Barbara Perkel, John Perkel, Charlotte Kolczynski, Frank Villella, Phillip Huscher, Eric Moskowitz, and Lisa Tuite for their generous assistance. I also wish to thank Carol J. Oja, Thomas Forrest Kelly, Alexander Rehding, Elizabeth Craft, Glenda Goodman, Luci Mok, Anne Searcy, and Hannah Lewis for their helpful comments on versions of this chapter, as well as Jeremy Barham and others involved in the Mahler Centenary Conference at the University of Surrey in July 2011, where this material was first presented.

the third and fifth movements, but even smaller cuts have been seen to invalidate entire recordings. The Polish conductor Paul Kletzki's cut toward the end of the finale of Mahler's First Symphony prevented Smoley from recommending Kletzki's interpretation.[6] In David Pickett's study of Mahler recordings, the author considered the tape of Dimitri Mitropoulos's performance of Mahler's Third Symphony with the New York Philharmonic from 15 April 1956 to be 'best forgotten' due partly to deletions in three movements that Mitropoulos 'allowed himself to make'.[7] And Smoley considered Mitropoulos's cuts here as among 'the most unforgivable commissions' in what he called a 'pitiful performance' to be 'relegated to oblivion of the archive shelves'.[8]

On the surface, Fülöp's catalogue and the recent reactions to those abridged performances would seem to suggest that abbreviations in Mahler's symphonies were anomalous in the long performance history of his music. But the story is far more complex. Focusing specifically on the United States, which became home to several important Mahler conductors with transnational reputations during the twentieth century, it becomes clear through newspaper reviews and other archival materials that abridging Mahler's symphonies was once a common practice. This included American premieres. Ernst Kunwald shortened Mahler's Third Symphony when he led the first American performance in 1914 with the Cincinnati Symphony Orchestra, and Frederick Stock did the same with Mahler's Seventh in its American premiere in 1921 with the Chicago Symphony Orchestra.[9] Later, the Hungarian conductor Ernö Rapée shortened the Eighth Symphony in a highly anticipated concert with the Radio City Music Hall Symphony Orchestra in 1942, which was broadcast to Latin America.[10]

Indeed, the practice of abridging Mahler's works was once so typical that it ought to be considered not with censorious handwringing but rather as an opportunity to clarify its historical context. Here I focus on two sets of concerts as case studies: the Austrian conductor Wilhelm Gericke's performances of Mahler's Fifth Symphony in 1906 with the Boston Symphony Orchestra (BSO), which marked the first time the work was heard in several major US cities; and Serge Koussevitzky's performances of the Ninth Symphony with the same group in Boston and New York between 1931 and 1941, which included the American premiere. In Gericke's case, Mahler himself sent revisions to be incorporated into Gericke's performance of the Fifth Symphony, but Gericke also made cuts in the work. In 1931 and afterward, scores and orchestral part books show that Koussevitzky, known in his time as one of America's leading Mahler advocates, regularly conducted Mahler's Ninth Symphony with deletions in the first three movements. By shortening Mahler's Ninth, Koussevitzky made choices that aligned with his views about a conductor's authority to interpret a musical text. And both Gericke and Koussevitzky tempered Mahler's reputation for having composed inaccessibly long symphonies.

In addition to shedding new light on a forgotten but once-prevalent practice in the performance of Mahler's music, this research raises larger issues within the study of performance practice. Lurking beneath criticisms of abridged performances of works by any composer is the assumption that by condensing or otherwise significantly altering a complete artwork, performers carelessly and unjustifiably violate the composer's intentions or the integrity of a composition. This is an especially attractive assumption in the case of Mahler, who left a surfeit of score directions and other evidence about how he likely understood, conducted, and expected others to perform his own music.[11] But whatever specific performance decisions Mahler himself might or might not have endorsed, the cases of Gericke and Koussevitzky show that in contrast to today's typical view of Mahler's symphonies as inviolably complete works of art, a major concern in the early twentieth century was the basic necessity of transmitting those works in the concert hall. In this sense, abridgement of Mahler's works may be profitably viewed as part of what Richard Taruskin has called an oral tradition in Western art music—a tradition of which, as I show in the following, archival documentation of performances exposes a lost but significant part.[12] Sources such as conducting scores and orchestral parts expand discussions of performance practice beyond how Mahler's music, and that by other composers, supposedly *should have been* performed to include, instead, the significance of how it once *was* communicated to audiences.

Wilhelm Gericke and Mahler's Fifth Symphony

In 1906, when the Austrian conductor Wilhelm Gericke led performances of Mahler's Fifth Symphony in Boston and on tour in New York, Philadelphia, and Baltimore, Mahler's music was quite new to the United States and had sparked passionate responses, both positive and negative. The Fifth Symphony had its American premiere in Cincinnati on 24 March 1905 and was only the second of Mahler's symphonies to have been heard in the United States. It was less than two years earlier, on 6 November 1904, that Walter Damrosch and the New York Symphony Orchestra led the Fourth Symphony in the first concert of any music by Mahler in the United States.[13]

As Mahler's published letters show, the composer was deeply invested in the success of Gericke's plans to perform the Fifth Symphony.[14] Late in 1905, three months before Gericke first conducted the composition on 2 February 1906 in Boston, Mahler thanked him for programming the composition and informed him about revisions that he considered essential for the performances. About a month later, Mahler explained to Gericke that he had just successfully used these revisions when conducting the work in Vienna; Mahler even sent his own score to the conductor from which to transfer those changes to Gericke's copy of the score and the orchestral parts.[15]

In addition to any revisions he copied from Mahler's score, Gericke also apparently made his own deletions in the work—a decision that the public was allowed to believe originated with the composer himself and that therefore countered typical views of Mahler's works as fatally long-winded. Henry Taylor Parker, writing in the *Boston Evening Transcript* on 3 February 1906, reported that Gericke's performance of the Fifth symphony lasted fifty-five minutes; this duration was so short that, as Henry-Louis de La Grange has speculated, the symphony must have been abridged or played at an exceedingly quick tempo.[16] Moreover, when Karl Muck conducted the work with the Boston Symphony Orchestra seven years later, on 21–22 November 1913, those concerts were advertised in the program notes as unabridged performances specifically in contrast to Gericke's from 1906.[17] When Henry Taylor Parker reported on the surprisingly short length of the work in 1906, he could only infer that it was because of Mahler's latest revisions:

> As for the musical world outside of Germany and Austria, it has been told to weariness that these symphonies were of extraordinary length and that they required extraordinary forces to perform them ... But the fifth of Mahler's symphonies, that Mr. Gericke put on his programme, hardly bore out even these premonitory warnings. Report had declared that to perform it required an hour and a half. In fact, it lasted fifty-five minutes, perhaps ten or fifteen minutes longer than does an ordinary symphony of large dimensions, but it held the interest of the audience to the end, with fewer desertions than are usual at the afternoon concerts and with no visible signs of weariness ... Perhaps the new version of the score which Mahler himself prepared only two months ago and which Mr. Gericke used accounts for these surprises.[18]

Parker's guess that Mahler had recently shortened the score from ninety minutes (already a high estimate) to fifty-five gave the composer credit for a version of the symphony whose length—likely through Gericke's intervention—the critic found surprisingly manageable. But the programme notes for Gericke's performances simply announced that the score the orchestra used was the same one Mahler revised for performance in Vienna the previous December;[19] these notes did not outline the specific nature of Mahler's changes and thus left open the possibility for Boston audiences to believe that the composer himself had made the symphony thirty-five minutes shorter than they expected it to last. (Although the score Mahler sent to Gericke is now lost, there is no reason to believe that cuts would have been among the revisions Mahler suggested to Boston's conductor.)[20]

It is not clear if Mahler knew that Gericke made cuts in the symphony, but he might have acquiesced in the conductor's abridgements. As for what Mahler may have known of those cuts, in his letter to Gericke after the performances the composer referred to the positive reviews the symphony received and to a report Gericke had sent him;[21] it is unknown whether the materials Mahler received from Gericke contained any allusions to the fact that Gericke made cuts.[22] This could have included actual copies of reviews, such as Parker's or Henry Krehbiel's,[23] that would have made clear to Mahler that cuts were applied, or a summary of the performances and their reception that incorporated the information that Gericke made deletions. If he did indeed discover that detail, then Mahler would have had to concede that the decision to pare down symphonic works fell within the conductor's purview, as evidenced by Mahler's own well-documented decision to trim down and otherwise edit the works of other composers.[24] What is more, Mahler's only documented reaction to Gericke's performances was gratitude for programming the work and for garnering a positive response from audiences.[25] Not only did Mahler appreciate the publicity Gericke gave his composition, but the composer was surely thrilled that a group with as shining a reputation as the Boston Symphony Orchestra was performing his music for the first time; Mahler later told Willem Mengelberg that the orchestra was the best in North America.[26] Given the Boston Symphony Orchestra's stature and his own developing profile as a composer in the United States, Mahler may not have objected to Gericke's deletions in the Fifth Symphony if he did know of them.

Thus, from the standpoint of the conductor, the audience, and even the composer, the Fifth Symphony was a flexible entity when Gericke performed it in 1906. Perhaps more was at stake for Gericke and Mahler than missing pages in a score that the composer was continuing to revise. Looking back on Gericke's performances, it is tempting to view the conductor as having slyly avoided notice for the supposed intellectual crime of abridging a symphony and, to make matters worse, having deceptively shoved responsibility for that abridgement on to the very composer who trusted Gericke to implement the latest revisions. But when seen in the context of contemporary attitudes toward Mahler's music, Gericke's actions emerge as those of a performer trying to ensure the best possible reception for the works he was introducing to his audience. As for audience members who may have known that Gericke, not Mahler, was responsible for the symphony's shorter-than-expected length, it likely would not have fazed them, either; in a review in the *Musical Courier*, Leonard Liebling highlighted the conductor's interpretive authority by writing that Mahler's Fifth Symphony, 'in Gericke's version', lasted under one hour.[27]

Serge Koussevitzky and Mahler's Ninth Symphony

By the time Serge Koussevitzky introduced Mahler's Ninth Symphony to the United States on 16 October 1931 with the Boston Symphony Orchestra, Americans knew Mahler's music considerably better than when Gericke performed it in 1906. Mahler himself had conducted his own First, Second, and Fourth symphonies in New York during his time in that city from 1907 to 1911.

Since Mahler's death in 1911, many conductors, including Ernst Kunwald, Leopold Stokowski, Frederick Stock, Willem Mengelberg, and Bruno Walter, had performed Mahler's symphonies in the United States. Specifically with the Boston Symphony Orchestra, Karl Muck had led the Fifth Symphony in 1913 and 1914, and the Second Symphony in 1918, and Pierre Monteux had conducted the First Symphony in 1923 (in an abridged performance).[28] Koussevitzky had already introduced *Das Lied von der Erde* to Boston in 1928, repeating it in 1930. And in 1931, the year Koussevitzky first led the Ninth Symphony, the Bruckner Society of America was formed with the goal of promoting the works of Mahler and Bruckner in the United States.

An array of documentary evidence clearly demonstrates that when Serge Koussevitzky led the American premiere of the Ninth, he deleted a number of passages. Not only did critics' reviews of that concert report that cuts were applied, as will be seen below, but at least some of the deletions themselves are preserved in three sources: Koussevitzky's full score of the Ninth Symphony and his four-hand piano reduction, both held in the Boston Public Library's Koussevitzky Collection, and a set of string parts (with which are mingled some hand-copied percussion and wind parts), located in the Boston Symphony Orchestra's library.[29] The full and piano scores contain marks in blue and lead pencil as well as corner folds and impressions of paperclips that at one time yoked pages together, all indicating passages Koussevitzky skipped or considered omitting. The parts preserve Koussevitzky's deletions with marks in blue, red, and lead pencil. (The orchestra used these same parts again in the 1951–52 season, when Richard Burgin conducted the work; these parts also show Burgin's deletions, some of which were the same as Koussevitzky's but some of which were Burgin's own.) Koussevitzky's specific abridgements are discussed in further detail below, but Fig. 16.1 shows a cut in the third movement as labeled in Koussevitzky's piano score (with marks in blue and lead pencil), and Fig. 16.2 shows the end of the same cut as labeled in the full score (in blue pencil).

Between Gericke's and Koussevitzky's tenures, the friendly climate persisted in which conductors would sometimes abridge works. David Ewen wrote of Koussevitzky that he 'does not hesitate to change tempi, to make deletions, to revise scoring or to alter dynamics if he feels that the music profits by such a treatment'.[30] Indeed, at the BSO, Koussevitzky made cuts in other compositions, including Mahler's Fifth Symphony in 1937 and Liszt's *Faust* Symphony in 1948.[31] Furthermore, Ewen linked Koussevitzky's interpretive practices to Mahler's own precedent.

> The very great interpreter whose taste and judgment are discerning can afford such indulgences, with which lesser artists can only spell ruin. [Hans] Von Bülow, Mahler, and [Arthur] Nikisch more often than not brought about new, brilliant, and eloquent qualities in the music they conducted as a result of their discriminating revisions. And Koussevitzky has done so too.[32]

Fig. 16.1 Deletion marked in Koussevitzky's piano score of Mahler's Ninth Symphony. Courtesy of the Trustees of the Boston Public Library. Reproduced by permission of the Serge Koussevitzky Music Foundation, Inc., copyright owner. All rights, including the right of further reproduction or transmission, are reserved.

Koussevitzky himself articulated a rationale for such editing that implied that revising scores could actually serve as a way to honor, not defy, a composer's wishes, although he did not specifically mention deletions:

> Today we often hear 'musical authorities' declare, when discussing a performance: 'Let music speak for itself'. That up-to-date motto is dangerous, because

Fig. 16.2 Deletion marked in Koussevitzky's full score of Mahler's Ninth Symphony. Courtesy of the Trustees of the Boston Public Library. Reproduced by permission of the Serge Koussevitzky Music Foundation, Inc., copyright owner. All rights, including the right of further reproduction or transmission, are reserved.

it paves the way for mediocre performers to come and accurately play over a composition from beginning to end, claiming that they 'let the music speak for itself' ... A perfect interpretation may have two different aspects, equally faithful to the score of the composer. One may be called mechanically perfect, the other organically perfect. The first gives the beauty of mathematical balance, symmetry, and clarity; the second is the indivisible, living, pulsating

élan vital of the composition. One aims to present a beautified surface or reflection of the composition. In the other, the composition—its central idea—
lives as a reality . . . Like a mystic experience, the organic interpretation puts
the listener in direct touch with the absolute reality hidden in the great work.[33]

Koussevitzky's idea of going beyond a 'beautified surface or reflection' of the
composition suggests that alterations—including deletions—were an accept-
able way of unearthing some deeper meaning and still remaining, as he put it,
'faithful to the score of the composer'.

The idea that elisions in a score could enable a conductor to present a more
vibrant realisation of a work is reflected quite literally in an article in the *New
Republic* by the influential critic Paul Rosenfeld, written after a New York performance of Mahler's Ninth by Koussevitzky in 1932. Rosenfeld asserted of
Mahler's symphonies that some 'will have to be edited, and the Mahlerites will
have to choose between half the loaf or none at all' and that 'the time when conductors will have the wit to detach the living pages from the sick trunk of the
whole cannot be remote.'[34] Here, the critic was referring to the related practice
of performing individual movements instead of whole works. But his belief in
a conductor's freedom to reduce a Mahler symphony to its so-called living essence accords with Koussevitzky's claims that his own adjustments to others'
works unearthed deeper musical truths than if scores were treated as fixed texts.

Reviews of the American premiere of Mahler's Ninth suggest that even with
his deletions, Koussevitzky was much appreciated for bringing this Mahler
composition across the Atlantic for the first time—almost twenty years after
Bruno Walter led the world premiere in Vienna on 26 June 1912 with the Vienna
Philharmonic. On 17 October 1931—the day after the American premiere—
Warren Storey Smith, a Mahler enthusiast writing for the *Boston Post*, remarked
on the rarity of the 'experience of hearing novel music that is also great and
moving music'.[35] The same day in the *Boston Globe*, P.R. (Penfield Roberts) commented that the Ninth Symphony 'impressed one hearing it for the first time as
a masterpiece deserving a permanent place in the repertory, and frequent performance'.[36] And Leslie A. Sloper of the *Christian Science Monitor* remarked that
the work 'had a popular success that was exceptional for a newly heard work'.[37]

Some critics in 1931 knew that Koussevitzky had abridged the Ninth—and
this knowledge did not impinge negatively on their appreciation of it. The critic
Moses Smith reported in the *Boston American* the day after the American premiere, that the Ninth Symphony 'would have been even longer but for some
cuts that Mr. Koussevitzky made in the score', and continued, 'Apparently, these
cuts were merited—if they ever are—for even as heard yesterday there are pages
which induce an unedifying slumber.'[38] For Henry Taylor Parker of the *Boston
Evening Transcript*,

> Perhaps it would have been fairer to play the music note for note . . . with
> the tacit consent of an audience that, having listened through sixty minutes,

would hardly have rebelled at seventy or eighty. Perhaps, again, Mahler's iro-
nies and mockeries are repetitive and ran sufficiently charactered through
the version of Friday.[39]

For some, however, Koussevitzky could apparently have done even more to
shrink Mahler's Symphony. After a New York performance of the work with
the BSO, the critic and noted Mahler skeptic Deems Taylor commented,

> The Ninth Symphony, as [Mahler] wrote it, lasts a few minutes short of an
> hour. Prune it down until nothing is left save Mahler's musical ideas and
> the amount of development that they are worth, and the Ninth Symphony
> would last about 20 minutes. Some day, some real friend of Mahler will do
> just that—take a pruning knife and reduce his works to the length that they
> would have been if the composer had not stretched them out of shape; and
> then the great Mahler war will be over.[40]

Of course, as with Gericke, it was Koussevitzky, not Mahler, who was responsible for the sub-hour length of the work—and Taylor was apparently unaware
of any cuts the conductor made in the Ninth Symphony. But Taylor's remark,
however facetious it may have been, shows the extent to which abridgement
served as a viable solution to the works' extreme length.

By considering the markings from the various scores that document
Koussevitzky's performances, one may identify specific sections that the conductor eliminated in the Ninth (and attempt to distinguish those from Burgin's
own deletions, which are typically labeled in the parts as having been in use in
1952). Deletions that Koussevitzky likely made or considered making during
his performances, some of which overlap and most of which appeared in the
third movement, are listed in Table 16.1. The table includes those deletions that
are indicated in the full score, and it designates if evidence exists for those cuts
in the piano score or the parts. (Omitted here are other passages that markings
in parts suggest Koussevitzky may have deleted, but for which there is no clear
evidence in the full score.) Here, I indicate the location of cuts in terms of distance from rehearsal numbers, which are in bold; for instance, in the cut beginning at **37** + 1, the first deleted bar is the first after Rehearsal Figure 37, while
the final bar within the cut, **38**-11, is the eleventh before Rehearsal Figure 38.

It is unclear which cuts applied to which of Koussevitzky's performances
between 16 October 1931 and 13 March 1941, when he last conducted it.
Performance dates recorded by the musicians on some of the part books indicate that at least a portion of these books were used in Koussevitzky's performances of the Ninth as early as 8 December 1933 and as late as 28 February
1941; it is possible that the musicians even used these same books for the
American premiere on 16 October 1931 but simply did not write down that
particular date. Furthermore, in Koussevitzky's full score, some of the marks
for cuts are themselves struck through or partially erased, showing that he
did not always perform the work with the same omissions. Similarly, assorted

Table 16.1 Deletions in Serge Koussevitzky's Full Score of Mahler's Ninth Symphony

Movement	First bar of cut	Last bar of cut	Length of cut (bars)	Also indicated in piano score (P); orchestral parts (O)
1	16+1	16+52	52	P; O
2	21+32	22+50	115	P; O
2	26-2	27+12	38	O
3	33-29	35+15	131	P; O
3	36+26	39+12	104	P; O
3	37-6	38-11	20	P
3	37+1	38-11	14	O
3	38+21	39+12	34	P; O
3	39+3	39+12	10	P
3	40-23	40-13	11	P; O
3	42-7	43+21	44	P; O

conducting marks even appear within sections that were, at one time or another, slated for deletion.

A few details offer clues into the chronology of some of the deletions. One of the part books is a handwritten copy of the third French horn part dated 25 March 1936, two days before Koussevitzky conducted it that season. In this copy, presumably made in time for the 1936 performances, no signs exist of the large, 104-bar cut of nearly the entire D major episode in the third movement, from **36** + 26 to **39** + 12. But markings for the shorter deletions within that section, from **37** + 1 to **38**-11 and **38** + 21 to **39** + 12, are visible in this 1936 part book. Meanwhile, other part books include the longer cut (although the markings for it are only barely visible, having been faintly erased), suggesting that this cut was applied in at least some of Koussevitzky's performances before 1936 but not that year or afterward.

Far from indiscriminately slashing passages to make the Ninth Symphony shorter, then, Koussevitzky continually wrestled with decisions about precisely which portions to remove from the symphony. The conductor could simply have retained the same cuts through all his performances of the work, but as Table 16.1 shows, he reevaluated and shifted them, especially in the Rondo Burleske; the cut ending at **39** + 12 had three different possible starting points. Adding or subtracting time alone does not appear to have motivated these

evolving decisions about where to make omissions in the score, as the timings of the complete symphony from year to year were relatively consistent;
the first page of Koussevitzky's full score lists 63 minutes for performances in
1931 to 1932 and 64½ minutes for 1936; a first violin part reported 64 minutes
on 28 February 1941, while another reported 63 minutes for the previous day
(probably in a rehearsal, as the official concert dates were 28 February and
1 March). Koussevitzky likely revisited the cuts each season he programmed
it, and he may well have even made adjustments between consecutive performances within one programme, as he apparently did later with Mahler's
Seventh Symphony, which he performed in 1948; a list of timings recorded in
a blank page at the beginning of the score of Mahler's Seventh at the Boston
Symphony Orchestra's library explicitly states that Koussevitzky did not make
a cut in the finale of that work on 15 October 1948 but did abridge the movement for the next day's performance.[41]

Rather than viewing these deletions as assaults on Mahler's music, one
might instead consider what they accomplished for Koussevitzky and his audiences. Some of Koussevitzky's elisions actually lent more consistent overall
sound profiles to individual movements; in the first and third movements, the
deleted sections contain music that stands out as strikingly different from the
surrounding material. Koussevitzky's first abridgement includes the Misterioso
passage in the first movement; that digressive section contains some of the
movement's sparsest scoring and most melodically and rhythmically unstable
music. Later in the symphony, the wistful, tonally transparent D major episode
in the Rondo Burleske is similarly conspicuous against the intense polyphonic
background of the rest of that movement. In his survey of the symphonies,
Constantin Floros suggests that this D major episode 'seems like a foreign
body' in the movement.[42] Indeed, it is closer in orchestration and tempo to the
final *Adagio* than to the rest of the movement. And by removing nearly the
entire episode in some performances, Koussevitzky allowed the similar turn
figures in the following Adagio movement to seem fresher when they first appeared. Moreover, by omitting repeated material, Koussevitzky also tightened
the work's structure in ways that actually suggest a closer engagement with
the music than the analogous decision many conductors have made to leave
out the verbatim repeats in Mahler's First and Sixth symphonies.[43] The 131-
bar portion that Koussevitzky removed from the Rondo Burleske was a varied
repetition of what Floros identified as the movement's first three sections, A,
fugato, and B.[44] Similarly, but on a smaller scale, the eleven bars Koussevitzy
removed from **40**-23 to **40**-13 are a varied repeat of the previous eleven.

Koussevitzky also made deletions in Mahler's Ninth by finding repeated figures and simply skipping to the second iterations of those figures, thus rendering practically unnoticeable the act of deleting material for first-time listeners
and, as a consequence, creating the illusion that the work was shorter. In the
115-bar deletion in the second movement, Koussevitzky jumped directly to the

second statement of the Ländler, which begins almost identically to the first statement, except for a flute trill in the second statement.[45] The other cut in the movement was similarly imperceptible in that Koussevitzky merely skipped from one descending passage in the horns to the next, identical one. Not all of Koussevitzky's cuts were so graceful; the large deletion in the third movement from **36** + **26** to **39** + **12**, of nearly the entire D major episode, bluntly interrupts the trumpet phrase that inaugurates the episode. The smaller cut from **37** + 1 to **38**-11 is smoother; at the starting and ending points of that deletion, the violin states a version of the section's opening turn figure, and Koussevitzky simply removed the intervening material. In a critical environment that supported abridgement, and in which Mahler was frequently viewed as 'appallingly long-winded' (as the Boston critic and program annotator Philip Hale put it in the *Boston Herald* the day after the American premiere of the Ninth in 1931),[46] such subtle tightening perhaps helped Mahler's symphonies match audience expectations to hear shorter works.

The cases of Gericke and Koussevitzky likely only scratch the surface of the practice of abridgement in Mahler's symphonies; further research into the performances of Mahler's music in both Europe and the United States in the first half of the twentieth century will surely reveal a wealth of evidence for performances in which Mahler's works were abridged. Reviews, conducting scores, and orchestral parts will continue to emerge as rich sources of information about this little-known aspect of performance practice. To evaluate thoroughly the significance of these performances, scholars ought to take abridgements seriously and view them not as liberties taken with an established repertory but rather as ways of estimating conductors' views of their own roles as musicians and of their audience's needs, and as a practice that preceded the modern one documented in discographies and recordings. Today's Mahler aficionados may not take kindly to shortening the symphonies, but in the early twentieth century, many of them would have had no choice but to accept—and even embrace—abridgement.

Notes

1. See Fülöp, *Mahler Discography*, 512–68.
2. These were performances by Hans Schmidt-Isserstedt with the Nordwestdeutscher Rundfunk Symphony Orchestra in 1956, and Leopold Stokowski with the Philadelphia Orchestra in 1967 (See Fülöp, *Mahler Discography*, 518).
3. See Fülöp, *Mahler Discography*, 530.
4. Banks, "Aspects of Mahler's Fifth Symphony", 265.
5. Smoley, *Gustav Mahler's Symphonies*, 131.
6. Smoley, *Gustav Mahler's Symphonies*, 9.

7. Pickett, "Mahler on Record", 359.

8. Smoley, *Gustav Mahler's Symphonies*, 70 and 71.

9. See Krehbiel, "Mahler's Symphony Heard First Time" and Hackett, "Orchestra Plays Mahler's Music in Brilliant Style".

10. See Straus, "Erno Rapee Leads Mahler's Eighth".

11. On the relationships between Mahler's views of his own works and the decisions of other conductors, see Pickett, "Mahler on Record", 346–47; Kaplan, "Adagietto: From Mahler with Love"; Kaplan and Franklin, "Mahler and Tradition"; and Banks, "Aspects of Mahler's Fifth Symphony". The author of this paper is grateful to the Kaplan Foundation for support in the form of a fellowship for graduate study at Harvard University from 2006 to 2008.

12. Taruskin, "Tradition and Authority", 179. My argument builds on recent commentary on this subject by Rockwell ("Leinsdorf's Mahler as Act of Boldness"). In a *New York Times* review of an abridged performance of Mahler's Seventh Symphony by Erich Leinsdorf and the New York Philharmonic in 1990, Rockwell justified Leinsdorf's decision by noting: 'Cuts in Mahler's own music after his death were common enough—so common that Mr. Leinsdorf's reversion to the practice can be called a kind of "authentic" performance practice.' Similarly, Zychowicz ("Mahler: Symphony No. 3") connected the practice in Mahler's music to a similar one in the performance history of Bruckner's. See also Metzger, *Perspektiven der Rezeption Gustav Mahlers*, 204, and Kolleritsch, "Gespräch mit einem Mahler-Interpreten", 101–2.

13. Reilly, "Mahler in America", 422–23. For specific details on early performances of Mahler's music in the United States, and samples of reviews, see Lang, "Mahler's American Debut".

14. See Reilly, "Gustav Mahler and Wilhelm Gericke".

15. Reilly, "Gustav Mahler and Wilhelm Gericke", 62.

16. La Grange, *Gustav Mahler*. Vol. 3, 313, fn.115. A review in the *New York Tribune* from 1906, attributed by La Grange (on p. 315, fn.124) to Henry Krehbiel corroborates Parker's sub-hour timing. Krehbiel reported that the orchestra's performance of the Fifth Symphony on 15 February 1906 at Carnegie Hall (in its New York premiere) lasted fifty-nine minutes, and that the work had 'been revised and benignantly curtailed'.

17. Hale, "Programme of the Sixth Rehearsal and Concert", 347.

18. Parker, "A Symphony by Mahler for the First Time".

19. Hale, "Programme of the Fourteenth Rehearsal and Concert", 1033.

20. On the complex story of the sources and revisions of Mahler's Fifth Symphony, see Kubik, "Vorwort".

21. Reilly, "Gustav Mahler and Wilhelm Gericke", 63.

22. In his discussion of these performances and their correspondence, La Grange (*Gustav Mahler*. Vol. 3, 315) wrote that Gericke sent copies of positive reviews to Mahler, but Mahler's letter to Gericke is ambiguous on the matter.

23. Parker, "A Symphony by Mahler for the First Time", and Krehbiel (attr.), "A Symphony by Mahler".

24. For details on some of Mahler's cuts in symphonic works, see Pickett, "Gustav Mahler as Interpreter", 209–10 and 488–92, and Pickett, "Arrangements and *Retuschen*: Mahler and *Werktreue*", 191–93. Some recent commentators have mentioned, alongside their discussions of conductors' manipulations of Mahler's works, the fact that Mahler himself edited other composers' music; see Banks, "Aspects of Mahler's Fifth Symphony", 265, fn. 32; Pickett, "Mahler on Record", 357, fn. 15; and Kaplan, "Adagietto: From Mahler with Love", 385.

25. Reilly, "Gustav Mahler and Wilhelm Gericke", 63.

26. Roman, *Mahler's American Years*, 93.

27. Liebling, "Variations", 262.

28. That Monteux shortened the Symphony is indicated in a list of timings in the score (no. 784) in the Boston Symphony Orchestra's library. The sheet specifically noted when certain performances contained deletions.

29. In the Boston Public Library, the full score (Universal-Edition, no. 3395) is found at Kous.M1001.M21 no. 9 1912bx folio, and the piano score (Universal-Edition, no. 3397) at Kous.M209.M22 no. 9 1912x. The parts (Universal-Edition, no. 3396a-e) are found in Box G.O.B. 10 in the BSO's library.

30. Ewen, *Dictators of the Baton*, 97.

31. See Durgin, Review of Fifth Symphony and "Mayes Cello Soloist at Symphony".

32. Ewen, *Dictators of the Baton*, 97.

33. Koussevitsky, "Poetry and Music", 3.

34. Rosenfeld, "After Mahler's 'Ninth'", 245.

35. Smith, "Symphony in Mahler's Great 9th".

36. P.R. (Penfield Roberts), Review of Ninth Symphony.

37. Sloper, Review of Ninth Symphony.

38. Smith, "Mahler's Ninth Symphony Wins Favor".

39. Parker, "Mahler Makes Impression".

40. Taylor, "Words and Music".

41. In this score (no. 769), the movement timing is listed as 14:32 under the date 15 October 1948, but under 16 October 1948, the last movement is labeled 'with cut' next to a time of 9:07.

42. Floros, *Gustav Mahler. The Symphonies*, 290.

43. See Pickett, "Mahler on Record", 349.

44. Floros, *Gustav Mahler. The Symphonies*, 287.

45. Paul Kletzki removed the same passage in his 1955 recording with the Israel Philharmonic Orchestra.

46. Hale, Review of Ninth Symphony.

17

Mahler and the Game of History

Jeremy Barham

All memory is presence . . .

Only the gaze that is turned backward
Can bring us forward,
For the gaze that is turned forward
Leads us backward.[1]

Historiography in Progress

Issues of time, memory, and history have long preoccupied creative literary minds. Proustian concerns, for example, seem to colour Milan Kundera's exploration of the novel:

> man is separated from the past . . . by two forces . . . the force of forgetting (which erases) and the force of memory (which transforms) . . . What becomes of our certainties about the past, and what becomes of History itself . . . ? Beyond the slender margin of the incontestable . . . stretches an infinite realm: the realm of the approximate, the invented, the deformed, the simplistic, the exaggerated, the misconstrued, an infinite realm of nontruths that copulate, multiply like rats, and become immortal.[2]

Similarly, Julian Barnes's recent Booker-Prize–winning novel *The Sense of an Ending* (2011) addresses time and history in a fictionalising and narrativising of Frank Kermode's famous work of literary criticism of the same name. Kermode's study stemmed from what he describes as the 'need to know the shape of life in relation to the perspectives of time'.[3] The protagonists in Barnes's novel similarly suggest the following:

> We live in time—it holds us and moulds us—but I've never felt I understood it very well . . . I mean ordinary, everyday time, which clocks and watches assure us passes regularly . . . Is there anything more plausible than a second hand? And yet it takes only the smallest pleasure or pain to teach us time's malleability. Some emotions speed it up, others slow it down; occasionally, it seems to go missing—until the eventual point when it really does go missing, never to return . . . I need to return briefly to a few incidents that have grown

into anecdotes, to some approximate memories which time has deformed into certainty. If I can't be sure of the actual events any more, I can at least be true to the impressions those facts left. That's the best I can manage.[4]

'History is the lies of the victors' ... 'it is also the self-delusions of the defeated' ... 'History is a raw onion sandwich ... It just repeats ... Same old story, same old oscillation between tyranny and rebellion, war and peace, prosperity and impoverishment' ... 'History is that certainty produced at the point where the imperfections of memory meet the inadequacies of documentation.'[5]

If the origins of a 'modern idea of history' founded on contemporary doubts of an unalterable, objective outer world can be traced back to the sixteenth and seventeenth centuries according to Hannah Arendt,[6] it was from the late nineteenth century and especially the mid-twentieth century that even stronger notions of a destabilised, relativised historiography and the dangers of a universal historicism rooted in ideologies of relentless progress gained particular momentum within varied political and philosophical contexts. For example, only four years separated Walter Benjamin's final anti-fascist critique of historicism in 'Theses on the Philosophy of History' (1940) written in the year of his suicide as he attempted to escape the German regime, and Karl Popper's *The Poverty of Historicism* which began life in 1936 and was dedicated to 'the countless men and women ... who fell victims to the fascist and communist belief in Inexorable Laws of Historical Destiny'.[7] These critiques respectively emanated from neo-Marxist and liberal-Western contexts but had similar aims of releasing historiography from the mechanical constraints of a predominantly universalist, scientific, and quantitative approach, and liberating human consciousness from the requirement to conform to one technocratic form of totalitarianism or another.

Notably this desire to re-engage with theories of historical understanding and to rethink temporalities of human existence not only straddled political divides but also cut across the intellectual and critical spectrum. Folded into very different responses to the entire Enlightenment legacy were, on the one hand, Nietzsche's elitist and iconoclastic idea of the 'suprahistorical man' for whom 'the past and present are one', and the living man's critical stance towards history which eschews the historicist 'blind rage for collecting' and is confident enough to lend to humankind 'a past in which one would like to originate in opposition to that in which one did originate.'[8] On the other hand, from a post-second-world-war leftist perspective came Sartre's remarkably similar claim that 'I totalize myself on the basis of centuries of history ... This means that my life itself is centuries old.' In a shift of focus from diachronic history to synchronic culture common among historians of this period, Sartre the philosopher talks of the 'synthetic bonds' of history and past-present '*reciprocity*' from which we may 'select the best examples ... from the past which we did not live, but which is nevertheless, through the *medium* of culture, completely ours'[9]—a past which, as myth or even lie, is, according to Hayden White, 'what we decide to remember of it', and which has 'no existence apart from our consciousness of it'.[10] It was not necessary to be a political radical to hold such views, as demonstrated by Gadamer in his work on history and hermeneutics in the mid-1970s:

> Time is no longer primarily a gulf to be bridged because it separates; it is actually the supportive ground of the course of events in which the present is rooted. Hence temporal distance is not something that must be overcome. This was, rather, the naïve assumption of historicism, namely that we must transpose ourselves into the spirit of the age, think with its ideas and its thoughts, not with our own, and thus advance toward historical objectivity. In fact the important thing is to recognize temporal distance as a positive and productive condition enabling understanding. It is not a yawning abyss but is filled with the continuity of custom and tradition, in the light of which everything handed down presents itself to us.[11]

The twin tendencies, apparent from the above, to de-objectify historical studies and to play with the linearity of temporal progression upon which they have been understandably constructed, stemmed from increasing inroads into the discipline made during the twentieth century by waves of literary theory, social science, Marxist thinking, and poststructuralist philosophy: from American New Criticism, through critical anthropology and historical materialism, to continental deconstruction. There is no need to rehearse the entire history of historiographic theory here,[12] but it is worth noting that such desires to escape from the grand narrative of Western rationalism, however ideologically circumscribed, have continually had to wrestle with claims and counter-claims regarding the possibility/impossibility of working with any degree of acceptance of (a) objective fact; (b) a reliable, defined past; or (c) the irreversibility of chronological time. Hayden White set out to demonstrate in the 1970s, for example, that 'there are no criteria of truth in historical narratives',[13] 'the contents of which are as much *invented* as *found*',[14] and, calling on Lévi-Strauss, that 'appeal to the chronological sequence affords no relief from the charge that the coherency of the historical account is mythological in nature'.[15] Simultaneous echoes and subsequent developments and intensification of these challenges to presumed norms of the discipline, largely under the impress of the so-called linguistic turn of the 1970s and contemporary politicising trends in historical theory, can be found in disparate regions of a twentieth-century intellectual landscape that includes Barthes, Veyne, Deleuze and Guattari, Koselleck, Ricoeur, Baudrillard, Kellner, Ankersmit and Kellner, Jenkins, and Rancière, with important precursors among the so-called *Annales* School of French historians culminating in the work of Fernand Braudel.[16] Arguably, the impact of a radical postmodernism on historical studies has waned somewhat in recent years. But to a large extent the shifts in conceptual and methodological emphasis such thinking encouraged between objectivity and plausibility, scholarly inquiry and rhetoric, and rational and metaphorical discourses were only articulating semi-submerged and unacknowledged ambiguities that had long existed in the discipline and were liberating the historical imagination to explore neglected yet always inherent historiographical possibilities. Such possibilities may be suggested in historians' and philosophers' attempts to find answers to questions such as these:

- Is there anything like a specifically historical time that differs from natural time?[17]
- Is 'the very notion of a modernist historiography modeled on the ['disemplotment' of the] modernist, anti-narrativist novel' a 'contradiction in terms'?[18]
- Is it possible, in a historiographically meaningful way, to 'grasp "the plural unity of future, past, and present"'?[19]
- Can meaningful use be made of those operations of chance or apparently meaningless coincidence that since the time of Enlightenment theorists have been overtly excluded from the true 'representational art of historiography'?[20]
- Is history a form of fiction?[21]

Not so much to call for a new type of history but more to encourage greater awareness of the advantages and disadvantages of differing, extant historiographical methods (though something of the former may indeed emerge from the latter), in what follows I bring three approaches of the historical project into operation in relation to Mahler, a composer whose music began, at a critical juncture in Western sociopolitical development, to democratise and destabilise identities, as well as to play with teleologies, causalities, and temporalities, both structurally within works and in terms of its incitement to rethink larger contexts of backward- and forward-looking historical trajectories in music and culture.

Historicism

Resistance to the postmodernising of historical study has been strong in some quarters. In a consideration of chaos theory, historical contingency, and counterfactuals, Aviezer Tucker asserts:

> Evaluating how contingent, complex, and chaotic history is can only be done empirically: it is the work of historians and social scientists. There is no philosophical superhighway to bypass the careful historiographical study of concrete historical processes and events. Instead of speculation, the only way to examine the contingency of history is to study it empirically.[22]

Iggers similarly suggests that it would be a mistake to throw the Enlightenment baby out with the bath water, since, by charting the Enlightenment's supposedly inevitable lapse into totalitarianism and universal utopianism, thinkers from Adorno to Foucault have somewhat misrepresented its legacy at the expense of acknowledging the 'autonomy of the enlightened individual' who is in fact empowered to exert 'determined opposition to all forms of arbitrary authority and total control'. If, according to Iggers, 'the alternative to an albeit chastened Enlightenment is barbarism',[23] then that of an empirically rooted historiography may be meaningless or at least highly speculative relativism.

The indebtedness of a generation of Mahler scholars to Henry-Louis de La Grange for his monumental factual persistence in ca. 4,000 pages of biography, nevertheless should not prevent the questioning of a type of relentless reportage that has the capacity, even the tendency, to mould artificial fixity out of actual uncertainty and disorder in a drive to control the individual subject. The logical conclusion of de La Grange's project would be to attempt to chart every moment of every day of Mahler's existence (including his subconscious psyche)—to insert oneself into his purported inner and outer life's trajectory in an act of testimonial surrogacy. Given that not even Mahler's closest associates and family members could ever gain complete understanding of the depths and shallows of his human nature and his creative and mental processes, and given that Mahler himself could not always explain them either, not only can such biographical activity never attain total objectivity and universal knowledge, but also sooner or later it confronts the 'imperfections of memory' and 'the inadequacies of documentation' in the form of empiricism's limits, the varied reliability of evidence, and the intentional fallacy.

Every biographer has to be aware of these circumstances and of the point at which reporting ends and interpretation begins. For the most part, de La Grange negotiates this line by remaining on the side of reporter, both of historical events and of the analysis and interpretation of other scholars. Less persuasive are his own forays into musical analysis, hermeneutics, and cultural commentary, and, for the purposes of this study, his (albeit necessarily) selective quotation of sources, especially contemporary critical reviews of performances. In a study of Mahler's Hamburg years,[24] Bernd Shabbing has since shown how intensifying documentary zeal yet further in the surveying and citation of contemporary criticism can go some way towards providing a corrective. He has revealed, for example, that the critical fraternity of this period wielded much less power than is usually assumed, and that supposed opponents of the composer such as Sittard and Krause were far more supportive and generous than previously thought. It is all too easy to manipulate sources (whether consciously or unconsciously) in the support of particular readings, and for readings to harden into received opinion. At the risk of arriving at a less sensational representation of reality, one way to guard against this is to adopt a policy of documentary macro-criticism. The logical extension of Schabbing's

approach in turn would, for instance, be to publish a long-overdue comprehensive anthology of unabridged concert reviews of the period, thereby trans-
ferring the responsibility of interpreting the data to each individual reader.
Even then, however, readers would naturally absorb and respond selectively,
the hidden agendas of critics and the papers for whom they wrote would need
to be taken into account, and the often neglected and underrated problem of
translation would rear its head, requiring careful editorial intervention and
thus re-introducing an element of authorial control in an unresolvable, eternally regressive contest between a mutually tempering subjectivity and objectivity that would generate almost limitless metacritique. Tendencies towards
extreme documentary, then, cannot necessarily prevent the construction or
intimation of subjective stories, although, with the diminished presence of a
third-party filtering and interpreting mind, in certain cases they retain the
potential to resist, defer, or inflect these.

As for Schabbing, like almost all for whom a historicist recounting of the
past is an end in itself, or for those who invest heavily in this to construct readings, he encounters the age-old problem of how to traverse the gulf between
biography/documentary and critique: what Boulez (ironically in the preface
to de La Grange's first French volume) called the 'separation between life and
creation ... the shifting and elusive slide that interposes itself between the
event and its elaboration'.[25] Modes of traversal have varying degrees of per-
suasiveness, and perhaps none can be completely successful. But if empirical
fact-gathering and biographical accounts are to have significance in a wider
project of 'understanding', it may not be enough, for example, in relation to
Mahler's performance habits, for Schabbing to assume a direct parallel between the composer's (empirically documented) conducting of 'programmatic'
music and the qualities of his own compositional aesthetic;[26] or in the case of
sketch studies, for Hartmut Schaefer, taking his lead from Constantin Floros,[27]
to suggest unmediated linkages between vivid scrawling on manuscripts and
either the composer's 'stormy temperament' or the 'inner drama of [a] passage';[28] or, in the case of establishing a particular cultural reading, for K. M.
Knittel to base claims of an all-pervasive legacy and continued presence of
anti-Semitism in Mahler criticism on, among other things, highly selective
quotation of somewhat de-contextualised sources.[29]

The 'residue of mystery' in the creative process and the distinction between
historical event as cause and as content of art works were concepts well understood by Mahler.[30] Together they may seem to risk crippling any approach to
studying the composer which purports to uncover truths that are more than
a matter of mundane incontestable historical record—the kind of mythmak-
ing prevalent in Floros's *Gustav Mahler: Visionär und Despot. Porträt einer
Persönlichkeit* (1998) built on an extensive but inevitably selective exercise in
documentary *Textkritik* that conflates intellectual preoccupations with supposed personality traits and compositional impulse with semantic content in

unmediated correlation. This is not to invalidate the collecting of supposed historical data and documentation per se. The benefits of, for example, volumes of correspondence or Knud Martner's chronology of Mahler's entire performance career are considerable.[31] But it is rather to warn in the first place against the illusion that political and cultural agendas can be eradicated from historicism; secondly against uncritical, prima facie acceptance of incontestability; thirdly against the idea that this is all there is, against the belief that the past's mysteries have thereby been solved, its significances and complexities grasped, the end of the historiographical project reached; and finally against any simplistic or over-determined extrapolation that conveniently transforms the chaotic, formerly 'unexpected' into the orderly, retrospectively 'inevitable'—turns the 'unforeseen' into an 'epic', as Philip Roth puts it.[32] It is neither necessary nor even desirable to reject or refute the processes of historicism, but only to be aware of their limitations and those of a mindset that does not accept further historiographical possibilities. Conversely, resisting the powerfully seductive siren call of a post-rationalist historiography that suppresses the need for regulated critique carries its own obvious benefits.[33] Historical materialism suggests something of a middle path.

Historical Materialism

Walter Benjamin critiques historicism for its reverential attitude to history as an '"eternal" image of the past', assured of, and finding security in, continual progress.[34] The facts, '"the way it really was"',[35] will always be there waiting for our contemplation of them, according to this model, 'the opiate of the intellectuals'.[36] '"Once upon a time"' is the whore in historicism's brothel, he writes, presupposing 'homogeneous, empty time' which it attempts to fill with 'a mass of data', and relating the sequence of events like the beads of a rosary.[37] With a then-current anti-authoritarian political disdain, Benjamin counters historicism with a version of historical materialism which, unlike its Hegelian precursor, sees history as radically fragmented. Whereas for historicism '"the truth will not run away from us"',[38] historical materialism has to 'seize' the past as it 'flits by', to 'seize hold of a memory as it flashes up at a moment of danger'.[39] Because the past is precarious, dynamic, broken, 'a pile of debris' that 'grows skyward', the historical materialist is drawn, perhaps involuntarily, to charged moments that 'blast open the continuum of history' through revolutionary action.[40] The provocative image that Benjamin calls upon to illustrate this is Paul Klee's 1920 painting 'Angelus Novus' (see Fig. 17.1). He writes:

> 'Angelus Novus' shows an angel looking as though he is about to move away from something he is fixedly contemplating. His eyes are staring, his mouth is open, his wings are spread. This is how one pictures the angel of history.

Fig. 17.1 Paul Klee, 'Angelus Novus' (1920)

His face is turned toward the past. Where we perceive a chain of events, he sees one single catastrophe which keeps piling wreckage upon wreckage and hurls it in front of his feet. The angel would like to stay, awaken the dead, and make whole what has been smashed. But a storm is blowing from Paradise; it has got caught in his wings with such violence that the angel can no longer close them. This storm irresistibly propels him into the future to which his back is turned, while the pile of debris before him grows skyward. This storm is what we call progress.[41]

With such an abolition of historical time had previously come Benjamin's dialectics at a standstill, in which 'what has been comes together in a flash with the now to form a constellation',[42] and where history is 'the subject of a structure whose site is ... filled by the presence of the now [*Jetztzeit*]',[43]—an absolute contraction of 'instantaneous, particular and always perishing *Jetzt* and the chronological, general, and durative *Zeit*'.[44] As Hansen suggests,[45] Benjamin's temporally complex philosophy of history is inextricable from his critical theorising of film media, the latter built as they are on illusory movement created by the rapid succession of fleetingly grasped still images whose persistent and abrupt change constitutes for him 'the shock effect of the film'.[46] If such media offer 'revolutionary criticism of traditional concepts of art' and in some cases 'revolutionary criticism of social conditions',[47] politically radical film repertoire such as that of the New German Cinema in particular does so in the manner of Benjamin's materialist historian by 'renounc[ing] the epic element in history', 'blast[ing] the epoch out of the reified "continuity of history"' and 'explod[ing] the homogeneity of the epoch, interspersing it with ruins'.[48] Indeed, the capacity of film to shed magnifying light on the wreckage, debris, myths, and missing pieces of history—as the negative presence of the oppressed and defeated—by 'burst[ing]' the 'prison-world' of our surroundings 'asunder by the dynamite of the tenth of a second',[49] goes some way to explaining Benjamin's otherwise enigmatic statement in *The Arcades Project* which appears to situate film at the very core of his historiographical thinking and critique of modernism: 'the refuse- and decay-phenomena as precursors, in some degree mirages, of the great syntheses that follow. These worlds <?> of static realities are to be looked for everywhere. Film, their center. ◻ Historical Materialism ◻.'[50]

The highly politicised films of Rainer Werner Fassbinder are notable in this regard and for their use of Mahler's music,[51] but Hans Jürgen Syberberg's *Hitler, a Film from Germany* (1977) comes closest to fulfilling the Benjaminian ideal. A monumental work of expiative mourning that echoes Benjamin's own early preoccupation with the genre of baroque *Trauerspiel*, with its 'Protestant baroque . . . tendencies to modernity and fragmentation' and its 'Catholic baroque . . . tendencies to reaction and totality',[52] *Hitler* assembles a kaleidoscopic juxtaposition of historical and cultural allusions, figures, texts, recordings, voice-over, music, stage and filmic clutter, memorabilia, and imagery in a Germanic, carnival phantasmagoria of *tableaux vivants* that, like the *Trauerspiel*, 'mourns the loss of totality but makes no attempt to restore it'.[53] Not only does it form a Benjaminian past-present constellation par excellence, substituting time-bound narrative representational organisation with timeless, anachronistic contemplation, but also it typifies Syberberg's belief that 'film has the possibility of creating new magical worlds according to its own inner laws, which, in my experience, are closer to those of music than any comparable realm of cultural history.'[54] Near the beginning of Part 2, 'A German Dream . . . Until the End of the World', after recordings of pro- and anti-German wartime exhortations by Goebbels and Einstein, respectively (heard over the opening of Wagner's *Parsifal*), images of an all-seeing, self-reflexively filmic eye with the Nazi eagle at its centre, and, held before it, a

Fig. 17.2 Still from Syberberg, *Hitler, a Film from Germany*, Part 2, 'A German Dream . . . Until the End of the World' (1977)

small glass ball of the type that encases a snowy landscape (an object of great fascination for Benjamin),[55] merge over a portentous poetic-philosophical voice-over authored by the director (see Fig. 17.2):

> And in us, the horror images of the paradise of hell; the loneliest corner of the deepest cold of our misunderstanding; and in the hand the crystal grail of longing with a bleak house of our bloodiest memories of eternal homesickness. The old glowing chalice of madness on the lips full of guilt; and in it the new miracle to grasp the world simultaneously from inside and outside, and to live divided by new unity in sacred excitement, according to the rules of film.

The glass ball is shaken to reveal inside it a model of Edison's famous 'Black Maria' film studio, reputedly the first of its kind, constructed in 1893 in West Orange, New Jersey. With this in close-up, the voice-over later continues:

> Let's imagine an absolutely quiet situation, like before falling asleep, in the cellars of our cities and shelters of our soul, light and shadow falling, projections from outside, from the other world, from above, from without. We see each other standing on a mountain by the sea, in a forest, the forest of times past or the future.

At this point a passage from towards the end of the finale of Mahler's Symphony 2 takes over from the Wagner: bars 631–56, which includes the end of the choral interlude leading into the final passage for alto and soprano soloists, and which tonally ascends from deep on the flat side (B♭ minor/D♭ major) to A♭ for the soloists' verse, in preparation for the subsequent final return to E♭ for the movement's close:

> Chorus: 'Cease from trembling! Prepare thyself to live!'

> Alto and Soprano solo: 'O Pain, thou piercer of all things, From thee have I been wrested! O Death, thou masterer of all things, Now art thou mastered!'

Shortly after the beginning of the excerpt, the image within the eye shifts to a scene from Syberberg's 1974 film *Karl May. In Search of Paradise Lost*, in which the same music had accompanied the dying May's figurative entrance into that paradise (in the form of a chapel decorated with vast apocalyptic statues). The narration continues, leading to May's warning for the future (shown at the end of the quotation below), at which moment a shift in the music, also taken from the 1974 film, transports us to the final heavenly vision from near the end of Mahler's song 'Das himmlische Leben' (piano version, bars 124–26), with its gently rocking melody over tonic pedal in E major:

> Worlds are born as projections. Let's assume we are arriving, lost, confused, in the depths of that forest. We are creeping deep into ourselves, moving along the path to our inner self, into the midst of our lives, searching for deliverance from the collective guilt of the world, in the endless country of our soul, through the history of our most recent past. Seeking advice from another seeker of God, who said: 'All of us are guilty of the deed of the individual. It has to be forgiven for itself.' Another said at the end of his life: 'Beware if the wrong one comes along.'

The Mahlerian constellation resumes and concludes some three minutes later when a fragment from the first choral verse in Symphony 2's finale (bars 478^3–488^2, '. . . short rest! Immortal life! Immortal life, He who called thee . . .') fades in and out during the narration's final phrases:

> And they wanted one who wanted the impossible, a misunderstood one, torn by love and hatred, the laurel wreath of the dying hero. Not a politician, but an artist and god, one all of them could follow by simply believing. The man from their midst, that's what they wanted and that's what they created from their midst.

After the intervening scene of a young girl alongside a puppet of King Ludwig II of Bavaria (a reference to another of Syberberg's previous films and a further de-humanising, temporally arresting ploy), the interior of the glass ball returns for the narration cited above, now against the backdrop of a winged seraph, before the image changes once again, in further allusion to a scene from *Karl May*, with snow being sprinkled on a model of May's town of birth, the clouds of paradise pictured behind. The hitherto long-sustained, momentous scenario of transcendence is then abruptly overwritten in a thoroughly Mahlerian about-face by street-music fanfares heralding a magic show and a master of ceremonies announcing: 'Ladies and gentlemen. This is the masseur of Heinrich Himmler, the Reichsführer of the SS.'

This complex audio-visual assemblage extends vertically and laterally in a profound historico-cultural matrix of meaning with Mahler at or near its centre: the humble birth of Benjamin's modernist revolutionary art of cinema (with whose context Mahler was both historically and aesthetically—though not practically—related) is aligned with deep-seated resonances of German artistic achievement and cultural mythologies in Wagner, *Parsifal* and the grail quest on the one hand, and on the other, in the relative kitsch of May's populist, ingenuous, but no less sincere escapist fare, the work of ' "the last great German mystic" in an age of dying legends' according to Syberberg.[56] The apocalyptic and theatrical sense of Mahler's 'Resurrection' Symphony continues and intensifies the Wagnerian musical context in accord with the spoken and visual sentiments. The seismic shift of gear to the childlike innocence of 'Das himmlische Leben' echoes May's principal audience and his reflection on his childhood origins, and it suggests a contrasting Blochian anti-teleology of pure innocence, akin to Mahler's re-contextualising of the song as the gossamer endpoint of Symphony 4, in which 'the true Genesis is not at the beginning, but at the end ... Once the [creative human] has grasped himself and that which is his, without alienation and based in real democracy, so there will arise in the world something that shines into everyone's childhood, but where no one has yet been: Heimat.'[57] Facing in multiple directions, the ' "*historical-revolutionary*" experience' of Mahler's music,[58] like that of Kafka's fables in the eyes of Benjamin, lay in the modernist reworking of the archaic childhood fairy tale.

The penchant of Mahler—like Syberberg an 'emigrant in his own country'[59]—for the most earnest forms of intellectual and spiritual engagement with German high culture, alongside brusque flirtations with triviality and kitsch, his early forms of bricolage, as well as his search in the musical past of the baroque, classicism and early romanticism for a way in which, as one of the most dedicated of Wagnerians, he could establish a post-Wagnerian existence for himself, all mirror Syberberg's historically explosive projection of a postwar, spiritually dispossessed Germany's struggle for equanimity in the face of the shameless kitsch and historical determinism and falsification of its fascist past. Like Syberberg's film, they link backwards in time to the Counter-Reformation *Trauerspiel*'s recurrent theme of redemption through death, and the 'worthlessness of all mortal life, bound as it is to an inevitable decline and decay', illustrated through exaggerated morbidity and the 'piles of corpses which cluttered the stage',[60] and forwards in time to what Fredric Jameson calls a 'moment of crisis in modern culture . . . at which culture and emergent mass culture began to split apart from one another and to develop seemingly autonomous structures and languages', the resultant heterogeneous collage ready to 'blow the entire system sky-high'.[61] Moreover, Mahler's stylistic, and Benjamin's historiographical, constellations share the same extra-temporal desire of Syberberg's *Hitler* to 'say everything', to 'be everything', its 'insistence on occupying different spaces and times simultaneously', and perhaps more specifically its questioning, if not 'refusal of modern industrial civilization',[62] and the most deleterious effects of the latter's materialism and rationalism.

The populist practice of appropriating Mahler's music as material for film soundtracks is already one which plays with historical time in a loosely Benjaminian sense.[63] But within this, 'charged moments' of 'revolutionary action' are few and far between. Alongside Syberberg and Fassbinder might also be mentioned German leftist filmmaker Harun Farocki's *Zwischen zwei Kriegen* (*Between Two Wars*, 1978), an elegiac 'Trauerarbeit', according to Wilhelm Roth,[64] on inter-war oppression at the hands of capitalism and heavy industry, and a film characterised by drab imagery and solemn sociopolitical and philosophical pronouncements. Interspersed throughout are short instrumental cues from the final movement, 'Der Abschied', of Mahler's *Das Lied von der Erde*. Some are used as means of eliding scenes, and almost all comprise the funereal slow tread, drooping paired quaver figures, and swooning appoggiatura material, whether from near the beginning of the movement or from the long orchestral approach to the concluding vocal leave-taking that begins: 'He alighted from his horse and handed him the drink of farewell' (for example, bars 1–4, 9–18, 302–8, 312–16, 323–32). One rare exception is the use of bars 130–37, part of the more ardently striving orchestral interlude, marked 'zart leidenschaftlich' in first violins, that forms an eventual katabasis from more strenuous chromatic writing around E♭ minor and D♭ major to a static and desolate A minor, and comes between the final lines of the second sung verse: 'Weary mortals wend homewards. So that, in sleep, they may learn anew forgotten joy and youth,' and 'The birds huddle silent on their branches. The world is falling asleep!' Occurring at the conclusion of an earnest discussion among the characters about problems of international industrial cooperation versus competition, war, and the life of workers, the cue coincides with one character displaying his own crude pictorial political interpretation of the rapacious 'bird of the night' preying on the good of humankind (see Fig. 17.3), emblem of an empty modernisation in which the 'representation of the always-the-same as the "new" . . . characterises the consumption of commodities under capitalism.'[65]

Subscribing to an Adornian co-option of Mahler for mid-twentieth-century leftist causes is of course problematic. As I have discussed elsewhere,[66] Mahler's putative socialist tendencies were of a very different order from the political concerns that emerged after two world wars and a failed German republic.

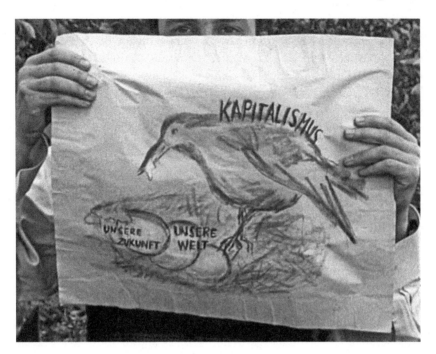

Fig. 17.3 Still from Farocki, *Zwischen zwei Kriegen* (*Between Two Wars*), 1978

Nevertheless, it is in this kind of coercive historical nexus that the value of historical materialism lies. As one character articulates the key Benjaminian philosophical cornerstone of the film, concerning the difference between conceptions of time in the lives of workers and the lives of bourgeois profiteers ('From all that happens to them, they are able to create a connection between what has gone before and what is to come, while in the meantime our entire way of life melts away'), and as, in one cue, the arrival at bar 303 of the tonic C minor on tremolo double basses near the beginning of the long orchestral approach mentioned above (returning us to the starting point of the whole movement) synchronises with the appearance on screen of torch-lit urban graffiti ('HITLER—DAS IST DER KRIEG'), one is continually reminded of how the histories of Germany and romanticism are closely intertwined; how some, like Thomas Mann and Syberberg, believe Nazism to have been the 'grotesque fulfilment—and betrayal—of German Romanticism';[67] and how Mahler and his music embody that emergent historical and cultural-political ambiguity of a democratic levelling of musical material carried out amid resolutely high-art, imperial, and establishment contexts and ambitions. *Das Lied von der Erde* combines drinking songs, delicate chinoiserie, and intense meditations on death couched in very personal as well as universal terms. It develops an attenuated harmonic and textural language beyond the Wagnerian, as well as a strophic-linear formal complexity that plays with conceptions of time and dissolution, marking both the waning of some (German) romantic traditions and the nurturing of new, perhaps more internationalist, ones.

The longest music cue in *Zwischen zwei Kriegen* is reserved for the end. A woman speaks: 'In this second war then, which began at the latest in 1933, the dead have nothing more to tell the living. Why they died, we could already have learnt from a previous war. In this war my diary remains empty. Learning is not encouraged.' The dirge-like journey back to the C minor tonic during bars 342^4–74, the moments of brief outpouring in strings and woodwind, the plodding quaver duplets, and the gradual thinning of texture, then accompany a slow-panning crane shot over the sill of an apartment window to reveal the chalked outline several stories below where the body of one of the politically oppressed characters fell to his death in a presumed suicide. Rain falls, slowly dissolving the outline, the white-tinged water flowing along the street and disappearing down the grill of a drain. The luxury of 'Der Abschied''s magical dissolutional conclusion is not afforded to us here, but this cue's length and sense of completion provide interim closure to what has been a filmic indictment of an impersonal system's exploitation of the individual and its inability to avoid or learn from the history of weaponised conflict in the drive for expansion of capital, land, and resources. The rest of Mahler's output is replete with militaristic references (marches, fanfares, bugle calls, drum strokes) and his *Wunderhorn* songs personalise notions of sacrifice, homeland, absence, and soldierly conduct almost certainly inspired by regular visitations and departures of military personnel in Iglau, his childhood home. There is even a brief possible militaristic reference in 'Von der Schönheit' in *Das Lied von der Erde* as the glittering young lads on horseback distract the young maidens from their flower-picking idyll (from bar 43).[68] The collision of Mahler and Farocki raises questions of, for example, how far nineteenth-century paternalistic culture has been able to extend into more recent times and form the engine of growth and destruction; the degree to which ideological appropriation is able silently to morph into political misconception; the way in which the New German Cinema's heyday and Mahler's resurrected popular reception coincided in the 1970s as agencies and symptoms of an extreme sociocultural mourning that risked airbrushing optimism out of consciousness in their pervasive 'exportable Weltschmerz'[69] and in the mass melancholy attributed to the German people; and the success, or otherwise, with which Mahler in musical terms, and more widely the twentieth-century globalised individual, political party, ethnic or religious grouping, society, and nation in human terms, have been able to deal with the precarious, dynamic, broken past, and to make coherent sense of its ever-proliferating 'pile of debris'.

Just how far Mahler's music can effectively be enlisted for the all-inclusive, extra-temporal, humanitarian world project is difficult to discern. A more controversial dimension to this process is introduced when his music is utilised in specifically Judaic film contexts. The juxtaposition of the opening of Mahler's Symphony 1 and the Middle Eastern sand dunes and camels of 1940 Palestine in Amos Gitai's film *Eden* (2001) is odd. Its prosaic story of conflicting political views (and interpersonal relationships) prior to the birth of the Jewish state of Israel has two main characters as left-wing American Zionists, who, along with an expatriate German bookseller, nevertheless promote non-discrimination between Jew and Arab, whilst another arrives to build Jewish settlements purely for financial reasons, and a fourth advocates an entirely separate state for the Jewish population and carries out acts of terrorism against the occupying British forces. If there is an undertone of Herzl and Jewish triumphalism, this might be said to be exacerbated by the soundtrack cues containing Mahler's exultant, though offstage, fanfare figures from the first movement's introduction, even though in the real world, as Karen Painter has plausibly argued,[70] the aspirations of Mahler's Zionist contemporary (Herzl's *Der Judenstaat* was published in Vienna in 1896) would seem far removed from the composer's assimilationist trajectory. On the other hand, the score of the film is built on a repeated inability to achieve completion or continuation, since not until the very end do any of the cues get past the movement's ruminative and fragmented introductory material. Perhaps this relentless provisionality is the fate of most film music; perhaps it is a deliberate ploy to render the music a metaphor for the troubled beginnings of Israel and the continuing instability of the region (in addition to the characters' failed relationships and the suicide of the bookseller, the greatest humanitarian among them, in the face of loss and lack of hope). If this is too simplistic, then perhaps the failure to cohere should be regarded as part of the very nature of the critical filmic repertoire Benjamin extolled, and as something that Mahler often musically celebrated even as he attempted at the same time to overcome it in his finished works—the inevitable but truly authentic fate of a post-romantic epigone of the type favoured in Benjamin's philosophy of history because their fragmented art works 'undercut the illusory Enlightenment vision of cumulative historical progress and ... the infinite perfectibility of man'.[71] 'Those who are born after such great spirits as Beethoven and Wagner, the epigones, have no easy task. For the harvest is already gathered in, and there remain only a few solitary ears of corn to glean,' as Mahler reportedly said in 1893.[72] As opposed to the eternal repetition and the myth of homogeneous, progressive historical time, this is Benjaminian Messianic time: ruptured, stretching to past and future, intensely felt, and made up of monadic instants, concentrates, or configurations. Near the end of the film, after the shock of discovering the suicide, the principal female Zionist character walks determinedly out into the street. We see her turn a corner and somehow emerge seamlessly and unchanged sixty years later into modern-day metropolitan Israel, where it may be that we are invited to contemplate what is now the fully functioning successful outcome of her early sociopolitical efforts, or are encouraged to lament the fact that in terms of instability, oppression, and mutual antagonism, nothing has changed in the region. This cross-temporal shift occurs during the same Mahler cue, which for the first time in the film continues past the introduction and into the more confidently striding 'Immer sehr gemächlich' of the 'Ging heut' Morgen über's Feld' song adaptation. Has coherence, continuity, integration at last been achieved? If it has, it appears to be too late as the black-screen end credit sequence is already under way by the time this musical point is reached, and we are by now outside the film and into the framing device that reveals its boundary and the artifice of its apparatus. Though *Eden* may not be particularly successful as a political film, it nevertheless avoids giving easy answers to intractable questions. The history of Mahler's music and its function within history are both implicated and reconfigured here, as his Symphony, co-opted rightly or wrongly as old-European but Janus-faced Jewish émigré in a twentieth-century Middle Eastern environment, and shifted back and forth through time, partakes in ' "the plural unity of future, past, and present" '.[73]

Rhizome

As Rolf Tiedemann observes, Benjamin's critique of traditional philosophy of history was that with its gaze 'happily turned towards the future, it is not concerned by the debris behind it [and] knows nothing of the prevailing catastrophe'. Because of this, his most cherished aim of redeeming the past 'is not compatible with the linear concept of teleological progress'.[74] Michael Löwy goes as far as to suggest that Benjamin's fragmented Messianic time 'draw[s] on the Jewish religious tradition to contest the model of thought that is common to Christian theodicy, the Enlightenment and the Hegelian philosophy of history'.[75] Whether theologically inspired or not, the abandonment of these models loosens history 'from a time of necessity to a time of possibilities, a random time, open at any moment to the unforeseeable irruption of the new'.[76] The wider implications of this have been mined since Benjamin's time by a variety of historians and philosophers, some of whom were listed near the beginning of this chapter. Siegfried Kracauer, for example, diagnosed Proust's radical de-emphasising of chronological history in terms of a 'discontinuous, non-causal succession of situations, or worlds, or periods' built on 'time atoms'.[77] Reinhart Koselleck viewed chance relatively and perspectivally as not 'unhistorical' but instead a 'motivational trace' that invites critique of the historiography of a set of conditions.[78] Jacques Rancière followed Benjamin's lead directly in advocating that history 'first gets interested in the exploration of the multiple paths at the unforeseen intersections . . . which constitute the uniqueness of the democratic age and also follow the rethinking of other ages'.[79] Since for him the 'real must be fictionalized in order to be thought', '[w]riting history and writing stories come under the same regime of truth', and the constructed fictions of politics and art connect 'what is done and what can be done', blurring the 'logic of facts' and the 'logic of fiction'.[80] Even Frank Ankersmit's attempted rehabilitation of historicism suggests, 'All that is of real importance in historical writing begins only once we have left time and chronology behind us.'[81] Empiricist chronicles and annals lack depth, scope, structure, and coherence. By contrast, 'it is the essence of historical narratives to *obliterate* or *transcend* time as much as possible,'[82] partly because, as individuals, we rarely experience the world and its historical representations in ordered sequence, but rather piecemeal, randomly, and with only the intermittent and not always reliable intervention of hindsight. If this is the case, then the implications of much earlier theorisations of time can be more fully realised. Jonathan Gorman summarises the temporal theory of R. G. Collingwood: 'time is a succession of past, present, and future, existing all at once *in thought*.'[83] This concept has been re-articulated by Preston King much more recently: 'The past is not *chronologically* present. But there is no escaping the fact that much of it is *substantively* so.'[84] The late twentieth-century end of utopian top-down conceptions of coherent historical continuity and processes of change or development mirrored shifts in political perceptions and realities. The repercussions of such de-objectification combined with de-temporalisation are manifold: past expectations do not align with present experience; the future is not implied by the past and present; the sudden, the surprising, and the chance create the unpredictable; the past is an unstable, shifting projection of present and future; the present becomes the centre, the focal point of convergence, but present moments do not necessarily follow in coherent and contiguous sequence, instead existing as mutually independent individual histories with their own past and future trajectories.[85]

In the midst of the 1980s 'postmodern turn', John Toews indicated how such an emerging 'new history' might operate:

> The heterogeneous historical experiences and cultural perspectives that ground the new history (or histories) are after all related to each other and to the official, unitary history they confront in specific, historically identifiable, empirically reconstructable ways. The connecting ties are horizontal, secular, contingent, dynamically changing and proliferating lines of opposition and reciprocity, of domination, subordination, and mutual recognition, not vertical lines with predetermined trajectories that merge in, or derive from, a common metahistorical essence or center. The empirical reconstruction and critical extension of these lines of connection, not from one privileged and dominating center but from many different locations within the open-ended web of relations, would seem to be the appropriate task of a potentially democratic and global history, a history in which all human beings would be recognized as active makers of their own history, even as they suffer and are molded as objects in the history of others.[86]

With freedom comes responsibility, however, and it would seem naïve to project the idea that purveyors of history have one and the same objective, evidentiary criteria, or even approach to 'truth', especially under the impress of the so-called linguistic turn. Nancy Partner refers to the fictionalising trend in popular and mass-media arenas on the one hand as a 'pandemic' ignored by, or beyond the control of, historical representations from the academy,[87] but on the other hand suggests that this ignores the 'more ancient and more popular view of fiction as a form of "invention" which could represent the meaning of reality in a way that expressively "concretizes", deepens and extends rather than undermines, the historian's task of truth-telling'.[88]

How might we then characterise the state of historiography in relation to Mahler in current times of apparently unlimited proliferation of information about, and accessibility to, the past? To call upon Paul Klee once again, his prophetically named 1922 painting *The Twittering Machine* could form an appropriate starting point (see Fig. 17.4). Though digital social media have recently been serving as catalyst and conduit for very real political change, a less conducive reading might see us act like hand-cranked organic automatons, tethered to the technological machinery of superabundant randomised communication and miscommunication, continually nudged into unthinking reception and regurgitation of each other's half-digested, self-purveyed, unreflective, everyday history. Nevertheless, such inter-communication may amount to just the kind of anti-historical, undifferentiated, 'disemplotted' chronicle and proliferating network of chance comments that many post-linguistic-turn radical historiographers wished to legitimise. Something like Proust's complex 'texture of reflections, analogies, reminiscences' and 'zigzag routes spreading over the whole scroll of the past',[89] and Rancière's determinedly non-arborescent attempt 'to think in terms of horizontal distributions, combinations between systems of possibilities' rather than in terms of 'surface and substratum'[90] might find a theoretical correlate in the radical leftist historiographical model of the rhizome propounded by Gilles Deleuze.

This image signifies a non-hierarchical mode of philosophical and historical inquiry contrary to the vertical and linear mode of arborescent thought based on the continual branching and division of organic growth, on beginnings and ends, and resulting binary oppositions. The rhizomatic model recognises multiplicities, shifting identities, the free flow of connecting operations, and blurred boundaries between phenomena rather than rigidly determined hierarchies and totalising historical perceptions. In short, this model acknowledges the circular, cyclic, and chaotic nature of the world: 'jumping from one already differentiated line to another', the rhizome's 'transversal communications between different lines scramble the genealogical trees ... The rhizome is antigenealogy.'[91] Its open-ended, fluid map of connections replaces, in even more extreme terms than Benjamin's, the teleological journey paradigm of history 'like a stream without beginning or end'.[92] This model has the potential to

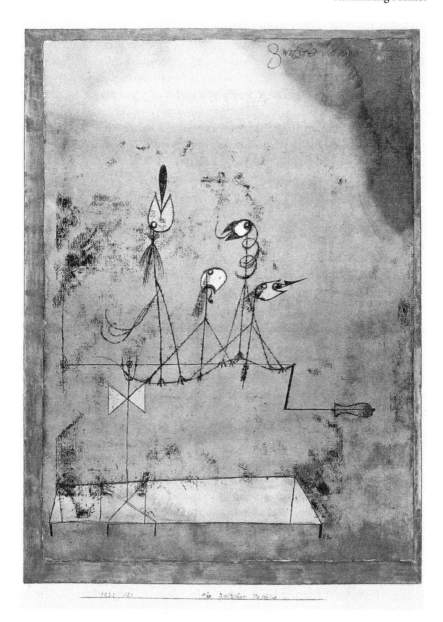

Fig. 17.4 Paul Klee, 'The Twittering Machine' (1922)

counter the epistemological difficulties confronting any conventionally linear historiographical project, and though there is a risk that the rhizome's rather desperate clamour for the freedom to think outside socially imposed norms (particularly, for Deleuze, outside the Western capitalist framework) can degenerate into self-indulgence, it might otherwise provide a fruitful means of addressing irregular, less consciously determined, surprising, and perhaps in-advertent, lateral offshoots between cultural phenomena that develop into what Deleuze calls a 'plateau' of shared meaning, content or form. Therefore, despite minimal or undeclared evidence to suggest direct intertextual reference, the rhizome model may at least encourage us to think again, when we project back through history and alight on the plateaus generated by the following.

It is difficult to establish whether there is any value in noting the similari-ties between the distinctive phrase in bars 1–2 of Paul McCartney's mid-1960s song 'Yesterday' and the violin solo in bars 101–2 from the fourth movement of Mahler's Third Symphony (see Ex.17.1). Though it is an exact melodic and tonal match, the McCartney occurs over a II7 – V7 – I progression in D minor, while the Mahler is underpinned by a static, implied second-inversion, trem-olo D minor chord in violas. Can one usefully compare the musical contexts of thirty-two-bar popular-song form with a larger, through-composed move-ment from seventy years earlier, with only vestiges of strophic structure? It is perhaps interesting that both pieces share a preoccupation with repeated fall-ing stepwise motion, some of which is combined with appoggiatura harmonic function: McCartney begins bars 1, 3, and 5 with 9–8, 9–8 and 4–3 appoggia-turas, respectively; Mahler opens the first ten bars of the movement with just the two alternating pitches A and B, has the voice produce a series of unre-solved downward appoggiaturas on 'Gib Acht!' and 'Ich Schlief!' (bars 20–21, 22–23, 37–38, and 39–40), and uses exactly the same appoggiatura effect in the violin solo mentioned above, between two vocal iterations of 'Deep is [the world's] woe!', as McCartney does in bar 3 of his song. Both musicians are here keenly aware of the expressive power of this technique in contexts of yearning. The two works are associated with the pain of absence in different ways, and, under the shadow of something dark, articulate an impossible longing for the eternity of what is lost or past, or indeed for an escape from time altogether: McCartney's song only believes in yesterday, Mahler's movement supposedly projects the hope that pain can be overcome by something deeper, and does so by calling on material from the symphony's real-time past—the trumpet motive from an early, faltering, stage of the first movement, bars 83–90—(but which is also from its creative future, since this movement was the last to be composed), and surrounding it with transformative, major-mode variants (horns bars 24–31, violins bars 58–67 and 119–29).

If it is very unlikely that McCartney had heard Mahler's Third Symphony by 1965 (the work was first broadcast by the BBC in 1947 and not given its public premiere (in London) until 1961),[93] then it is only marginally more conceiv-able that it was heard by popular songwriter Sammy Fain (1902–89), despite the fact that he lived and worked in New York where Willem Mengelberg gave four performances with the New York Philharmonic in 1922. Sixteen years later with Irving Kahal, Fain composed the song 'I'll be Seeing You', which became a major hit after being used in the 1944 romantic film of the

Ex. 17.1 (a) opening bars of McCartney's 'Yesterday'; and (b) bars 101–2, 24–27, and 119–21 of Mahler's Third Symphony, fourth movement

a)

b)

same title starring Ginger Rogers and Joseph Cotten. It has long been recognised that the principal phrase of the refrain bears a striking resemblance to the motive from the final movement of the symphony first heard in the cellos, bars 8–12,[94] and which recurs three further times as part of the main chorale complex (bars 99, 206, and 275), always in the strings (the last two appearances reinforced by flutes and horns, respectively), with varied harmonisations and degrees of chromatic alteration, and always as the second theme after restoration of the D major chorale, mediating between this and subsequent collapse (except for the final iteration which leads to the movement's triumphant conclusion) (see Ex. 17.2). Apart from the distinctive shared melodic shape reliant on frequent chromatic turn figures, it is notable that in versions 1, 3, and 4 Mahler uses the exact same 'false secondary dominant' idea as Fain to progress from chords I to II via a chromatically raised 5th either suggesting or stating a major version of chord III as preparation for a presumed cadence to chord VI/the relative minor, but which slides to chord II instead. Although Fain utilises a simpler harmonic language, the phrase structure of both is the same, comprising 4- or 2-bar periods, and marking a steady overall ascent in pitch. Symphony and song attempt to express 'what love tells them' from the perspective of temporal quandaries: the finale of the symphony revels in present achievement after past struggle, by including, and making strenuous efforts to overcome, troubling dissolutional material from the first movement; the song evokes a mixture of nostalgic loss and pathetic imaginative projection, as the protagonist envisions his loved one in future thoughts of cherished past experiences, rather like the archetypal work of popular melancholy longing, Irving Berlin's 'White Christmas' (1940) built on hopes for the future that are embedded in the past, and which opens with the same chromatic turn figure used in the Mahler and to a greater extent in the last movement of Symphony 9—perhaps one of the most intense expressions of the struggle between longing for an edenic past or future whilst struggling to accept its unattainability (see Fig. 17.5).[95] Audiences of the 1944 film, which centres on the idea of love overcoming past darknesses of trauma and crime, would presumably have felt the sentiments of the Fain/Kahal song even more strongly in a collective longing for the relationship of the two protagonists to succeed. In personal trajectories of experience within the histories of mass and 'high' culture, Mahler's nostalgic mode may well be seen as one chronological origin of Hollywood musical schmaltz but at the same time can be understood, in part, as its aesthetic goal, or culminating refinement. In that sense history is conceptualised a-chronologically, the lines of rhizomatic flight extending in multiple directions that defy or distort causality and teleology.

   This network of interconnections—direct or indirect, fortuitous or intended, historically focused or chronologically scattered—suggests potentially powerful acts of conceptual, creative, and aesthetic blending on the part of Mahler and us, his interpreters. How far can this process be taken? Capturing in music something of humanity's inner, spiritual nature in the face of the steady increase in contemporaneous erosion of such concerns at the hands of certain areas of scientific, political, and cultural activity is a Mahlerian preoccupation shared—to cast the rhizomatic net much more widely—in popular and mass media work by, for example, latter-day musician-philosopher David

Ex. 17.2 (a) opening bars of the refrain from 'I'll Be Seeing You'; and (b) the four statements of the secondary motive in Mahler's Third Symphony, last movement: (i) bars 8–11; (ii) bars 99–102; (iii) bars 206–8; and (iv) bars 275–78

Bowie who had an abiding interest in the displaced, post-Enlightenment human condition, and by philosophising filmmaker Christopher Nolan (via composer Hans Zimmer), who displays a persistent interest in forms of temporal non-linearity and ambiguity.

I'll be seeing you	I'll be seeing you	I'll be seeing you
In all the old familiar places	In every lovely summer's day;	In every lovely summer's day;
That this heart of mine	In every thing that's light	In every thing that's light
embraces	and gay.	and gay.
All day through.	I'll always think of you that way.	I'll always think of you that way.
In that small cafe;	I'll find you	I'll find you
The park across the way;	In the morning sun	In the morning sun
The children's carousel;	And when the night is new.	And when the night is new.
The chestnut trees;	I'll be looking at the moon,	I'll be looking at the moon,
The wishin' well.	But I'll be seeing you.	But I'll be seeing you.

I'm dreaming of a white Christmas,
Just like the ones I used to know.
Where the tree-tops glisten,
And children listen
To hear sleighbells in the snow.

Fig. 17.5 Lyrics of 'I'll Be Seeing You' and first verse of 'White Christmas'

Piecing together my own disemplotted historical reception and understanding of the track 'Slip Away' from Bowie's 2002 album *Heathen* suggests challenging possibilities: (1) a chance hearing on TV at the time of release; (2) an initial and growing sense of its appeal and depth; (3) purchase in 2003 revealing the CD booklet's provocative cultural context of vandalised 'high-art' renaissance paintings (among them, as identified in 2015, Reni's *The Slaughter of the Innocents* (1611), Dolci's *Maria Maddalena* (1660), and an unidentified version of *La Pietà*), along with, most strikingly, leather-bound folios of Einstein's *The General Theory of Relativity*, Freud's *The Interpretation of Dreams*, and Nietzsche's *The Gay Science* pictured together on a bookshelf (all works marking the birth of modernism in different ways, and originating in Mahler's cultural and geographical environment, the last of which provided the temporary title of his Third Symphony in summer 1895); (4) thirteen years later reading that Bowie acknowledged the influential role that the music of Mahler played at the time of the *Heathen* recording sessions,[96] and locating Bowie's spoken comments on the album's concern with alienation, isolation, barbarian or philistine thought, destruction alongside democratisation of culture, the early modernist overturning of cherished scientific, psychological, and religious beliefs by Einstein, Freud, and Nietzsche, and the need to re-purpose the human condition, to recast inner spiritual life in the absence of a fixed, reassuring 'masterplan.'[97]

   In musical analytical terms, the emerging plateau attains a degree of consistency by considering Mahler's most commercially prominent movement, the Adagietto from Symphony no. 5 as a 'composing out', on different levels, of significant structural elements of the track. Both are built to an extent on the use of substitute dominants often involving chromatic neighbour-note movement, in an F major tonal context. The track's opening four bars of instrumental introduction, as well as melodically inscribing the semitonal descent from 5 to 3 characteristic of early jazz, music-hall, and McCartney's 'When I'm Sixty-Four', crystallise the use of E7 and diminished chord on G—either side of the tonic—as alternative paths to that tonic subsequently used within verses and between refrain/verse and refrain/coda.[98] Mahler's movement dramatises such chromatic substitution (especially E7(9) – F) at moments of highly tensioned returns to the tonic (see Ex. 17.3).

The four-bar coda to 'Slip Away' oscillates between tonic chords of the song's two principal tonal areas (F major for verse/a minor for refrain), melodically alluding to the Mahler (rising C – D – E over F major chord)—as also do the verses' ascending, and the refrains' descending, stepwise movement.[99] The Adagietto offers a more extended compositional exploration of the same two principal tonal areas that are not only suggested in a local sense by the melodic and tonal ambiguity of the opening C – A pitch combination and the persistent use of F maj7 sonorities, but also clearly established through statement and modulation in the opening twenty bars. This exploration comprises subsequent structural shifts to keys immediately and chromatically adjacent to F: G♭ major from bar 47, E major (as the dominant of a minor) from bar 60, as well as D major (as subdominant of a minor) from bar 63, all approached via chromatic substitute dominants, as shown in Ex. 17.3.

Composed prior to, but released soon after, the events of 9/11, *Heathen* has acquired an association with those events, as if it somehow impossibly represents Bowie's prescient 'response' to them. In particular, 'Slip Away', its lyrics ostensibly inspired by characters from the TV programme 'The Uncle Floyd Show' syndicated in 1982, projects acute nostalgia for recent 'simpler times' with its sonic echoes of old-time bar piano and 1970s stylophone. At an even further chronological remove, Mahler's Adagietto has similarly accrued elegiac meaning in wider consciousness and has developed over the last fifteen years into a staple part of public commemorative activity surrounding the 2001 attacks. Music created chronologically before a major geo-political event becomes part of the subsequent history of that event, which, particularly in this case, has the power to change the nature of the pre-existent music in turn by reconstituting all of past time, and by cementing patterns of reception. Despite Bowie's declared belief in his album's generally more positive sentiments compared with most of his other work, and despite the biographical context known to have surrounded the Adagietto,[100] the pressures of societal re-description have proved irresistible.

It is in the nature of Hollywood to commodify things for its own purposes. In scoring terms, this often takes the form of isolating, fragmenting, and re-processing musical gestures, usually those that are craved for or feared most. Christopher Nolan's *Interstellar* (2014) provides a filmic realisation of the kind

Ex. 17. 3 (a) 'Slip Away': opening bars and shift from chorus back to verse; chromatic dominant substitutions; (b) Mahler 'Adagietto', chromatic dominant substitutions, bars 15, 28–30, 46, 59–60, 62–64, 71–72, 94–95

of historico-temporal unification at issue in the Deleuzian model, and indeed in the present chapter as a whole. Time is both transcended and is a terrifying oppressor, as heroic astronauts willingly sacrifice decades of relative time back home (a matter of mere hours in their own existence) in their pursuit of salvation for the human race, and are also mystically granted access to, and the ability to affect, their own past in a way which reveals the simultaneously

Ex. 17.3 Continued

horrific and transformative circularity of temporal phenomena. In the film's central relationship, after long separation a father is ultimately enabled to reunite with his daughter (now far older than himself) in fulfillment of a long-held promise—a glimpse into devoted familial longevity that in the real world Mahler was of course denied in the case of Maria (his eldest daughter who pre-deceased him in 1907) and her younger sibling Anna because of his own early death, except indirectly through the expressive legacy of his music. A secondary musical mode in Zimmer's score re-purposes that Mahlerian legacy as found in the chromatic, appoggiatura-laden harmonic language and string-dominated textures of Symphonies 9 and 10. As father and child work together near the beginning of the film to solve inexplicable gravitational phenomena that will eventually bring their own and humanity's salvation, the music alludes strongly to the *Kindertotenlieder* quotation towards the end of Mahler's Symphony no. 9 (Ex. 17.4).

Ex. 17.4 (a) reduction of *Interstellar* score at 19:18; (b) Mahler, Symphony no. 9, fourth movement, bars 165–67

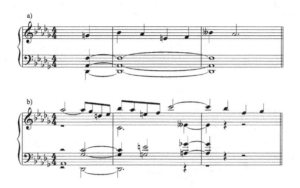

At the father's poignant leave-taking from his family, and later at the two remaining astronauts' emotionally charged departure from the all-important space-time 'wormhole'—one going forwards and the other effectively 'back' in time—Zimmer thematises a simple but potent gesture found throughout the final movement of Mahler's Symphony no. 10, a work which time did not allow the composer to complete. A signal part of the yearning adagio formal component that occurs either side of and between its allegro counterparts, the gesture comprises melodic rising 4th or 7th landing on a 4–3 appoggiatura (becoming a 7–6 when the chord over which the dissonance is heard is stated in second inversion), which Mahler expands and elaborates organically in his signature multi-voiced, slowly unfolding, and harmonically dense and directional chorale idiom. On two occasions, however, the rising incipit appears to stall and get stuck in its own reiterations: bars 66–77 in a fervent B major and over a return of the movement's opening drum strokes, after which the problem is temporarily set aside by the ensuing allegro section; and bars 186–217, infiltrating and halting the allegro, reintroducing the 'resolution' part of the gesture in major, minor, and mixed-mode variants, and heralding a brief oasis of calm B major from bar 225, before the return and collapse of the allegro into a reprise of the nine-note cataclysm from the first movement, and then the final ambiguously radiant-defiant-accepting apotheosis of the signal gesture in the movement's closing adagio section from bar 298, eventually reaching a tonally conclusive F♯ major. Zimmer fixatedly repeats his version of the gesture in F♯ tonality with major and minor resolutions (see Ex. 17.5), and later in the film (2:10:43–2:12:25) stretches it out over much more static harmonic underpinning with achingly Mahlerian chromatic passing notes and appoggiaturas in the upper string melody.

Zimmer has the luxury of not having to address long-term musical continuity, overall coherence, or completion since, for one thing, the film can

Ex. 17.5 Reduction of *Interstellar* score at 38:42 (first and second systems) and 39:59 (third system); Mahler, Symphony no. 10, fifth movement, bars 29–31, 66–68, 322–24 and 352–54

continue without his scoring. Mahler has to struggle, or to depict a struggle, to find an organic way to end that nevertheless suggests continuation, particularly in the Ninth and Tenth Symphonies where closure is so painfully resisted and deferred. Hearing Zimmer's reiteration of the same, tonally unchanging but sensorially overwhelming gesture of extreme tension-and-release returns us over and over again into a looping temporal cul-de-sac where larger-scale resolution is suppressed in favour of the repeated (pleasurable) re-living of micro-teleological advance followed by retreat. Seen through that lens, Mahler's attenuated yet contextually integrated, abstract yet strongly structured tonal and thematic treatment of the gesture appears not only to suggest ways of assimilating the irresolution/temporary resolution paradigm and ways of incorporating it into a developmental symphonic language that transcend the purveying of a single idea, but also to provide an organic escape from temporal inertia and circularity that extends even beyond the phenomenal boundaries of the finished work: a way, through structural-musical means, of coming to terms with, without denying, the extreme pain of past loss, and of generating hope for future fulfilment whilst always accepting the possibility of its unobtainability.

Conclusion

In the context of postwar music historiography, as early as 1967 in an attempt to free music historians from the grip of rigid historicism, Leo Treitler challenged the essentialism of 'the historical theory in which the causes of events are sought in developmental processes'.[101] Calling on diverse literary and philosophical sources from the 1950s to the 1980s (including Wittgenstein's remarkable pre-Deleuzian idea of language development as a mesh of intertwining fibres, from *Philosophical Investigations*), Treitler subsequently reinforced the value of a-temporal perspectives, the past's reciprocal contingency on changing presents, the role of accident and individual variation, contradiction and fragmentation, the constructed nature of the historical project, and the restrictiveness of purely chronological, causal, and evolutionary models.[102] The richness and pliability of the approach I have espoused here can go a long way towards addressing these issues as well as Carl Dahlhaus's canonic problematising of music history, since it is no longer flanked on the one hand 'by the dictates of "aesthetic autonomy"', or on the other hand 'by a theory of history that clings to the concept of "continuity"',[103] but rather, like historiography in general, as Anne Shreffler and George Iggers observe, it operates on more of an interpersonal, granulated micro-level than an impersonal, institutional macro-level.[104]

Mahler's time may have come, but it has done so in a complex, transient play of sociocultural regressiveness and progressiveness, aesthetics and commerce, chaos and discontinuity that he could not have envisaged, and that has not been fully appreciated. After all, he lived in precisely that era when the culmination of 'confidence in the beneficence of historical development' sat alongside increasingly 'deep uncertainty about the quality of modern life' played out in the kind of conflict between clinging to (or abandoning) mythic-poetic meaning and succumbing to (or accepting) potentially nihilistic rationalism that also underpinned the development of contemporaneous historiographic theory.[105] While they chronologically followed Mahler, these screen and popular composers and arrangers in many ways aesthetically, structurally, and idiomatically 'preceded' him—the musical-historical goal of their creativity is located in their forebear. Approaching Mahler in reverse through the lens of these artists of popular culture and mass media, and acknowledging the lines of proliferation that extend towards and from his music provide a glimpse into Deleuze's 'radically historical concept of "stratigraphic" time' or 'untimely series of events' in which 'every new occurrence opens up a potential to refigure all time' because each new artwork allows, even compels, us 'to view the entire history of [art] differently',[106] and encourages us to 'delineate the internal dynamisms of all kinds of events and the manner in which these unfold in reality', and to accept '"all kinds of correlations and movements back and forth between [history and becoming]"'.[107] The jury may still be out on whether it is legitimate to subscribe to the strong version of reading history backwards whereby in the network outlined above, McCartney, Bowie, and Zimmer would be taken as precursors to Mahler, or whether this can only ever be a metaphorical formulation, the most that can be said being 'that a later event might influence, or reconfigure, interpretation of an earlier event, in a meeting of hermeneutic horizons'.[108] In a sense, it does not matter, for the Deleuzian impulse is one which revels in widely divergent (sub)cultural ideas, movements and practices becoming 'fully' cultural through, in this case, music historiography 'as a protean, performative rhizome of interlinked scholarly praxes',[109] in which 'the simultaneity of the convergence . . . make[s] all succession vanish.'[110]

The challenge is to negotiate a meaningful path between not allowing history-telling to degenerate into a reactionary, one-dimensional enterprise, and yet policing the imaginative but potentially irresponsibly porous boundaries between fiction and historical representation, 'natural' time and historical time: a wavering balance of fluid process and temporary permanence. The idea of such a challenge is not new. Turning back to look forward: as successor to Benjamin *avant la lettre*, Schlegel wrote in 1798 that 'the historian is a prophet turned backwards';[111] just as Deleuze and Guattari state that history's function is 'to translate a co-existence of becomings into a succession',[112] two hundred years earlier Novalis was already aware that 'that which makes history into history [is] uniting the diversity of chance events into a pleasing and instructive whole . . . a writer of history must necessarily also be a poet.'[113] The true value of this poesy of history—as Nietzsche would argue in terms that presciently befitted Mahler and that grasped its abiding dilemma between construction and reconstruction—'will be seen to consist in its taking a familiar, perhaps commonplace theme, an everyday melody, and composing inspired variations on it, enhancing it, elevating it to a comprehensive symbol, and thus disclosing in the original theme a whole world of profundity, power and beauty'.[114]

Notes

1. "Alle Erinnerung ist Gegenwart"; 'Nur der rückwärtsgekehrte Blick bringt vorwärts, da der vorwärtsgekehrte Blick rückwärts führt.' Novalis, "Fragmente", in *Schriften*, 270 and 291.

2. Kundera, *The Curtain*, 148–49.

3. Kermode, *The Sense of an Ending*, 3.

4. Barnes, *The Sense of an Ending*, 3–4.

5. Barnes, *The Sense of an Ending*, 16–17.

6. Arendt, "The Modern Concept of History", 581.

7. Popper, *The Poverty of Historicism*, iii.

8. Nietzsche, "On the Use and Abuse of History for Life", in *Untimely Meditations*, 66, 75 and 76.

9. Sartre, *Critique of Dialectical Reason*, 54 and 56.

10. White, "The Burden of History", 123.

11. Gadamer, *Truth and Method*, 297.

12. A plethora of articles in the pages of the journal *History and Theory* from the 1960s to the present day by theorists such as Siegfried Kracauer, W. von Leyden, Hayden White, Murray Krieger, John R. Hall, Irving Wohlfarth, George A. Reisch, Michael Shermer, John E. Toews, Aviezer Tucker, and Helge Jordheim, as well as Robert Berkhofer's (1997), Michael Bentley's (1999) and Georg Iggers's (2005) book-length studies, and Bentley's voluminous anthology (1997) together give excellent insight into the development of, and challenges facing, the discipline of historiography.

13. Iggers, *Historiography in the Twentieth Century*, 118.

14. White, *Tropics of Discourse*, 82. Emphasis in the original.

15. White, "Interpretation in History", 289.

16. Barthes, "The Discourse of History"; Veyne, *Writing History*; Deleuze and Guattari, *Anti-Oedipus: Capitalism and Schizophrenia* and *A Thousand Plateaus*; Koselleck, *Futures Past. On the Semantics of Historical Time*; Ricoeur, "Narrative Time"; Baudrillard, "History: A Retro Scenario"; Kellner, *Language and Historical Representation*; Ankersmit and Kellner (eds.), *A New Philosophy of History*; Jenkins, *The Postmodern History Reader*; and Rancière, *The Names of History, The Politics of Aesthetics*, and *Figures of History*.

17. Koselleck, *The Practice of Conceptual History*, 101.

18. White, *The Content of the Form*, 173.

19. White, *The Content of the Form*, 51, citing Ricoeur, "Narrative Time", 171.

20. Koselleck, *Futures Past*, 126–27.

21. Rancière, *The Politics of Aesthetics*, 35.

22. Tucker, "Review of Niall Ferguson, *Virtual History: Alternatives and Counterfactuals*", 273.

23. Iggers, *Historiography in the Twentieth Century*, 147.

24. Schabbing, *Gustav Mahler als Konzert- und Operndirigent in Hamburg*.

25. Boulez, "La Biographie, Porquoi?," 3.

26. Schabbing, *Gustav Mahler als Konzert- und Operndirigent in Hamburg*, 74–76.

27. Floros, *Gustav Mahler. Visionär und Despot*, 84–86.

28. Schaefer, "Die Musikautographen von Gustav Mahler", 132 and 137. The practice of sketch studies becomes fraught with philosophical problems once it strays beyond the confines of establishing basic chronologies of the creative process. See Barham, "Review of *Gustav Mahler: Briefe und Musikautographen aus den Moldenhauer-Archiven*" for brief discussion of these issues.

29. Knittel, *Seeing Mahler. Music and the Language of Antisemitism in fin-de-siècle Vienna*.

30. See letters from Mahler in Blaukopf (ed.), *Gustav Mahler Briefe*, 163, 171–73, 206, and 277; English translations in Martner (ed.), *Selected Letters*, 172, 178–81, 201, and 262.

31. Martner, *Mahler's Concerts*. Martner almost entirely eschews value judgment in favour of dispassionate chronicling but cannot resist making unfounded remarks about Mahler's 'futile studies at the University' in 1879–80 (25), and the lack of influence of Weber's music on Mahler's creative activity in 1888 (the time of his completion of *Die drei Pintos*) (61).

32. 'Turned wrong way round, the relentless unforeseen was what we schoolchildren studied as "History," harmless history, where everything unexpected in its own time is chronicled on the page as inevitable. The terror of the unforeseen is what the science of history hides, turning a disaster into an epic' (Roth, *The Plot against America*, 113–14).

33. This is the type of approach I have attempted to adopt elsewhere in a revisionist account of Mahler's intellectual and political concerns, using the touchstone of contemporary journalism and authorial comments, along with wider contextual exploration, in a combined macro- and micro-historical mode: Barham, "'Mit der Dummheit kämpfen Götter selbst vergebens'".

34. Benjamin, "Theses on the Philosophy of History", 254.

35. Benjamin, "Theses on the Philosophy of History", 247.

36. Wohlfarth, "Smashing the Kaleidoscope", 197.

37. Benjamin, "Theses on the Philosophy of History", 254.

38. Benjamin is purportedly citing Gottfried Keller, but the source has yet to be identified.

39. Benjamin, "Theses on the Philosophy of History", 247.

40. Benjamin, "Theses on the Philosophy of History", 249 and 254.

41. Benjamin, "Theses on the Philosophy of History", 249.

42. Benjamin, *The Arcades Project* 462.

43. Benjamin, "Theses on the Philosophy of History," 252–53.

44. Fioretos, "Contraction: (Benjamin, Reading, History)", 564.

45. Hansen, *Cinema and Experience*, 76.

46. Benjamin, "The Work of Art in the Age of Mechanical Reproduction", 232.

47. Benjamin, "The Work of Art in the Age of Mechanical Reproduction", 224.

48. Benjamin, *The Arcades Project*, 474.

49. Benjamin, "The Work of Art in the Age of Mechanical Reproduction", 229.

50. Benjamin, *The Arcades Project*, 672.

51. I have explored elsewhere Fassbinder's use of Mahler's Eighth Symphony in the soundtrack of *Chinese Roulette* (1976), *Lili Marleen* (1980), and *Berlin Alexanderplatz* (1980) (see Barham, "'A Time of Gifts'").

52. Steinberg, "Introduction: Benjamin and the Critique of Allegorical Reason", 15.

53. Steinberg, "Introduction: Benjamin and the Critique of Allegorical Reason", 16.

54. Syberberg, *Syberbergs Filmbuch*, 14.

55. According to Adorno: 'He was drawn to the petrified, frozen or obsolete elements of civilization ... Small glass balls containing a landscape upon which snow fell when shook were among his favourite objects' (Adorno, "A Portrait of Walter Benjamin", 233).

56. Syberberg, "Filmography", 50.

57. Bloch, *Das Prinzip Hoffnung*, 1628.

58. Osborne, "Small-scale Victories, Large-scale Defeats", 95.

59. Kaes, *From Hitler to Heimat*, 72.

60. Wolin, *Walter Benjamin. An Aesthetic of Redemption*, 62.

61. Jameson, *Signatures of the Visible*, 71 and 74.

62. Sontag, "Syberberg's Hitler", 23 and 25.

63. See Barham, "Plundering Cultural Archives", "'A Time of Gifts'", and "Programming Mahler" for fuller historical and theoretical discussion of the more than 130 examples of filmic use of Mahler's music.

64. Roth, Excerpt from article on Harun Farocki, 11.

65. Wolin, *Walter Benjamin. An Aesthetic of Redemption*, 51.

66. Barham, "'Mit der Dummheit kämpfen Götter selbst vergebens'".

67. Sontag, "Syberberg's Hitler", 18.

68. Compare especially bar 50 onwards with the concluding Allegro Vivace section of Tchaikovsky's *1812 Overture*.

69. Krabbe, "Die Neuen Caligaris", 59.

70. Painter, "From Zionism to Assimilation".

71. Wolin, *Walter Benjamin. An Aesthetic of Redemption*, 59.

72. Bauer-Lechner, *Recollections of Gustav Mahler*, 38.

73. White, *The Content of the Form*, 51, citing Ricoeur, "Narrative Time", 171.

74. Tiedemann, *Studien zur Philosophie Walter Benjamins*, 138.

75. Löwy, *Fire Alarm. Reading Walter Benjamin's 'On the Concept of History,'* 102.

76. Löwy, *Fire Alarm*, 102.

77. Kracauer, "Time and History", 76.

78. Koselleck, *Futures Past*, 115–16.

79. Rancière, *The Names of History*, 102–3.

80. Rancière, *The Politics of Aesthetics*, 38 and 39.

81. Ankersmit, *Meaning, Truth and Reference*, 39.

82. Ankersmit, *Meaning, Truth and Reference*, 40. See Jansen, "Time, Narrative, and Fiction" for a useful investigation of forms of historiographical time.

83. Gorman, "The Limits of Historiographical Choice in Temporal Distinctions", 163, referring to Collingwood, "Some Perplexities about Time; with an Attempted Solution".

84. King, *Thinking Past a Problem*, 55.

85. Paraphrased from Hölscher, "Mysteries of Historical Order", 139.

86. Toews, "Perspectives on 'The Old History and the New'", 698.

87. Partner, "Historicity in an Age of Reality-Fictions", 23–24. See also Toews, "Review: A New Philosophy of History?" for a response to this.

88. Partner, "Historicity in an Age of Reality-Fictions", paraphrased in Toews, "Review: A New Philosophy of History?" 239.

89. Kracauer, "Time and History", 76.

90. Rancière, *The Politics of Aesthetics*, 49.

91. Deleuze and Guattari, *A Thousand Plateaus*, 11 and 12.

92. Deleuze and Guattari, *A Thousand Plateaus*, 28.

93. I am grateful to Sybille Werner for this information on the first performances of the Third Symphony. McCartney reputedly 'composed' his song in a dream and was initially concerned that he had unconsciously plagiarised the melody from another artist's work (see Turner, *A Hard Day's Write*, 83).

94. Most likely Deryck Cooke was the first to note this in a radio broadcast of 1970. This in turn was observed by Hans Keller in the article "Truth & Music", in *Music and Musicians Magazine*, November 1970.

95. The song's poetic reference to children and sleighbells is also suggestive of the opening of Mahler's Fourth Symphony, a work which makes its way to a state of paradisiac past/future innocence by means of a retrospective historical channeling and re-working of eighteenth-century idioms.

96. See Pegg, *The Complete David Bowie*, 405 and 422.

97. See Bowie, "A Philosophical Conversation with David Bowie", "'Heathen' cd interview", and "David Bowie 2002 Heathen interview".

98. A version of the song produced a year earlier for the never-released *Toy* album, contains an additional instance of the E7 – F shift in the verse's return, instead of Gdim – F, at 'some of us will always stay behind'.

99. Bowie's more exact model for parts of the verse might have been the Bach-Gounod *Ave Maria* (1853)—itself a play with, through the overwriting of, past material—with which it shares very similar sequential movement and diminished

harmony: compare bars 1–6 of Bowie's verse with bars 16–21 of the Bach-Gounod piece which may well have been heard in the Bowie household on radio or vocalised by his mother who was a keen singer of related repertoire such as Mendelssohn's 'O for the Wings of a Dove' from *Hear My Prayer* (1844) (TV interview with Michael Parkinson, 2002, https://www.youtube.com/watch?v=N2EhAR8mMWc, accessed July 2015).

100. See Kaplan, "Adagietto: From Mahler with Love".

101. Treitler, "On Historical Criticism". 201.

102. See Treitler, "The Present as History", "What Kind of Story Is History?," and "History and Music."

103. Dahlhaus, *Foundations of Music History*, 19.

104. See Schreffler, "Berlin Walls: Dahlhaus, Knepler, and Ideologies of Music History", 523, and Iggers, *Historiography in the Twentieth Century*, 99.

105. Iggers, *Historiography in the Twentieth Century*, 141.

106. Colebrook, "Introduction," 26–27. A reiteration, curiously, of modernist T. S. Eliot's statement in the 1921 essay "Tradition and the Individual Talent": 'What happens when a new work of art is created is something that happens simultaneously to all the works of art which preceded it' (*Selected Essays*. London: Faber & Faber, 1951, 15).

107. Patton, "Events, Becoming and History", 49 and 50, citing Deleuze, *Two Regimes of Madness*, 377.

108. Williams, "Review of Michael Klein. *Intertextuality in Western Art Music*", 319. See Lampert's discussion of 'backward', 'quantum', or 'co-existent' causality in the context of Deleuzian historical theory, in Lampert, *Deleuze and Guattari's Philosophy of History*, 156–58 and 162–64.

109. Kügle, "Past Perfect", 85.

110. Lampert, *Deleuze and Guattari's Philosophy of History*, 84. It is in this historiographical spirit that the recent phenomenon of Mahler remixes may best be approached—an aesthetic seemingly predicated on a mashing up of historical time, a scrambling of musical structure into disemplotted 'time atoms' within settings of intense repetition (see Barham, " 'Not Necessarily Mahler' ").

111. Athenaeum Fragment no. 80, in Schlegel, *Philosophical Fragments*, 27.

112. Deleuze and Guattari, *A Thousand Plateaus*, 430.

113. *Heinrich von Ofterdingen*, publ. 1802, cited in Koselleck, *Futures Past*, 127.

114. Nietzsche, "On the Use and Abuse of History for Life", in *Untimely Meditations*, 93.

Bibliography

Abbate, Carolyn. *Unsung Voices: Opera and Music Narrative in the Nineteenth Century*. Princeton: Princeton University Press, 1991.

Adler, Emma. "Biografie Victor Adlers". Vienna: Verein für Geschichte der Arbeiterinnenbewegung, n.d. Adler-Archiv, Mappe 29, 1115 (photocopy, Internationale Gustav Mahler Gesellschaft, Vienna).

Adorno, Theodor W. *Mahler: eine musikalische Physiognomik*. Frankfurt: Suhrkamp Verlag, 1960.

Adorno, Theodor W. *Ästhetische Theorie*. Gesammelte Schriften, 7. Frankfurt am Main: Suhrkamp, 1970.

Adorno, Theodor W. "Mahler. Eine musikalische Physiognomik". In *Die musikalischen Monographien*, 149–320. Gesammelte Schriften, 13. Frankfurt am Main: Suhrkamp, 1971.

Adorno, Theodor W. *In Search of Wagner*. Transl. R. Livingstone. London: Verso, 1981.

Adorno, Theodor W. "A Portrait of Walter Benjamin". In *Prisms*, 227–42. Theodor Adorno Transl. Samuel Weber and Shierry Weber. Cambridge, Mass.: MIT Press, [1967] 1981.

Adorno, Theodor W. *Mahler: A Musical Physiognomy*. Transl. Edmund Jephcott. Chicago: University of Chicago Press, 1992.

Adorno, Theodor W. "Mahler (Centenary Address, Vienna 1960)". In *Quasi Una Fantasia: Essays on Modern Music*, 81–110. Transl. Edmund Jephcott. London: Verso, 1998.

Agawu, V. Kofi. "Structural 'Highpoints' in Schumann's *Dichterliebe*". *Music Analysis* 3 (1984): 159–80.

Agawu, V. Kofi. "Mahler's Tonal Strategies: A Study of the Song Cycles". *Journal of Musicological Research* 6 (1986): 1–47.

Agawu, V. Kofi. "Tonal Strategy in the First Movement of Mahler's Tenth Symphony". *19th-Century Music* 9 (1986): 222–33.

Agawu, V. Kofi. "Theory and Practice in the Analysis of the Nineteenth-Century Lied". *Music Analysis* 11 (1992): 3–36.

Agawu, V. Kofi. "Prolonged Counterpoint in Mahler". In *Mahler Studies*, 217–47. Ed. Stephen E. Hefling. Cambridge: Cambridge University Press, 1997.

Agawu, V. Kofi. *Music as Discourse: Semiotic Adventures in Romantic Music*. Oxford: Oxford University Press, 2009.

Almén, Byron. *A Theory of Musical Narrative*. Bloomington: Indiana University Press, 2008.

Alpert, Hollis. "The Murder of Mahler". *Saturday Review*, 8 February 1975: 39.

Andraschke, Peter. *Gustav Mahlers IX. Symphonie. Kompositionsprozess und Analyse*. Wiesbaden: Franz Steiner, 1976.

Ankersmit, Frank. *Meaning, Truth and Reference in Historical Representation*. New York: Cornell University Press, 2012.

Ankersmit, Frank and Hans Kellner (eds.). *A New Philosophy of History*. London: Reaktion Books, 1995.

Anonymous. Review of Visconti's *Death in Venice*. *Guardian*, 4 March 1971: 8.

Appel, Bernhard R. "Humoreske". In *Die Musik in Geschichte und Gegenwart, Sachteil*, Vol. 4, 454–58. Ed. Ludwig Finscher. Kassel: Bärenreiter Metzler, 1996.

Arendt, Hannah. "The Modern Concept of History". *Review of Politics* 20/4 (1958): 570–90.

Armstrong, Charles. *Romantic Organicism: From Idealist Origins to Ambivalent Afterlife*. Basingstoke: Palgrave Macmillan, 2003.

Ashby, Arved. *Absolute Music, Mechanical Reproduction*. Berkeley: University of California Press, 2010.

Bailey, Robert. "*Die Meistersinger* Act II: Syntax and Structure". Unpublished paper read at the International Wagner-Verdi Congress, Ithaca, NY, 1984.

Balázs, Béla. *Early Film Theory: Visible Man and the Spirit of Film*. Transl. Rodney Livingstone. Ed. Erica Carter. New York: Berghahn Books, 2010.

Banks, Paul. "Mahler 2: Some Answers?" *Musical Times* 128/1730 (April 1987): 203, 205–6.

Banks, Paul. "Aspects of Mahler's Fifth Symphony: Performance Practice and Interpretation". *Musical Times* 130/1755 (1989): 258–65.

Barham, Jeremy. "Mahler the Thinker: The Books of the Alma Mahler-Werfel Collection". In *Perspectives on Gustav Mahler*, 37–151. Ed. Jeremy Barham. Aldershot: Ashgate, 2005.

Barham, Jeremy. "Review of *Gustav Mahler: Briefe und Musikautographen aus den Moldenhauer-Archiven in der Bayerischen Staatsbibliothek* (Munich: Bayerische Staatsbibliothek und Kulturstiftung der Länder, March 2003)". *Music & Letters*, 87/1 (2006): 147–53.

Barham, Jeremy. (ed.). *The Cambridge Companion to Mahler*. Cambridge: Cambridge University Press, 2007.

Barham, Jeremy. "Plundering Cultural Archives and Transcending Diegetics: Mahler's Music as 'Overscore'". *Music and the Moving Image* (Illinois) 3/1 (2010): 1–24.

Barham, Jeremy. "'A Time of Gifts': Mahler's Eighth, Fassbinder's Cinema, and Musical Politics". In *The Total Work of Art: Mahler's Eighth Symphony in Context. Studien zur Wertungsforschung* 52, 61–80. Ed. Elisabeth Kappel. Vienna: Universal Edition, 2011.

Barham, Jeremy. "Programming Mahler: Meaning, Redescription, and the Post-Adornian Counterlife". *Nineteenth-Century Music Review* (issue guest edited by Jeremy Barham: "Mahler: Centenary Commentaries on Musical Meaning") 8/2 (November 2011): 255–71.

Barham, Jeremy. "'Not Necessarily Mahler': Remix, Samples and Borrowing in the Age of 'Wiki'". *Contemporary Music Review* 33/2 (2014): 1–20.

Barham, Jeremy. "'Mit der Dummheit kämpfen Götter selbst vergebens'. Mahler, the Politics of Reason, and the Metaphysics of Spiritualism." In *Naturlauf: Scholarly Journeys Toward Gustav Mahler, Essays in Honour of Henry-Louis de La Grange at His Ninetieth Birthday*, 73–109. Ed. Paul-André Bempéchat. Berne: Peter Lang, 2016.

Barham, Jeremy. *Post-Centenary Mahler: Revaluing Musical Meaning*. Bloomington: Indiana University Press, forthcoming.

Barnes, Julian. *The Sense of an Ending*. London: Jonathan Cape, 2011.

Barry, Barbara. "In Search of an Ending: Reframing Mahler's Contexts of Closure". *Journal of Musicological Research* 26 (2007): 55–68.

Barthes, Roland. "The Discourse of History" [1967]. Transl. Stephen Bann. *Comparative Criticism* 3 (1981): 7–20.

Batka, Richard. "Viertes philharmonisches Konzert. (Neues Deutsches Theater)". *Prager Tagblatt*, February 26, 1904: n.p.

Baudrillard, Jean. "History: A Retro Scenario" [1981]. In *Simulacra and Simulation*, 43–48. Transl. Sheila Faria Glaser. Ann Arbor: University of Michigan Press, 1994.

Bauer-Lechner, Natalie. *Fragmente: Gelerntes und Gelebtes*. Vienna: R. Lechner, 1907.

Bauer-Lechner, Natalie. *Errinerungen an Gustav Mahler*. Leipzig: E. P. Tal, 1923.

Bauer-Lechner, Natalie. *Recollections of Gustav Mahler* [1923]. Transl. Dika Newlin. Ed. Peter Franklin. London: Faber Music, 1980.

Bauer-Lechner, Natalie. *Gustav Mahler in den Erinnerungen von Natalie Bauer-Lechner*. Ed. Herbert Killian. Hamburg: Karl Dieter Wagner, 1984.

Bauer-Lechner, Natalie. "Brief über Mahlers Lieben an Hans Riehl". *The Musical Quarterly* 97/1 (2014): 21–65; reprinted in corrected layout, *The Musical Quarterly* 97/3 (2014): 497–541.

Bauman, Zygmunt. *Modernity and Ambivalence*. Cambridge: Polity Press, 1991.

Baumgarten, Franz Ferdinand. *Zirkus Reinhardt*. Potsdam: Tillgner, 1920.

Bazin, André. *What Is Cinema?* Vol. 1. Transl. Hugh Gray. 1967; reprint ed., Berkeley: University of California Press, 2005.

Beiner, Ronald. "Walter Benjamin's Philosophy of History". *Political Theory* 12/3 (August 1984): 423–34.

Bekker, Paul. *Die Sinfonie von Beethoven bis Mahler*. Berlin: Schuster & Loeffler, 1918.

Bekker, Paul. *Gustav Mahlers Sinfonien*. Berlin: Schuster and Loeffler, 1921.

Bempéchat, Paul-André (ed.). *Naturlauf. Scholarly Journeys Toward Gustav Mahler. Essays in Honour of Henry-Louis de La Grange for His 90th Birthday*. New York: Peter Lang, 2016.

Benjamin, Walter. *The Arcades Project* [1928–40]. Transl. Howard Eiland and Kevin McLaughlin. Cambridge, Mass: Belknap Press of Harvard University Press, 1999.

Benjamin, Walter. "Theses on the Philosophy of History". In *Illuminations*, 245–55. Ed. Hannah Arendt. London: Pimlico, [1950] 1999.

Benjamin, Walter. "The Work of Art in the Age of Mechanical Reproduction" [1950]. In *Illuminations*, 211–44. Ed. Hannah Arendt. London: Pimlico, 1999.

Bentley, Michael (ed.). *Companion to Historiography*. London: Routledge, 1997.

Berger, Christian and Schnitzler, Günter (eds.). *Bahnbrüche: Gustav Mahler*. Freiburg: Rombach, 2015.

Berger, Karol. "Diegesis and Mimesis: The Poetic Modes and the Matter of Artistic Presentation". *Journal of Musicology* 12 (1994): 407–33.

Berger, Karol. *Modern Historiography*. London: Routledge, 1999.

Bergson, Henri. *Essai sur les données immédiates de la conscience*. Paris: Alcan, 1889.

Bergson, Henri. *Time and Free Will*. Transl. F. L. Pogson. London: George Allen, 1913.

Berkhofer, Robert F., Jr. *Beyond the Great Story: History as Text and Discourse*. Cambridge, Mass.: The Belknap Press of Harvard University Press, 1997.

Bhabha, Homi. *The Location of Culture*. London: Routledge, 1994.

Biebuyck, Benjamin, Praet, Danny, and Vanden Poel, Isabelle. 'Cults and Migrations: Nietzsche's Meditations on Orphism, Pythagoreanism, and the Greek Mysteries". In *Nietzsche and Antiquity: His Reaction to the Classical Tradition*, 151–69. Ed. Paul Bishop. Rochester, N.Y.: Camden House, 2004.

Blaukopf, Herta (ed.). *Gustav Mahler—Richard Strauss Correspondence 1888–1911*. Transl. Edmund Jephcott. London: Faber and Faber, 1984.

Blaukopf, Herta (ed.). *Mahler's Unknown Letters*. Transl. Richard Stokes. London: Victor Gollancz, 1986.

Blaukopf, Herta (ed.). *Gustav Mahler Briefe*. Rev. edn. Vienna: Zsolnay, 1996.

Blaukopf, Kurt. *Mahler oder der Zeitgenosse der Zukunft*. Vienna: Fritz Molden, 1969. Transl. Inge Goodwin as *Gustav Mahler*. London: Allen Lane, 1973.

Bloch, Ernst. *Das Prinzip Hoffnung*. Frankfurt: Suhrkamp, 1959.

Bloch, Ernst. "Über Beckmesser's Preis-Lied Text". In *Literarische Aufsätze*, 178–84. Frankfurt Am Main: Suhrkamp, 1965.

Bogue, Ronald. *Deleuze on Cinema*. New York: Routledge, 2003.

Bohrer, Karl Heinz. *Suddenness. On the Moment of Aesthetic Experience*. New York: Columbia University Press, 1994.

Bonds, Mark Evan. *After Beethoven. Imperatives of Originality in the Symphony*. Cambridge, Mass.: Harvard University Press, 1996.

Borio, Gianmario. "Le parole cancellate e le tracce: sul primo movimento della Prima Sinfonia di Mahler". In *Studi sul Novecento musicale in memoria di Ugo Duse*, 15–28. Ed. Nino Albarosa and Roberto Calabretto. Udine: Forum, 2000.

Borio, Gianmario. "Über Sinn und Bedeutung in der Musik. Ein Blick auf Adornos Musikphilosophie". In *Die Lebendigkeit der kritischen Gesellschaftstheorie*, 109–29. Ed. Andreas Gruschka and Ulrich Oevermann. Weltzer: Buchse der Pandora, 2004.

Bösch, Gabriele. "Die Kunst des inneren Sehens: Ernst Stöhr—Leben und Werk". Unpubl. diss. Philipps-Universität, Marburg, 1992.

Botstein, Leon. "Whose Gustav Mahler? Reception, Interpretation, and History". In *Mahler and His World*, 1–53. Ed. Karen Painter. Princeton: Princeton University Press, 2002.

Boulez, Pierre. "La Biographie, Pourquoi?" In Henry-Louis de La Grange, *Gustav Mahler. Chronique d'Une Vie I. Vers La Gloire 1860-1900*, 1–3. Paris: Fayard, 1979.

Boulez, Pierre. "Mahler: Our Contemporary?" In *Pierre Boulez. Orientations*, 295–303. Ed. Jean-Jacques Nattiez. Transl. Martin Cooper. London: Faber and Faber, 1986. [Orig. "Mahler actuel?" in *Gustav Mahler et Vienne*, 11–26. Paris: Librairie Générale Française, 1979.]

Bowie, Andrew. *Aesthetics and Subjectivity: from Kant to Nietzsche*, 2nd edn. Manchester: Manchester University Press, 2003.

Bowie, David. "A Philosophical Conversation with David Bowie". Interview with Guillaume Durand on *Heathen* album, for French television, 2002. https://www.youtube.com/watch?v=TajCh41y17I accessed July 2015.

Bowie, David. "David Bowie 2002 Heathen interview". https://www.youtube.com/watch?v=CLCRSP5TCAA accessed July 2015.

Bowie, David. "'Heathen' cd interview.'" Interview with Kay Rush for Spanish television, part 1, 2002: https://www.youtube.com/watch?v=ohb3IAWt4cs; part 2, 2002: https://www.youtube.com/watch?v=Ah3VANVlCA0 accessed July 2015.

Boyle, Nicholas. "Goethe, Johann Wolfgang von". *Routledge Encyclopedia of Philosophy*. Ed. E. Craig. London: Routledge, 1998. Retrieved August 21, 2012, from http://www.rep.routledge.com/article/DC030.

Bradbury, Malcolm. *The Social Context of Modern English Literature*. Oxford: Blackwell, 1971.

Bradshaw, Peter. "Ken Russell: His Film Career Was One Colossal, Chaotic Rhapsody". *Guardian*, 28 November 2011: http://www.guardian.co.uk/film/2011/nov/28/ken-russell-appreciation-peter-bradshaw?intcmp=239.

Braun, Emily. "Klimtomania/Klimtophobia". In *Gustav Klimt: Modernism in the Making*, 40–53. Ed. Colin B. Bailey. New York and Ottawa: Harry N. Abrams and National Gallery of Canada, 2001.

Breckling, Molly M. "Tears from a Nightingale: Analytical Duality in Gustav Mahler's 'Wo die schönen Trompeten blasen'". *Music Research Forum* 19 (2004): 49–70.

Breckling, Molly M. "Narrative Strategies in Gustav Mahler's Balladic *Wunderhorn Lieder*". Unpublished Ph.D. diss. University of North Carolina, Chapel Hill, 2010.

Brinkmann, Reinhold. "In the Time of the Eroica". In *Beethoven and His World*, 1–26. Ed. Scott Burnham and Michael P. Steinberg. Transl. Irene Zedlacher. Princeton: Princeton University Press, 2000.

Brod, Max. "Gustav Mahlers jüdische Melodien". *Musikblätter des Anbruch* 2/10-2 (1920): 378–79.

Brotbeck, Roman. "Verdrängung und Abwehr. Die verpaßte Vergangenheitsbewältigung in Friedrich Blumes Enzyklopädie *Die Musik in Geschichte und Gegenwart*". In *Musikwissenschaft—eine verspätete Disziplin? Die akademische Musikforschung zwischen Fortschrittsglauben und Modernitätsverweigerung*, 347–84. Ed. Anselm Gerhard. Stuttgart: Metzler, 2000.

Bruckner, Anton. *IX. Symphonie D-Moll (1. Satz—Scherzo & Trio—Adagio)*. Sämtliche Werke IX, Studienpartitur, Kritische Neuausgabe, unter berücksichtigung der Arbeiten von Alfred Orel und Leopold Nowak, vorgelegt von Benjamin Gunnar Cohrs. Wien: Musikwissenschaftlicher Verlag der Internationalen Bruckner-Gesellschaft, 2000.

Buhler, James. "'Breakthrough' as Critique of Form: The Finale of Mahler's First Symphony". *19th-Century Music* 20/2 (1996): 125–43.

Buhler, James. "Theme, Thematic Process, and Variant-Form in the Andante moderato of Mahler's Sixth Symphony". In *Perspectives on Gustav Mahler*, 255–88. Ed. Jeremy Barham. Aldershot: Ashgate Press, 2005.

Calinescu, Matei. *Faces of Modernity: Avant-Garde, Decadence, Kitsch.* Bloomington: Indiana University Press, 1977.

Caplin, William E. *Classical Form: A Theory of Formal Functions for the Instrumental Music of Haydn, Mozart, and Beethoven.* New York: Oxford University Press, 2000.

Caplin, William E. "The Classical Cadence: Conceptions and Misconceptions". *Journal of the American Musicological Society* 57/1 (2004): 51–117.

Cardus, Neville. "Mahler, Warts and All". *Guardian*, 16 April 1966: 7.

Cardus, Neville. "Alma's Mahler". *Guardian*, 29 November 1968: 9.

Cardus, Neville. "Glorious John". *Guardian*, 30 July 1970: 11.

Cardus, Neville. "More of Mahler". *Guardian*, 19 July 1973: 9.

Cardus, Neville. "Review of 1973 edition of Alma Mahler, *Memories and Letters*". *Guardian*, 10 December 1973: 10.

Celestini, Federico. "Der Trivialitätsvorwurf an Gustav Mahler: eine diskursanalytische Betrachtung (1889–1911)". *Archiv für Musikwissenschaft* 62 (2005): 165–76.

Celestini, Federico. *Die Unordnung der Dinge. Das Groteske in der Wiener Moderne.* Beihefte zum Archiv für Musikwissenschaft, 56. Stuttgart: Steiner Verlag, 2006.

Celestini, Federico. "Literature as Déjà-Vu? The Third Movement of Gustav Mahler's First Symphony". In *Phrase and Subject: Studies in Literature and Music*, 153–66. Ed. Delia da Sousa Correa. Oxford: Legenda, 2006.

Celestini, Federico. "The Acoustic Proximity of Temporal Distance. Auratic Sonority in Mahler's *Lieder eines fahrenden Gesellen*". In *Music as Social and Cultural Practice. Essays in Honour of Reinhard Strohm*, 355–73. Ed. Melania Bucciarelli and Berta Joncus. Woodbridge: Boydell & Brewer, 2007.

Celestini, Federico. "Gustav Mahlers Fünfte Symphonie". In *Gustav Mahler. Interpretationen seiner Werke*, 1–51. Ed. Peter Revers and Oliver Korte. 2nd Vol. Laaber: Laaber-Verlag, 2011.

Celestini, Federico. "Gustav Mahler und die jüdische Moderne". In *Gustav Mahler– Arnold Schönberg und die Wiener Moderne*, 11–25. Ed. Karl Katschthaler. Frankfurt am Main: Peter Lang Edition, 2013.

Celestini, Federico. *Nietzsches Musikphilosophie. Zur Performativität des Denkens.* Paderborn: Wilhelm Fink Verlag, 2016.

Chua, Daniel. "The Promise of Nothing: The Dialectic of Freedom in Adorno's Beethoven". *Beethoven Forum* 12, 13–35. Urbana-Champaign: University of Illinois Press, 2005.

Cohn, Richard. "Maximally Smooth Cycles, Hexatonic Systems, and the Analysis of Late-Romantic Triadic Progressions". *Music Analysis* 15/1 (1996): 9–40.

Cohrs, Benjamin Gunnar. "Vorwort". In Bruckner, *IX. Symphonie D-Moll*, VII–XII. *Sämtliche Werke IX, Studienpartitur, Kritische Neuausgabe, unter berücksichtigung der Arbeiten von Alfred Orel und Leopold Nowak, vorgelegt von Benjamin Gunnar Cohrs*. Wien: Musikwissenschaftlicher Verlag der Internationalen Bruckner-Gesellschaft, 2000.

Colebrook, Claire. "Introduction". In *Deleuze and History*, 1–32. Ed. Jeffrey A. Bell and Claire Colebrook. Edinburgh: Edinburgh University Press, 2009.

Coleman, John. "A Load of Symbolics". *New Statesman* 87 (5 April 1974): 488.

Collingwood, R. G. "Some Perplexities about Time; with an Attempted Solution". *Proceedings of the Aristotelian Society* 26 (1925–26): 135–50.

Comini, Alessandra. "Vampires, Virgins and Voyeurs in Imperial Vienna". In *Woman as Sex Object: Studies in Erotic Art, 1730–1970*, 207–21. Ed. Thomas B. Hess and Linda Nochlin. New York: Newsweek (Arts News Annual, 38), 1972.

Cooke, Deryck. *Gustav Mahler. An Introduction to His Music*. London: Faber Music, 1980.

Csáky, Moritz. "Die Wiener Moderne. Ein Beitrag zu einer Theorie der Moderne in Zentraleuropa". In *Nach kakanien. Annäherung an die Moderne*, 59–102. Studien zur Moderne, 1. Ed. Rudolf Haller. Wien: Böhlau, 1996.

Csáky, Moritz, Johannes Feichtinger, Peter Karoshi, and Volker Munz. "Pluralitäten, Heterogenitäten, Differenzen. Zentraleuropas Paradigmen für die Moderne". In *Kultur, Identität, Differenz. Wien und Zentraleuropa in der Moderne*, 13–43. Gedächtnis—Kultur—Identität, 4. Ed. Moritz Csáky, Astrid Kury, and Ulrich Tragatschnig. Innsbruck: StudienVerlag, 2004.

Dahlhaus, Carl. *Foundations of Music History*. Transl. J. B. Robinson. Cambridge: Cambridge University Press, 1983.

Dahlhaus, Carl. *Realism in Nineteenth-Century Music*. Transl. Mary Whittall. Cambridge: Cambridge University Press, 1985.

Dahlhaus, Carl. *Nineteenth-Century Music*. Transl. J. Bradford Robinson. Berkeley: University of California Press, 1989.

Dalle Vacche, Angela. "The Difference of Cinema in the System of the Arts". In *Opening Bazin: Postwar Film Theory and Its Afterlife*, 142–52. Ed. Dudley Andrew and Herve Joubert-Laurencin. New York: Oxford University Press, 2011.

Darcy, Warren. "Rotational Form, Teleological Genesis, and Fantasy Projection in the Slow Movement of Mahler's Sixth Symphony". *19th-Century Music* 25/1 (2001): 49–74.

Darcy, Warren. "In Search of C major: Tonal Structure and Formal Design in Act III of Die Meistersinger". In *Richard Wagner for the New Millenium: Essays in Music and Culture*, 111–28. Ed. Matthew Bribitzer-Stull, Alex Lubet and Gottfried Wagner. New York: Palgrave, 2007.

Daverio, John. *Nineteenth-Century Music and the German Romantic Ideology*. New York: Macmillan, 1993.

Davison, Peter. "The *Nachtmusiken* from Mahler's Seventh Symphony: Analysis and Reappraisal". Unpubl. PhD diss. Jesus College, Cambridge, 1985.

Davison, Peter. "Nachtmusik II: 'Nothing but Love, Love, Love'?" In *The Seventh Symphony of Gustav Mahler: A Symposium*, 89–97. Ed. James Zychowicz. Cincinnati: University of Cincinnati, 1990.

Decsey, Ernst. "Stunden mit Mahler". Pts. 1 and 2. *Die Musik* 10/18 (1911): 352–56; 10/21 (1911): 143–53.

Decsey, Ernst. *Johann Strauss: Ein Wiener Buch*. Stuttgart: Deutsche Verlags-Anstalt, 1922.

Deleuze, Gilles and Félix Guattari. *Anti-Oedipus: Capitalism and Schizophrenia*. Transl. Robert Hurley, Mark Seem, and Helen R. Lane. New York: Viking Press, 1977.

Deleuze, Gilles and Félix Guattari. *A Thousand Plateaus: Capitalism and Schizophrenia*. Transl. Brian Massumi. London: Continuum, 1987.

Deleuze, Gilles. *Cinema 1: The Movement-Image*. Transl. Hugh Tomlinson and Barbara Habberjam. Minneapolis: University of Minnesota Press, 1986.

Deleuze, Gilles. *Cinema 2: The Time-Image*. Transl. Hugh Tomlinson and Robert Geleta. Minneapolis: University of Minnesota Press, 1989.

Deleuze, Gilles. *Two Regimes of Madness: Texts and Interviews 1975–1995*. Transl. Ames Hodges and Mike Taormina. New York: Semiotext(e), 2006.

Dijkstra, Bram. *Idols of Perversity: Fantasies of Feminine Evil in Fin-de-Siècle Culture*. New York: Oxford University Press, 1986.

Downes, Stephen. *Music and Decadence in European Modernism: The Case of Central and Eastern Europe*. New York: Cambridge University Press, 2010.

Draughon, Francesca. "Dance of Decadence: Class, Gender and Modernity in the Scherzo of Mahler's Ninth Symphony". *Journal of Musicology*, 20/3 (2003): 388–413.

Draughon, Francesca and Knapp, Raymond. "Gustav Mahler and the Crisis of Jewish Identity". *ECHO: A Music-Centered Journal* 3/2 (2001): n.p.

Düntzer, Heinrich. *Goethes Faust, erster und zweiter Theil, zum ersten Mal vollständig erläutert*. Leipzig: Dyk, 1851.

Düntzer, Heinrich. *Göthe's Faust in seiner Einheit und Ganzheit wider seine Gegner dargestellt*. Cologne: Verlag von F. C. Eisen, 1836.

Düntzer, Heinrich (ed.). *Goethes Werke, Zwölfter Teil: Faust*. Deutsche National-Litteratur: Historisch kritische Ausgabe. Ed. Joseph Kirschner, vol. 93. Berlin: Verlag von W. Spemann, 1882.

C.W.D. (Durgin, Cyrus W.) Review of Fifth Symphony. *Boston Globe*, 23 October 1937: 12.

Durgin, Cyrus W. "Mayes Cello Soloist at Symphony; Liszt's 'Faust' Score Revived". *Boston Globe*, 27 November 1948, 14.

Düsel, Friedrich. "Dramatische Rundschau". *Westermanns Monatshefte* 55/109 (1910–11): 782–88.

Eckermann, Johann Peter. *Gespräche mit Goethe in den letzten Jahren seines Lebens, 1823–1832*. Leipzig: Brockhaus, 1837.

Eggebrecht, Hans Heinrich. *Die Musik Gustav Mahlers*. Munich: Piper 1982.

Eisenberg, Evan. *The Recording Angel: Explorations in Phonography*. New York: McGraw-Hill, 1987.

Eley, Geoff and Ronald Grigor (eds.). *Becoming National: A Reader*. New York: Oxford University Press, 1996.

Eliot, T. S. "Four Quartets". In *The Complete Poems and Plays of T S Eliot*. London: Faber and Faber, 1969.

Elliott, J. H. "The Growing Cult of Mahler". *Guardian*, 17 December 1962: 8.

Elsaesser, Thomas. *New German Cinema. A History*. London: Macmillan, 1989.

Elsaesser, Thomas. *Fassbinder's Germany. History, Identity, Subject*. Amsterdam: Amsterdam University Press, 1996.

Epstein, Max. *Max Reinhardt*. Berlin: Winckelmann, 1918.

Erk, Ludwig and Franz M. Böhme (eds.). *Deutscher Liederhort: Auswahl der vorzüglicheren Deutschen Volkslieder, nach Wort und Weise aus Vorzeit und Gegenwart*. Rev. edn., Vol. 2. Leipzig: Breitkopf & Härtel, 1893.

Ewen, David. *Dictators of the Baton*. Chicago: Alliance Book Corporation, 1943.

Figlio, Karl. "Historical Imagination/Psychoanalytic Imagination". *History Workshop Journal* 45 (Spring 1998): 199–221.

Finson, Jon W. "The Reception of Gustav Mahler's *Wunderhorn* Lieder". *The Journal of Musicology* 5/1 (Winter 1987): 91–116.

Finson, Jon W. *Robert Schumann: the Book of Songs*. Cambridge, Mass.: Harvard University Press, 2007.

Fioretos, Aris. "Contraction: (Benjamin, Reading, History)". *Modern Language Notes*, 110/3 (German Issue, 1995): 540–64.

Fischer, Jens Malte. *Gustav Mahler*. Transl. Stewart Spencer. New Haven: Yale University Press, 2011.

Fischer, Kurt von. "Gustav Mahlers Umgang mit Wunderhorntexten". *Melos/NZ* 2 (1978): 103–7.

Fischer-Lichte, Erika. *Theatre, Sacrifice, Ritual. Exploring Forms of Political Theatre*. London: Routledge, 2005.

Fischer-Lichte, Erika. "Sinne und Sensationen—Wie Max Reinhardt Theater neu erfand". In *Max Reinhardt und das deutsche Theater*, 13–27. Ed. Roland Koberg, Bernd Stegemann, and Henrike Thomsen. Blätter des Deutschen Theaters, No. 2. Berlin: Henschel, 2005.

Flinn, Caryl. "Strategies of Remembrance: Music and History in the [New] German Cinema". In *Music and Cinema*, 118–41. Ed. James Buhler, Caryl Flinn, and David Neumeyer. Hanover: Wesleyan University Press, 2000.

Floros, Constantin. *Gustav Mahler II. Mahler und die Symphonik des 19. Jahrhunderts in neuer Darstellung*. Wiesbaden: Breitkopf & Härtel, 1977. [2nd edn., 1987].

Floros, Constantin. "Prinzipien des Liedschaffens von Gustav Mahler". *Österreichische Zeitschrift* 45 (1990): 7–14.

Floros, Constantin. *Gustav Mahler. The Symphonies*. Transl. Vernon Wicker. Aldershot: Scolar Press, 1994.

Floros, Constantin. "Tag und Nacht in Wagner's *Tristan* und in Mahlers Siebenter Symphonie". *Österreichische Musikzeitschrift* 49/1 (1994): 9–17.

Floros, Constantin. *Gustav Mahler. Visionär und Despot*. Zürich: Arche Verlag, 1998.

Franklin, Peter. *Mahler: Symphony No. 3*. Cambridge: Cambridge University Press, 1991.

Freeze, Timothy. "'Fit for an Operetta': Mahler and the Popular Music of His Day". In *Mahler im Kontext/Contextualizing Mahler*, 357–88. Ed. Erich Wolfgang Partsch and Morten Solvik. Vienna: Böhlau Verlag, 2010.

Freitag, Christian. *Ballade*. Themen—Texte—Interpretationen. Vol. 6, ed. Hans Gerd Rötzer. Bamberg: C.C. Buchners Verlag, 1986.

Freud, Sigmund. "Das Unbehagen in der Kultur". In *Fragen der Gesellschaft— Ursprünge der Religion*, 191–270. Studienausgabe, 9. Frankfurt am Main: Fischer Verlag, 2000.

Friese, Heidrun (ed.). *The Moment: Time and Rupture in Modern Thought*. Liverpool: Liverpool University Press, 2001.

Fuhrich, Edda and Gisela Prossnitz (eds.). *Max Reinhardt. Die Träume des Magiers*. Transl. Sophie Kidd and Peter Waugh as *Max Reinhardt. The Magician's Dreams*. Salzburg: Residenz-Verlag 1993.

Fülöp, Péter. *Mahler Discography*. Toronto: Mikrokosmos, 2010.

Gadamer, Hans-Georg. *Truth and Method*. Transl. Joel Weinsheimer and Donald G. Marshall. London: Sheed & Ward, 1989.

Gilliam, Bryan. "The Annexation of Anton Bruckner: Nazi Revisionism and the Politics of Appropriation". *Musical Quarterly* 78 (1994): 584–604.

Goeres, Ralf. "Sensualistischer Phänomenalismus und Denkökonomie. Zur Wissenschaftskonzeption Ernst Machs". *Journal for General Philosophy of Science/Zeitschrift für allgemeine Wissenschaftstheorie*, 35/1 (2004): 41–70.

Gorman, Jonathan. "The Limits of Historiographical Choice in Temporal Distinctions". In *Breaking Up Time. Negotiating the Borders between Present, Past and Future*, 155–75. Ed. Chris Lorenz and Berber Bevernage. Göttingen: Vandenhoeck & Ruprecht, 2013.

Graf, Max. "Die dritte Symphonie Gustav Mahlers". *Neues Wiener Journal*, December 20, 1904: n.p.

Greisenegger, Wolfgang. "Alfred Roller: Neubedeutung des szenischen Raumes". *Studia Musicologica Academiae Scientiarum Hungaricae* 31/1–4 (1989): 271–81.

Grey, Thomas. "Masters and Their Critics: Wagner, Hanslick, Beckmesser, and *Die Meistersinger*". In *Wagner's* Meistersinger. *Performance, History, Representation*, 165–89. Ed. Nicholas Vazsonyi. Rochester, N.Y.: University of Rochester Press, 2003.

Gumbert, Friedrich and Karl Thieme (eds.). *Posthornschule und Posthorn-Taschenliederbuch. Sammlung beliebter Volkslieder, Arien, Märsche etc. für Posthorn, Trompete oder Cornet à Pistons leicht ausführbar eingerichtet*. Leipzig: Carl Merseburger, 1903.

Gutmann, Emil. "Gustav Mahler als Organisator". In *Gustav Mahler. Unbekannte Briefe*, 87–91. Ed. Herta Blaukopf. Vienna: Paul Zsolnay, 1983. [Orig. "Gustav Mahler als Organisator". *Die Musik* 18/2 (July 1911): 364–68.]

Gutmann, Emil. "Gustav Mahler as Organizer". In *Mahler's Unknown Letters*, 84–88. Ed. Herta Blaukopf. Transl. Richard Stokes. London: Victor Gollancz, 1986.

Hackett, Karleton. "Orchestra Plays Mahler's Music in Brilliant Style". *Chicago Evening Post*, 16 April 1921, n.p.

Hale, Philip. "Programme of the Fourteenth Rehearsal and Concert, Boston Symphony Orchestra". 2–3 February 1906, 997–1049.

Hale, Philip. "Programme of the Sixth Rehearsal and Concert, Boston Symphony Orchestra". 21–22 November 1913, 347–91.

Hale, Philip. Review of Ninth Symphony. *Boston Herald*, 17 October 1931, n.p.

Hall, Stuart. "Kulturelle Identität und Globalisierung". In *Widerspenstige Kulturen. Cultural Studies als Herausforderung*, 393–441. Ed. Karl H. Hörning and Rainer Winter. Frankfurt am Main: Suhrkamp, 1999.

Hansen, Matthias. *Gustav Mahler*. Stuttgart: Philipp Reclam, 1996.

Hansen, Miriam Bratu. *Cinema and Experience. Siegfried Kracauer, Walter Benjamin, and Theodor W. Adorno*. Berkeley: University of California Press, 2012.

Hanslick, Eduard. *On the Musically Beautiful*. Transl. G. Payzant. Indianapolis: Hackett, 1986.

Haskell, Eric T. "Illustrations for Baudelaire's *Les Fleurs du mal*: Symbolist Dreams and Decadent Nightmares". *Symposium: A Quarterly Journal in Modern Literatures* 38/3 (1984): 179–95.

Head, Matthew. (1997), "Birdsong and the Origins of Music". *Journal of the Royal Music Association* 122 (1997): 1–23.

Hefling, Stephen E. (ed.). *Mahler Studies*. Cambridge: Cambridge University Press, 1997.

Hefling, Stephen E. (ed.). "'Ihm in die Lieder zu blicken': Mahler's Seventh Symphony Sketchbook". In *Mahler Studies*, 169–216. Ed. Stephen E. Hefling. Cambridge: Cambridge University Press, 1997.

Hefling, Stephen E. (ed.). *Mahler: Das Lied von der Erde*. Cambridge: Cambridge University Press, 2000.

Hefling, Stephen E. "Techniques of Irony in Mahler's Oeuvre". In *Gustav Mahler et l'ironie dans la culture viennoise au tournant du siècle: Actes du Colloque Gustav Mahler Montpellier 1996*, 99–142. Ed. André Castagné, Michel Chalon, and Patrick Florençon. Castelnau-le-Lez: Editions Climats, 2001.

Hefling, Stephen E. "Aspects of Mahler's Late Style". In *Mahler and His World*, 199–223. Ed. Karen Painter. Princeton: Princeton University Press, 2002.

Hefling, Stephen E. "Gustav Mahler: Romantic Culmination". In *German Lieder in the Nineteenth* Century, 273–331. Ed. Rufus Hallmark. New York: Routledge, 2010.

Hepokoski, James and Warren Darcy. *Elements of Sonata Theory: Norms, Types, and Deformations in the Late-Eighteenth-Century Sonata*. New York: Oxford University Press, 2006.

Heyworth, Peter. "Mahler and the Lost Generation". *Observer*, 4 November 1962: 28.

Heyworth, Peter. "Catching Up with Mahler: *Mahler* by Henry-Louis de La Grange". *Observer*, 21 April 1974: 36.

Hiller, Albert. *Das große Buch vom Posthorn*. Wilhelmshaven: Heinrichshofens Verlag, 1985.

Hiller, Ferdinand. *Aus dem Tonleben unserer Zeit: Gelegentliches von Ferdinand Hiller*. Leipzig: F. E. C. Leuckart, 1871.

Hillman, Roger. *Unsettling Scores. German Film, Music, and Ideology*. Bloomington: Indiana University Press, 2005.

Hilmar-Voit, Renate. *Im Wunderhorn-Ton: Gustav Mahlers sprachliches Kompositionsmaterial bis 1900*. Tutzing: Hans Schneider, 1988.

Hirschfeld, Robert. "Konzerte". *Wiener Abendpost*, 28 December 1904: n.p.

Hirschfeld, Robert. "Mahler und Strauß in Wien". *Österreichische Rundschau* 1 (1905): 535–40.

Hoeckner, Berthold. *Programming the Absolute: Nineteenth-Century German Music and the Hermeneutics of the Moment*. Princeton: Princeton University Press, 2002.

Hofmannsthal, Hugo von. "Der Dichter und diese Zeit". *Die neue Rundschau* 18/3 (1907): 257–76.

Hofmannsthal, Hugo von. "Reinhardt bei der Arbeit". In Hugo von Hofmannsthal, *Gesammelte Werke: Reden und Aufsätze II. 1914–1924*, 295–309. Frankfurt am Main: Fischer-Taschenbuchverlag, 1979.

Hölscher, Lucian. "Mysteries of Historical Order: Ruptures, Simultaneity and the Relationship of the Past, the Present and the Future". In *Breaking Up Time. Negotiating the Borders between Present, Past and Future*, 134–51. Ed. Chris Lorenz and Berber Bevernage. Göttingen: Vandenhoeck & Ruprecht, 2013.

Hope-Wallace, Philip. "Alma's Martyr". *Guardian*, 4 April 1974: 10.

Hopkins, Robert. *Closure and Mahler's Music. The Role of Secondary Parameters*. Philadelphia: University of Pennsylvania Press, 1990.

Huckvale, David. "The Composing Machine: Wagner and Popular Culture". In *A Night at the Opera: Media Representations of Opera*, 113–43. Ed. Jeremy Tambling. London: John Libbey, 1994.

Huesmann, Heinrich. *Welttheater Reinhardt*. Munich: Prestel 1983.

Iggers, Georg G. *Historiography in the Twentieth Century*. 2nd edn. Middletown, Conn.: Wesleyan University Press, 2005.

Jameson, Frederic. *Signatures of the Visible*. New York: Routledge, 1992.

Jansen, Harry. "Time, Narrative, and Fiction: The Uneasy Relationship between Ricoeur and a Heterogeneous Temporality". *History and Theory* 54 (2015): 1–24.

Jean Paul. *Vorschule der Ästhetik*. Ed. Norbert Miller. Munich: Hanser, 1963.

Jenkins, Keith (ed.). *The Postmodern History Reader*. London: Routledge, 1997.

Johnson, Julian. "Mahler and the Idea of Nature". In *Perspectives on Gustav Mahler*, 23–36. Ed. Jeremy Barham. Aldershot: Ashgate, 2005.

Johnson, Julian. *Mahler's Voices. Expression and Irony in the Songs and Symphonies*. New York: Oxford University Press, 2009.

Johnson, Julian. "The Breaking of the Voice". *Nineteenth-Century Music Review* 8/2 (2011): 179–95.

Kaes, Anton. *From Hitler to Heimat. The Return of History as Film*. Cambridge, Mass.: Harvard University Press, 1989.

Kalbeck, Max. "Feuilleton. Das populäre Concert". *Neues Wiener Tagblatt*, 11 November 1897.

Kangas, Ryan. "Classical Style, Childhood and Nostalgia in Mahler's Fourth Symphony". *Nineteenth-Century Music Review* 8/2 (2011): 219–36.

Kant, Immanuel. *Critique of Judgement*. Transl. James Creed Meredith. Oxford: Clarendon Press, 1986.

Kaplan, Gilbert. "Adagietto: From Mahler with Love". In *Perspectives on Gustav Mahler*, 379–400. Ed. Jeremy Barham. Aldershot: Ashgate, 2005.

Kaplan, Gilbert and Peter Franklin. "Mahler and Tradition". *Musical Times* 133/1797 (1992): 559–63.

Kaplan, Richard A. "The Interaction of Diatonic Collections in the Adagio of Mahler's Tenth Symphony". *In Theory Only* 6 (1981): 29–39.

Kaplan, Richard A. "Temporal Fusion and Climax in the Symphonies of Mahler". *Journal of Musicology* 14 (1996): 213–32.

Kapp, Reinhard. "Schumann-Reminiszenzen bei Mahler". In *Musik-Konzepte Sonderband. Gustav Mahler*, 325–61. Ed. Heinz-Klaus Metzger and Rainer Riehn. Munich: edition text + kritik, 1989.

Karbusicky, Vladimír. *Gustav Mahler und seine Umwelt*. Darmstadt: Wissenschaftliche Buchgesellschaft, 1978.

Kellner, Hans. *Language and Historical Representation*. Madison: University of Wisconsin Press, 1989.

Kermode, Frank. *The Sense of an Ending*. Oxford: Oxford University Press, 1967.

Kinderman, William. *The Creative Process in Music from Mozart to Kurtág*. Urbana: University of Illinois Press, 2012.

King, Preston. *Thinking Past a Problem: Essays on the History of Ideas*. London: Routledge, 2000.

Kittler, Friedrich A. *Discourse Networks 1800/1900*. Transl. Michael Metteer. Stanford: Stanford University Press, 1990.

Klatte, Wilhelm. "Die 38. Tonkünstler-Versammlung des Allgemeinen Deutschen Musikvereins zu Krefeld". *Die Musik* 1/19 (1902): 1761–66.

Knapp, Raymond. "Suffering Children: Perspectives on Innocence and Vulnerability in Mahler's Fourth Symphony". *19th-Century Music* 22/3 (Spring 1999): 233–67.

Knapp, Raymond. *Symphonic Metamorphoses: Subjectivity and Alienation in Mahler's Re-Cycled Songs*. Middletown: Wesleyan University Press, 2003.

Knittel, K. M. *Seeing Mahler. Music and the Language of Antisemitism in fin-de-siècle Vienna*. Farnham: Ashgate, 2010.

Kolleritsch, Otto. "Gespräch mit einem Mahler-Interpreten". In *Gustav Mahler, Sinfonie und Wirklichkeit*, 93–102. Ed. Otto Kolleritsch. Graz: Universal-Edition für Institut für Wertungsforschung, 1977.

Korngold, Julius. "Feuilleton. Musik. (Außerordentliches Gesellschaftskonzert: Mahlers Dritte Symphonie". *Neue Freie Presse*, 17 December 1904: 1–3.

Korngold, Julius. "Feuilleton. Mahler's Seventh Symphony". *Neue Freie Presse*, 6 November 1909. Transl. Karen Painter and Bettina Varwig. In *Mahler and His World*, 327–32. Ed. Karen Painter. Princeton: Princeton University Press, 2002.

Koselleck, Reinhart. *Futures Past. On the Semantics of Historical Time,* Transl. Keith Tribe. New York: Columbia University Press, 2004.

Koselleck, Reinhart. *The Practice of Conceptual History*. Transl. Todd Samuel Presner and others. Stanford: Stanford University Press, 2002.

Koussevitsky, Serge. "Poetry and Music; Musical Interpretation; and Some Remarks about American Orchestras". *Proceedings of the American Academy of Arts and Sciences* 73/1 (1938): 1–4.

Krabbe, Jörg Friedrich. "Die Neuen Caligaris". *Neues Forum* (July/August 1976): 59–64.

Kracauer, Siegfried. "Time and History". *History and Theory* 6/6 (1966): 65–78.

Kramer, Jonathan. "Postmodern Concepts of Musical Time". *Indiana Theory Review* 17/2 (1996): 21–62.

Krebs, Wolfgang. "Zum Verhältnis von musikalischer Syntax und Höhepunktsgestaltung in der zweiten Hälfte des 19. Jahrhunderts". *Musiktheorie* 13 (1998): 31–41.

Krehbiel, Henry (attr.). "A Symphony by Mahler". *New York Tribune*, 16 February 1906: 7.

Krehbiel, Henry. "Mahler's Symphony Heard First Time: Affords Novelty Last Day of Cincinnati Music Festival". *New York Tribune*, 10 May 1914: 11.

Krekeler, Friedrich (ed.). *Anleitung zum Blasen des Signal-Posthorns (oder der sogenannte Posttrompete)*. Leipzig: Breitkopf & Härtel, 1905.

Krummacher, Friedhelm. *Gustav Mahlers III. Symphonie*. Kassel: Bärenreiter, 1991.

Kubik, Reinhold. "Vorwort". In *Gustav Mahler: Sämtliche Werke, Band V, Symphonie Nr. 5*, I–XI. Frankfurt: C. F. Peters, 2002.

Kubik, Reinhold. "Spuren in die Vergangenheit. Gustav Mahler und die Tradition der musikalischen Rhetorik". In *Mahler-Gespräche. Rezeptionsfragen— literarischer Horizont—musikalische Darstellung*, 144–77. Ed. Friedbert Aspetsberger and Erich Wolfgang Partsch. Innsbruck: StudienVerlag, 2002.

Kügle, Karl. "Past Perfect: Richard Taruskin and Music Historiography in the Early Twenty-First Century". *Tijdschrift van de Koninklijke Vereniging voor Nederlandse Muziekgeschiedenis* 58/1 (2008): 69–85.

Kundera, Milan. *The Curtain. An Essay in Seven Parts*. Transl. Linda Asher. London: Faber & Faber, 2007.

Kurth, Ernst. *Bruckner*. Hildesheim: Olms, 2000 [orig. edn.: *Bruckner*. Berlin: Hesse, 1925].

Kuspit, Donald B. *The Dialectic of Decadence: Between Advance and Decline in Art*. New York: Allworth, 2000.

La Grange, Henry-Louis de. *Gustav Mahler*, Vol. 1. Garden City, N.Y.: Doubleday, 1973; London: Victor Gollancz, 1974 & 1976.

La Grange, Henry-Louis de. *Gustav Mahler. Chronique d'Une Vie I. Vers La Gloire 1860–1900*. Paris: Fayard, 1979.

La Grange, Henry-Louis de. *Gustav Mahler*, Vol. 2: *Vienna, the Years of Challenge (1897–1904)*. Oxford: Oxford University Press, 1995.

La Grange, Henry-Louis de. "Music about Music in Mahler: Reminiscences, Allusions or Quotations?" In *Mahler Studies*, 122–68. Ed. Stephen E. Hefling. Cambridge: Cambridge University Press, 1997.

La Grange, Henry-Louis de. *Gustav Mahler,* Vol. 3: *Vienna: Triumph and Disillusion (1904–1907).* Oxford: Oxford University Press, 1999.

La Grange, Henry-Louis de. *Gustav Mahler,* Vol. 4: *A New Life Cut Short (1907–1911).* Oxford: Oxford University Press, 2008.

La Grange, Henry-Louis de and Günther Weiß (eds.). *Ein Gluck ohne Ruh': Die Briefe Gustav Mahlers an Alma.* Berlin: Siedler Verlag, 1995.

La Grange, Henry-Louis de and Günther Weiß (eds.). *Gustav Mahler: Letters to His Wife.* Rev. and transl. Antony Beaumont. Ithaca: Cornell University Press, 1995.

Lake, William E. "Hermeneutic Music Structures in 'Das irdische Leben' by Gustav Mahler". *In Theory Only* 12/7 (1994): 3–14.

Lamb, Andrew. "Orphée aux enfers". In *The New Grove Dictionary of Opera, Grove Music Online, Oxford Music Online.* Ed. Stanley Sadie.

Lampert, Jay. *Deleuze and Guattari's Philosophy of History.* London: Continuum, 2006.

Lang, Zoë. "Mahler's American Debut". In *Mahler and His World,* 227–63. Ed. Karen Painter. Princeton: Princeton University Press, 2002.

Langley, Lee. "Passion in an Ornate Period Frame". *Guardian,* 5 March 1971: 10.

Lastra, James. *Sound Technology and the American Cinema: Perception, Representation, Modernity.* New York: Columbia University Press, 2000.

Leclerc, Michel. *Analyse Formelle du Premier Mouvement de la Neuvième Symphonie de Mahler.* Laval: University of Laval, 1988.

Le Rider, Jacques. *Modernity and Crisis of Identity.* Transl. Rosemary Morris. New York: Continuum, 1993.

Lewis, Christopher O. *Tonal Coherence in Mahler's Ninth Symphony.* Ann Arbor: UMI Research Press, 1984.

Liebling, Leonard. "Variations" [Review of Mahler's Fifth Symphony]. *The Musical Courier* 21 February 1906. In "Mahler's American Debut", 258–62. Ed. Zoë Lang. In *Mahler and His World,* 227–63. Ed. Karen Painter. Princeton: Princeton University Press, 2002.

Lipiner, Siegfried. *Über die Elemente einer Erneuerung religiöser Ideen in der Gegenwart.* Vienna: Leseverein der deutschen Studenten Wiens, 1878. Reproduced in Stephen E. Hefling, "Siegfried Lipiner's *On the Elements of a Renewal of Religious Ideas in the Present*: Introduction and Translation (with Original German Text)". In *Mahler im Kontext/Contextualizing Mahler,* 89–144. Ed. Erich Wolfgang Partsch and Morten Solvik. Vienna: Böhlau, 2011.

Lipiner, Siegfried. "Die künstlerische Neuerung in Goethe's 'Faust'". *Deutsche Zeitung,* no. 3259, 30 January 1881, morning edn.: 1–3.

Lipiner, Siegfried. "Homunkulus: Eine Studie über Faust und die Philosophie Goethes". D. Phil. diss. University of Vienna, 1894 [lost].

Lipiner, Siegfried. Letter to Alma Mahler, 12 March 1906 (photocopy of typescript, Internationale Gustav Mahler Gesellschaft, Vienna).

Löwy, Michael. *Fire Alarm. Reading Walter Benjamin's "On the Concept of History".* London: Verso, 2005.

Lyotard, Jean-François. "Answering the Question: What Is Postmodernism?" In *The Postmodern Condition: A Report on Knowledge*, 71–82. Transl. Geoff Bennington and Brian Massumi. Manchester: Manchester University Press, 1986.

Mach, Ernst. "Introductory Remarks: Antimetaphysical". In *The Analysis of Sensations and the Relation of the Physical to the Psychical*. Transl. Cora May Williams, rev. and supplemented from the 5th German, ed. Sydney Waterlow. New York: Dover 1959.

Mahler, Alma. *Gustav Mahler. Erinnerungen und Briefe*. Allert de Lange: Amsterdam, 1940.

Mahler, Alma. *Gustav Mahler: Memories and Letters*. Transl. Basil Creighton. London: Murray, and New York: Viking Press, 1946.

Mahler, Alma. *Gustav Mahler: Memories and Letters*. Rev. edn. Ed. Donald Mitchell. Transl. Basil Creighton. London: Murray, 1968.

Mahler, Alma. *Gustav Mahler: Memories and Letters*. Rev. edn. Ed. Donald Mitchell. Transl. Basil Creighton. New York: Viking Press, 1969.

Mahler, Alma. *Gustav Mahler: Erinnerungen und Briefe*. Ed. Donald Mitchell. Frankfurt am Main: Ullstein, 1971.

Mahler, Alma. *Gustav Mahler: Memories and Letters*. 3rd rev. edn. Ed. Donald Mitchell. Transl. Basil Creighton. London: Murray, 1973.

Mahler, Alma. *Gustav Mahler: Memories and Letters*. 4th rev. edn. Ed. Donald Mitchell and Knud Martner. Transl. Basil Creighton. London: Cardinal, 1990.

Mahler, Gustav. Autograph letter to Alma Mahler [22 (?) June 1909]. Morgan Library and Museum, New York. Reproduced in *Ein Gluck ohne Ruh'*, 388–90. Ed. Henry-Louis de La Grange and Günther Weiß. Also in Alma Mahler, *Gustav Mahler: Erinnerungen und Briefe*, 436–39. Amsterdam: Allert de Lange, 1949.

Mahler, Gustav. "The Influence of the Folk-Song on German Musical Art". Interview in *The Etude* (May 1911): 301–2.

Mahler, Gustav. *Symphonie Nr. 1 in vier Sätzen für großes Orchester*. Sämtliche Werke I, Partitur, verbesserte Ausgabe, Kritische Gesamtausgabe, Leitung: Karl Heinz Füssl, herausgegeben von der Internationalen Gustav Mahler Gesellschaft, Wien; Vorwort und Revisionsbericht: Sander Wilkens. Wien: Universal Edition, 1992.

Mandelkow, Karl Robert (ed.). *Goethe im Urteil seiner Kritiker: Dokumente zur Wirkungsgeschichte Goethes in Deutschland. Teil III: 1870–1918*. Munich: Verlag C. H. Beck, 1979.

Mann, Thomas. *Death in Venice*. Transl. and ed. Clayton Koelb. New York: Norton, 1994.

Martner, Knud (ed.). *Selected Letters of Gustav Mahler*. Transl. Eithne Wilkins, Ernst Kaiser, and Bill Hopkins. London: Faber and Faber, 1979.

Martner, Knud. "Mahler im Opernhaus". In *Neue Mahleriana*, 163–73. Ed. Günther Weiss. Berne: Peter Lang, 1997.

Martner, Knud (ed.). *Mahler's Concerts*. London: Duckworth, 2010.

Marx, Peter W. *Max Reinhardt—Vom bürgerlichen Theater zur metropolitanen Kultur*. Tübingen: Francke, 2006.

Matthews, Colin. "Mahler at Work: Some Observations on the Ninth and Tenth Symphony Sketches". *Soundings: A Music Journal* 4 (1974): 76–86.

Maurer-Zenck, Claudia. "Technik und Gehalt im Scherzo von Mahlers Zweiter Symphonie". *Melos/Neue Zeitschrift für Musik* 2/3 (1976): 179–84.

Maximilian in Bayern, Herzog (ed.). *Posthorn-Klänge*. Munich: Braun & Schneider, 1869.

McClatchie, Stephen. "The Gustav Mahler—Alfred Rosé Collection at the University of Western Ontario". *Notes* 52/2 (1995): 385–406.

McClatchie, Stephen (ed. and transl.). *The Mahler Family Letters*. Oxford: Oxford University Press, 2006.

McClatchie, Stephen (ed.). *'Liebste Justi!' Briefe an die Familie*. Bonn: Weidle Verlag, 2006.

Meier-Graefe, Julius. *Modern Art (Being a Contribution to a New System of Aesthetics)*. Transl. Florence Simmonds and George W. Chrystal. New York: Arno Press (Arno Contemporary Art, 16), 1968.

Melly, George. "A Triumph of Seduction". *Observer*, 7 March 1971: 23.

Metzger, Christoph. *Perspektiven der Rezeption Gustav Mahlers*. Wilhelmshaven: F. Noetzel, 2000.

Mey, Curt. *Der Meistergesang in Geschichte und Kunst*. Leipzig: Hermann Seemann Nachfolger, 1901.

Meyer, Leonard B. "Exploiting Limits: Creation, Archetypes, and Style Change". *Daedalus* 109 (1980): 177–205.

Meylan, Claude (ed.). *William Ritter. Chevalier de Gustav Mahler: Ecrits, Correspondance, Documents*. Bern: Peter Lang, 2000.

Millington, Barry. "Nuremberg Trial: Is There Anti-Semitism in *Die Meistersinger*?" *Cambridge Opera Journal*, 3/3 (1991): 247–61.

Mitchell, Donald. "Influences and Anticipations". In *Gustav Mahler: The Wunderhorn Years*, 333–62. Berkeley: University of California Press. 1975.

Mitchell, Donald. *Gustav Mahler: The Early Years*. Rev. edn. Ed. Paul Banks and David Matthews. Berkeley: University of California Press, 1980.

Mitchell, Donald. *Gustav Mahler*. Volume III: *Songs and Symphonies of Life and Death*. London: Faber & Faber, 1985.

Mitchell, Donald. *Gustav Mahler: The Wunderhorn Years*. Rev. edn. Ed. Paul Banks and David Matthews. Berkeley: University of California Press, 1995.

Mitchell, Donald. "'Swallowing the Programme'. Mahler's Fourth Symphony". In *The Mahler Companion*, 187–216. Ed. Donald Mitchell and Andrew Nicholson. Oxford: Oxford University Press 1999.

Mitchell, Donald. "The Mahler Renaissance in England: Its Origins and Chronology". In *The Mahler Companion*, 547–64. Ed. Donald Mitchell and Andrew Nicholson. Oxford: Oxford University Press, 1999.

Mitchell, Donald. "*Das klagende Lied*: Mahler's 'Opus 1'". In *Discovering Mahler: Writings on Mahler, 1955–2005*, 73–90. Ed. Gastón Fournier-Facio. Woodbridge: Boydell Press, 2007.

Mitchell, Donald. "Mahler's Eighth Symphony: The Triumph of Eros". In Donald Mitchell, *Discovering Mahler. Writings on Mahler 1955–2005*, 447–55. Ed. Gastón Fournier-Facio. Woodbridge: Boydell Press, 2007.

Mitchell, Donald and Andrew Nicholson (eds.). *The Mahler Companion*. 2nd rev. edn. Oxford: Oxford University Press, 2002.

Mitchell, Donald and Edward Reilly (eds.). *Gustav Mahler, Facsimile of the Seventh Symphony*. Amsterdam: Rosbeek, 1995.

Monahan, Seth. "'I Have Tried to Capture You . . . ': Rethinking the 'Alma' Theme from Mahler's Sixth Symphony". *Journal of the American Musicological Society* 64/1 (2011): 119–78.

Monahan, Seth. *Mahler's Symphonic Sonatas*. Oxford: Oxford University Press, 2015.

Monelle, Raymond. *The Sense of Music: Semiotic Essays*. Princeton: Princeton University Press, 2000.

Munz, Volker. "The Reception of a Philosophical Text: A Case Study". *Newsletter Moderne Zeitschrift des Spezialforschungsbereichs 'Moderne—Wien und Zentraleuropa um 1900'* 7/2 (2004): 17–23.

Natorp, Paul. "Vorwort" in Siegfried Lipiner, *Adam: Ein Vorspiel/Hippolytos: Tragödie*, 3–13. Stuttgart: Verlag von W. Spemann, 1913.

Nattiez, Jean-Jacques. "Can One Speak of Narrativity in Music?" Transl. Katherine Ellis. *Journal of the Royal Musical Association* 115 (1990): 240–57.

Newcomb, Anthony. "Narrative Archetypes and Mahler's Ninth Symphony". In *Music and Text: Critical Inquiries*, 118–36. Ed. Steven Paul Scher. Cambridge: Cambridge University Press, 1992.

Newman, William S. "The Climax of Music". *Music Review* 13 (1952): 283–93.

Newsom, Jon and Alfred Mann (eds.). *The Rosaleen Moldenhauer Memorial: Music History from Primary Sources*. Washington, DC: Library of Congress, 2000.

Niekerk, Carl. *Reading Mahler. German Culture and Jewish Identity in Fin-de-Siècle Vienna*. New York: Camden House, 2010.

Nietzsche, Friedrich. *Untimely Meditations*. [1873] Transl. R. J. Hollingdale. Cambridge: Cambridge University Press, 1983.

Nietzsche, Friedrich. *Der Fall Wagner*. [1888]. Ed. Giorgio Colli and Mazzino Montinari. Kritische Studienausgabe, Vol. 6. Munich: de Gruyter, 1988.

Nietzsche, Friedrich. *Nachlaß 1869–1874*. Kritische Studienausgabe, 7. Munich: de Gruyter, 1999.

Nietzsche, Friedrich. "Das griechische Musikdrama". In *Die Geburt der Tragödie—Unzeitgemäße Betrachtungen*, 515–32. Kritische Studienausgabe, 1. München: de Gruyter, 1999.

Nixon, Mark. "The Construction of Closure and Cadence in Gustav Mahler's Ninth Symphony and *Das Lied von der Erde*". Unpubl. Ph.D. diss. Open University, 2008.

Notley, Margaret. "*Volksconcerte* in Vienna and Late Nineteenth-Century Ideology of the Symphony". *Journal of the American Musicological Society* 50/2–3 (1997): 421–53.

Novalis [Georg Philipp Friedrich Freiherr von Hardenberg]. *Schriften. Dritter Theil*. Ed. Ludwig Tieck and Eduard von Bülow. Berlin: Reimer, 1846.

Oltmanns, Michael. *Strophische Strukturen im Werk Gustav Mahlers: Untersuchungen zum Liedwerk und zur Symphonik.* Musikwissenschaftliche Studien, no. 1, Freiburg: Centaurus, 1988.

Osborne, Peter. "Small-scale Victories, Large-scale Defeats: Walter Benjamin's Politics of Time". In *Walter Benjamin's Philosophy: Destruction and Experience*, 59–109. Ed. Andrew Benjamin and Peter Osborne. London: Routledge, 1994.

Oswald, Peter. *Perspektiven des Neuen. Studien zum Spätwerk von Gustav Mahler.* Vienna: University of Vienna, 1982.

Paddison, Max. *Adorno's Aesthetics of Music.* Cambridge: Cambridge University Press, 1993.

Painter, Karen (ed.). *Mahler and His World.* Princeton: Princeton University Press, 2002.

Painter, Karen. "Jewish Identity and Anti-Semitic Critique in the Austro-German Reception of Mahler, 1900–1945". In *Perspectives on Gustav Mahler*, 175–94. Ed. Jeremy Barham. Aldershot: Ashgate, 2005.

Painter, Karen. "From Zionism to Assimilation: Theodor Herzl, Gustav Mahler, and the Aesthetics of Redemption". In *The Total Work of Art: Mahler's Eighth Symphony in Context*, 81–95. Ed. Elisabeth Kappel. Studien zur Wertungsforschung 52. Vienna: Universal Edition, 2011.

Papanikolaou, Eftychia. "Trauma as Memory in Ken Russell's *Mahler*". In *After Mahler's Death*, 72–89. Ed. Gerold W. Gruber, Morten Solvik and Jan Vičar. Olomouc: Palacký University, 2013.

H.T.P. (Parker, Henry Taylor.) "A Symphony by Mahler for the First Time". *Boston Evening Transcript*, 3 February 1906, n.p.

H.T.P. (Parker, Henry Taylor.) "Mahler Makes Impression as Never Before". *Boston Evening Transcript*, 17 October 1931, n.p.

Partner, Nancy. "Historicity in an Age of Reality-Fictions". In *A New Philosophy of History*, 21–39. Ed. Frank Ankersmit and Hans Kellner. Chicago: University of Chicago Press, 1995.

Partsch, Erich Wolfgang, "Alte Tonartensymbolik in Mahlers Liedschaffen?" In *Mahler-Gespräche. Rezeptionsfragen—literarischer Horizont—musikalische Darstellung*, 178–93. Ed. Friedbert Aspetsberger and Erich Wolfgang Partsch. Innsbruck: StudienVerlag, 2002.

Patton, Paul. "Events, Becoming and History". In *Deleuze and History*, 33–53. Ed. Jeffrey A. Bell and Claire Colebrook. Edinburgh: Edinburgh University Press, 2009.

Peattie, Thomas. "In Search of Lost Time: Memory and Mahler's Broken Pastoral". In *Mahler and His World*, 185–98. Ed. Karen Painter. Princeton: Princeton University Press, 2002.

Peattie, Thomas. "The *Fin-de-siècle* Metropolis, Memory, Modernity and the Music of Gustav Mahler". Unpubl. Ph.D. diss. Harvard University, 2006.

Peattie, Thomas. *Gustav Mahler's Symphonic Landscapes.* Cambridge: Cambridge University Press, 2015.

Pegg, Nicholas. *The Complete David Bowie.* London: Titan Books, 2011.

Pfistermeister, Fr. von (ed.). *Taschenliederbuch für Trompete, Cornet à Piston oder Posthorn: Eine Sammlung von über 100 Gebirgs- und Volksliedern, Opernarien, Ländlern, Märschen etc., leicht spielbar arrangirt.* Munich: Josef Seiling, 1892.

Phillips, Gene D. *Ken Russell*. Boston: Twayne, 1979.

Pickett, David. "Gustav Mahler as Interpreter. A Study of His Textural Alterations and Performance Practice in the Symphonic Repertoire". Unpubl. Ph.D. diss. University of Surrey, 1988.

Pickett, David. "Mahler on Record: The Spirit or the Letter?" In *Perspectives on Gustav Mahler*, 345–77. Ed. Jeremy Barham. Aldershot: Ashgate, 2005.

Pickett, David. "Arrangements and *Retuschen*: Mahler and *Werktreue*," in *The Cambridge Companion to Mahler*, 178–99. Ed. Jeremy Barham. Cambridge: Cambridge University Press, 2007.

Pisk, Paul A. "Zur Soziologie der Musik". *Der Kampf. Sozialdemokratische Monatsschrift* 18 (1925): 184–87.

Plato. "Ion". In *Plato in Twelve Volumes*. Vol. 9. Transl. Walter Rangeley Maitland Lamb. Cambridge: Harvard University Press; London: William Heinemann, 1925.

Plato. *Republic. Plato in Twelve Volumes*. Vols. 5 and 6. Transl. Paul Shorey. Cambridge: Harvard University Press; London, William Heinemann, 1969.

Poggioli, Renato. *The Poets of Russia, 1890–1930*. Cambridge: Harvard University Press, 1960.

Popper, Karl. *The Poverty of Historicism*. London: Routledge & Kegan Paul, 1957.

Proust, Marcel. *Finding Time Again*. Transl. Ian Patterson. London: Penguin Books, 2002.

Pynsent, Robert B. "Conclusory Essay: Decadence, Decay and Innovation". In *Decadence and Innovation. Austro-Hungarian Life and Art at the Turn of the Century*, 111–248. Ed. Robert Pynsent. London: Weidenfeld and Nicolson, 1989.

Pynsent, Robert B. "Czech Decadence". In *History of the Literary Cultures of East-Central Europe: Junctures and Disjunctures in the 19th and 20th centuries*, Vol. 1, 348–63. Ed. Marcel Cornis-Pope and John Neubauer. Amsterdam: John Benjamin, 2004.

Rancière, Jacques. *The Names of History*. Transl. Hassan Melehy. Minneapolis: University of Minnesota Press, 1994.

Rancière, Jacques. *The Politics of Aesthetics*. Transl. Gabriel Rockhill. London: Continuum, 2004.

Rancière, Jacques. *Figures of History*. Transl. Julie Rose. Cambridge: Polity, 2014.

Rasch, Wolfdietrich. *Die literarische Décadence um 1900*. Munich: Beck, 1986.

Ratcliffe, Michael. "The Pattern of Mahler's Existence". *The Times*, 18 April 1974: 7.

Ratz, Erwin, "Zum Formproblem bei Gustav Mahler". In *Gustav Mahler*, 90–141. Arnold Schönberg et al. Tübingen: Rainer Wunderlich, 1966.

Rauch, Angelika. "Post-Traumatic Hermeneutics: Melancholia in the Wake of Trauma". *Diacritics* 28/4 (Winter 1998): 111–20.

Reilly, Edward R. "Gustav Mahler and Wilhelm Gericke". In *Mahler's Unknown Letters*, 59–63. Ed. Herta Blaukopf. Transl. Richard Stokes. London: Victor Gollancz, 1986.

Reilly, Edward R. "Mahler in America". In *The Mahler Companion*, 422–37. Ed. Donald Mitchell and Andrew Nicholson. New York: Oxford University Press, 1999.

Reilly, Edward R. "Gustav Mahler Sketches in the Moldenhauer Archives". In *The Rosaleen Moldenhauer Memorial: Music History from Primary Sources*, 301–12. Ed. Jon Newsom and Alfred Mann. Washington, DC: Library of Congress, 2000.

Reinhardt, Max. "From an Interview with Max Reinhardt. Concerning the Direction of Crowd Scenes". *Berliner Lokal-Anzeiger*, 10 May 1914. In *Max Reinhardt. The Magician's Dreams*, 76–78. Ed. Edda Fuhrich and Gisela Prossnitz. Transl. Sophie Kidd and Peter Waugh. Salzburg: Residenz-Verlag 1993.

Reinhardt, Max. "Autobiographical Sketches: The Promptbook". In *Max Reinhardt. The Magician's Dreams*, 59–62. Ed. Edda Fuhrich and Gisela Prossnitz. Transl. Sophie Kidd and Peter Waugh. Salzburg: Residenz-Verlag 1993.

Revers, Peter. "Return to the Idyll: The Night Pieces in Gustav Mahler's Seventh Symphony". In *Colloque International Gustav Mahler: 25, 26, 27 Janvier 1985*, 40–51. Paris: Association Gustav Mahler, 1986.

Revers, Peter. "Latente Orchestrierung in den Klavierliedern Gustav Mahlers". In *De Editional Musices: Festschrift Gerhard Croll zum 65. Geburtstag*, 65–77. Ed. Wolfgang Gratzer and Andrea Lindmayr. Laaber: Laaber, 1992.

Revers, Peter. "Gustav Mahler und Anton Bruckner". In *Neue Mahleriana: Essays in Honour of Henry-Louis de La Grange on His Seventieth Birthday*, 265–96. Ed. Günther Weiß. Bern: Lang, 1997.

Revers, Peter. *Mahlers Lieder: Ein musikalischer Werkführer*. Munich: Verlag C. H. Beck, 2000.

Revers, Peter and Oliver Korte (eds). *Gustav Mahler. Interpretationen seiner Werke*. 2 Vols. Laaber: Laaber Verlag, 2011.

Richard, Father Noël. *Le mouvement Décadent: Dandys, Esthètes et Quintessents*. Paris: Librairie Nizet, 1968.

Ricoeur, Paul. "Narrative Time". *Critical Inquiry* 7/1 (1980): 169–90.

Ringer, Alexander L. "Johann Strauß und Gustav Mahler". In *Johann Strauß. Zwischen Kunstanspruch und Volksvergnügen*, 147–57. Ed. Ludwig Finscher and Albrecht Riethmüller. Darmstadt: Wissenschaftliche Buchgesellschaft, 1995.

P.R. (Roberts, Penfield.) Review of Ninth Symphony. *Boston Globe*, 17 October 1931, 4.

Robinson, David. "Poor Mahler Gets the Russell Treatment". *The Times*, 5 April 1974: 9.

Rockwell, John. "Leinsdorf's Mahler as Act of Boldness". *New York Times*, arts section, 2 June 1990, 14.

Roller, Alfred. "Bühne und Bühnenhandwerk". In *Thespis: das Theaterjahrbuch*, 137–45. Ed. Rudolph Roessler. Berlin: Bühnenvolksbundverlag, 1930.

Roman, Zoltan. "Structure as a Factor in the Genesis of Mahler's Songs". *Music Review* 31 (1974): 157–66.

Roman, Zoltan. *Mahler's American Years, 1907–1911: A Documentary History*. Stuyvestant, N.Y.: Pendragon Press, 1989.

Roman, Zoltan. "Between *Jugendstil* and Expressionism: The Orient as Symbol and Artifice in *Das Lied von der Erde* (or 'Warum ist Mahlers Werk so schwer verständlich?')". In *Tradition and Its Future in Music*, 301–8. Ed. Yosihiko Tokamaru et al. Osaka: Mita Press (Report of the 4th Symposium of the IMS [SIMS 1990 Osaka]), 1991.

Roman, Zoltan. "Song and Symphony (I). *Lieder und Gesänge*, Vol. 1: *Lieder eines fahrenden Gesellen* and the First Symphony: Compositional Patterns for the Future". In *The Cambridge Companion to Mahler*, 72–88. Ed. Jeremy Barham. Cambridge: Cambridge University Press, 2007.

Roman, Zoltan. *Mahler és Magyarország*. Transl. Inez Kemenes and Lujza Havas. Budapest: Geopen, 2010.

Rose, Bernard. "Hi Ken, Sorry I Stole Your Movie". *Guardian*, 14 September 2008: http://www.guardian.co.uk/film/2008/sep/15/biography?intcmp=239.

Rosen, Charles. *The Classical Style*. New York: Norton, 1998.

Rosenfeld, Paul, "After Mahler's 'Ninth'". *New Republic*, 13 January 1932, 244–45.

Roth, Philip. *The Plot against America*. London: Vintage, 2005.

Roth, Wilhelm. Excerpt from article on Harun Farocki, *Süddeutsche Zeitung*, 18 June 1979 in booklet to *Harun Farocki Filme 1967–2005*, 11. Berlin: Absolut Medien, 2009.

Russell, Ken. *Directing Film: From Pitch to Première*. London: BT Batsford, 2000.

Ruzicka, Peter (ed.). *Mahler: Eine Herausforderung*. Wiesbaden: Breitkopf & Härtel, 1977.

Samuels, Robert. "Music as Text: Mahler, Schumann and Issues in Analysis". In *Theory, Analysis & Meaning in Music*, 152–63. Ed. Anthony Pople. Cambridge: Cambridge University Press, 1994.

Sartre, Jean-Paul. *Critique of Dialectical Reason. I. Theory of Practical Ensembles*. [1960] Transl. Alan Sheridan-Smith. London: NLB, 1976.

Schabbing, Bernd. *Gustav Mahler als Konzert- und Operndirigent in Hamburg*. Berlin: Verlag Ernst Kuhn, 2002.

Schaefer, Hartmut. "Die Musikautographen von Gustav Mahler". In *Gustav Mahler Briefe und Musikautographen aus den Moldenhauer-Archiven in der Bayerischen Staatsbibliothek*, 69–237. Munich: Kulturstiftung der Länder und der Bayerischen Staatsbibliothek, 2003.

Schein, Ida. "Die Gedanken- und Ideenwelt Siegfried Lipiners". Unpubl. D. Phil. diss. University of Vienna, 1936.

Scherlein, Anton (ed.). *Anleitung zum Blasen eines einfachen Posthornes nebst einem Anhang von Postrufen, Fanfaren, Ländler, Walzer, Lieder etc.* Augsburg: Böhm & Sohn, 1886.

Scherzinger, Martin. "The Finale of Mahler's Seventh Symphony: A Deconstructive Reading". *Music Analysis* 14/1 (1995): 69–88.

Schiller, Friedrich. *On the Aesthetic Education of Man*. Transl. Elizabeth Wilkinson and L. A. Willoughby. Oxford: Clarendon Press, [1794] 1967.

Schlegel, Wilhelm Friedrich. *Charakteristiken und Kritiken (1796–1801)*. Ed. Hans Eichner. Vol. 2 of *Kritische Ausgabe*. Paderborn: Schöningh, 1967.

Schlegel, Wilhelm Friedrich. *Philosophische Lehrjahre (1796–1806)*. Ed. Ernst Behler. Vol. 18 of *Kritische Ausgabe*. Paderborn: Schöningh, 1962.

Schlegel, Wilhelm Friedrich. *Philosophical Fragments*. Transl. Peter Frichow. Minneapolis: University of Minneapolis Press, 1991.

Schmidt, Jochen. *Goethes Faust: Erster und zweiter Teil: Grundlagen, Werk, Wirkung*. Munich: Verlag C. H. Beck, 2001.

Schnebel, Dieter. "Mahlers Spätwerk als Neue Musik". In *Denkbare Musik: Schriften 1952–1972*, 70–84. Köln: Dumont Schauberg, 1974.

Schnebel, Dieter. "Über Mahlers Dritte". In *Mahler: Eine Herausforderung*, 151–70. Ed. Peter Ruzicka. Wiesbaden: Breitkopf & Härtel, 1977.

Schoenberg, Arnold. *Harmonielehre*. Vienna: Universal, 1911.

Schoenberg, Arnold. *Harmonielehre*, 2nd ed. Vienna: Universal, 1922.

Schoenberg, Arnold. *Fundamentals of Musical Composition*. Ed. Gerald Strang and Leonard Stein. London: Faber and Faber, 1967.

Schoenberg, Arnold. *Theory of Harmony* [1922]. Transl. Roy E. Carter. London: Faber and Faber, 1978.

Schönberg, Arnold, Ernst Bloch, Otto Klemperer, Erwin Ratz, Hans Mayer, Dieter Schnebel, and Theodor W. Adorno. *Gustav Mahler*. Tübingen: Rainer Wunderlich, 1966.

Schopenhauer, Arthur. *On the Will in Nature*. Ed. David E. Cartwright. Transl. E. F. J. Payne. Berg: Oxford, 1992.

Schwerte, Hans. *Faust und das Faustische: Ein Kapital deutscher Ideologie*. Stuttgart: Ernst Klett Verlag, 1962.

Seelig, August. "Die Wiener Orchesterfrage". *Musikalische Rundschau* 5 (1890): 63–65.

Sheinbaum, John. "'The Artifice of the Natural': Mahler's Orchestration at Cadences". *Journal of Musicological Research* 24/2 (2005): 91–121.

Shreffler, Anne C. "Berlin Walls: Dahlhaus, Knepler, and Ideologies of Music History". *Journal of Musicology* 20/4 (2003): 498–525.

L.A.S. (Sloper, Leslie A.) Review of Ninth Symphony. *Christian Science Monitor*, 17 October 1931, n.p.

Smith, Moses. "Mahler's Ninth Symphony Wins Favor under Koussevitzky". *Boston American*, 17 October 1931 n.p.

Smith, Warren Storey. "Symphony in Mahler's Great 9th". *Boston Post*, 17 October 1931, n.p.

Smoley, Lewis M. *The Symphonies of Gustav Mahler: A Critical Discography*. New York: Greenwood Press, 1986.

Smoley, Lewis M. *Gustav Mahler's Symphonies: Critical Commentary on Recordings since 1986*. Westport, Conn.: Greenwood Press, 1996.

Smoley, Lewis M. "Mahler Conducted and Recorded: From the Concert Hall to DVD". In *The Cambridge Companion to Mahler*, 243–61. Ed. Jeremy Barham. Cambridge: Cambridge University Press, 2007.

Solvik Olsen, Morten. "Culture and the Creative Imagination: The Genesis of Gustav Mahler's Third Symphony". Unpubl. Ph.D. diss. University of Pennsylvania, 1992.

Solvik Olsen, Morten. "Biography and Musical Meaning in the Posthorn Solo of Mahler's Third Symphony". In *Neue Mahleriana: Essays in Honour of*

Henry-Louis de La Grange on His Seventieth Birthday, 339–60. Ed. Günther Weiß, Berne: Peter Lang, 1997.

Solvik Olsen, Morten. "The International Bruckner Society and the N.S.D.A.P.: A Case Study of Robert Haas and the Critical Edition". *Musical Quarterly* 82 (1998): 262–82.

Solvik Olsen, Morten, and Stephen E. Hefling. "Natalie Bauer-Lechner on Mahler and Women: A Newly Discovered Document". *The Musical Quarterly* 97/1 (2014): 12–65; reprinted in corrected layout, *The Musical Quarterly* 97/3 (2014): 488–541.

Sontag, Susan. "Syberberg's Hitler" [1979]. In *Syberberg. A Filmmaker from Germany*, 13–25. London: BFI, 1992.

Specht, Richard. *Gustav Mahlers VIII. Symphonie. Thematische Analyse.* Leipzig, 1912.

Specht, Richard. *Gustav Mahler.* Berlin: Schuster & Loeffler, 1913.

Specht, Richard. "Zu Mahlers Achter Symphonie". *Tagespost Graz* 59/150 (14 June 1914): 9.

Spiering, Theodore. "Zwei Jahre mit Gustav Mahler in New York". [1911] In *Mahler: His Life, Work and World*, 227–28. Ed. Kurt Blaukopf and Herta Blaukopf. London: Thames & Hudson, 1991.

Spinnler, Burkard. "Zur Angemessenheit traditioneller Formbegriffe in der Analyse Mahlerscher Symphonik—Eine Untersuchung des ersten Satzes der Neunten Symphonie". In *Form & Idee in Gustav Mahlers Instrumentalmusik*, 223–76. Ed. Klaus Hinrich Stahmer. Wilhelmshaven: Heinrichshofen, 1980.

Sponheuer, Bernd. *Logik des Zerfalls. Untersuchungen zum Finalproblem in den Symphonien Gustav Mahlers.* Tutzing: Schneider, 1978.

Sponheuer, Bernd. "Einleitung: Gustav Mahler (1860–1911)—Gustav Mahler (1960–)". In *Mahler Handbuch*, 2–12. Ed. Bernd Sponheuer and Wolfram Steinbeck. Stuttgart: Metzler, 2010.

Sponheuer, Bernd and Wolfram Steinbeck (eds.). *Gustav Mahler und die Symphonik des 19. Jahrhunderts.* Frankfurt: Peter Lang, 2001.

St John, Michael (ed.). *Romancing Decay: Ideas of Decadence in European Culture.* Aldershot: Ashgate, 1999.

Steinbeck, Wolfram. "Gustav Mahler und das Scherzo". In *Gustav Mahler und die Symphonik des 19. Jahrhunderts*, 63–79. Ed. Bernd Sponheuer. Frankfurt am Main: Peter Lang, 2001.

Steinbeck, Wolfram. *Anton Bruckner: Neunte Symphonie d-moll.* München: Fink, 2003.

Steinberg, Michael. "Introduction: Benjamin and the Critique of Allegorical Reason". In *Walter Benjamin and the Demands of History*, 1–23. Ed. Michael Steinberg. Ithaca: Cornell University Press, 1996.

Steinberg, Michael. *Listening to Reason. Culture, Subjectivity, and Nineteenth-Century Music.* Princeton: Princeton University Press, 2004.

Sternfeld, Richard. "Symphonie der Tausend". *Allgemeine Musik-Zeitung* 39/17 (26 April 1912): 444–45.

Stöhr, Ernst. *Ver Sacrum*, 2/12 (1899) (complete issue available at https://www.belvedere.at/jart/prj3/belvedere/data//documents/dokumente/downloads/digitale-bibliothek/ver-sacrum/1899_versacrum_v13_72dpi.pdf).

bibliography

Straus, Noel. "Erno Rapee Leads Mahler's Eighth: Playing of Symphony Marks 500th Program of Radio City Music Hall of the Air". *New York Times*, 13 April 1942, 13.

Sutcliffe, Tom. "Mahler Record". *Guardian*, 22 April 1974: 8.

Syberberg, Hans Jürgen. *Syberbergs Filmbuch*. Frankfurt: Fischer, 1979.

Syberberg, Hans Jürgen. "Filmography". In *Syberberg. A Filmmaker from Germany*, 44–57. London: BFI, 1992.

Tallián, Tibor. "Intézménytörténet 1884–1911". In *A budapesti Operaház 100 éve*, 63–115. Ed. Géza Staud. Budapest: Zeneműkiadó, 1984.

Taruskin, Richard. "Tradition and Authority". In *Text and Act: Essays on Music and Performance*, 173–97. New York: Oxford University Press, 1995.

Tawaststjerna, Erik. *Sibelius. II: 1904–1914*. Transl. Robert Layton. London: Faber, 1986.

Taylor, Deems. "Words and Music". *Albany Times-Union*, 27 November 1931, n.p.

Tibbetts, John C. *Composers in the Movies: Studies in Musical Biography*. New Haven: Yale University Press, 2005.

Tiedemann, Rolf. *Studien zur Philosophie Walter Benjamins*. Frankfurt: Suhrkamp, 1973.

Tischler, Hans. "Mahler's Impact on the Crisis of Tonality". *Music Review* 12 (1951): 113–21.

Toews, John E. "Perspectives on 'The Old History and the New': A Comment". *American Historical Review* 94/3 (1989): 693–98.

Toews, John E. "Review: A New Philosophy of History? Reflections on Postmodern Historicizing". *History and Theory* 36/2 (1997): 235–48.

Toulmin, Stephen. *Cosmopolis: The Hidden Agenda of Modernity*. New York: Free Press, 1990.

Tovey, Donald. *Essays in Musical Analysis*. Vol. I: *Symphonies*. London: Oxford University Press, 1935.

Tovey, Donald. *A Companion to Beethoven's Pianoforte Sonatas*. London: Associated Board of the Royal Schools of Music, 1935.

Trakl, Georg. *Aus goldenem Kelch: Die Jugendgedichten*. Ed. Erhard Buschbeck. Salzburg: Otto Müller, 1939.

Treitler, Leo. "On Historical Criticism". *Musical Quarterly* 53/2 (1967): 188–205.

Treitler, Leo. "The Present as History". *Perspectives of New Music* 7/2 (1969): 1–58.

Treitler, Leo. "What Kind of Story Is History?" *19th-Century Music* 7/3 (1984): 363–73.

Treitler, Leo. "History and Music". *New Literary History* 21/2 (1990): 299–319.

Tucker, Aviezer. "Review of Niall Ferguson, *Virtual History: Alternatives and Counterfactuals*". *History and Theory* 38/2 (May, 1999): 264–76.

Turner, Steve. *A Hard Day's Write: The Stories behind Every Beatles Song*. London: Carlton Books, 2010.

Vaget, Hans Rudolf. "'Du warst mein Feind von je': The Beckmesser Controversy Revisited". In *Wagner's* Meistersinger. *Performance, History, Representation*, 190–208. Ed. Nicholas Vazsonyi. Rochester, N.Y.: University of Rochester Press, 2003.

Vancsa, Max. Review of Mahler's Third Symphony. *Neue Musikalische Presse*, 23/24 December 1904: n.p.

Van Roosbroeck, Gustave Leopold. *The Legend of the Decadents*. New York: Institut des études françaises [Columbia University], 1927.

Vazsonyi, Nicholas (ed.). *Wagner's* Meistersinger. *Performance, History, Representation*. Rochester, N.Y.: University of Rochester Press, 2003.

Veyne, Paul. *Writing History*. [1970] Transl. Mina Moore-Rinvolucri. Middletown, CT: Wesleyan University Press, 1984.

Von Reibnitz, Barbara. "Vom 'Sprachkunstwerk' zur 'Leseliteratur'. Nietzsches Blick auf die griechische Literaturgeschichte als Gegenentwurf zur aristotelischen Poetik". In *'Centauren-Geburten'. Wissenschaft, Kunst und Philosophie beim jungen Nietzsche*, 47–66. Monographien und Texte zur Nietzsche-Forschung, 27. Ed. Tilman Borsche, Federico Gerratana, and Aldo Venturelli Berlin. New York: de Gruyter 1994.

Walter, Bruno. "Gustav Mahlers Weg: Ein Erinnerungsblatt". *Der Merker* 3/5 (1912): 166–71.

Walter, Bruno. *Gustav Mahler*. Vienna: Herbert Reichner, 1936.

Walter, Bruno. *Theme and Variations: An Autobiography*. Transl. James A. Galston. New York: Knopf, 1946.

Wandel, Juliane. *Die Rezeption der Symphonien Gustav Mahlers zu Lebzeiten des Komponisten*. Frankfurt am Main: Lang, 1999.

Weiner, Marc A. *Richard Wagner and the Anti-Semitic Imagination*. Lincoln: University of Nebraska Press, 1995.

Weir, Donald. *Decadence and the Making of Modernism*. Amherst: University of Massachusetts Press, 1995.

Weiss, Günther (ed.). *Neue Mahleriana: Essays in Honour of Henry-Louis de La Grange on His Seventieth Birthday*. Berne: Peter Lang, 1997.

Werner, Sybille. "The Popularity of Mahler's Music in Vienna between 1911 and 1938". In *Naturlauf. Scholarly Journeys toward Gustav Mahler. Essays in Honour of Henry-Louis de La Grange for his 90th Birthday*, 553–72. Ed. Paul-André Bempéchat. New York: Peter Lang, 2016.

White, Hayden. "The Burden of History". *History and Theory* 5/2 (1966): 111–34.

White, Hayden. "Interpretation in History". *New Literary History* 4/2 (1973): 281–314.

White, Hayden. *Tropics of Discourse*. Baltimore: Johns Hopkins University Press, 1978.

White, Hayden. *The Content of the Form. Narrative Discourse and Historical Representation*. Baltimore: Johns Hopkins University Press, 1987.

Whitehead, Alfred North. *Process and Reality. An Essay in Cosmology. Gifford Lectures, University of Edinburgh 1927–28*. Corrected edition. Eds David Ray Griffin and Donald W. Sherburne. New York: The Free Press, 1978.

Whitworth, Paul John. "Aspects of Mahler's Musical Language. An Analytical Study". Unpubl. Ph.D. diss. Cornell University, 2002.

Wildhagen, Christian. *Die Achte Symphonie von Gustav Mahler. Konzeption einer universalen Symphonik*. Frankfurt a.M.: Peter Lang, 2000.

Wildhagen, Christian. "The 'Greatest' and the 'Most Personal': The Eighth Symphony and *Das Lied von der Erde*". In *The Cambridge Companion to Mahler*, 128–42. Ed. Jeremy Barham. Cambridge: Cambridge University Press, 2007.

Wilkens, Sander. "Vorwort". In Mahler, *Symphonie Nr. 1 in vier Sätzen für großes Orchester*, V–XII. Vienna: Universal Edition, 1992.

Will, Richard. "Time, Morality and Humanity in Beethoven's *Pastoral* Symphony". *Journal of the American Musicological Society* 50/2–3 (1997): 271–329.

Williams, Alastair. "Review of Michael Klein. *Intertextuality in Western Art Music*. Indiana University Press, 2005". *Music Theory Spectrum* 28/2 (2006): 316–20.

Williams, Christopher Alan. "Mahler's Seventh Symphony and the Emergence of a Post-Tonal Harmonic Vocabulary". Unpubl. paper presented at the annual meeting of the American Musicological Society, Minneapolis, 1994.

Williamson, John G. "Deceptive Cadences in the Last Movement of Mahler's Seventh Symphony". *Soundings* 9 (1982): 87–96.

Williamson, John G. "Mahler, Hermeneutics and Analysis". *Music Analysis* 10 (1991): 357–73.

Williamson, John G. "Prolonged Counterpoint in Mahler". In *Mahler Studies*, 217–47. Ed. Stephen E. Hefling. Cambridge: Cambridge University Press, 1997.

Wohlfarth, Irving. "History, Literature and the Text: The Case of Walter Benjamin". *MLN* 96/5, Comparative Literature (December 1981): 1002–14.

Wohlfarth, Irving. "Smashing the Kaleidoscope: Walter Benjamin's Critique of Cultural History". In *Walter Benjamin and the Demands of History*, 190–205. Ed. Michael Steinberg. Ithaca: Cornell University Press, 1996.

Wolin, Richard. *Walter Benjamin. An Aesthetic of Redemption*. New York: Columbia University Press, 1982.

Young, Gavin. "Gavin Young Takes It Extremely Easy in the South of France". *Observer*, 6 June 1971: 36.

Zaenker, Karl A. "The Bedeviled Beckmesser: Another Look at Anti-Semitic Stereotypes in *Die Meistersinger von Nürnberg*". *German Studies Review*, 22/1 (1999): 1–20.

Zychowicz, James. *Mahler's Fourth Symphony*. Oxford: Oxford University Press, 2000.

Zychowicz, James. "Mahler: Symphony No. 3". *Opera Today* [online], 20 November 2006, available at http://www.operatoday.com/content/2006/11/mahler_symphony.php, accessed 16 April 2012.

Index

Abblasen, 192

Abravanel, Maurice, 166

abridgment of Mahler symphonies,
299–301, 311
　Symphony No. 5, 301–3, 312n16
　Symphony No. 9, 303–11

'Ach, wie ist's möglich denn', 193–94

action-image, 146–47

Adam, Adolphe, 191

Adler, Emma, 273

Adler, Guido, 245

Adorno, Theodor W.
　on Benjamin, 349n55
　on 'breakthrough', 97, 101
　on 'Das himmlische Leben', 135
　on historical connection of Mahler
　　and Bruckner, 85
　on interpretative tools for studying
　　Mahler's music, 243–44
　on Mahler's fractures, 225
　on Mahler's historical
　　positioning, 51
　on Mahler's repetition of past
　　material, 70
　on Mahler's tendency towards
　　bass-lessness, 60
　'material theory of musical form',
　　86, 96–101
　on mimesis, 246
　portrayal of Mahler, 73
　on Seventh and Eighth
　　Symphonies, 122n6

on Symphony No. 2, 244

on Symphony No. 3's third
　movement posthorn
　solos, 184

on Symphony No. 4, 3, 4, 6,
　9, 23n28

on Symphony No. 8, 203

on thematic variants, 246

on tonality as means of
　representation, 212

on unfinished cadence in *Das
　Lied*, 69, 70

affect(ion)-image, 155, 157, 158,
　160n16

Agawu, Kofi, 52, 64, 87–88

alfresco technique, 155, 158

Alpert, Hollis, 174

Ankersmit, Frank, 332

Appel, Bernhard R., 134

appoggiaturas
　in 'Der Abschied', 60
　in Symphony No. 4, 11, 12*ex.*
　in 'Yesterday' and Symphony
　　No. 3, 335

arch form, in 'Des Antonius von
　Padua Fischpredigt', 35–37

Arendt, Hannah, 316

Aristaeus, 128*ex.*, 129–30, 131, 133

Ashby, Arved, 172

Augenblick, 220–21, 222.
　See also moment

Augustine, St., 254

Bach, Johann Sebastian, 134
Bahr, Hermann, 242, 259
Bailey, Robert, 114
Balázs, Béla, 153
ballads. See also *Des Knaben Wunderhorn: Alte Deutsche Lieder*
    based on texts from *Des Knaben Wunderhorn*, 26–28t
    tools used in Mahler, 25
Banks, Paul, 299
Barbirolli, Sir John, 166
bar forms, in *Des Knaben Wunderhorn*, 38–41
Barnes, Julian, 315–16
Batka, Richard, 187
Baudelaire, Charles
    Les Fleurs du mal, 255–56
    'Le Voyage', 255–56, 261
Bauer-Lechner, Natalie, 105, 120, 199n8, 271, 273–74
Bauman, Zygmunt, 243
Baumgarten, Franz Ferdinand, 208
Bazin, André, 141, 150
Beethoven, Ludwig von
    and deceptive cadence, 54, 67
    dramatic succession in works of, 9
    and establishment of scherzo style, 74–75
    tension of music of, 221
    use of sonata form, 7
    WORKS
    String Quartet in F minor, op. 95, 54
    String Quartet op. 131, 87
    Symphony No. 3 (*Eroica*), 74–75, 227–28
    Symphony No. 6, 75
    Symphony No. 8, 9
    Symphony No. 9, 228
Bekker, Paul, 134, 196, 210

Benjamin, Walter, 254, 316, 321–23, 330, 331, 349n55
Bergson, Henri, 144, 230, 232, 247
Berlin, Irving
    Cheek to Cheek, 23n24
    'White Christmas', 337, 339*fig.*
Berlioz, Hector, 87, 244
Bernstein, Leonard, 166
Bhabha, Homi, 242–43
Blaukopf, Kurt, 167
Bode, Karl, 134
Bohrer, Karl Heinz, 221
Botstein, Leon, 165, 178, 266
Boulez, Pierre, xxvii, 320
Bowie, Andrew, 69
Bowie, David, 337–40, 350–51n99
    Heathen, 339–40
    'Slip Away', 339–40, 341*ex.*
Bradbury, Malcolm, 257
Bradshaw, Peter, 179
Brahms, Johannes
    death of, 23n28
    Symphony No. 4, 8–9
breakdown of musical subject, 243–44
'breakthrough', 97, 101
Brentano, Clemens, 134
Brinkmann, Reinhold, 227
Britten, Benjamin, xxvi, 167
Brod, Max, 250
Bruckner, Anton
    death of, 23n28
    energetic deployment and formal organisation in late, 90–96
    historical connection between Mahler and, 85, 97
    Kurth on morphology of, 89, 90
    scherzos of, 75, 79
    Symphony No. 4, 63, 79
    Symphony No. 9, 90–96
Burgin, Richard, 304, 308

cadence(s), 51–52
   'conflated', 52, 54–55, 64
   digression, 62–65
   hybrid, 52–54
   modulating deceptive
      perfect, 56–58
   phrase ending and function
      of, 70n11
   Schlegel and, 65–67
   simple deceptive perfect, 55–56
   in Symphony No. 7 and *Die
      Meistersinger*, 108*ex.*, 109, 110
   unfinished, 67–71
   V–VI–I sequences, 54–62
Calinescu, Matei, 265–66
Caplin, William, 70n11
Cardus, Neville, 166, 167, 168
Challier, Ernst, 184
chromatic elaboration, in Symphony
      No. 9 and *Das Lied von der
      Erde*, 58–60
Chua, Daniel, 220
cinema. *See also* Russell, Ken
   forms of action in, 145–49
   forms of time in, 143–45, 159–160n9
   and historical materialism, 323–31
   musical portraiture and mirror of,
      152–57
   myth of total, 141–42
   observer in, 158–59
   realism in, 149–52
circus theatre, 208
classical music, stylistic distinc-
      tion between romantic and,
      87, 89–90
climax, 85–86
   and formal organisation in late
      Bruckner, 90–96
   and material theory of form and
      energetic organisation in
      Mahler, 96–101

   theoretical debate on role of, 86–90
close-up, cinematic, 153, 154
closure, secondary parameters
      in, 88, 90
Coleman, John, 174
Collingwood, R. G., 332
colloquial tone (*umgangssprachlichen
      Ton*), 194, 195–97, 201n31
comma, musical, 222
conclusions, of Mahler works, 66
'conflated' cadences, 52, 54–55, 64
Cooke, Deryck, 3, 121n6, 166, 350n94
Creighton, Basil, 167
Crémieux, Hector, 132
crowds, theatrical handling
      of, 207–13
crystal-image, 150, 155
Csáky, Moritz, 240

Dahlhaus, Carl, 142, 149, 196, 345
Damrosch, Walter, 301
Darcy, Warren, 124n33, 153
Daverio, John, 66
decadence, 253, 254, 255, 256
deceptive cadences, 52–54, 64–67,
      71n37, 109, 110*ex.*
deceptive perfect cadences, 55–58,
      65, 66, 67–70
Decsey, Ernst, 186, 198
de-identification
   in Mahler's work, 243–50
   Nietzsche on aesthetic, 239–40
   Plato on aesthetic, 237–38
   reception of, 240–43
Deleuze, Gilles, 144–46, 150, 154, 155,
      158, 159, 160n16, 333–35, 346
denial, in Symphony No. 4, 6–9, 11
Derrida, Jacques, 254
'Des Antonius von Padua
      Fischpredigt', 35–38
Deutsche Reichspost, 192

digression(s), 62–67

Dionysos/Dionysian, 239

distance effects, 190–91, 227

documentary
    macro-criticism, 319–20

double return, in Symphony No. 4,
    7–9, 19

Downes, Stephen, 254

Draughon, Francesca, 78, 79

Düntzer, Heinrich, 275–78

Dvorak, Antonin
    symbolic demise of, 23n28
    Symphony No. 8, 8–9, 18*fig.*

dynamism, in Symphony No. 4, 11

early romanticism, 67

Eggebrecht, Hans Heinrich, 194,
    201nn31, 37

ego, 241–42

Eliot, T. S., 351n106

Elliott, J. H., 166

energetic organisation, and material
    theory of form in Symphony
    No. 1, 96–101

Enlightenment, 319

enriched voice leading, in Symphony
    No. 9 and *Das Lied von der
    Erde*, 60–62

Epstein, Max, 206–8

evasion, Symphony No. 4, 6–9

evolution of musical language, scher-
    zos as impulses for, 73–83

Ewen, David, 304

face, 155

faceicity, 154, 155, 158, 161n40

faceification, 154, 155, 157, 161n40

Fain, Sammy, 335–37,
    338*ex.*, 339*fig.*

fake exposition repeat, 8, 23n31

Fall, Leo, 191

Farocki, Harun, 327–29

Fassbinder, Rainer Werner, 323

Faust letter, 280–83*t*, 290–94

Faust Notebook, 271, 272*fig.*, 274*fig.*
    annotations and commentary in,
        284–94
    authorship of, 271, 275–76, 278, 283
    comparison to Mahler's *Faust*
        letter, 290–94
    context of, 271–82
    dating, 275–76
    discussion on language, 276–77
    relevance to Mahler's
        understanding of *Faust*,
        280–83
    translated excerpt from, 284–89

Felix, Benedikt, 120

fictionalising trend, 333

film media. *See* cinema

fin-de-siècle, 253, 254, 258–61

Finson, Jon, 52

Fischer, Jens Malte, 295

Floros, Constantin, 3, 135, 136,
    310, 320

folk music, 75, 193–94, 247

form
    Adorno's material theory of,
        86, 96–101
    hybridity of, 249
    Kurth's theory of, 89–90
    in late Bruckner, 90–96
    meaning of music in, 123n20

formal tension, 93–96, 99–101

'fragment', 65–66

fragmentation, 240

free forms, in *Des Knaben
    Wunderhorn*, 41–48

Freud, Sigmund, 242–43

Friese, Heidrun, 220

Fülöp, Péter, 299, 300

fusion, 88–89

Gadamer, Hans-Georg, 317
Gericke, Wilhelm, 300, 301–3,
    311, 312n22
German Romanticism, 328–29
'Ging heut' Morgen über's Feld', 97
Gitai, Amos, 330–31
Gluck, Christoph Willibald, 132
Goethe, Johann Wolfgang von
    'An Schwager Kronos', 198
    on ballads, 25
    Faust, 211, 213, 271–95
Gorman, Jonathan, 332
grace note, 127
Graf, Max, 197
Greenfield, Edward, 167
Greisenegger, Wolfang, 210
grotesque destabilisation, 244–45
Gutmann, Albert, 210
Gutmann, Emil, 203, 205, 206

Habsburg monarchy, 240–41
Haitink, Bernard, 166–67
Hale, Philip, 311
Halévy, Ludovic, 132
Hall, Stuart, 241
Hansen, Miriam Bratu, 323
Hanslick, Eduard, 123n20
Haydn, Joseph, 74
Heath, Edward, 179, 182n52
heaven, in Symphony No. 4, 5–6
Hefling, Stephen, 65, 66, 84n14,
    123n26, 133
Heraclitus, 256, 257
Heyworth, Peter, 165–66, 169, 173, 178
highpoints. *See* climax
Hiller, Ferdinand, 186
Hirschfeld, Robert, 121–22n6,
    191, 196
historical materialism, 321–31
historicism, 318–21, 332
historiography, 315–18, 333

history, critique of traditional philos-
    ophy of, 331–33
Hoeckner, Berthold, 220
Hoffmann, E. T. A., 133
Hofmannsthal, Hugo von, 193,
    210, 242
Homunculus, 279–80, 292
Hope-Wallace, Philip, 174
Hopkins, Robert, 51, 88
Horenstein, Jascha, 166
Humoreske, 133–34
humour, 133–35, 245
hybrid cadences, 52–54, 55*ex.*, 67
hybridity, 247–49

Iggers, George, 319, 345
integration, climax and, 86
'intermediate state(s)', 257–58,
    261, 262–63
irony, 65, 69, 245–46

Jameson, Fredric, 326–27
Jean Paul, 133–34, 245
Jewish stereotypes, 120–21,
    125n42, 250
Johnson, Julian, 66, 120, 134, 141–42,
    245, 266

Kahal, Irving, 335–37, 338*ex.*, 339*fig.*
Kangas, Ryan, 11–14
Kant, Immanuel, 226–27
Kaplan, Richard, 87, 88–89
Karbusicky, Vladimír, 75, 201n37
Keller, Hans, 350n94
Kermode, Frank, 315
Kinderman, William, 120, 124n35
King, Preston, 332
Klee, Paul
    'Angelus Novus', 321–22
    The Twittering Machine, 333, 334*fig.*
Kleist, Heinrich von, 221

Kletzki, Paul, 300, 313n45
Klimt, Gustav, 259
Klopstock, Friedrich, 198
Knapp, Raymond, 135, 136
Knittel, K. M., 121, 125n41, 320
Korngold, Julius, xxvi, 192–93
Koselleck, Reinhart, 228, 331
Koussevitzky, Serge, 300, 301, 303–11
Kracauer, Siegfried, 331
Kramer, Jonathan, 123n21
Krebs, Wolfgang, 89
Krehbiel, Henry, 312n16
Kundera, Milan, 315
Kunstballaden, 29–30
Kunwald, Ernst, 300
Kurth, Ernst, 86, 89–94

La Grange, Henry-Louis de, 3,
        131, 168–69, 173, 302,
        312n22, 319
Ländler, 74–82, 225–26
Langer, Susanne, 144
language, scherzos as impulses for
        evolution of musical, 73–83
Lastra, James, 151
Leibling, Leonard, 249–50
Leinsdorf, Erich, 312n12
Lenau, Nicolas, 185, 198
Lévi-Strauss, Claude, 317
lingering, and time in cinema, 143
Lipiner, Siegfried, 251n25, 271–83
        Adam, 271, 275*fig.*
        'The Artistic Reform in Goethe's
                "Faust," 274–75
        'On Homunculus: A Study
                of Faust and Goethe's
                Philosophy', 272–73
Losey, Joseph, 181n31
Löwy, Michael, 331
LP recordings, 166–67
Luftpause, 222

lyrical turn, 187–88
lyric time, 143–44

Mach, Ernst, 241–42
Mahler, Alma, 29, 152, 153, 167–69,
        181n43, 278, 283
Mahler, Anna, 168, 342
Mahler, Gustav
        on composing music, 151
        conversion of, 175–78,
                181n43, 254–55
        historical positioning of, 51, 67
        identification with
                Beckmesser, 120–21
        illness of, 180n2
        letter to Alma Mahler, 280–83
        letter to Justine Rosé, 273*fig.*
        popularity in 1950s and
                1960s, 165–67
        reawakening of, xxv–xxvi
        rehearsing Symphony No. 8,
                206*fig.*
        scholarly approaches to, xxvi–xxvii
        on Wagner's *Die Meistersinger*, 105
        WORKS
        'Der Abschied'
                enriched voice leading in, 60,
                        61*ex.*, 62*ex.*
                in Farocki's *Zwischen zwei
                        Kriegen*, 327, 329
                parallel with Finale of
                        Symphony No. 1, 233–35
                temporal location of, 263
                transition and progression in,
                        261, 262
        Blumine, 187
        *Des Knaben Wunderhorn: Alte
                Deutsche Lieder*
                ballads based on texts
                        from, 26–28t
                bar forms in, 38–41

formal structure as narrative
device in, 25–29, 48
free forms in, 41–48
modified strophic forms
in, 29–34
Symphony No. 3 and, 194
ternary forms in, 35–38
'Der Einsame im Herbst',
60, 61*ex.*
'Es wird scho glei dumpa', 249*ex.*
Fünf Humoresken, 134
'Das himmlische Leben', 127–36,
325, 326
Das Klagende Lied, 30
Lieder eines fahrenden Gesellen,
30, 97, 231, 248*ex.*, 249*ex.*
Das Lied von der Erde
chromatic elaboration in, 60
'conflated' cadences in, 54–55
'Das Trinklied Jammer der
Erde,' bars 147–53, 58*ex.*
'Das Trinklied Jammer der
Erde,' bars 225–30, 55*ex.*
'Das Trinklied Jammer der
Erde,' bars 311–26, 68–69*ex.*
deceptive cadences in,
55–56, 71n37
'Der Einsame im Herbst,' bars
98–103, 60*ex.*, 61*ex.*
enriched voice leading in, 60,
61*ex.*, 62*ex.*
in Farocki's *Zwischen zwei
Kriegen*, 327, 329
and German
Romanticism, 328–29
middleground digressions
in, 64–65
modulating deceptive cadence
in, 52, 53*ex.*, 54, 56–58
parallel with Finale of
Symphony No. 1, 233–35

transitional characteristics
of, 261–63
unfinished cadence in, 67–70
'Von der Jugend,' bars 107–11,
57*ex.*
'Von der Jugend,' bars 22–25,
56*ex.*
'Nicht Wiedersehen!', 38–41
'Revelge', 41
'Der Schildwache
Nachtlied', 30–34
Songs of a Wayfarer, 247, 248*ex.*
Symphony No. 1
Augenblick in, 220–21, 222
Blumine, 167, 187
double return in, 8
folk music themes in, 75
in Gitai's *Eden*, 330
material theory of form and
energetic organisation
in, 96–101
octave leaps in, 75*ex.*
parallel with *Das Lied von der
Erde*, 233–35
scherzos in, 83
temporal purposiveness in, 227
time in Funeral March, 229
viola gesture in Finale of, 219–21
Zusammenbruch in Finale of, 244
Symphony No. 2
abridgment of, 299
contrast between middle and
outside movements in, 223–26
double return in, 8
in *Hitler, a Film from
Germany*, 325–26
scherzo in, 83
temporal purposiveness in, 227
Zusammenbruch in, 244
Symphony No. 3
abridgment of, 300

Mahler, Gustav (*cont.*)
  double return in, 8
  hybridity of form in, 249
  Mahler on, 152
  plurality of voices in, 245
  posthorn episodes of,
    187–98
  Scherzo in, 79
  similarities to 'I'll be Seeing
    You', 335–37, 338*ex.*
  similarities to 'Yesterday', 335,
    336*ex.*, 350n93
  temporality in, 222
  temporal purposiveness
    in, 227
  Zusammenbruch in, 244
Symphony No. 4
  Augenblick in, 222–23
  collapsing gestures in first
    movement, 21*ex.*, 24n41
  conclusion of, 66
  crisis in, 19–22
  development in, 14–19
  double return in, 7–8
  as escapist fantasy, 11–14
  evasion and denial in, 6–7
  fake exposition repeat in,
    8–9, 23n31
  final movement, 4–6
  first movement, appoggiatura
    functions, 12*ex.*
  first movement, bars 233–38,
    10*ex.*
  first movement, bars 237–41,
    224*ex.*
  first movement, bars 330–37,
    225*ex.*
  first movement, 'dream ocarina'
    bars, 18*fig.*
  first movement, melodic
    recycling, 13*ex.*

  first movement, sequence and
    'clone', bars 187–99 and
    199–212, 20*ex.*
  'Das himmlische Leben',
    127–36, 325, 326
  innocence in, 350n95
  motivic metamorphosis in, 246
  relationship to first three
    symphonies, 9–10
  Scherzo in, 79
  scholarship on, 3–4
  tonal centres in first
    movement, 14–17
  Zusammenbruch in, 244
Symphony No. 5
  abridgment of, 299–300,
    301–3, 312n16
  'Adagietto', 52, 54*ex.*
  and Bowie's 'Slip Away', 339–40,
    341–42*ex.*
  connections with Seventh and
    Meistersinger, 120, 124n35
  folk music themes in, 75
  Meyer on second movement
    of, 101
  moments of self-reflection in, 226
  motivic metamorphosis in, 246
Symphony No. 6
  abridgment of, 299
  collapsing gestures in first
    movement, 21*ex.*, 24n41
  connections with Seventh and
    Meistersinger, 115–17
  first movement as musical
    portraiture, 152–59
  formal structure of, 147–49
  temporal purposiveness
    in, 230–31
  time in, 228
Symphony No. 7
  abridgment of, 300

Adorno on, 122n6
conclusion of, 66
deceptive cadences in, 64
discarded sketches for,
    115–17, 123n26
erosion of structural unity
    in, 230
first movement, end of
    introduction, bars 45–50,
    113ex.
Meistersinger references in
    Finale, 106–10
night and day in,
    119–20, 124n32
quartal harmony in
    Meistersinger and, 112–15
reception of, 105–6
remnants of Meistersinger in
    Finale, 110–12
traditional structures in
    Finale, 123n21
Symphony No. 8
abridgment of, 300
Adorno on, 122n6
performance site of
    premiere, 205–6
public aspect of, 203–5
rehearsal of, 206fig.
and Reinhardt's concept of
    Massenregie, 207–13
Symphony No. 9
abridgment of, 300,
    303–11, 313n28
chromatic elaboration in, 58–59
'conflated' cadences in, 54–55
deceptive cadences in, 56, 71n37
enriched voice leading in, 62
final movement, bars 180–85, 233
first bars of the second Ländler,
    bars 218–21, 81ex.
first movement, bars 1–7, 264ex.

first movement, bars 53–54,
    53ex.
harmonic reduction of first
    Ländler's section in scherzo
    of, 78ex.
harmonic reduction of the waltz
    theme, bars 90–102, 80ex.
as impulse for evolution of mu-
    sical language, 73–83
and Interstellar score, 342,
    343ex., 344ex., 345
Ländler-theme in the scherzo
    of, 77ex.
Mahler on, 66
middleground digressions
    in, 64–65
second movement, bars 295–99,
    63ex., 64ex.
second movement, bars 429–32,
    57ex.
second movement, bars 564–71,
    59ex.
structural outline of Scherzo,
    81ex., 82ex.
third movement, bars 1–7,
    265ex.
transitional characteristics
    of, 263–65
Symphony No. 10, 88–89, 166, 343,
    344ex., 345
'Das Trinklied Jammer der Erde'
    bars 147–53, 58ex.
    bars 311–26, 68–69ex.
    hybrid cadence in, 55ex.
    modulating deceptive perfect
        cadences in, 56–58
'Von der Jugend'
    bars 107–11, 57ex.
    bars 22–25, 56ex.
    deceptive perfect cadences
        in, 55–56

Mahler, Gustav (*cont.*)
  'Wer hat dies Liedlein
    erdacht?!', 134
  'Wo die schönen Trompeten
    blasen', 41–48
Mahler, Maria, 342
Mann, Thomas, 171–72, 181n32
march genre, 229
Marschalk, Max, 194
Martner, Knud, 321, 348n31
Massenregie, 207–13
materialism, historical, 321–31
'material theory of musical form',
    86, 96–101
Matthews, Colin, 82
McCartney, Paul
  'When I'm Sixty-Four', 340
  'Yesterday', 335, 336*ex.*, 350n93
meaning, 5
Meier-Graefe, Julius, 258–59, 261
melodic recycling, in Symphony
    No. 4, 11–14
memory, 232
Mengelberg, Willem, 204–5, 335
metamorphosis, 246
Meyer, Leonard, 87, 101
middleground digressions, 64–65
milieux, realism and, 146
Mime (*Die Meistersinger*), 120–21,
    124–25n40
mimesis, 246
Mitchell, Donald, 4, 14, 124n32, 134,
    135, 136, 167, 212
Mitropoulos, Dimitri, 166, 300
modernist historiography, 315–18
modernity/modernism, 232, 265–66
modified strophic forms, in *Des
    Knaben Wunderhorn*, 29–34
modulating deceptive cadence, 52–54
modulating deceptive perfect
    cadences, 56–58

moment. See also *Augenblick*
  in Mahler symphonies, 221–22
  ordering of time and potency
    of, 226–27
  in Symphony No. 1, 219–21, 222
  in Symphony No. 2, 223–26
  in Symphony No. 4, 222–23
  in Symphony No. 5, 226
Monahan, Seth, xxvi, 3, 152, 155
Monelle, Raymond, 141, 143, 144,
    145, 151
montage, 142, 147
Monteux, Pierre, 304, 313n28
movement-image, 145, 146, 160n16
Muck, Karl, 302, 304
Müller, Adolf Sr., 185
Munch, Edward, 260
Munz, Volker, 242
musical comma, 222
musical language, scherzos as impulses
    for evolution of, 73–83
musical portraiture, 152–57
musical subject, tragic breakdown
    of, 243–44
musical time, forms of, 143–45
Musikfesthalle, 206–7
Musil, Robert, 242
myth of total cinema, 141
myth of total symphony, 152

Nachträglichkeit, xxvii–xxviii
Natorp, Paul, 272–73
natural time, 144–45
nature, 151–52
Nazi regime and Nazism, 85, 328
neo-Catholicism, 254
Nessler, Viktor, 186, 187, 188–91,
    186*ex.*, 189*ex.*
Nestroy, Johann, 131
Neue Musik-Festhalle, 205–6
'new history', 332

Newman, William, 86
Nietzsche, Friedrich, 205, 239–43,
    255, 316
  Beyond Good and Evil, 240
  The Birth of Tragedy out of the
    Spirit of Music, 239
Nolan, Christopher, 338, 340–45
'nominalism', 86
Novalis, 346–47
Now, Voyager, 147, 148*fig.*

objective time, 144–45
observer, 150, 151, 158–59
Offenbach, Jacques, 127–36
Oswald. Peter, 76
Otherness, 243

Painter, Karen, 121, 330
paired verse forms, 30
Parker, Henry Taylor, 302, 307–8
particularity
  and erosion of structural
    unity, 230
  and failure to deliver temporal
    purposiveness, 229–30
  of horns in Symphony No. 5, 226
  in Mahler and Proust, 232
  of viola gesture in Symphony No. 1
    Finale, 219–21, 233
Partner, Nancy, 333
pastoral musical tradition, in *Orphée*
    aux Enfers and 'Das
    himmlische Leben', 131, 133
Peattie, Thomas, xxvi, 232
per aspera ad astra, 244–45
perfect cadences, 52, 55–56, 65,
    108, 109
Pickett, David, 166, 300
Pisk, Paul Amadeus, 210
Plato, 237–38
Plötzlichkeit, 221

pluralism, 240
plurality of voices, 245–46
poetry, Plato's rejection of, 238
Poggioli, Renato, 256
Popper, Karl, 316
popular music
  invoked in Mahler, Nessler, and
    Schäffer works, 186–91
  invoked in Symphony No. 3, 196–97
  posthorns in, 183–86
portraiture, musical, 152–57
posthorn and posthorn solos
  appeal of, 184
  dualistic character of, 184–87
  interpretive traditions of, 183–84
  popular music conventions
    invoked by, 186–93
  in Symphony No. 3, 194–98
primary parameters, 88, 90
progressive time, 144–45
Proust, Marcel, 232, 250, 331, 333
publicity, 203, 204*fig.*
purposiveness, 227, 228, 229
Pynsent, Robert B., 258

quartal harmony, in Symphony No. 7
    and *Die Meistersinger*, 112–15

Rancière, Jacques, 331–32, 333
Rapée, Ernö, 300
Rassenfosse, Armand, 256
Ratcliffe, Michael, 168–69
Ratz, Erwin, 73
realism, 143, 146, 149–52
recollection, 232
recordings, 151, 166–67
Reilly, Edward, 123n29
Reinhardt, Max, 206–13
Revers, Peter, 85, 124n37
rhizome, 333–35, 346
Richter, Hans, 23n28, 121n1

Richter, Johann Paul Friedrich, 133–34

Ringer, Alexander L., 252n43

Ritter, William, 119

Robinson, David, 174–75

Rockwell, John, 312n12

Roller, Alfred, 209–10

romanticism, 67, 328–29

romantic music, stylistic
    distinction between classical
    and, 87, 89–90

Rondo-Burleske, 265

Rosé, Arnold, 199n8

Rose, Bernard, 179

Rosé, Justine Mahler, 271, 273*fig.*.
    See also *Faust* Notebook

Rosen, Charles, 7

Rosenfeld, Paul, 307

Roth, Philip, 321

Roth, Wilhelm, 327

Russell, Ken, 163–65, 168, 169–71,
    172, 173, 174–80

St Matthew Passion (Bach), 134

Samuels, Robert, 3

Sartre, Jean-Paul, 316–17

Schaefer, Hartmut, 320

Schäffer, Heinrich, 187, 188*ex.*, 189–90

Scheffel, Victor von, 186

Scherchen, Hermann, 299–300

Scherzinger, Martin, 123n21

scherzos
    erosion of temporal purposiveness
        through particularity in, 230
    as impulses for evolution of
        musical language, 73–83

'scherzo style', 74–75

Schiller, Friedrich, 228

Schlegel, Wilhelm Friedrich, 65–67,
    69, 221, 227, 346

Schnebel, Dieter, 83

Schnitzler, Arthur, 242

Schoenberg, Arnold
    change of attitude towards
        Mahler's music, 121
    on deceptive cadence, 64, 66
    differentiation of Mahler's music
        from, 221
    Mahler's influence on, 51
    and onset of musical
        modernism, 266

Schopenhauer, Arthur, xxvi

Schubert, Franz, 75

Schumann, Robert, 52–54, 67, 88, 133

Scruton, Roger, 6

Secessionist movement, 259

Second Viennese School, 51, 67

Seelig, Adolf, 210

seer, 150, 158

sentimental trumpet solo,
    185–87, 190–91

September 11 terrorist attacks, 340

Shabbing, Bernd, 319–20

Sheinbaum, John, 51

Shreffler, Anne, 345

'Sisyphean sequence', 87

sketchbook, 115–17, 123n26

Sloper, L. A., 307

slow motion, 159–160n9

Smetana, Bedřich, 199n8

Smith, Moses, 307

Smith, Warren Storey, 307

Smoley, Lewis, 124n37, 179, 299

sonata form, 7–8, 82–83, 96, 223

song form, 29. See also *Des
    Knaben Wunderhorn: Alte
    Deutsche Lieder*

Spiering, Theodore, 63

Spohr, Louis, 199n8

statistical climax, 87

Steinbeck, Wolfram, 74

Steinberg, Michael P., 222

Sterneld, Richard, 205

Stock, Frederick, 300
Stöhr, Ernst, 259–60
Strauss, Johann, 23n28, 193
    'Eine Nacht in Venedig', 249*ex.*
Strauss, Richard, 219
strophic forms, modified, in *Des
        Knaben Wunderhorn*, 29–34
Sturm, Peter (Nikolaus)
        Marcelin, 133
'suprahistorical man', 316
Sutcliffe, Tom, 173
Syberberg, Hans Jürgen
    Hitler, a Film from Germany,
        323–26, 327
    *Karl May. In Search of Paradise
        Lost*, 325–26
Symons, Arthur, 258
symphonic breakdown, 243–44
symphonism, 142
syntactic climax, 87, 97, 101

Taruskin, Richard, 301
Taylor, Deems, 308
temporal distance, 317
temporal purposiveness, 222, 226,
        227, 228, 229–31
tension, formal, 93–96, 99–101
ternary forms, in *Des Knaben
        Wunderhorn*, 35–38
Tiedemann, Rolf, 331
time
    of *Eroica*, 227–28
    forms of musical, 143–45, 159–60n9
    historiography and, 315–16
    in *Interstellar*, 341–43
    in *Mahler*, 163
    in Mahler symphonies, 228–29
    potency of moments and ordering
        of, 226–27
    romantic, 227
    sudden intrusions and, 221–22

in Symphony No. 2, 223–26
in Symphony No. 5, 226
theorisations of, 332
time-images, 145, 150, 155
Tischler, Hans, 51
Toews, John, 332
Tönnies, Ferdinand, 231
total cinema, myth of, 141–42
total symphony, myth of, 152
Toulmin, Stephen, 243
tradition, in Symphony No. 7 and
        Die Meistersinger, 110–11
Tragic, 239–40, 251n25
tragic breakdown of musical
        subject, 243–44
Trakl, Georg, 261
transition, 253, 254, 255–58, 260–66
Treitler, Leo, 345
trio
    in Scherzo of Symphony No. 9, 79
    in scherzos of Mahler
        symphonies, 83
trumpet solo, sentimental,
        185–87, 190–91
Tucker, Aviezer, 318

Umlauf, Friedrich, 241
unfinished cadence, 67–70
'unsaveable I', 242

Vancsa, Max, 187
vertical differentiation, 240
Vienna, at turn of century,
        240–43, 258–61
Virgil, 133
Visconti, Luchino, 171–73, 174, 181n31
Vitalism, 89
voice leading, in Symphony No.
        9 and *Das Lied von der
        Erde*, 60–62
voices, plurality of, 245–46

von Arnim, Achim, 134

Wagner, Cosima, 175–78, 181n43
Wagner, Richard
  on Jewish composers, 250
  Kurth on morphology of, 89, 90
  and Nietzsche's musical
    thinking, 239–40
  WORKS
  Das Rheingold, 249*ex.*
  Götterdämmerung, 118–19
  *Die Meistersinger von
    Nürnberg*, 105–6
    Mahler on Mime and
      Beckmesser, 120–21
    night and day in, 117–19, 124n32
    quartal harmony in Symphony
      No. 7 and, 112–15
    references to, in Symphony
      No. 7 Finale, 106–10
    remnants of, in Symphony
      No. 7, 110–12

Das Rheingold, 249*ex.*
Der Ring des Nibelungen, 118–19,
  124–25n40
Walter, Bruno, 3, 66, 271–72
waltzes, 79–82, 193
Webern, Anton, 228
White, Hayden, 317
Whitehead, Alfred North, 257
Wildhagen, Christian,
  213, 295
Will, Richard, 231
Williams, Christopher,
  123n22, 124n37
Williamson, John, 51, 64, 66, 70n17
Wilson, Harold, 179, 182n52
Wittgenstein, Ludwig, 136
Wolf, Hugo, 23n28

Zimmer, Hans, 342, 342–45
Zuckerkandl, Emil, 242
Zusammenbruch, 243–44
Zychowicz, James, 3, 312n12